PRUDENT LENDING
RESTORED

YASUYUKI FUCHITA
RICHARD J. HERRING
ROBERT E. LITAN
Editors

PRUDENT LENDING RESTORED

Securitization after the Mortgage Meltdown

NOMURA INSTITUTE OF CAPITAL MARKETS RESEARCH
Tokyo

BROOKINGS INSTITUTION PRESS
Washington, D.C.

Prudent Lending Restored: Securitization after the Mortgage Meltdown
may be ordered from:
BROOKINGS INSTITUTION PRESS, C/O HFS
P.O. Box 50370, Baltimore, MD 21211-4370
Tel.: 800/537-5487; 410/516-6956; Fax: 410/516-6998
Internet: www.brookings.edu

Library of Congress Cataloging-in-Publication data

Prudent lending restored : securitization after the mortgage meltdown / Yasuyuki Fuchita,
Richard J. Herring, and Robert E. Litan, editors.
     p.   cm.
Includes bibliographical references and index.
Summary: "Examining growth of complex securitized structures in U.S. and world markets,
provides a timeline of key events, proposing explanations for the resulting financial crisis.
Offers suggestions on securitization reform, including a solution to insure the mortgage market
against default risk. Provides strategies to increase transparency and encourage more prudent
lending"—Provided by publisher.
   ISBN 978-0-8157-0336-5 (pbk. : alk. paper)
   1. Asset-backed financing.   2. Mortgage loans.   3. Financial crises.   I. Fuchita,
Yasuyuki, 1958–   II. Herring, Richard.   III. Litan, Robert E., 1950–   IV. Title.

   HG4028.A84P78 2009
   332.63'27—dc22   2009023362

9 8 7 6 5 4 3 2 1

Typeset in Adobe Garamond

Composition by R. Lynn Rivenbark
Macon, Georgia

Tokyo Club Foundation for Global Studies has underwritten
the production of *Prudent Lending Restored.*

Contents

Preface

IN 2004 THE Brookings Institution was approached by the Tokyo Club Foundation for Global Studies to showcase research on selected topics in financial market structure and regulation of interest to policymakers, scholars, and citizens in the United States and Japan and elsewhere. This collaboration, led by Brookings senior fellow Robert E. Litan and Yasuyuki Fuchita, senior managing director of the Nomura Institute of Capital Markets Research, has resulted in four conferences and the publication of three volumes: *Financial Gatekeepers: Can They Protect Investors?* (2006), *New Financial Instruments and Institutions: Opportunities and Policy Challenges* (2007), and *Pooling Money: The Future of Mutual Funds* (2008).

In 2008, the Financial Institutions Center at the Wharton School of Finance at the University of Pennsylvania, led by Richard Herring, joined the collaboration. Brookings has cosponsored with the Financial Institutions Center the *Brookings-Wharton Papers on Financial Services* and is currently collaborating with Janet Rothenberg Pack of Wharton in producing the *Brookings-Wharton Papers on Urban Affairs.*

The chapters in this volume are based on papers presented at a conference on October 16, 2008, that focused on the future of securitization. As outlined in the following introduction, this topic has become of great interest since the subprime mortgage crisis emerged in 2007 as the precursor to a major economic recession in the United States, Japan, and many other countries. All of the chapters represent the views of the authors and not necessarily those of the staff, officers, or trustees of the Brookings Institution, the Nomura Institute of Capital Markets Research, or the Wharton Financial Institutions Center.

The editors thank Adriane Fresh for research assistance and Lindsey Wilson for organizing the conference and providing administrative assistance. Thanks also to Eileen Hughes of the Brookings Institution Press for editing the book.

YASUYUKI FUCHITA
RICHARD J. HERRING
ROBERT E. LITAN

1

The Future
of Securitization:
An Introduction

SINCE ITS DEVELOPMENT over a period of more than three decades, the securitization of loans—the process by which many individual loans (initially mortgages and since then many other types of loans as well) are packaged together in trusts and used as collateral for securities—has been hailed as one of the more important and socially useful financial innovations of recent times. The securitization process has allowed Wall Street to more efficiently finance Main Street, bringing capital from securities markets to loan originators, relieving them of the need to finance and maintain loans on their balance sheets. Further, by effectively splitting the ownership of loans into many smaller units—through the sale of securities—the process was thought to diversify credit risk more widely across national and, indeed, global capital markets rather than concentrate that risk on the balance sheets of the institutions that originated the loans.

However, the meltdown since late 2006 of the subprime mortgage market, coupled with the severe recession that has since followed, has caused many to reconsider what they may have believed about the securitization process. Although there is little basis for questioning the lower cost of credit that securitization affords for prime quality borrowers, there is now widespread skepticism of the net benefits of the more complex securitized structures that facilitated the explosion of subprime mortgage credit in the United States during the last three years of the 2002–06 economic expansion. Moreover, it is now broadly accepted that the securitization process did not disperse credit risk as broadly as was once thought but instead may have simply shifted it, in concentrated forms, across a limited number of financial entities, some of which are systemically important.

What, then, is the future of securitization? And what can be done to ensure that in the future securitization continues to deliver benefits—cheaper loans and more liquidity in lending markets—without causing harm? The chapters in this volume seek to answer those questions.

The authors come at the issues from a variety of perspectives. In chapter 2, Robert A. Eisenbeis sets the stage for the later chapters by analyzing the causes of the subprime mortgage crisis, concentrating on what he argues was excessively lax monetary policy. Joseph R. Mason describes in chapter 3 how the creation of an alphabet soup of complex securities and structures—constant proportion debt obligations (CPDOs), structured investment vehicles (SIVs), and auction rate securities (ARSs)—played a key role in facilitating the rapid growth and eventual implosion of the subprime mortgage market. In chapter 4, Günter Franke and Jan P. Krahnen examine the flaws in the policy framework and the misalignment of incentives that they believe allowed the securitization process to run off the rails and suggest changes to put it back on a constructive track. In chapter 5, Jennifer E. Bethel, Allen Ferrell, and Gang Hu take up the legal and economic issues from the litigation that has arisen and is likely to arise in the future from the 2007–08 credit crisis. Jack Guttentag and Igor Roitburg offer in chapter 6 a specific proposal for improving the alignment of incentives in mortgage markets. In chapter 7, Eiichi Sekine, Kei Kodachi, and Tetsuya Kamiyama conclude this volume with a penetrating comparison of securitization in Asia, especially in Japan, and that in the United States. Ironically, the fact that securitization has grown more slowly in Asia and has simpler structures that are easier to value has so far better insulated Asian economies from the financial problems recently experienced in the United States, if not from the subsequent recession. A brief summary of the contents of each of these chapters follows below.

Eisenbeis begins in chapter 2 by providing a timeline of the key events that characterized the financial crisis in the United States and subsequently elsewhere, through October 2008 (the time of the conference on which in this volume is based). Eisenbeis places heavy emphasis on the low interest rate environment since 2002 as a major contributing cause of the crisis. Policy actions in several parts of the world made that possible: loose monetary policy in both the United States and Japan and the willingness of central banks in countries such as China to purchase U.S. Treasury securities even in the face of large U.S. federal budget and trade deficits. Eisenbeis is also critical of financial institutions for their laxity in originating subprime mortgages and of the credit rating agencies for their failure to analyze the securities secured by these mortgages with sufficient rigor.

In discussing the sequence of events that led up to the crisis and its aftermath, Eisenbeis highlights the different responses by central banks and finance ministries in various developed economies. At first, the reactions were uncoordinated: the European Central Bank injected massive amounts of liquidity into European banks, while the Federal Reserve cut rates and expanded its liquidity facilities to cover primary dealers of U.S. Treasury securities. The Fed followed with its term auction facilities for banks, while the FDIC expanded its insurance coverage of bank deposits and extended coverage to some long-term debt. Only when those actions seemed insufficient to stem the crisis did central banks begin to coordinate their rate cuts and liquidity facilities, in a massive and unprecedented fashion. Throughout the crisis period, the different responses by various central banks permitted different interest rates to prevail in the affected countries, despite the fact that all were confronting similar crisis conditions.

Although Eisenbeis finds that no one country responded optimally to the crisis and that, taken together, the varied central bank actions had only limited success in mitigating it, he applauds both the European Central Bank and the Fed for responding quickly and decisively. At the same time, the Fed's extraordinary actions have exposed it and U.S. taxpayers to future losses, while greatly expanding and radically changing the composition of the Fed's balance sheet.

Eisenbeis worries about the long-term consequences of such deep government involvement in the financial system, for which no exit strategy or coherent plan for moving forward was apparent in October 2008. In particular, the massive injection of funds into the banking systems by governments in the United States and Europe leaves few protections for taxpayers. Eisenbeis highlights other distortions: the consolidation of banking systems—leading to ever-larger, too-big-to-manage and too-big-to-fail banks (much like the failed government-sponsored enterprises, Fannie Mae and Freddie Mac)—which put banks without government support at a disadvantage relative to those that receive government funds, and the failure of policymakers to reduce the leverage in the financial system, which undoubtedly exacerbated the crisis.

Eisenbeis concludes by identifying four ways in which policymakers could reduce the frequency and severity of future financial crises. First, he calls for ending the blanket guarantees of all bank deposits. Second, he urges policymakers to adopt better ways to handle the failure of both bank and nonbank financial institutions. In his view, governments in the United States and Europe were forced to take over failed financial institutions and/or to guarantee their creditors because of inadequate bankruptcy procedures. Third, Eisenbeis urges policymakers to find ways of discouraging regulators from taking an excessively short-run view by attempting to make sure that financial institutions do not "fail" on their watch without regard for the longer-term consequences for systemic stability. Finally, he concludes that there is an urgent need to limit leverage, by both borrowers and the financial institutions that often are all too willing to lend to them.

How was it possible that securities backed by subprime debt—less than prime quality loans—gained such popularity until the middle of 2007? In chapter 3 Mason answers that question, in part, by explaining how three financial "innovations"—in the securities themselves and in the institutions that were formed to sell or hold them—contributed to the acceptance of those securities and laid the foundation for the crisis that followed. Ironically, each of the innovations also proved to be a victim of the crisis.

The first such innovation is the collateralized debt obligation (CDO), a refinement of the mortgage-backed security (MBS), a pioneering financial innovation of the 1970s. In the typical (pass-through) MBS structure, investors receive, on a pro rata basis, the principal and interest payments on the underlying mortgages. In later innovations, MBSs were structured into various "tranches," with the top layer having first claim to the mortgage payments and with additional payments cascading to each lower tranche after the claims of the more senior tranches had been fully satisfied. The CDO differs from the MBS in several respects: the pools of assets securitized by CDOs are actively managed rather than static; CDO transactions often are closed before the pool of underlying assets is fully formed; and CDOs often contain far fewer assets than conventional MBSs. As a result of those features, the value of a CDO tranche is much more opaque than the value of an MBS tranche. Moreover, secondary markets in CDOs are thinner than those for MBSs; thus prices of CDO tranches can be much more volatile than those of MBS tranches. Mason is critical (as are many others) of the credit rating agencies, whose excessively optimistic ratings of CDO tranches facilitated their easy sale to investors.

Although created in the late 1980s, structured investment vehicles (SIVs), the second key innovation that Mason singles out, did not become popular until the middle of this decade, when commercial banks discovered their advantages as an off–balance sheet means of financing the purchase of CDOs and other structured products that the banks manufactured and marketed. The typical SIV was funded by asset-backed commercial paper (ABCP), which, until the subprime mortgage market collapsed, was readily sold to investors seeking highly rated, short-term securities promising higher returns than those available on more traditional money market instruments. By funding long-term assets with short-term liabilities, SIVs were vulnerable to funding risk. They could function only as long as investors were willing to purchase (or roll over their purchases of) ABCP. Moreover, SIVs had relatively thin capital cushions, at 5 to 10 percent of assets, which made them vulnerable to a loss of confidence in the value of their assets. That instability became manifest in 2007, when, after investors saw home prices beginning to decline in many parts of the country, SIVs were unable to roll over their ABCP as it matured. Following a failed attempt by the U.S. Treasury to organize a private sector financing facility for them, the banks that created them felt compelled (for reputational reasons) to purchase their assets or liabilities, weakening the banks' own balance sheets in the process. In the end, concern over reputational risk undermined the attempt to transfer credit risk.

Auction rate securities, the third innovation that Mason discusses, predate SIVs, and like them, they were developed as a way to fund pools of debt, in this case municipal bonds. The rates on ARSs are set periodically by auction. Mason explains how in recent years, ARS structures grew more complex and proved to be far less liquid than many investors expected. As the financial crisis deepened, the auctions for the securities failed, so that investors could not sell them. Mason describes how eventually the banks that created and marketed the securities became the buyers of last resort (much like the banks that purchased SIV assets and liabilities).

Given the clear flaws in the more complex securitizations of recent years, what changes—by private actors or the government or both—are necessary to preserve the benefits that earlier securitizations achieved? Franke and Krahnen tackle that subject in chapter 4. As a predicate to their suggestions, the authors begin with their own diagnosis of what went wrong. In their view, the principal villains were flawed financial engineering, lack of transparency, and compensation systems that rewarded excessive risk taking in the short run at the expense of longer-term stability. The authors agree that housing speculation clearly helped lay the foundation for the crisis, but they argue that the factors that they emphasize are evidence of much deeper problems in financial markets and institutions that require fundamental reform.

Like Mason, the authors begin by focusing on both the benefits and the costs of securitization. In their view, securitization turned sour because of the failure to preserve incentives for loan originators to be prudent. The lack of transparency throughout the various stages of the securitization process, including by the financial institutions that marketed and ended up holding the securities, also was an important contributing cause of the crisis.

Compensation structures aggravated those problems. Too many managers at financial institutions had incentives to choose riskier, more leveraged financial structures, when given a choice. At the same time, the authors are skeptical that regulators have sufficient knowledge to mandate more appropriate compensation systems. A more promising approach might be for regulators to require more transparency in compensation systems so that key stakeholders—creditors and shareholders—are better positioned to influence the development of more suitable compensation arrangements.

More broadly, the authors conclude that given current compensation systems and the permissive regulatory environment, the financial crisis shares features of what Gerrit Hardin has described as the "tragedy of the commons." Financial stability, argue Franke and Krahnen, is a commons that can be and has been eroded by overleveraged positions, deteriorating underwriting standards, and unsound financial engineering. How can that undesirable result be avoided in the future? The authors suggest that the best course is for policymakers to mandate the disclosure of information by issuers of securities so that market participants can more fully understand the risks of and the potential for incentive misalignments. They predict that in the future investors will require issuers to absorb first losses of securitized instruments, thereby encouraging issuers to be more prudent throughout the securitization process. Although they reject direct regulation of credit rating agencies, here too they believe that fuller disclosure of the incentives of the parties structuring asset-backed securities is required. They also suggest that regulators publish the performance of the rating agencies, which would subject those entities to greater market discipline. Finally, the authors urge that capital standards be revised to encourage greater transparency, so that henceforth regulated financial institutions pay a greater price for engaging in practices or business strategies that obscure the risks that they are taking. In effect, capital requirements would rise with an institution's opacity.

One certain outcome of any financial crisis, at least in the United States, is litigation: lawsuits by aggrieved parties seeking some recompense for the losses that they have suffered. In chapter 5, Bethel, Ferrell, and Hu examine the litigation that has been spawned so far by the financial crisis of 2007–08 and speculate about the kinds and consequences of crisis-related litigation that may occur in the future.

After explaining how home mortgage loans are securitized, the authors survey the status of crisis-generated litigation as of October 2008. Among other things, the crisis has been associated with a nearly 50 percent increase in securities class action filings. Various government authorities—the FBI, the attorneys general of Connecticut and New York, and the SEC—have launched investigations of the practices of certain commercial and investment banks. Litigation under the Employee Retirement Income Security Act (ERISA) also has been filed against large financial companies, including Citigroup, MBIA, Merrill Lynch, Morgan Stanley, and State Street Bank.

The authors offer their views, based on their analysis of applicable statutes and prior court rulings, about what other kinds of litigation may ensue in the wake of the crisis, the legal theories that plaintiffs might advance, and the likely judicial responses. They begin by examining what cases might be brought by securities purchasers, specifically those who bought CDOs and MBSs. CDOs were sold principally under rule 144A, which applies to securities purchased by institutional investors. Such purchasers are not protected by the antifraud provisions of rule 10b-5; their claims therefore must be based on violation of a contract with a CDO manager. In contrast, individuals who purchased MBSs may have claims, depending on the facts, for false or misleading registration statements by MBS issuers with respect to documentation, disclosure of underwriting standards, and pricing of the MBS tranches. The authors suggest that plaintiffs might also sue the firms that performed due diligence for underwriters of the securities as well as the commercial (and formerly independent) investment banks that sold the securities. Some suits might also be filed on behalf of pension funds under ERISA against banks and mortgage originators for facilitating imprudent investments by plan trustees. And, of course, some litigation against the rating agencies is likely, even though the agencies have so far been able to defeat actions against them on First Amendment grounds.

It is difficult, of course, to predict which of these classes of lawsuit—or whether any particular lawsuit—might be successful. Indeed, the authors highlight a number of the procedural and doctrinal hurdles that plaintiffs must overcome if they are to prevail. At the same time, however, given the magnitude of the claimed losses at stake, it is likely that some of the defendants will settle. Any future losses from future litigation, of course, are not likely to be reflected in the current balance sheets of possible future defendants.

Clearly, the subprime mortgage crisis has revealed that too many parties—loan originators, securitizers, and purchasers of securities backed by subprime debt—significantly underestimated the default risk of subprime mortgages, in particular those originated toward the end of the subprime mortgage boom, in 2005 and 2006. In chapter 6, Guttentag and Roitburg examine the flaws in the mortgage finance system that led to this result.

Under the traditional system of mortgage finance, borrowers theoretically are charged a risk-based interest rate. Higher-risk borrowers pay higher interest rates than prime borrowers. Guttentag and Roitburg argue that this system fails to properly account for default risk. They propose instead a new system of mortgage insurance that would require borrowers to purchase insurance whose premiums reflect default risk. Such mortgage insurance would protect investors after default from any drop in home value and from foreclosure costs if the property ends up in foreclosure. Such a system, in their view, would better insulate the financial system against a fall in house prices and do so at lower cost to borrowers than under the current system.

More broadly, the authors argue that the principles underlying their proposed system have wider market applicability. The key to making their system work is what they call transaction-based reserving (TBR), which ensures that a portion of the risk premium on a given transaction is reserved and withdrawn and used only upon the occurrence of certain events defined in advance. In principle, TBR is immune to the tendency for lending standards and reserves to decline in a boom, rendering the financial system more vulnerable to future exogenous shocks. During the economic boom years preceding the financial crisis, loan originators promoted riskier loans and lenders were not required to increase their capital or reserves to provide an added cushion against loss from those riskier assets. Guttentag and Roitburg argue that had their TBR system been in place, riskier assets would have carried higher premiums, which would have funded larger reserves against loss, an outcome that would have helped to insulate the financial system against the shocks that in fact occurred.

Although some Japanese banks have suffered losses from U.S. mortgage securities, by and large, the Japanese financial system has escaped the worst (at least as of October 2008). In chapter 7, Sekine, Kodachi, and Kamiyama conclude this volume by explaining how and why that occurred.

In brief, the authors credit Asia's more favorable experience with securitization to the fact that securitization in Asia is less complex and less extensive than in the United States. For example, only as of 2006 had the issuance of new securitized instruments in major Asian markets reached the level seen in the United States in 1995. Despite the financial turmoil triggered by the flaws of securitization in the United States, the authors predict the importance of securitization should continue to grow in Japan in the future. The challenge for private actors and policymakers everywhere is to ensure that all parties properly understand the risks of both the securities and the mortgages that underlie them.

The authors explain that even though securitization is less developed in Asian capital markets than in the U.S. capital market, it still plays an important role for two reasons. First, bond markets in Asia (except in Japan) also are relatively underdeveloped; asset-backed securities therefore fill an important need for investors looking for fixed-income products. Second, Asian companies depend heavily on banks for funds, which leads to a concentration of risk in Asian banking systems. Securitization has the potential for reducing the concentration of risk by transferring some proportion to other hands. That potential was not realized in the United States largely because the complexity of financial engineering out-paced the ability of the rating agencies and investors to fully understand the risks of the securities. In contrast, securitized instruments offered in Japan have much simpler structures and consequently are much easier to understand and value.

Securitization originally developed in Japan and China for somewhat different reasons than in the United States. In both countries, public officials encouraged the process largely as a way of enabling banks to dispose of nonperforming loans, although Japan viewed mortgage-backed securities also as a means of enhancing liquidity in mortgage markets. In China in particular, the government helps to ensure the quality of securitized instruments by tightly overseeing what kinds of debt can be securitized. In response to the financial crisis, China's bank regulator tightened the rules in that regard, to the point that no new securitized instrument was approved for sale between May 2008 and October 2008.

Sekine, Kodachi, and Kamiyama cite data indicating that at least as of the time that their paper was presented, the Japanese economy was weathering the diffi-culties in securitized instruments reasonably well. Downgrades and defaults of securitized debt were quite low relative to those in other countries. However, the authors do point out one major vulnerability. They are concerned that collateral-ized bond obligations (CBOs) may have considerably higher losses in the near future, due to credit downgrades of the bonds underlying those obligations. Inter-estingly, the authors argue that this vulnerability resembles some of the flaws in the subprime mortgage-backed CDO market in the United States, with CBOs relying excessively on inadequate quantitative risk management models, insuffi-cient model calibration periods, and faulty assumptions by the rating agencies with respect to likely annual defaults.

Sekine, Kodachi, and Kamiyama also explain the central role that the Japan Housing Finance Agency has played in facilitating mortgage securitization in Japan. For much of the post–World War II period, the Government Housing Loan Corporation (GHLC) provided mortgage loans directly. In 2005, the GHLC began to put more emphasis on securitizing rather than originating mortgage loans. In 2007, the GHLC was formally transformed into the Japan Housing Finance Agency (JHF), which continues the securitization function. The JHF is modeled on the operations of similar government-sponsored enterprises in the United States, but with an important difference: the JHF requires overcollateral-ization for the securities that it guarantees, and unlike Fannie Mae or Freddie Mac, the JHF does *not* seek additional profits by trading mortgage-backed securities or derivatives. At the time that the authors' paper was presented, the future of the JHF was being actively debated in Japan, with some advocating its privatization. Sekine, Kodachi, and Kamiyama argue that Japanese policymakers should wait until the financial crisis eases and the future of the housing government-sponsored enterprises (GSEs) in the United States is resolved before making any final decisions about the JHF.

The authors conclude by offering some perspectives on how the United States might learn from Asian economies when thinking about the future of securitization. Perhaps most important, they suggest that U.S. market participants and authorities copy the Asian practice of ensuring that loan originators retain at least some subordinate position in asset-backed securities so that they have a greater incentive to act prudently. Further, in Asia, mortgage loans are almost always originated by commercial banks rather than specialized mortgage banks or brokers. Although that tends to concentrate more credit risk in banks, it also encourages more prudence in originating loans. Finally, although Japanese taxpayers are at risk, like their U.S. counterparts, for the risks underwritten by their quasi-governmental mortgage agencies, the authors argue that the JHF faces less risk because it is engaged only in securitization, not in trading.

In sum, the chapters in this volume document the factors that have led to the growth of securitization in both U.S. and other markets as well as the flaws in the securitization process in the United States that helped lead to the subprime mortgage crisis. Those flaws can and should be corrected. Once they are, however, securitization has a bright, more secure future because properly redesigned securitizations can yield significant benefits to both borrowers and lenders, without jeopardizing the stability of the financial system.

ROBERT A. EISENBEIS

2

Financial Turmoil and Central Bank Responses in the United States, United Kingdom, European Union, and Japan

T HE PROTRACTED FINANCIAL market turmoil now affecting most industrial countries, which had its genesis in the U.S. subprime mortgage market, initially elicited significantly different responses from various central banks (principally, the Federal Reserve, the European Central Bank, the Bank of England, and the Bank of Japan). It also exposed significantly different structural defects in the national safety nets across the world's major financial markets, most notably in the United States, United Kingdom, and European Union. The resulting issues run the gamut from questions about how central banks and more generally governments should respond to a financial crisis and provide needed liquidity when market disruptions arise to concerns about how to structure deposit guarantee systems and financial safety nets. The purpose of this chapter[1] is to describe the market disruptions that took place from the fall of 2007 through November 2008 and to discuss and assess the various central bank and government policy responses to the turmoil.[2] The chapter then goes on to point out defects in safety net design and suggests needed reforms to address those defects.

I am indebted to Edward Kane, George Kaufman, and Larry Wall for helpful comments on earlier versions of this chapter.

1. An earlier version of this chapter was presented at the Brookings–Tokyo Club–Wharton Conference, "Prudent Lending Restored: Securitization after the 2007 Mortgage Securities Meltdown," Washington, October 16, 2008.

2. For other discussions, see Chailloux and others (2008).

The Market Turmoil and What Contributed to It

The market turmoil that unsettled financial markets in the fall of 2007 is widely blamed on problems in the U.S. subprime mortgage market. However, the case can also be made that the subprime market was simply where the financial market imbalances resulting in large measure from a series of international and domestic macroeconomic fiscal and monetary policy mistakes came unwound first. Those policy mistakes are important, and they are not confined to the United States.

There were four major policy problems. First, following the dotcom bust, the continued slowdown in the rate of inflation, and the investment-led recession, the U.S. Federal Reserve cut interest rates drastically, from 6.5 percent for federal funds in 2000 to 1 percent in 2003, in order to stimulate the economy, forestall the recession, and avoid so-called unwanted deflation. Rates were kept low for a protracted period of time, and the resulting stimulus for housing and strong consumer spending fueled a huge run-up in housing construction and home prices (see figure 2-1). Strong housing demand combined with a flat yield curve stimulated increased leverage on the part of both consumers and lenders.

Second, the large and persistent federal deficits and growing trade imbalance interacted with the policies of foreign governments, mainly in China and Japan, to keep their currencies undervalued; created the conditions for a perfect storm that supported and isolated the U.S. economy in the short term from some of the natural economic equilibrating forces; and supported continuing and growing imbalances rather than acting to limit them. In order to create jobs and stimulate economic growth through exports, the Chinese government kept its exchange rate artificially low. The trade surplus with the United States in particular resulted in the Chinese accumulating huge dollar reserves, which flowed back into U.S. financial markets in the form of increased demand for U.S. Treasury liabilities (which were in ample supply, because of the fiscal deficit).

A third contributing policy problem was the zero interest rate policy pursued by the Japanese in an attempt to stimulate their economy into finally recovering from the malaise of the 1990s. The Bank of Japan flooded the market with liquidity, which gave rise to and stimulated the yen carry trade, in which investors borrowed low-cost funds in Japan and purchased higher yielding U.S. Treasuries or other high-quality government-issued assets in other countries.[3] That was a relatively riskless arbitrage as long as exchange rates did not move against the trade in what were very large and liquid markets. When combined with leverage, returns could

---

3. See Hattori and Shin (2007).

be very large. Japan's policies to stabilize interest rates, combined with both the carry trade and Chinese demand for U.S. Treasuries, helped to keep downward pressure on U.S. interest rates, especially on the long end of the yield curve. It also meant that foreigners and foreign governments were financing the U.S. fiscal and trade deficits by keeping the demand for U.S. dollars high, and it made the conduct of monetary policy easier than it would have been if the Federal Reserve had had to purchase U.S. Treasuries in the market to keep the federal funds rate at its low target level. This external financing of the U.S. deficit also helped keep domestic inflation low by limiting growth of the U.S. money supply.

The fourth problem was that low U.S. interest rates not only encouraged and supported growth of the U.S. housing industry but also, when combined with financial engineering techniques, contributed to the widespread use of leverage on the part of borrowers (that is, subprime borrowers) and increased risk taking by exposing low-quality borrowers to interest rate risk if interest rates were significantly higher when their variable-rate loans with low teaser rates began to be repriced.[4] Of course, the Federal Reserve did begin to tighten monetary policy in June 2004 and continued to do so with eighteen 25-basis-point cuts ending in the fall of 2007. Short-term interest rates, to which variable-rate subprime mortgages were tied, moved up, with predictable consequences for repayment performance.

Increased leverage not only characterized the housing market but also was a more general problem. The flood of liquidity combined with a relatively flat yield curve and declining risk spreads more generally encouraged the use of greater leverage by many market participants, including banks that sought to get loans off their balance sheets through the use of special purpose entities in order to avoid capital adequacy constraints but retain their fees for loan origination and loan servicing. Again, the growth of derivatives and the use of loan conduits and structured investment vehicles (SIVs), all of which were highly leveraged and financed in the short-term commercial paper market, enabled firms generating high volumes of loans to place them in the capital markets. Many of those techniques were used to sell off subprime and other types of loans and/or to sell the credit risk to those who—willingly or unwittingly—took that risk by using credit default swaps and other forms of credit derivatives. The common ground here, whether one is talking about borrowers or lenders, was the use of extreme leverage enabled by ample liquidity and low risk spreads.

Of course, a description of what went wrong would not be complete without some recognition that misplaced private sector incentives emphasized fee and asset generation with little regard for the inherent risks in the assets, since they

4. Taylor (2009) considers this to be a major contributing cause of the crisis.

Figure 2-1. *U.S. Federal Funds Target Rate to December 5, 2008*

Percent

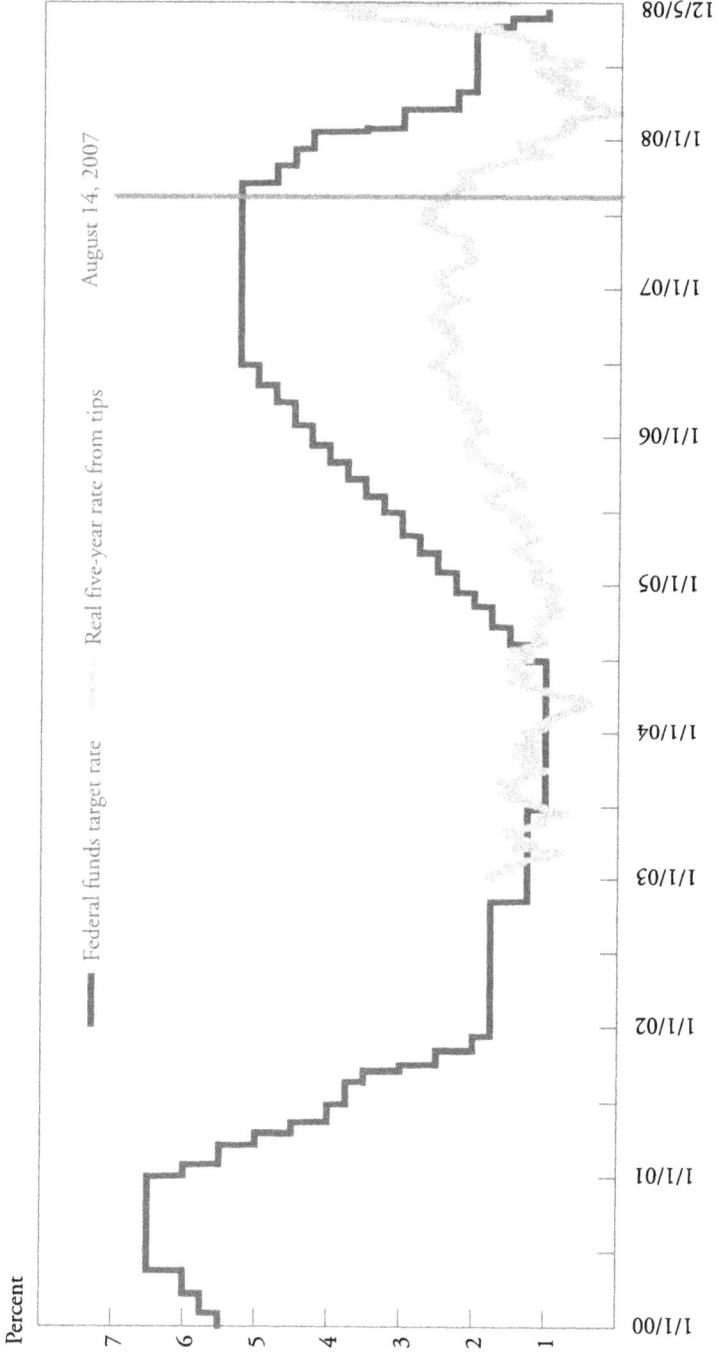

Source: Board of Governors of the Federal Reserve System (www.federalreserve.gov/fomc/fundsrate.htm) and the U.S. Treasury Department.

would be sold. That together with lender outsourcing of due diligence to credit rating agencies also were important in placing financial institutions in a precarious financial position. Financial engineering and the use of complex pricing models to turn payment streams into designer instruments intended to meet customer cash flow needs also drove fee-oriented structures. The institutions that originated assets earned a fee for doing so, but they were not responsible for assessing and monitoring the risks associated with low-quality mortgages. That meant that less attention was paid to the actual risks in the loans because the originator usually was not held responsible for any losses that might occur.

Especially problematic were the conflicted incentives in the credit rating industry. The credit rating agencies were paid by the originators of the assets to assess the underlying credit quality of the loans and derivative assets being created. Originators had an incentive to shop for favorable ratings while the rating agencies had an incentive to provide them because of the fees that they were paid to "work with" the originators to create assets with the desired risk characteristics. Ratings were created that had the same letter grades as corporate and municipal bonds, but in fact the ratings were not designed to mean the same thing. Kane (2008a, 2008b) points out that ratings of complex mortgage structures really should have been based on probabilities, with two-sided ranges on the likely risks in the instruments, rather than indicated simply by a letter grade. That practice encouraged the creation of instruments that just met the threshold for the desired rating but had a very high likelihood of being of lower quality.

The point here is that both macroeconomic policy problems and defective managerial incentives involving financial institution managers and the rating agencies created an environment that proved vulnerable when asset prices declined. And when housing prices defied expectations and actually did begin to decline because of oversupply in many markets—such as in California, Florida, Nevada, and Arizona in particular—excessive leverage only exacerbated the consequences of the fall in housing prices.

The Initial Problem

While it is always difficult to pinpoint an exact catalyst for the sudden unwinding of an unsustainable financial position, problems in the subprime market were clearly already developing by the start of 2006 and festered for the early part of 2007 before creditors suddenly began to have questions about the quality of assets backed by mortgages, whether subprime or conventional. Positions became increasingly difficult to finance. Financial markets began to reprice and reevaluate risk and essentially seized up in late August 2007. The problems and policy responses, however, were different in the three main markets affected—the European Union, United Kingdom, and United States. The appendix provides a detailed chronology of the key emerging developments and the policy responses to them as background to the discussion that follows. That chronology suggests that the first signs of problems appeared in early 2007 with the failure of ResMAE, a large residential mortgage lender, and the subsequent emergence of problems in other U.S. lenders as well as in lenders in other parts of the world. Those would include losses by and withdrawal of funding to the U.S. investment bank Bear Stearns; the rescue of two real estate–oriented, state-owned German banks; problems in the sponsored hedge funds of BNP Paribas; the takeover of the troubled mortgage lender, Countrywide; and the nationalization of the U.K. lender Northern Rock.

All of these events had their genesis in the emerging problems in the U.S. real estate markets. The U.S. housing market began to slow in late 2005, whether measured by declining sales of new and existing houses or by the falloff in new construction and issuance of new permits. At the same time, signs of deterioration began to appear in the quality of outstanding mortgages, particularly so-called subprime adjustable rate mortgages, whose delinquency rates began to reverse in 2005 the steady decline that they had exhibited beginning in 2002. Subprime fixed-rate loans and prime adjustable rate loans maintained good performance through 2005 and did not begin to show significant signs of weakness until 2006.

About the time that U.S. housing markets began to exhibit the first signs of weakness, the growth of mortgage-related derivatives activities took off. In particular, the securitization of mortgages spread far beyond conventional mortgages (which had prospered under the sponsorship of Fannie Mae and Freddie Mac) to include subprime and Alt-A mortgages and they became a significant part of the market. The Bank of England's 2007 *Financial Stability Report* documents the fact that the growth in the issuance of real estate mortgage–backed securities backed by subprime loans jumped to more than $125 billion in 2004 but then almost doubled by the end of 2006, just when major problems hit the U.S. housing market.[5] Equally interesting, the report also suggests why the impacts of the problems in the U.S. mortgage market hit investment banks especially hard and quickly spread abroad. The main issuers of residential mortgage–backed securities (RMBSs) backed by subprime mortgages were investment banks, large European financial institutions, and U.K. financial institutions; by comparison, U.S. commercial banks were relatively minor participants. Subsequently, it was not surprising that

---

5. Bank of England (2007, chart 2-14).

there were large losses and a movement by institutions to put assets back on their balance sheets in order to preserve their reputations, particularly by investment banks and to some extent by the large money center banks. In part, the reputational effect reflected the fact that fee generation and trading revenues dominated the revenue generation activities of the large, complex financial institutions. The report also documents how dominant those activities had become compared with traditional intermediation.[6] Traditional lending accounted for only about a quarter of the earnings of large, complex financial institutions while commissions and fees and trading income accounted for the bulk of their earnings.

The financial problems triggered by the U.S. real estate slowdown manifested themselves somewhat differently in the international money markets, in part because of some differences in institutions and practices. At first, problems were seen as being mainly short-term liquidity problems that affected spreads. However, as time progressed, it became apparent that deeper issues were involved, not just a temporary pullback by cautious liquidity providers. Differences in perceptions of the problems and their causes conditioned the responses of central bankers and regulators to the financial market turmoil that ensued. The responses were divided into what now appear to be two separate phases. The first phase consisted of largely independent country and institution responses, which persisted up through approximately mid-October 2008. More recently, responses have become more coordinated across central banks and governments as they attempt to address what now seem to be increasing risks to real economies stemming from the financial turmoil. The first-phase responses are discussed below, followed by a brief summary of the coordinated, second-phase responses.

Phase 1 Responses in Germany, the European Union, and the European Central Bank

The credit quality problem in the U.S. subprime market claimed its first casualty in the European Union (EU) with Germany's IKB Deutsche Industriebank AG. Originally a second-tier institution specializing in lending to businesses of intermediate size, IKB began investing in complex fixed-income securities, collateralized debt obligations (CDOs), and derivatives through its subsidiary Rhineland Funding Capital Corporation.[7] Those relatively longer-term assets, which included but were not limited to securities backed by U.S. subprime loans, were funded by Rhineland with shorter-term debt instruments placed with investors

---

6. Bank of England (2007, chart 2-16).

7. See Mollenkamp, Taylor, and McDonald (2007) for a detailed discussion of IKB. The initial package was valued at about 3.5 billion euros (US$4.8 billion).

throughout the world. The funding-short and lending-long strategy worked as long as credit risk spreads and interest rates remained low, but it began to unravel in early 2007 when U.S. subprime defaults began to increase and the value of the securities that they supported began to decline in value. As investors became increasingly concerned about refunding asset-backed commercial paper in general, IKB began to experience problems rolling over its funding. On July 27, instead of honoring a credit line that it had extended to IKB, Deutsche Bank reported IKB's 2007 funding difficulties to BaFin (Bundesanstalt für Finanzdienstleistungsaufsicht), the German financial regulator. BaFin arranged a rescue package for IKB that included an injection of funds by KfW Group, which was a state-owned institution and a major shareholder in IKB. Other participants included other German banks, the Association of German Banks, and other banking organizations. By involving other institutions, BaFin probably hoped that depositors and other sources of funding would be reassured that the institution was sound.[8]

About the same time that German institutions experienced problems in valuing holdings of subprime mortgages, similar problems began to surface in other markets. In the United States, for example, Bear Stearns was experiencing large losses on mortgage securities in two of its sponsored hedge funds. On July 31, 2007, shortly after the rescue of the German banks, two hedge funds sponsored by Bear Stearns filed for bankruptcy protection. Bear Sterns also invoked a lockout on another hedge fund.

Back in Germany, problems began to surface in other institutions. Two German mutual fund managers (Union Investment and Frankfurt Trust) suspended withdrawals.[9] Finally, on August 17, 2007, a second German banking organization, SachsenLB, which was owned by the German state of Saxony, was rescued with a package that amounted to 17.3 billion euros (US$23.3 billion). The bailout was triggered when the bank's conduit, Ormond Quay, was unable to continue funding its operations because of its holdings of U.S. subprime mortgages.[10] Shortly

---

8. Central bankers commonly enlist other bankers to help rescue troubled financial institutions, which is likely to be a misguided policy. Regulators should seek to make bank failures isolated events to prevent problems in one institution from infecting healthy institutions. By inducing healthy institutions to lend to or provide financial support to troubled institutions, regulators only prove to the marketplace, if there was uncertainty about potential contagion effects, that contagion effects are certain. It is partly for that reason that the U.S. system seeks to shut down institutions before they become economically insolvent and does not rely on cross-bank lending support. The United States has not always been immune to the problem. Money center banks were induced by Fed chairman Paul Volcker to provide funds to Continental Illinois Bank when it experienced financial difficulties in 1984.

9. See Boyd (2007). Union Trust's action was on August 3.

10. See Beams (2007).

Figure 2-2. *Euro-LIBOR Rates, August 1–17, 2007*

Percent

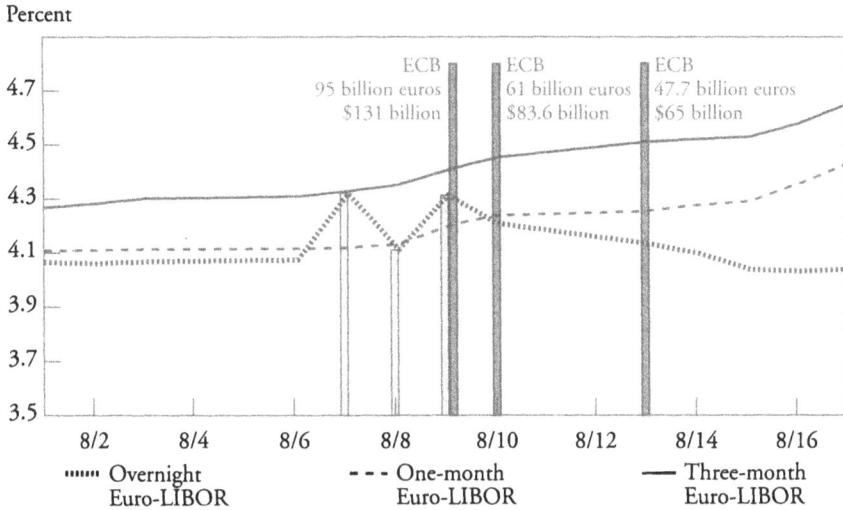

ECB	ECB	ECB
95 billion euros	61 billion euros	47.7 billion euros
$131 billion	$83.6 billion	$65 billion

▪▪▪▪▪ Overnight   - - - One-month   —— Three-month
Euro-LIBOR   Euro-LIBOR   Euro-LIBOR

Source: British Bankers Association (www.bba.org.uk/bba/jsp/polopoly.jsp?d=141&a=15151).

thereafter problems began to spread more widely within the EU as BNP Paribas SA suspended withdrawals from three of its funds because of difficulties in valuing its U.S. subprime mortgage holdings.[11]

Uncertainty about the quality of assets in financial institutions and those backing up derivative and related securities manifested themselves differently in Europe and the United States, and the responses of central banks also were markedly different. In Europe, where banks were the primary source of financial intermediation, credit spreads widened significantly in the interbank market, which was the most important channel for short-term funding of highly leveraged institutions, affiliates, and conduits. One month asset-backed commercial paper and eurodollar rates spiked after averaging less than 10 basis points prior to the turmoil, and the spread between the rates on asset-backed paper and financial commercial paper widened significantly.

Figure 2-2 highlights what happened to short-term euro-LIBOR rates over the month of August as the turmoil began to unfold in response to certain triggering events and central bank interventions. On August 7, overnight euro-LIBOR rates spiked nearly 20 basis points (but virtually no significant movement was observed in the one- and three-month rates on that day). The overnight rate declined on

11. See Boyd (2007).

August 8 but then spiked again on August 9, at which point the European Central Bank (ECB) made the first liquidity injection (for 95 billion euros) of several that it made in an attempt to bring rates down again and reinvigorate the interbank market, which many observers claimed had stopped functioning. The ECB followed with two more significant actions—for 61 billion euros on Friday, August 10, and 48 billion euros on August 13.[12] The spike in rates reportedly was in response to an announcement by BNP Paribas that it was suspending payments from two of its hedge funds because the assets were too hard to value. In total, the major central banks supplied $154 billion in funds on August 9, 2007, and another $135.7 billion on August 10, the bulk of which—about $215 billion (see figure 2-2)—was supplied by the ECB. Central banks followed up on August 13 with more fund injections: 47.7 billion euros (US$65 billion) from the ECB and smaller amounts of $5 billion from the Bank of Japan and $2 billion from the Federal Reserve.[13]

The injections of funds appeared to work, because the overnight rate returned to its pre-turmoil level or below and remained quiet until the end of August.[14] Interestingly, figure 2-2 shows that there were no movements in the one- and three-month euro-LIBOR rates that were parallel to those of the overnight rate except for an upward drift consistent with the expectation that the ECB might continue its tightening of policy by raising rates, which had been in progress prior to the turmoil. Euro-LIBOR markets remained calmed until the beginning of September, when attention focused on problems in the U.S. mortgage market and the likely spillover effects on other markets and institutions. Difficulties again hit home outside the United States when the credit problems in the U.K. mortgage lending institution Northern Rock began to become public and the focus of the turmoil turned to the United Kingdom (figure 2-3) when the overnight LIBOR rate spiked.

Phase I Problems in the United Kingdom

On September 10, 2007, rumors surfaced that the U.K. mortgage lender Northern Rock might become a takeover target because of funding problems in rolling over its short-term debt.[15] On September 13, the BBC disclosed that Northern Rock had asked for financial assistance from the Bank of England, and

---

12. *Economist* (2007).

13. Associated Press (2007).

14. In a statement issued August 15, ECB president Jean-Claude Trichet indicated that he believed that the financial turmoil was largely over and that market conditions had largely returned to normal (Dougherty 2007).

15. See Thompson (2007).

Figure 2-3. *U.K. Overnight, One-Month, and Three-Month LIBOR Rates for September 2007*

Percent

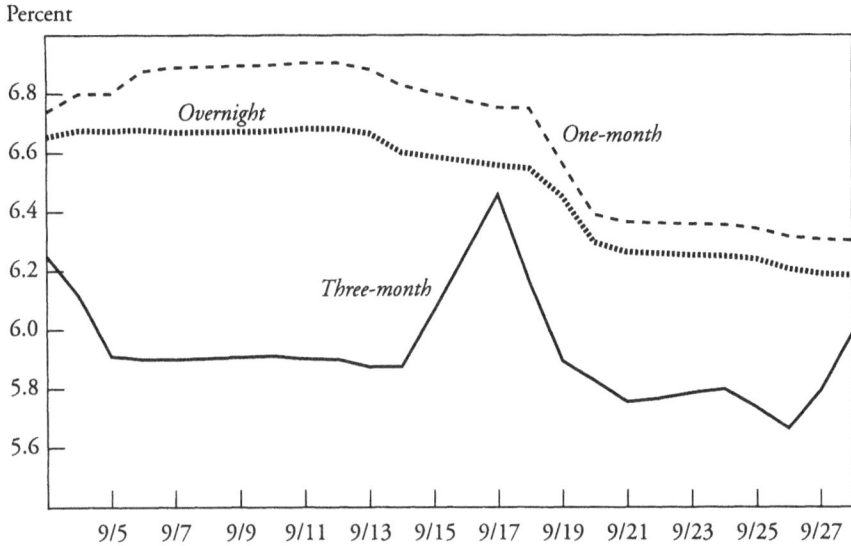

Source: British Bankers Association (www.bba.org.uk/bba/jsp/polopoly.jsp?d=141&a=15151).

on September 14, British television showed lines outside of branches of Northern Rock as customers began withdrawing their deposits, kindling the first bank run in the United Kingdom in more than 100 years. At the same time, the overnight but not the one-month or three-month LIBOR rates spiked (see figure 2-3).

On September 17, Alistair Darling, U.K. chancellor of the exchequer, took the extreme measure of jettisoning the existing deposit guarantee structure by providing a 100 percent guarantee of all of Northern Rock's liabilities. Finally, U.K. authorities—the Bank of England, the Financial Services Authority (FSA), and Her Majesty's Treasury (H.M. Treasury)—followed up the guarantee of Northern Rock's deposits with the unprecedented declaration that government guarantees would be extended to any other bank that experienced financial difficulties.[16] Bank lending continued to be disrupted as U.K. rates again jumped for two days before settling back down.

The U.K. response to the turmoil has been extremely interesting. It also has important implications for how safety nets should and should not be constructed for the efficacy of deposit guarantee schemes; for what the appropriate division of

16. Darling (2007).

powers should be between a central bank, a banking supervisory agency, and a government; and for the usefulness of memorandums of understanding (MOUs) when more financial disruptions occur.

At the time that the initial U.K. market problems with Northern Rock appeared, the governor of the Bank of England, Mervyn King, announced on September 12 that while the bank was prepared to provide funding to institutions that needed it, it would do so only on the traditional terms that were consistent with the tenets of Walter Bagehot. That is, the Bank of England would lend only against the highest-quality collateral and at a penalty rate. King emphasized that moral hazard associated with the central banks' bailing out bad pricing and credit risk assessments had real long-run cost implications for an economy.[17] Within a couple of days, however, pressure from within the government led to an abrupt reversal, and the Bank of England, like the U.S. Federal Reserve and the European Central Bank, began a program of injecting additional liquidity into the marketplace. Shortly thereafter, U.K. LIBOR rates returned to where they were before the turmoil began, but they jumped again on September 26 with the announcement that the ECB's emergency liquidity fund had been tapped for 3.9 billion euros.

The political fallout from the turmoil in the United Kingdom was widespread, and it clearly was directed at the three main government agency heads, who were widely characterized as pursuing a bumbling approach to crisis management. Both Governor King and Sir Callum McCarthy, head of the FSA, were summoned before the House of Commons Treasury Select Committee to explain why they had pursued the policies that they did. Governor King justified the Bank of England's action in testimony before the committee as being necessary to stem the "liquidity crisis." Other actions that might have been taken were precluded by U.K. laws and/or directives that effectively limited the options available to the Bank of England and the FSA for resolving a financial institution's troubles. Specifically cited were mandated public disclosures governing the takeover of a listed company, problems with the design of the deposit insurance contract, and laws that pitted the interests of depositors against those of shareholders and would have required Northern Rock to publicly disclose that it had been granted access to emergency liquidity by the Bank of England, thereby signaling to financial markets that it was in dire straits.

---

17. "If central banks underwrite any maturity transformation that threatens to damage the economy as a whole, it encourages the view that as long as a bank takes the same sort of risks that other banks are taking then it is more likely that their liquidity problems will be insured ex post by the central bank. The provision of large liquidity facilities penalizes those financial institutions that sat out the dance, encourages herd behavior, and increases the intensity of future crises." See King (2007).

During their questioning of Governor King, members of Parliament also spread blame for the embarrassing fiasco on the tripartite division of responsibility for financial stability among the Bank of England, the FSA, and H.M. Treasury. However, the real problem lay in the existence of structural flaws in the design of the U.K. safety net (some of which have already been pointed out) and not in how it was administered; that explains why a Northern Rock–style run is less likely to happen in the United States.

Phase I Problems in the United States

The turmoil that erupted in Europe and the United Kingdom in particular hit primarily the interbank markets, which were the main sources of short-term funding for banks. Rates spiked, and banks stopped lending to each other. In contrast, in the United States the problems initially associated with the subprime mortgage market quickly hit the asset-backed commercial paper (ABCP) market first. The difference arose because of the role that ABCP played in financing the pipeline of mortgage-backed securities, which was critical to the transfer of mortgages through the "originate-and-distribute model" to the ultimate investors. It served as the major source of short-term financing for the mortgage conduits, financing the holdings of mortgages until securities backed by those mortgages could be issued and sold. Many of those conduits were essentially funding the temporary holding of longer-term assets with short-term liabilities, not unlike savings and loan institutions (S&Ls) of the past, except that the short term was really short term and the long term was just a bit longer. The profitability of the business depended on two things: the ability to continually roll over the short-term paper and a high degree of leverage.

The asset-backed commercial paper market had exploded beginning in mid-2005 and continued to expand into the fall of 2007. Asset-backed commercial paper was valued at about $690 billion at the start of 2005 and ballooned to more than $1.2 trillion in 2007. In contrast, both financial and nonfinancial paper had been on a steady upward trend since the end of 2003, and while certainly both were becoming more volatile, they remained on that path despite the turmoil. Note too that the huge rise in asset-backed commercial paper coincides with the period when slowing in the U.S. housing markets became evident and credit quality problems began to appear. As concerns about increases in mortgage default probabilities heightened through 2007 and questions arose about the likely quality of the more recent vintages of subprime mortgages in many of the pools of asset-backed securities, spreads widened and funding dried up. As a result, the asset-backed paper market collapsed to approximately pre-turmoil levels at the end of July 2008.

U.S. Mortgage Market

Low inflation and the low interest rate environment coupled with the long and steady appreciation of housing prices and the growth of securitization of jumbo, subprime, and Alt-A mortgage loans combined to fuel the large growth in housing construction and highly leveraged mortgage debt in the United States. The securitization of lower-quality, high-risk loans was the private sector's extension of the securitization of prime loans fostered by the two large government-sponsored enterprises (GSEs) dealing with mortgages, Freddie Mac and Fannie Mae. Under the Freddie-Fannie model, nonconforming mortgages were originated and sold to Fannie Mae and Freddie Mac, which in turn provided a credit guarantee that enabled the construction and issuance of securities against the mortgages at favorable rates.

The process offered many potential benefits to participants, including improved transparency of investments and enhanced diversification for securities holders since the mortgages in the pools were from many parts of the country. It increased the liquidity of the mortgages and permitted banks to use their capital more intensely because the mortgages that were originated were no longer retained on bank or investment bank balance sheets. But the key to the acceptability of the instruments in the marketplace was the credit guarantee provided by Freddie Mac or Fannie Mae, which was regarded by market participants as being implicitly guaranteed by the U.S. government.

Of course, there are limits to the kinds of mortgages that were eligible for the Freddie-Fannie programs, but financial innovations evolved that enabled the securitization by private entities of other mortgages and assets, particularly jumbo loans, so-called subprime loans, and Alt-A loans. The securitization of these instruments substituted external ratings by credit rating agencies, mathematical valuation models, and insurance provided by monoline and other insurance companies such as American International Group (AIG) for the guarantees supplied by Freddie Mac and Fannie Mae. Issuers employed special purpose, bankruptcy-remote vehicles—usually separately incorporated trusts that issued their own securities to fund the purchase of assets—relying on leverage and a spread to make the whole process work from a profit perspective. But each component involved sacrificing some of the transparency and other attributes of the securitized assets that originated in Freddie and Fannie pools. None of those problems were critical, however, as long as housing prices continued to increase and the housing market flourished.[18]

18. See the excellent discussion of this by Herring (2008).

Problems in Mortgage Lending Institutions

To date, more large financial institutions have experienced ruinous financial difficulties and failed in the United States than in other countries. The most important problems have involved both Fannie Mae and Freddie Mac as well as the primary dealer and nation's largest specialized mortgage lender, Countrywide Financial; the institution specializing in Alt-A mortgages, IndyMac; the investment bank and primary dealer Bear Stearns and Lehman Brothers; and the thrift Washington Mutual.[19] Virtually all the independent investment banks have been acquired by banks or have sought and been granted banking charters.[20]

A significant number of large institutions either failed or were merged. The U.S. Treasury and the Federal Housing Finance Agency (FHFA) placed both Freddie and Fannie into conservatorship on September 7, 2008 (table 2-1), cut dividend payments, provided protection to preferred stock and other debt holders, and began the process of shrinking the institutions. But the problems did not end there. In a series of stunning events, Lehman Brothers, a primary dealer, failed; Merrill Lynch sold itself to Bank of America; the insurance giant American International Group, which was a major player in providing credit insurance, was placed into conservatorship by the U.S. government; and the U.S. Treasury extended insurance to money market funds. In addition, major legislation is in process that would give the U.S. Treasury virtually blanket authority to buy mortgages to support the housing industry. Some of the key events that led up to this unprecedented U.S. government intervention into financial markets are discussed below.

COUNTRYWIDE

Countrywide Financial originated approximately 17 percent of the total mortgages underwritten in the United States in 2007. At that time, it was a financial services holding company and had a federal savings bank subsidiary, together with other subsidiaries, that conducted mortgage banking, trading and underwriting of mortgage-backed securities, and mortgage servicing. After growing very rapidly for several years, it began to experience financial difficulties at the end of 2006. Countrywide applied and was approved for conversion to a savings and loan holding company and for conversion of its bank to a federal savings bank. The conversion also enabled it to switch regulators from the Federal Reserve for its holding company and Comptroller of the Currency for its national bank subsidiary to the Office of Thrift Supervision (OTS).

19. The discussion in this section draws heavily on Eisenbeis and Kaufman (2008a).
20. The Comptroller of the Currency has even conceived of a shelf charter, which would enable non-banking firms to bid on failed or failing banks.

Table 2-1. *Forms of Federal Reserve Lending to Financial Institutions*

Conditions	Regular OMOs	Single-Tranche OMO Program (announced March 7, 2008)	Discount window[a]	Term Discount Window Program (announced August 17, 2007)	Term Auction Facility (announced December 12, 2007)	Primary Dealer Credit Facility (announced March 16, 2008)[b]	Transitional credit extensions (announced September 21, 2008)
Who can participate?	Primary dealers	Primary dealers	Depository institutions	Primary credit-eligible depository institutions	Primary credit-eligible depository institutions	Primary dealers	U.S. and London broker-dealer subsidiaries of Goldman Sachs, Morgan Stanley, and Merrill Lynch
What are they borrowing?	Funds	Funds	Funds	Funds	Funds	Funds	Funds
What collateral can be pledged?	U.S. Treasuries, agencies, and agency MBSs[h]	U.S. Treasuries, agencies, and agency MBSs but typically agency MBSs	Full range of discount window collateral	Full range of discount window collateral	Full range of discount window collateral	Full range of tri-party repo system collateral[i,j]	Full range of discount window collateral and tri-party repo system collateral[j]
Is there a reserve impact?	Yes	Yes	Yes	Yes	Yes	Yes	Yes
What is the term of loan?	Typically, term is overnight to 14 days[l]	28 days[m]	Typically overnight, but up to several weeks[n]	Up to 90 days[o]	28 days or 84 days[m,p]	Overnight	Overnight
Is prepayment allowed if term is greater than overnight?	No	No	Yes	Yes	No	. . .	. . .
Which reserve banks conduct operations?	FRBNY	FRBNY	All	All	All	FRBNY	FRBNY

Reciprocal currency arrangements (first announced December 12, 2007)c	Securities lending	Term Securities Lending Facility (announced March 11, 2008)b	Term Securities Lending Facility Options Program d (announced July 30, 2008)	ABCP Money Market Fund Liquidity Facility (announced September 19, 2008)b	Commercial Paper Funding Facility (announced October 7, 2008)	Money Market Investing Funding Facility (announced October 21, 2008)	Term Asset-Backed Securities Loan Facility e (announced November 25, 2008)
Select central banks to lend on to banks in their jurisdictions c	Primary dealers	Primary dealers	Primary dealers	Depository institutions, bank holding companies, and U.S. branches and agencies of foreign banks	Eligible CP issuers f	Eligible money market mutual funds g	All U.S. persons that own eligible collateral
U.S. dollars	U.S. Treasuries	U.S. Treasuries	U.S. Treasuries	Funds	Funds	Funds and subordinated notes	Funds
Central banks pledge foreign currency and lend against eligible collateral in their jurisdiction	U.S. Treasuries	Schedule 1: U.S. Treasuries, agencies, and agency MBSs; Schedule 2: Schedule 1 plus all investment-grade debt securities i	Schedule 2 TSLF collateral	First-tier ABCP	Newly issued three-month unsecured and ABCP from eligible U.S. issuers	U.S. dollar-denominated certificates of deposit, bank notes, and commercial paper issued by highly rated financial institutions	Recently originated U.S. dollar-denominated AAA ABSs k
Yes	No (loans are bond-for-bond)	No (loans are bond-for-bond)	. . .	Yes	Yes	Yes	Yes
Overnight to 3 months	Overnight	28 days m	Typically 2 weeks or less q	ABCP maturity date (270-day maximum)	3 months	N/A	At least one year
Yes	. . .	No	No	No	. . .	. . .	Yes
FRBNY	FRBNY	FRBNY	FRBNY	FRB Boston	FRBNY	FRBNY	FRBNY

(continued)

Table 2-1. *Forms of Federal Reserve Lending to Financial Institutions* (continued)

Conditions	Regular OMOs	Single-Tranche OMO Program (announced March 7, 2008)	Discount window[a]	Term Discount Window Program (announced August 17, 2007)	Term Auction Facility (announced December 12, 2007)	Primary Dealer Credit Facility (announced March 16, 2008)[b]	Transitional credit extensions (announced September 21, 2008)
How frequently is the program accessed?	Typically once or more daily	Typically weekly	As requested (standing facility)	As requested (standing facility)	As requested (standing facility)	Every other week, or as necessary[p]	As requested (standing facility)
Where are statistics reported publicly?	Temporary OMO activity[s]	Temporary OMO activity[s]	H.4.1 – Factors Affecting Reserve Balances[t]	H.4.1 – Factors Affecting Reserve Balances[t]	TAF activity[s]	H.4.1 – Factors Affecting Reserve Balances[t]	H.4.1 – Factors Affecting Reserve Balances[t]

Source: Federal Reserve Bank of New York, "Forms of Federal Reserve Lending to Financial Institutions" (www.newyorkfed.org/markets/index.html).

a. Discount window includes primary, secondary, and seasonal credit programs.

b. The Primary Dealer Credit Facility (PDCF), Term Securities Lending Facility (TSLF), and ABCP Money Market Fund Liquidity Facility (AMLF) remained in operation through April 30, 2009, per an announcement on December 2, 2008.

c. European Central Bank and Swiss National Bank announced December 12, 2007; Bank of Canada, Bank of England, and Bank of Japan announced September 18, 2008; Reserve Bank of Australia, Sveriges Riksbank, Danmarks Nationalbank, and Norges Bank announced September 24, 2008; Reserve Bank of New Zealand announced October 28, 2008; Banco Central do Brasil, Banco de Mexico, Bank of Korea, and Monetary Authority of Singapore announced October 29, 2008.

d. TOP auctions are sales of options granting the right to enter into TSLF borrowing.

e. The TALF was expected to go live around February 2009. The Federal Reserve reserves the right to review and make adjustments to these terms and conditions—including size of program, pricing, loan maturity, and asset and borrower eligibility requirements—consistent with the policy objectives of the TALF.

f. Through the Commercial Paper Funding Facility, the FRBNY (Federal Reserve Bank of New York) provides financing to a special purpose vehicle that purchases eligible three-month unsecured and asset-backed commercial paper from eligible issuers.

g. Through the Money Market Investing Funding Facility, the FRBNY will provide senior secured funding to a series of private sector SPVs to finance the purchase of certain money market instruments from eligible investors.

(continued)

Reciprocal currency arrangements (first announced December 12, 2007)[c]	Securities lending	Term Securities Lending Facility (announced March 11, 2008)[b]	Term Securities Lending Facility Options Program[d] (announced July 30, 2008)	ABCP Money Market Fund Liquidity Facility (announced September 19, 2008)[b]	Commercial Paper Funding Facility (announced October 7, 2008)	Money Market Investing Funding Facility (announced October 21, 2008)	Term Asset-Backed Securities Loan Facility[e] (announced November 25, 2008)
As requested (standing facility)	Typically on schedule with FRBNY TAF auctions or as requested by central banks	Schedule 1: Every other week Schedule 2: Weekly	As necessary[r]	As requested (standing facility)	As requested (standing facility)	As requested (standing facility)	Monthly
H.4.1 – Factors Affecting Reserve Balances[t]	Securities lending activity	Term Securities Lending Facility activity[s]	Term Securities Lending Facility Options Program activity[s]	H.4.1 – Factors Affecting Reserve Balances[t]	H.4.1 – Factors Affecting Reserve Balances[t]	H.4.1 – Factors Affecting Reserve Balances[t]	TALF activity[s]

h. Reverse repos are collateralized with U.S. Treasuries.

i. PDCF and TSLF collateral expanded on September 14, 2008.

j. Includes securities that are not denominated in U.S. dollars.

k. Includes auto loans, student loans, credit card loans, or small business loans guaranteed by the U.S. Small Business Administration.

l. Open market operations (OMOs)are authorized for terms of up to sixty-five business days.

m. Twenty-eight-day and eighty-four-day terms may vary slightly to account for maturity dates that fall on bank holidays.

n. Primary credit loans are generally overnight. Loans may be granted for terms beyond a few weeks to small banks, subject to additional administration.

o. Maximum maturity of term increased from overnight to thirty days on August 17, 2007, and to ninety days on March 16, 2008.

p. Forward-selling TAF auctions announced on September 29, 2008, will be conducted in November with terms designed to provide funding over year-end.

q. Loans are designed to span potentially stressed financing dates, such as quarter-ends.

r. TOP auctions may be conducted on multiple dates for a single loan and may be conducted well in advance of a loan period.

s. Data are available only for days when operations are conducted.

t. Data are published on Thursday, as of close of business on Wednesday.

Countrywide had adopted the originate-and-distribute model, which meant that it relied heavily on funding its mortgage warehousing business in the short-term asset-backed commercial paper market until it could securitize and sell the mortgages that it had originated. However, when short-term lenders suddenly abandoned the asset-backed commercial paper market in August 2007, Countrywide's ability to finance its mortgage warehousing business essentially vanished. The rating agencies downgraded its credit rating, which increased its cost of funds. As mortgage delinquencies and default problems began to accelerate for both subprime and Alt-A mortgages, its rating was downgraded further.

Countrywide's stock price plummeted, as had that of Northern Rock, which pursued a similar business model. By the middle of August, with the commercial paper market essentially closed to it, Countrywide began to draw down its bank credit lines for funding. Countrywide also turned increasingly to the Federal Home Loan Bank of Atlanta for funding. Advances (collateralized borrowings from the Home Loan Bank) increased to $50 billion from $30 billion by the end of September 2007, accounting for approximately 25 percent of its total liabilities. Countrywide also benefited from the Federal Reserve's 50-basis-point cut in the discount rate and broadening of the collateral eligible for overnight repurchase agreements with primary dealers (of which Countrywide was one).[21] However, the continuing hemorrhaging of Countrywide and the drop of its stock price to nearly zero made it clear to the OTS and other federal regulators that its failure was imminent. Consequently, the Federal Reserve encouraged its sale for about $4 billion, without financial assistance, to Bank of America, which had earlier made a strategic investment of nearly $2 billion in Countrywide.

IndyMac

Similar to Countrywide, IndyMac (Independent National Mortgage Corporation) was an originator and distributor of mortgage loans and mortgage-backed securities.[22] It specialized in originating and servicing jumbo and Alt-A mortgages. It too was a thrift holding company regulated and supervised by the OTS. Like Countrywide, IndyMac grew rapidly, nearly doubling its assets, from $17 billion to $32.5 billion, between March 2005 and December 2007.[23] Its funding depended heavily on Home Loan Bank advances, which accounted for from 32 percent to 45 percent of its total liabilities in any one quarter.

IndyMac began to evidence financial problems in the middle of 2007, which were reflected in the decline in its book-value capital from a high of $2.7 billion

21. This occurred on August 14, 2007, and again on September 18, 2007. See the appendix.
22. Interestingly, IndyMac was a spin-off of Countrywide Financial.
23. Data from FDIC Quarterly Reports of Condition and Income (www2.fdic.gov).

in June 2007 to $1.8 billion in March 2008 and in the rapid fall of its stock price. As it experienced funding problems, the bank began bidding aggressively for federally insured deposits under $100,000, and it was widely touted as one of the best places to purchase certificates of deposit (CDs) because its rates were so high. IndyMac also increased its reliance on Home Loan Bank advances.

OTS's January 2008 examination indicated that IndyMac was in financial difficulty, faced with a decline in its capital and negative earnings. Nevertheless, the agency still concluded that it was adequately capitalized and did not classify it as a problem institution. In fact, the bank's March 31, 2008, 10Q filing with the U.S. Securities and Exchange Commission (SEC) stated that IndyMac's Tier 1 capital leverage ratio stood at 5.74 percent, above the minimum 5 percent requirement for the bank to be classified as "well capitalized." Risk-based Tier 1 capital was 9 percent and total risk-based capital was 10.26 percent; minimum required ratios of 6 and 10 percent, respectively, were required for a bank to be considered well capitalized.

The decision to close IndyMac followed a run on the institution, albeit a run that did not take the form of Northern Rock's run. There was an outflow of about $1.3 billion, but it remains unclear what the mix of insured and uninsured deposits was. OTS maintained that it was actively seeking to resolve IndyMac, but those efforts were frustrated by release of a letter that Senator Charles Schumer had sent to OTS on June 26 that raised legitimate questions about the health of IndyMac. As a result, OTS closed IndyMac on July 11, and the Federal Deposit Insurance Corporation (FDIC) became the receiver.

Applicable law under the U.S. Federal Deposit Insurance Corporation Improvement Act of 1991 requires the responsible federal regulator to intervene as an institution's capital declines and to close the institution before its net worth goes to zero. The FDIC's initial estimates were that it expected to lose between $4 billion and $8 billion in resolving the failure, but its latest estimates now place that figure at $8.9 billion. Eisenbeis and Kaufman (2008a) states that "given that IndyMac was supposedly adequately capitalized and was done in by a relatively small $1.3 billion of deposits run off, it stretches credibility that the bank's closure on a more timely basis would lead [to] between $4 and $8 billion in losses." While a number of other smaller financial institutions also have failed, the experience with Countrywide and IndyMac raises serious questions about the quality of federal supervision of depository institutions similar to those raised in the United Kingdom about the supervision of Northern Rock by the FSA. In addition, unlike in the United Kingdom, which does not have a system of prompt corrective action (PCA) and early intervention, in the United States there is a continuing tendency of banking regulators to delay in closing institutions as they are required to do, with the resulting losses then having to be absorbed by other healthy institutions through higher FDIC insurance premiums. This suggests that there remain significant incentive problems within the banking agencies. One reason that supervisors are able to delay is the fact that PCA is based on using book value rather than fair market value to determine capital adequacy.

BEAR STEARNS

While the financial conditions underlying Bear Stearns were similar to those of Countrywide and IndyMac, the applicable regulatory regime and bankruptcy options were different. Like Countrywide and IndyMac, Bear Stearns was a major player in the mortgage derivatives market. It had highly leveraged positions that were financed in short-term money markets, especially the asset-backed commercial paper market. On March 14, 2008, the Federal Reserve arranged a short-term emergency loan to Bear Stearns through the discount window. However, over the following weekend it became clear that without longer-term drastic action, Bear Stearns would have to declare bankruptcy because its funding had dried up. In congressional hearings, Alan Schwartz, the new Bear Stearns chief executive, maintained that rumors had done the firm in and that if only the Federal Reserve had provided emergency funding earlier, the institution might have survived.

Bear Stearns's problems were widely painted as a liquidity problem (a de facto run in the short-term money market) due to a sudden inability to roll over its commercial paper. Management maintained that the institution was solvent. However, that assertion does not square with the facts. Bear Stearns had begun reporting problems with its real estate portfolio in 2006, and those reports were accompanied by a drop in the firm's equity position and an increase in its leverage. In June 2007 significant losses were reported in two of its hedge funds due to subprime losses. In mid-July, the firm notified investors in those funds that little value remained, and at the end of July, it suspended withdrawals from a third hedge fund. The firm also reported an actual loss for the fourth quarter of 2007, when it also became apparent that other mortgage lenders—namely Northern Rock and Countrywide—also were experiencing problems with their subprime loans. Financial stress was evident in the asset-backed paper market, and central banks began cutting rates and/or expanding lending facilities and injecting liquidity into markets.

By March, when Bear Stearns was finally acquired by JPMorgan Chase with unusual assistance provided by the Federal Reserve Bank of New York, the problems in the mortgage market were well known. Bear Stearns, with its highly leveraged position, clearly represented high risk to any knowledgeable investor.

There are many similarities between the Bear Stearns situation and that of Northern Rock. Both had minimal regulatory supervision and oversight. Bear Stearns actually enjoyed less oversight than Northern Rock because it was an investment bank, under the jurisdiction of the SEC, which provides oversight under a voluntary agreement with investment banks. The SEC did not employ bank-type supervision or regulation, nor did it regulate Bear Stearns's capital position or leverage. So like Northern Rock, which was subject to the "light touch" oversight of the FSA, Bear Stearns was essentially unsupervised.

More important, once the institution was faced with bankruptcy, its only available legal option was to rely on the general bankruptcy process, with all the delays and uncertainties that it entailed. In the case of Bear Stearns it was asserted that, because of its web of counterparty relationships with other financial institutions, its failure represented a systemic risk that required unusual, nonstandard treatment. Hence, the Federal Reserve stepped in and invoked emergency powers under section 13(3) of the Federal Reserve Act, which, because it permitted the Federal Reserve to lend to individuals, partnerships, or corporations temporarily in emergency situations, enabled it to create the primary dealer credit facility. Thus, the authority was employed to permit primary dealers, including investment banks, access to the discount window. The Fed also took the unusual step of helping to finance the arranged acquisition of Bear Stearns by JPMorgan Chase, with the understanding that JPMorgan Chase would honor all of Bear Stearns's derivative and counterparty commitments. The Federal Reserve Bank of New York created a special purpose Delaware institution (Maiden Lane), which purchased some $30 billion of Bear Stearns assets, funded with a $29 billion loan from the Federal Reserve Bank of New York. JPMorgan Chase provided $1 billion in financing and agreed to absorb the first $1 billion of losses on those assets.

Given the widely feared systemic consequences that a Bear Stearns bankruptcy might pose to the financial system and the fact that bank-like insolvency and resolution policies were not available to the responsible agencies, U.S. officials found themselves in a situation similar to that of the Bank of England, the FSA, and H.M. Treasury in the United Kingdom in dealing with Northern Rock. As a result, they were left with few options other than to facilitate the takeover of Bear Stearns. Financial support, which was provided in the form of ex post loss sharing by the public sector that protected certain creditors at the expense of taxpayers, raised concerns about the structure of regulation and the moral hazard that such support implies for investment banks.

Freddie Mac and Fannie Mae

The conservatorship of Freddie Mac and Fannie Mae represented the culmi-
nation of a long-standing series of problems with the underlying business model
of the two entities.[24] Originally created by Congress as government-sponsored
enterprises to provide stability and liquidity in the secondary mortgage market,
Fannie Mae was privatized in the late 1960s and Freddie Mac in 1989. Through
their direct investments in mortgages and their guarantee business, they amassed
a huge portfolio of loans and either directly or indirectly held or guaranteed the
bulk of the securities in the U.S. mortgage market. The business model flaw, of
course, was the privatization of the gains from their mortgage activities, but
because of their implicit government backing, they were able to expand without
the effective constraint of market discipline and leverage themselves in ways that
truly private sector firms were not. It also meant, as events have proven, that
should their leverage result in huge losses, those losses would have to be borne by
the U.S. taxpayer.

In recognition of the moral hazard that their business model represented,
Congress established a regulatory regime to provide safety and soundness regulation and oversight of the two institutions by the Office of Federal Housing
Enterprise Oversight (OFHEO). OFHEO was to enforce specific capital requirements and limits on their permissible activities. That oversight proved, for a number of reasons, to be ineffective. Both institutions engaged in heavy lobbying
activities, and they contributed substantial amounts to congressional and presi-
dential campaigns. Moreover, because OFHEO was subject to the appropriations
process for funding, the agency was continually subject to political meddling
whenever its activities threatened to affect the profitability of the firms or the
flow of funding to housing.

It was widely believed and argued that because historic losses on mortgage
loans of the kind that Freddie Mac and Fannie Mae supported were low, the portfolios of the institutions were geographically diversified, and the institutions engaged in sophisticated risk management practices, they could get by with high
leverage and a small capital cushion.[25] Not only were their assets highly diversified, but also their funding base was internationally diversified. Their debt and
preferred stock were widely held by investors within and outside the United
States, including substantial portions held by foreign governments (again, because
of their implicit U.S. government guarantee).

24. See discussions in Eisenbeis, Frame, and Wall (2007), Frame and White (2004, 2005), Passmore
(2005), and Passmore, Sparks, and Ingpen (2002).
25. See Eisenbeis, Frame, and Wall (2007).

Perverse incentives due to high executive pay and little market discipline resulted not only in rapid growth for both Freddie Mac and Fannie Mae but also led to serious accounting scandals in the early 2000s, in which the companies paid fines for misstating their earnings, and to civil securities fraud charges brought by federal regulators. The accounting problems led to constraints being imposed on the institutions' activities in 2006 and to the ouster of the management of both companies. Despite remedial efforts, both companies have had difficulties presenting audited financial statements for the last four or five years.

However, the combination of bad and negligent management with high leverage really hit the firms only when the U.S. mortgage market began to contract in 2006 and 2007. Losses continued into 2008 and finally reached such proportions that Congress passed emergency legislation in July giving both Freddie and Fannie access to the Federal Reserve discount window. In addition, the Treasury was authorized to inject equity funds into the institutions if necessary to keep them running because of their widely perceived importance to the functioning of the U.S. housing market. Both measures proved insufficient to enable the institutions to absorb the losses that they were facing, and in September the Treasury and the Office of Federal Housing Enterprise Oversight put both institutions into conservatorship. They now are being run by the U.S. Treasury, and in the short term, at least, their balance sheets will continue to expand in an effort to provide funds to housing.

LEHMAN BROTHERS AND OTHERS

Through the end of 2007, the profits of Lehman Brothers were up some 5 percent and the firm seemed to have dodged the mortgage market problems despite its large holdings of mortgage-related securities; moreover, its stock price remained near its high of about $65 per share into February 2008. However, following the Federal Reserve's financial support of the takeover of Bear Stearns and the placing of Freddie Mac and Fannie Mae into conservatorship under the Treasury, weaknesses in Lehman Brothers and Merrill Lynch gained market attention and their share prices fell drastically. By mid-September, on the heels of a reported loss of more than $7 billion due largely to deterioration in its mortgage and related assets, Lehman's share price was near $5. In an effort to save the firm, its chairman sought to sell one of its best assets, Neuberger Berman, its wealth management unit, but the firm was unable to find a price that management deemed acceptable. In addition, the firm announced that it would cut its real estate exposure to about $13 billion and reduce its commercial real estate lending to $32.5 billion. Those efforts only raised further questions about the quality of its assets, and funding to the institution essentially dried up.

Merger discussions with Barclays and Bank of America were terminated when their request for Maiden Lane–type assistance from the Federal Reserve was rejected. It was estimated that Lehman Brothers had more than $60 billion in questionable real estate assets and that government support in the neighborhood of $80 billion had been requested. Furthermore, Treasury Secretary Henry Paulson indicated that markets had been more aware of Lehman's problems than those leading to Bear Stearns's demise and therefore that the likely financial disruptions would be less than in the Bear Stearns case if Lehman Brothers declared bankruptcy. Lehman Brothers filed for bankruptcy on September 14, 2008. Fearful that its own real estate losses would lead to additional financial pressures, Merrill Lynch sought and reached a merger agreement to sell itself to Bank of America on September 15 for $50 billion.

The failure of the government to support the acquisition of Lehman Brothers after rescues of Fannie Mae, Freddie Mac, and Bear Stearns came as a shock to markets and was interpreted as an effort to draw a line in the sand against moral hazard and the market's assumption that all Wall Street primary dealers were too big to fail. That stand was quickly erased, however, when the government stepped in on September 16 to provide $85 billion in support to AIG, which proved to have large positions in credit default swaps with U.S. and other firms around the world that, should it fail, would have to be unwound. That support was followed by an injection of $37.8 billion on October 9, 2008. The package was further modified on November 10 in several ways. The Troubled Asset Relief Progam (TARP) purchased $40 billion in preferred stock, and AIG's loan was lowered from $80 billion to $60 billion. In addition, the Federal Reserve (2008) created two new lending facilities that would lend up to $85 billion to buy up residential mortgage–backed securities and purchase CDOs owned by AIG.[26]

The result of these on-again, off-again rescues of troubled firms in September created great uncertainty in financial markets and triggered a request by Congress on September 18 to provide more than $700 billion to the U.S. Treasury to purchase mortgage and other assets from the public, with virtually unfettered authority. Despite this intervention, financial markets had yet to settle down in early 2009. One thing, however, is certain: the approval by the Federal Reserve Board of emergency applications from Morgan Stanley and Goldman Sachs to become regulated bank holding companies spells the demise of independent investment banking, which had been a hallmark of U.S. financial markets for more than 150 years. These institutions will now be subject to prudential supervision and regulation, with the Federal Reserve as the umbrella supervisor, and will have to

26. Federal Reserve (2008).

begin the deleveraging process to meet current capital adequacy standards. Universal banking now seems to be the model for the United States, as it is for much of the rest of the world.

The Spread of Problems to Other Markets

Liquidity and spread problems not only have affected the mortgage market, banks, and investment banks, but also have spilled over to other asset markets and have hit the municipal bond market especially hard. In virtually all instances, part of the problem was associated with a perceived deterioration in the quality of guarantees and credit enhancements issued by either monoline insurance companies, in the case of municipal bonds, or a decline in credit ratings and questions about the quality of underlying assets in the case of asset-backed commercial paper. Typically, because of their tax treatment, municipal bonds trade at lower yields than Treasuries. But almost from the outset of the crisis in September 2007, municipals traded at rates above Treasuries with spreads as high as 100 basis points and more. Because of their tax-exempt status, high-quality municipal bonds should normally be priced at rates below Treasuries.

The segment of the municipal market that was especially decimated was the auction-rate securities component. Banks and investment banks had helped support the market through their provision of liquidity facilities, but as the ratings of the monoline insurers fell and they stopped backing up the weekly auctions to prevent auction failures, more and more of the weekly auctions failed and interest rates skyrocketed. It suddenly became quite common to see these tax-exempt securities suddenly begin to be priced as if the underlying insurance were worthless. Their rates also were inconsistent with the underlying creditworthiness of the issuing municipality and also substantially above Treasuries. Indeed, as large financial institutions began pulling back from this market, the attorneys general of many states, but especially New York, launched investigations into behavior in the market. The allegation was that the securities were represented and sold to investors as cash equivalents, but when auctions began to fail, they no longer proved to be liquid. Settlements resulting in nearly $1 billion in fines were reached with many large institutions, which agreed to buy the securities back at a loss and bring approximately $60 billion of them back onto their balance sheets as of mid-August 2008.[27] Issuance and pricing disparities continued to exist in these markets through the end of November 2008.

---

27. Merrill Lynch ($10–$12 billion), Goldman Sachs ($1 billion), JPMorgan Chase ($3.5 billion), Morgan Stanley ($4.5 billion), UBS ($27 billion), Citi ($7.3 billion), and Wachovia ($5.7 billion), to name just a few.

Phase I Central Bank and Government Responses

The Federal Reserve's responses to the crisis were more multidimensional than those of either the Bank of England or the European Central Bank, and they also were prompt. The Fed's initial responses to the August turndown were to inject funds, albeit of more modest amounts than those injected by the ECB; to cut its target federal funds rate on September 18 from 5.25 percent to 4.75 percent (figure 2-1); and to reduce the spread between the federal funds rate from 100 to 50 basis points. Six additional rate cuts were made, and the discount rate spread was cut by an additional 25 basis points. By April 30, 2008, the funds rate stood at 2 percent.

The macroeconomic policy decision to inject liquidity by cutting the funds rate (in order to cut the funds rate, the Federal Reserve had to purchase government securities and expand its portfolio) was accompanied by a series of innovations to expand access to the discount window in order to deal with the seizing up of financial markets and the drying up of liquidity. (See figure 2-4 for the time line and approximate dollar amounts associated with each program and table 2-1 for details describing the programs.) The innovations were of four types.[28]

First, in the hope of simply encouraging use of the discount window and reducing the stigma of borrowing, on August 17, 2007, the board of governors cut the differential between its federal funds target and the discount rate from 100 basis points to 50 basis points and lengthened the maximum maturity of borrowing to ninety days. Despite the attempt to encourage banks to come to the discount window, borrowing was limited. The stigma and the evidence of both continuing and mounting liquidity problems, despite the fact that by this time the Federal Reserve had lowered the federal funds rate to 4.25 percent through two more cuts, prompted the Fed to introduce its second funding innovation, the Term Auction Facility (TAF), on December 12. Through the TAF, the Fed auctioned off a series of twenty-eight-day funds to bidders anonymously. The two initial auctions were for $20 billion, and the term was for twenty-eight days.[29] In addition, currency swap arrangements were made with both the European Central Bank and Swiss National Bank, of $20 billion and $4 billion respectively, to support similar dollar auctions in the European Union and Switzerland.[30] The

28. This discussion does not consider the fact that the Federal Home Loan Banks injected significant liquidity into the banking system by extending loans against assets of questionable value. For example, Countrywide had borrowed more than $50 billion from the Federal Home Loan Bank of Atlanta.

29. The TAF was subsequently expanded in a series of actions to $150 billion outstanding by May 2008.

30. Swap arrangements were subsequently expanded so that the outstanding European TAF auctions for the ECB would be $110 billion and for the Swiss National Bank up to $27 billion. In addition, swap

Fed has subsequently lengthened the maturity of TAF transactions to include both twenty-eight-day and eighty-four-day auctions.

The third innovation (already discussed in the description of the problems with Bear Stearns) was to enable primary dealers that were investment banks to have temporary access to the discount window through the primary dealer credit facility. The fourth innovation was to expand the Fed's Term Securities Lending Facility (TSLF), which enables primary dealers (both banks and investment banks) to borrow Treasury securities for up to two weeks on an overnight basis. The TSLF effectively enabled primary dealers to swap their illiquid assets temporarily in exchange for Treasuries and to temporarily sell those Treasury securities through repurchase agreements or to borrow against them to ensure short-term overnight funding. This program was broadened in July 2008 to include options on securities borrowing. In virtually all four programs, the Fed broadened the range of eligible collateral to include not only Treasury and agency securities but also highly rated residential mortgage–backed securities, collateralized debt obligations, and other asset-backed securities. (See table 2-1 for the appropriate details for each program and how the terms and collateral were broadened in subsequent announcements.)

These actions amounted to the extension of forbearance by the Federal Reserve to institutions with bad assets by allowing depository institutions and primary dealers to continue to carry illiquid assets at very favorable rates. While the programs may ultimately result in potential losses to the Federal Reserve and the taxpayer, meanwhile they have radically changed the composition of the Federal Reserve's balance sheet. Figure 2-5 details both how the Federal Reserve's balance sheet changed and how its holdings of Treasuries have shrunk. Also included is the impact of the Fed's securities lending programs, which technically are off–balance sheet but do reflect the ability of participants to liquefy what otherwise might be illiquid assets on their own balance sheets. They can do that by temporarily swapping their illiquid assets for the Fed's Treasuries and then using the Treasuries as collateral in repurchase transactions. In its phase I response, the Fed effectively expanded use of its balance sheet by about $350 billion in total, with slightly more than half of that coming from the TSLF. The decline in the Fed's holdings of Treasury securities reflects the sterilization actions taken to offset what might otherwise be additional injections of high-powered money into the system, which would have implications for inflation. But when the securities lending program is

arrangements were established with the Bank of Japan ($60 billion), Bank of Canada ($10 billion), and Bank of England ($40 billion). The total foreign TAF was $247 billion as of September 19, 2008. See table 2-1 for more details.

Figure 2-4. *Timeline of Key Federal Reserve Liquidity Innovations and Changes Made*

Approximate dollar amounts, in billions

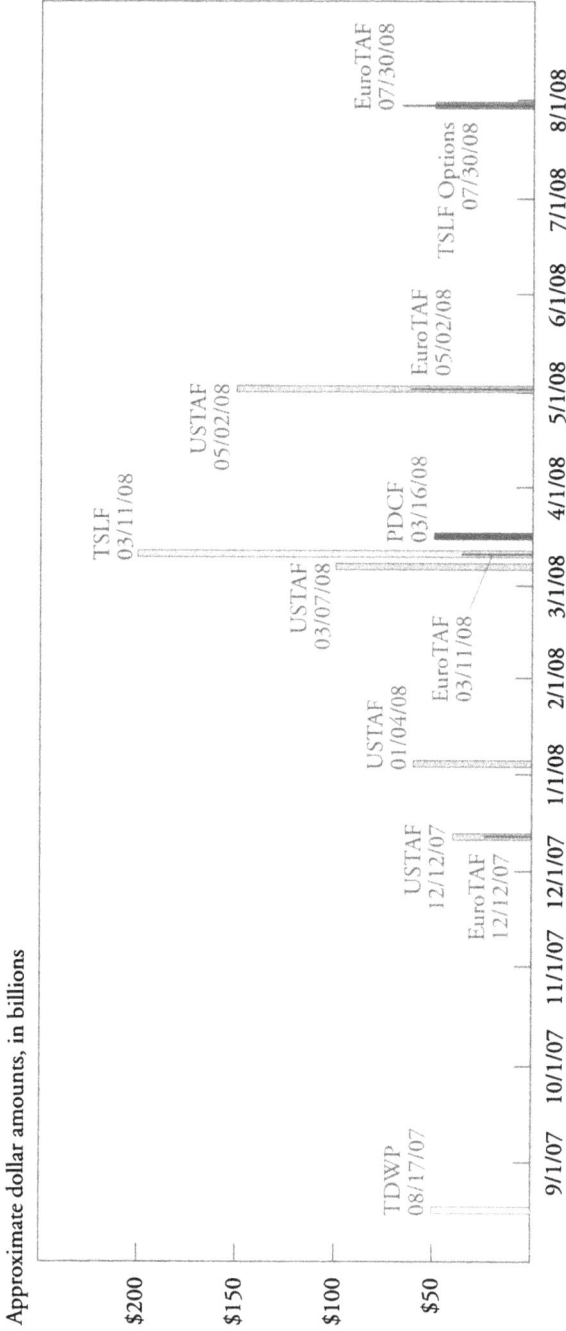

TDWP = Term Discount Window Program; TSLF = Term Securities Lending Facility; USTAF = U.S. Term Auction Facility; PDCF = Primary Dealer Credit Facility; EuroTAF = Euro Term Auction Facility.

Source: Federal Reserve Bank of New York, "Forms of Federal Reserve Lending to Financial Institutions," table 2 (www.newyorkfed.org/markets/index.html).

Figure 2-5. *Factors Adding to Reserves Plus Off–Balance Sheet TSLF from August 8, 2007, to November 12, 2008*

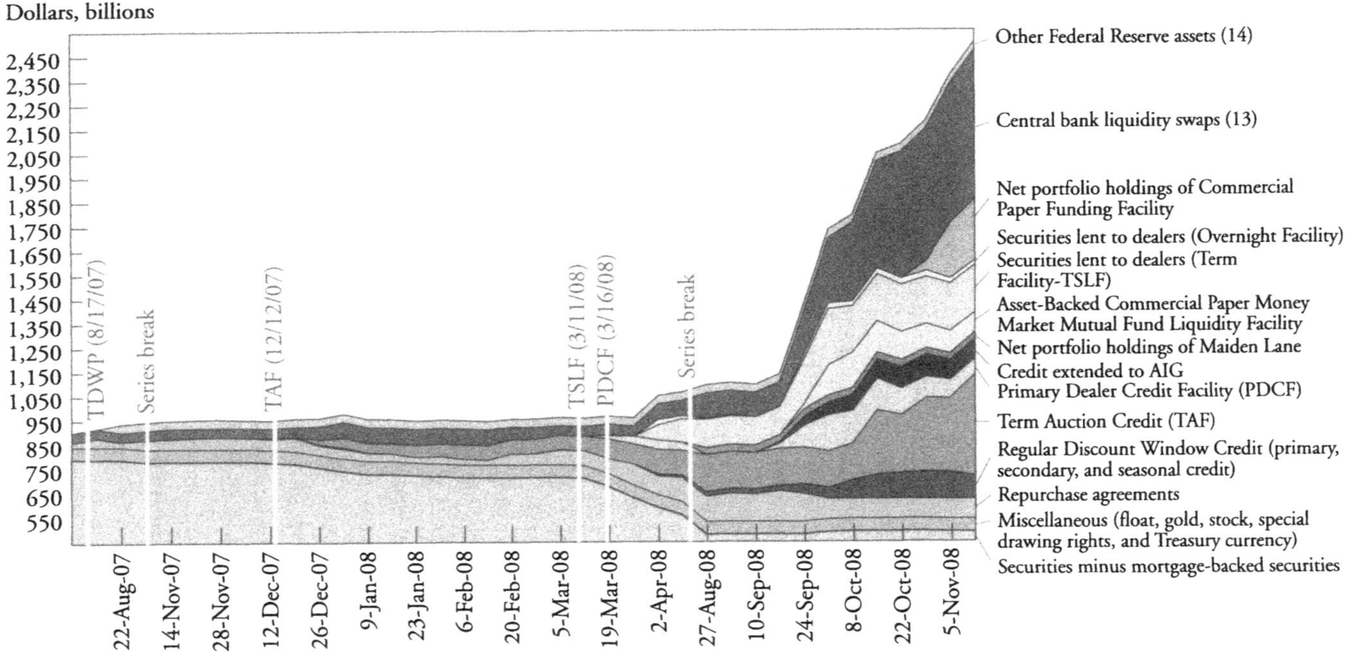

Dollars, billions
2,450
2,350
2,250
2,150
2,050
1,950
1,850
1,750
1,650
1,550
1,450
1,350
1,250
1,150
1,050
950
850
750
650
550
TDWP (8/17/07)
Series break
TAF (12/12/07)
TSLF (3/11/08)
PDCF (3/16/08)
Series break
22-Aug-07
14-Nov-07
28-Nov-07
12-Dec-07
26-Dec-07
9-Jan-08
23-Jan-08
6-Feb-08
20-Feb-08
5-Mar-08
19-Mar-08
2-Apr-08
27-Aug-08
10-Sep-08
24-Sep-08
8-Oct-08
22-Oct-08
5-Nov-08
Other Federal Reserve assets (14)
Central bank liquidity swaps (13)
Net portfolio holdings of Commercial Paper Funding Facility
Securities lent to dealers (Overnight Facility)
Securities lent to dealers (Term Facility-TSLF)
Asset-Backed Commercial Paper Money Market Mutual Fund Liquidity Facility
Net portfolio holdings of Maiden Lane
Credit extended to AIG
Primary Dealer Credit Facility (PDCF)
Term Auction Credit (TAF)
Regular Discount Window Credit (primary, secondary, and seasonal credit)
Repurchase agreements
Miscellaneous (float, gold, stock, special drawing rights, and Treasury currency)
Securities minus mortgage-backed securities

Source: Board of Governors of the Federal Reserve System, "H.4.1 Report" (www.federalreserve.gov/releases/h41).

considered in conjunction with the European TAF's lending of dollars against euro-denominated collateral, the effects have not been fully sterilized.

All these new programs, except the TAF, were limited to primary dealers, which numbered nineteen as of September 11, 2008. (See the website of the Federal Reserve Bank of New York for the current list.) These institutions were the main conduit through which the Open Market Desk conducted daily open market operations and supposedly were among the strongest, largest, best-run, and most secure institutions. However, that the support helped mainly primary dealers was more than coincidence; they were also among the institutions most significantly affected financially by the problems in the mortgage markets and auction-rate securities markets.[31]

Bianco Research periodically published a compilation of the losses that accumulated in major banks and investment banks as a result of the so-called subprime crisis.[32] The data shown in table 2-2 indicate that through the end of August 2008, more than sixty-four institutions recognized about $512 billion in mortgage-related losses. Some were able to replace the lost equity with new capital. Large institutions reported having raised $360 billion, but a large hole—$151 billion—remained to be filled just to get their equity back up to the level where it was before the crisis. The capital demands proved to be even greater since market participants appeared to have little confidence that all the losses had been identified, as reflected in the discounts at which the firms sold assets and attempted to raise funds. Losses were not concentrated solely in U.S. institutions. Bianco estimated that combined European and Asian losses were virtually equal to those of U.S. institutions: U.S. firms reported $261 billion in losses while European institutions reported $227.1 billion in losses and Asian institutions reported $23.8 billion.

The data also show that a large portion of the losses were concentrated in the primary dealers—the very institutions that reaped the greatest benefits from the Fed's liquidity injections. The data in table 2-2 were first sorted by primary dealer status and then by losses (the data also reflect the mergers that had taken place). The last column shows the ranking based solely on losses reported as of August 2008 without regard to primary dealer status. There was a close correlation between primary dealer status and loss ranking. The sixteen primary dealers listed dominated the group in terms of losses, having incurred $288 billion in losses, nearly 60 percent of the total. At the same time, they raised about $187.1 billion in new capital—about 53 percent of the total capital raised—leaving a shortfall

31. The discussion that follows on the loss experience of the primary dealers draws heavily upon Eisenbeis (2008).

32. See Bianco (2008).

Table 2-2. *Losses Recognized as of August 13, 2008*[a]

U.S. dollars, billions

Institution	Losses	Capital raised	Capital shortfall (losses minus capital raised)	Rank based on total losses recognized to date
Citigroup	55.1	49.1	–6	1
Merrill Lynch	51.8	29.9	–21.9	2
Bank of America	21.2	20.7	–.05	6
UBS	44.2	28.3	–15.9	3
HSBC	27.4	3.9	–23.5	4
Morgan Stanley	14.4	5.6	–8.8	10
JPMorgan Chase	14.3	7.9	–6.4	11
Bear Stearns	3.2	0	–3.2	38
Deutsche Bank	10.8	3.2	–7.6	12
Credit Suisse	10.5	2.7	–7.8	13
Barclays	9.1	18.6	9.5	15
Lehman Brothers	8.2	13.9	5.7	16
Canadian Imperial	6.3	2.7	–3.6	24
Dresdner	4.1	0	–4.1	31
BNP Paribas	4	0	–4	32
Goldman Sachs	3.8	0.6	–3.2	33
Wachovia	22.5	11	–11.5	5
IKB Deutsche	15.3	12.6	–2.7	7
Royal Bank of Scotland	14.9	24.4	9.5	8
Washington Mutual	14.8	12.1	–2.7	9
Wells Fargo	10	4.1	–5.9	14
Credit Agricole	8	8.8	0.8	17
Fortis	7.4	7.2	–0.2	18
European banks not on list	7.2	2.4	–4.8	19
Bayerische Landesbank	7.2	0	–7.2	20
HBOS plc	7	7.6	0.6	21
ING	6.9	4.8	–2.1	22
Societe Generale	6.8	9.7	2.9	23
Mizuho Financial Group	5.8	0	–5.8	25
National City	5.4	8.9	3.5	26
Lloyds TSB	5	4.9	–0.1	27
IndyMac	4.9	0	–4.9	28
West LB	4.7	7.5	2.8	29
Other Asian banks excluding Mizuho and Nomura	4.6	7.8	3.2	30

(continued)

Table 2-2. *Losses Recognized as of August 13, 2008*[a] (continued)
U.S. dollars, billions

Institution	Losses	Capital raised	Capital shortfall (losses minus capital raised)	Rank based on total losses recognized to date
LB Baden-Wurttemberg	3.8	0	−3.8	34
Etrade	3.6	2.4	−1.2	35
Natixis	3.3	6.7	3.4	36
Nomura Holdings	3.3	1.1	−2.2	37
Other U.S. firms	2.9	1.9	−1	39
HSH Nordbank	2.7	1.9	−0.8	40
Landesbank Sachsen	2.6	0	−2.6	41
Unicredit	2.6	0	−2.6	42
Commerzbank	2.4	0	−2.4	43
ABN Amro	2.3	0	−2.3	44
DZ Bank	2	0	−2	45
Bank of China	2	0	−2	46
Fifth Third Bancorp	1.9	2.6	0.7	47
Other Canadian banks (except CIBC)	1.8	0	−1.8	48
Bank Hapoalim	1.7	2.7	1	49
Rabobank	1.7	0	−1.7	50
Royal Bank of Canada	1.5	0	−1.5	51
Mitsubishi UFJ	1.5	1.5	0	52
Alliance and Leicester	1.4	0	−1.4	53
Marshall & Ilsley	1.4	0	−1.4	54
Dexia	1.3	0	−1.3	55
U.S. Bancorp	1.3	0	−1.3	56
Caisse d'Epargne	1.2	0	−1.2	57
KeyCorp	1.2	1.7	0.5	58
Hyo Real Estate	1	0	−1	59
Gulf International	1	1	0	60
Sovereign Bancorp	1	1.9	0.9	61
Sumitomo	0.9	4.9	4	62
Sumitomo Trust	0.7	1	0.3	63
DBS Group	0.2	1.1	0.9	64
	503.00	353.30	−149.25	

Sources: Bianco (2008) and Federal Reserve Bank of New York, "Forms of Federal Reserve Lending to Financial Institutions" (www.newyorkfed.org/markets/index.html).

a. Bold type indicates primary dealer designation.

of about $100 billion, or two-thirds of the total shortfall. Finally, only two of the primary dealers, Barclays and Lehman Brothers (prior to its failure), actually more than replaced the capital lost, while in some instances the rest, principally Merrill Lynch, UBS, and HSBC, faced serious capital shortfalls. Merrill Lynch's capital situation combined with uncertainty about its loss exposure clearly led management to sell the institution to Bank of America rather than risk a drop to zero in its market capital (stock price). Note too from the previous discussion that some of the firms that needed to raise more capital were the very ones that also were forced to bring auction-rate securities back onto their books.

In addition to injecting liquidity into the market, other central banks and governments actively intervened in other ways. As earlier discussions suggest and the appendix documents, the United Kingdom responded by nationalizing troubled banks and extending deposit insurance guarantees to cover virtually 100 percent of the liabilities of the affected institutions. EU entities actively intervened and nationalized banks. However, real intervention on a broad scale did not begin until mid-September 2008, when the responses entered what might be termed their second phase.

Phase II Responses by Central Banks and Governments

By the end of September 2008 it became clear that the financial turmoil had morphed into a full-blown financial crisis spanning financial markets throughout the world. After narrowing for a while from about June through August 2008, credit spreads over Treasuries widened across a wide variety of instruments and short-term maturities, including LIBOR, commercial paper, agency mortgage-backed securities and asset-backed securities, and credit default swap spreads compared with option adjusted spreads. Both the short- and long-term markets were affected, as were virtually all types of instruments, from shorter-term commercial paper to longer-term debt obligations.

In response, the Bank of England (see entry in the appendix for September 17, 2008, and table 2-3) expanded the drawdown on its special liquidity facility and the Federal Reserve expanded its swap arrangements with major foreign central banks, in turn increasing their lending of dollars against foreign-denominated collateral. Regulatory agencies, in a series of moves, prohibited the short selling of financial shares and broadened their guarantees and support of financial instruments and markets. For example, on September 19 the U.S. Treasury established a temporary guarantee program for money market mutual funds to prevent them from "breaking the buck" and having their value fall below one dollar.

Table 2-3. *Major Central Bank Operational Announcements from May to October 2008*[a]

Month	Bank of England	Federal Reserve	European Central Bank	Coordinated Central Bank Announcements[b]
May	Announcement that expanded three-month long-term repos will be maintained in June and July	Expansion of size of Term Auction Facility (TAF) Extension of collateral for Term Securities Lending Facility (TSLF)		Expansion of agreements between Federal Reserve and European Central Bank
July		Introduction of 84-day TAF Extension of Primary Dealer Credit Facility (PDCF) and TSLF to January 2009 Authorization of auction of options for primary dealers to borrow Treasury securities from the TSLF	Announcement that ECB will conduct operations under the 84-day TAF to provide U.S. dollars to European Central Bank counterparties Announcement that supplementary three-month, longer-term refinancing operations (LTROs) will be renewed in August and September	
September	Announcement that expanded three-month long-term repos will be maintained in September and October Announcement that long-term repo operations will be held weekly	Expansion of collateral for PDCF Expansion of size of and collateral for TSLF Announcement of provision of loans to banks to finance purchase of high-quality	Announcement that six-month LTROs will be renewed in October and three-month LTROs in November and December Conduct of Special Term Refinancing Operation.	Expansion of agreements between Federal Reserve and European Central Bank Establishment of swap agreements between Federal Reserve and Bank of England, subsequently expanded

October				
Extension of collateral for one-week U.S. dollar repos and for three-month long-term repos Extension of collateral of all extended-collateral, sterling, long-term repo operations; U.S. dollar repo operations; and the SLS to include bank-guaranteed debt under H.M. Treasury's bank debt guarantee scheme Announcement of Operational Standing Facilities and the Discount Window Facility, which together replace existing Standing Facilities	Extension of drawdown period for Special Liquidity Scheme (SLS)	Announcement of payment of interest on required and excess reserve balances Increase in size of TAFs Announcement of creation of the Commercial Paper Funding Facility	asset-backed commercial paper from money market mutual funds Increase in size of six-month supplementary LTROs Announcement of reduction in corridor of standing facilities from 200 basis points to 100 basis points around the interest rate on the main refinancing operations Introduction of swap agreements with Swiss National Bank	Announcement by Bank of England and European Central Bank, in conjunction with Federal Reserve, of an operation to lend U.S. dollars for one week over quarter-end, subsequently extended to scheduled weekly operations Announcement of schedules for TAFs and forward TAFs for auctions of U.S. dollar liquidity during the fourth quarter. Announcement by European Central Bank and Bank of England of tenders of U.S. dollar funding at 7-day, 28-day, and 84-day maturities at fixed interest rates or full allotment. Increase in swap agreements to accommodate required level of funding

Source: Bank of England (2008, table 3A, p. 18).
a. Data to close of business on October 20, 2008.
b. Coordinated actions also involved on one or more occasions some or all of the following central banks: Bank of Canada, Bank of Japan, Danmarks Nationalbank, Norges Bank, Reserve Bank of Australia, Sveriges Riksbank, and Swiss National Bank.

Foreign governments, such as Ireland's, guaranteed all bank deposits, and numerous banks were taken over or merged with government assistance. Not only were institutions rescued, but capital injections under government sponsorship were undertaken in the United States, the United Kingdom, and the Netherlands, just to name a few countries (see the appendix). On October 8, the Federal Reserve, Bank of Canada, Bank of England, European Central Bank, Sveriges Riksbank, and Swiss National Bank announced a coordinated interest rate cut of 50 basis points. Finally, on November 15, following a meeting in the United States of their finance ministers and central bank governors, leaders of the G-20 released a joint statement laying out some general principles for policy responses to what they had characterized as the worst financial crisis since the Great Depression. They presented guidelines for financial reforms to strengthen transparency and accountability, improve regulation, promote market integrity, and reform international institutions. The leaders also urged that a "college of supervisors" be set up to monitor the world's large complex financial institutions. Equally important, given the extensive involvement of government in the ownership of financial institutions, the group reaffirmed its support of free markets and expressed concern about increased protectionism.

When the crisis will end is not known, nor is it clear what a return to normal functioning of markets will actually mean. In the United States, a new administration has inherited the responsibility for resolving with the crisis and designing exit strategies as government support of markets and institutions is unwound. It seems clear, however, that more reforms will be proposed and implemented, and it is important to learn what has worked and what has not in the present regime and to direct reform efforts to those areas where key breakdowns have taken place or have been exposed.

Central Bank Responses: Which Was the Best?

The responses of the various central banks and their governments have been and likely will continue to be varied both in terms of the kinds of interventions pursued and the vigor with which liquidity has been provided. Their actions have been followed by many different criticisms. Commentators complain that some central banks responded too late to the initial problems (namely the Bank of England and Federal Reserve) or that their responses were insufficient as the downturn progressed (the ECB).[33] Others assert that some have overreacted to

---

33. See Atkins (2008).

the crisis, namely the Federal Reserve.[34] Finally, concerns have been raised that some central banks have put in place programs that will be difficult to unwind; that they set themselves up through their special lending programs to be and are now being arbitraged and are subsidizing leverage; that they have unduly broadened the safety net beyond banks to investment banks and other institutions in ways that may bring significant moral hazard and risks to taxpayers in the future; that they have subjected themselves to undue risk of political pressure and regulatory capture, jeopardizing their independence; that their actions mean that now more and more institutions may be regarded as "too big to fail"; and that they have created in market participants the expectation that governments will always attempt to insulate markets from downside risks.[35] Clearly, the United States is in the greatest risk position because of the takeover of Freddie Mac and Fannie Mae, the support extended to AIG, and the use of more than $700 billion in funds authorized under the Troubled Asset Relief Program.

Despite both the varied responses and complaints of critics, there is little convincing evidence that any of the central banks considered here significantly outperformed the others in terms of the quality of their responses. Financial turmoil is still with us, despite a year's worth of experimentation, rate cuts, and liquidity injections. While it is true that the general level of interest rates has come down, figure 2-6 shows that credit spreads remain atypically high, whether measured against LIBOR, U.S. agency debt, mortgage-backed securities, high-grade debt, or high-yield debt and that they have proved to be volatile. As far as the macro real economies are concerned, several, including the United States, have now slipped into official recession. Unemployment has moved up, and the massive injection of liquidity into financial markets implies that at some time in the near future, inflation is again likely to be a pressing problem. Major housing markets show no signs of having bottomed out yet, and institutions are continuing to experience financial stress and to fail.

The similarities in financial and economic performance are quite striking, given the variety of central bank responses. The ECB, for example, injected more funds into markets more quickly than did either the Fed or the Bank of England. The Fed cut its target policy rates more and did so more quickly than any other central bank. The Bank of England had cut rates three times by a total of 75 basis points, to 5 percent, in the early part of 2007, and it did not begin to cut rates again until the coordinated rate cuts on October 8, 2008 (see figure 2-6). The

34. Meltzer (2008). See also Kane (2007).

35. See Buiter (2008a, 2008b) for detailed criticisms, especially of the monetary policy errors that have been made.

Figure 2-6. *Central Bank Policy Rates, 2007–08*

Percent

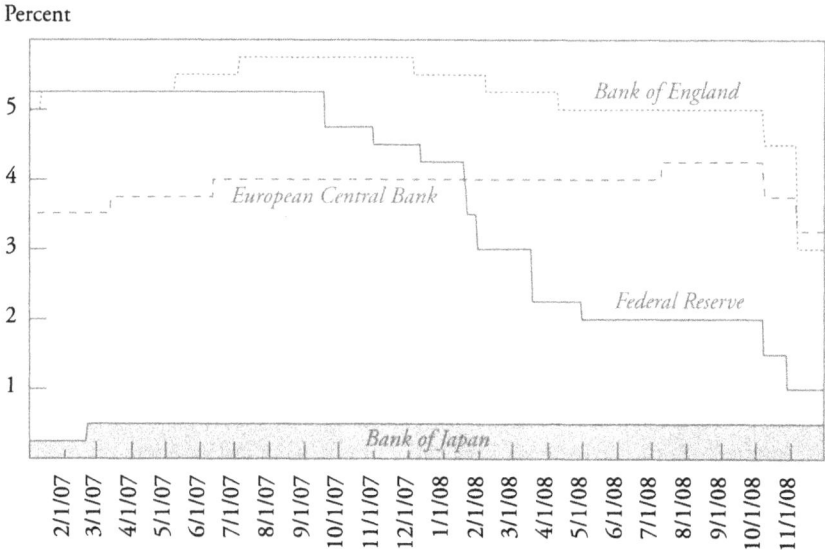

Sources: Federal Reserve (www.federalreserve.gov/fomc/fundsrate.htm); Bank of England (www.bank ofengland.co.uk/monetarypolicy/decisions.htm); Bank of Japan (www.boj.or.jp/en/theme/seisaku/kettei/ index.htm); European Central Bank (www.ecb.int/stats/monetary/rates/html/index.en.html).

Bank of Japan has held rates constant, mainly because its policy rates were so low that further cuts were nearly impossible. In contrast, the ECB actually increased rates by 25 basis points in July, whereas the Fed cut rates a total of seven times, from 5.25 percent to 2 percent (see figure 2-6) by May 2008, and then cut rates two more times, beginning with the coordinated October 8 cut, to 1 percent. The result is that while policy rates are clearly closer to each other than they were at the beginning of the crisis, current target policy rates remain widely divergent across the world in economies facing essentially the same significant external shocks to prices of energy, food, and other products.

In terms of liquidity provisions, the Fed received most of the attention because of the lending programs that it initiated, but the ECB stands out in terms of actually expanding liquidity. Figure 2-7 shows that the four main central banks—the Bank of Japan, Bank of England, Federal Reserve, and ECB—increased their balance sheets by slightly over $3 trillion, with about half being accounted for by the ECB and the remainder by the Federal Reserve. However, most of that happened after the coordinated rate increases on October 8, 2008. Before that action, the Fed (not considering its TSLF program, which was off–balance sheet)

Figure 2-7. *Assets, in Dollars, of Four Central Banks, July 31, 2007, through November 30, 2008*

Dollars, billions

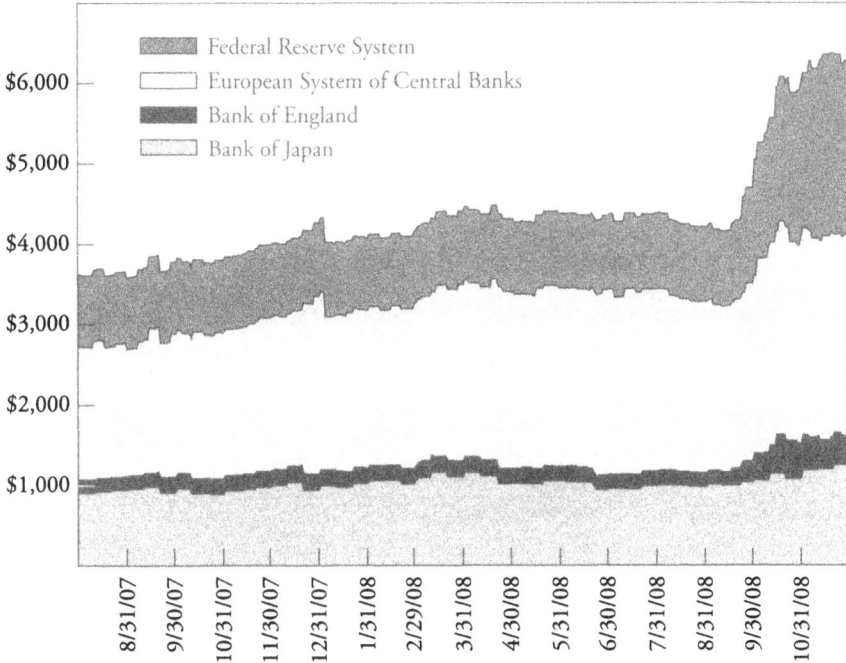

Sources: Board of Governors of the Federal Reserve System, "H.4.1 Report" (www.federalreserve.gov/ releases/h41); Bank of England (www.bankofengland.co.uk/mfsd/iadb/index.asp?first=yes&Section Required=B&HideNums=-1&ExtraInfo=false&Travel=NIxSTx); Bank of Japan (www.boj.or.jp/en/about/ kaikei/ac07/); Oesterreichische Nationalbank (for the European System of National Banks) (www.oenb.at/ en/stat_melders/datenangebot/oenb_eurosystem/kons_ausweis/consolidated_fi nancial_statement_of_the_eurosystem.jsp#tcm:16-3744).

accounted for 6 percent of the increase; the Bank of England, 2 percent; and the Bank of Japan, 13 percent. Review of the central bank responses suggests that initially monetary expansion was large only in the Eurozone countries, but more recently, the Federal Reserve has caught up the with the ECB's rate of monetary expansion. However, this assessment ignores the fungibility of funds and international currency flows.

The bottom line is that despite the efforts of the world's major central banks, as of the end of November 2008, there were few signs that any of the major economies had turned the corner; indeed, most had continued to contract despite those efforts.

Conclusions and Policy Recommendations

This contemporaneous account of the ongoing financial crisis has exposed several weaknesses in the existing financial structure and has already begun to suggest many areas where policy changes, consistent with the recommendations of the G-20 principals, are needed. They do, however, reach far beyond regulatory policy to include macroeconomic policy issues as well.

Macroeconomic Policy Issues

There are three major macro policy issues now confronting governments, central banks, and the Federal Reserve and the United States most particularly: how to unwind the massive liquidity and asset acquisition programs that have been put in place as velocity recovers and before a round of inflation breaks out; how to bring the stance of current policy back into equilibrium with world monetary polices when economies and financial markets are now global in scope; and how to change the day-to-day structure of the conduct of open market operations.

Unwinding Liquidity Programs and Facilitating
Deleveraging of the Financial System

The Federal Reserve has substantially altered the composition of its balance sheet. It has reduced significantly the amount of government securities that it holds and substantially expanded the array of collateral that it will take both at the discount window and through its repurchase agreements and other programs to include riskier securities. It also has put the taxpayer at risk through these programs as well as through its support of the Bear Stearns acquisition and lending to AIG. The Fed also has expanded the types of institutions besides federally regulated banks that have access to these programs—particularly investment banks, the Federal Home Loan Banks, and Freddie Mac and Fannie Mae. The key issues are whether access should be continued—and, if so, under what conditions—and what type of federal supervision and regulation should be required for private sector institutions now using Federal Reserve credit. In addition is the issue of what burdens the Federal Reserve and the Treasury, in particular, must now assume regarding transparency and disclosure of the performance of the assets that they have taken onto their balance sheets.

As for facilitating the deleveraging of the financial system, most of the liquidity facilities put in place have benefited mainly the select few institutions that constitute primary dealers. These are the institutions that have experienced the greatest financial pressures in terms of their dependence on the commercial paper market, their inability to fund substantial illiquid portfolios, and the largest losses on their portfolios. Most of the institutions also are highly leveraged and now face the need to raise more capital. That problem has been compounded by the Treasury's use of TARP monies to provide preferred stock capital injections into literally hundreds—and potentially thousands—of banking institutions.

While the nation's largest institutions have had some measure of success in raising additional capital, they still are hundreds of billions of dollars short of replacing capital that has been written off. As the Bank of England's 2008 *Financial Stability Report* clearly shows, reported losses have nearly doubled in the United Kingdom, European Union, and United States on a wide range of assets (table 2-4).[36] At the same time, institutions continue to fund illiquid portfolios temporarily by borrowing from the Federal Reserve, from other foreign central banks, and in the market. While seeking to delever their positions, they have met with only a modicum of success so far.[37] In fact, Bianco (2008) questions whether any significant degree of delevering has as yet taken place. Bianco estimated that in the U.S. case, the twenty primary dealers had cut the positions that they were carrying on their books by some $300 billion, or about 20 percent, reducing their holdings from $1.6 trillion to $1.3 trillion as of his August tabulations. But that was also about the amount that was being funded through the Federal Reserve's new lending programs. If that is true, then the primary impact of the aggressive restructuring of the Federal Reserve's portfolio may be to subsidize the primary dealers and other large financial institutions that essentially began relying on the Fed for about 20 to 25 percent of their leverage at below-market rates. Such subsidization combined with forbearance has long-lasting implications.

Unwinding Current Policy Ease

As the data on current policy rates in figure 2-6 show, there is substantial dispersion among policy rates, with the rate in Japan still being close to zero, the Bank of England rate currently at 3 percent, and the ECB rate at 3.25 percent. U.S. real interest rates were highly negative but more recently have moved into the positive range; however, they remain highly accommodative, despite concerns about inflation. These wide differences create arbitrage opportunities, of which the widely publicized Japanese carry trade was the primary example. The ability of institutions to put in place highly leveraged positions to arbitrage differences in policy rates has proved to be a continuing problem, and it is only likely to grow as a policy problem and constraint on monetary policy formation in the future.

36. Bank of England (2008).
37. Tobias and Shin (2007) suggests that substantial deleveraging has taken place in the Japanese carry trade market by major institutions.

Table 2-4. *Mark-to-Market Losses on Selected Financial Assets*[a,b]

Location	Outstanding amounts	April 2008 report of losses	October 2008 report of losses
United Kingdom (£ billions)			
Prime residential mortgage–backed securities	193	8.2	17.4
Nonconforming residential mortgage–backed securities	39	2.2	7.7
Commercial mortgage–backed securities	33	3.1	4.4
Investment-grade corporate bonds	450	46.2	86.5
High-yield corporate bonds	15	3	6.6
Total		62.7	122.6
United States (US$ billions)			
Home equity loan asset-backed securities (ABSs)[c]	757	255	309.9
Home equity loan ABS collateralized debt obligations (CDOs)[c,d]	421	236	277
Commercial mortgage–backed securities	700	79	97.2
Collateralized loan obligations	340	12.2	46.2
Investment-grade corporate bonds	3,308	80	600
High-yield corporate bonds	692	76	246.8
Total		738.8	1,577.3
Euro Area (€ billions)			
Residential mortgage–backed securities[e]	387	21.5	38.9
Commercial mortgage–backed securities[e]	34	2.8	4.1
Collateralized loan obligations	103	6.8	22.8
Investment-grade corporate bonds	5,324	283.8	642.9
High-yield corporate bonds	175	29.1	75.6
Total		344.1	784.6

Source: Bank of England (2008).

a. Estimated loss of market value since January 2007, except for U.S. collateralized loan obligations, which show losses since May 2007.

b. Data to close of business on October 20, 2008.

c. 2005 H1 to 2007 H2 vintages. The home equity loan asset class comprises mainly U.S. subprime mortgages, but it also includes, for example, other mortgages with high loan-to-value ratios. Home equity loans are of lower credit quality than U.S. Alt-A and prime residential mortgages.

d. High-grade and mezzanine ABS CDOs, excluding CDO²s (or CDOs squared).

e. Germany, Ireland, Italy, Netherlands, Portugal, and Spain.

Federal Reserve Open Market Operations

Over the longer run, the current difficulties raise serious questions about the structure of Federal Reserve daily open market operations and the wisdom of dealing with only a few institutions heavily concentrated in New York. We learned from 9/11 that serious events can jeopardize the smooth functioning of our money markets and payments systems. While one may have questioned the justification for permitting investment banks, among the biggest losers in the subprime debacle, to be primary dealers, that issue is now largely moot, given that they have since merged, failed, or converted to commercial bank charters. Nevertheless, current daily operating procedures, which rely on channeling funds to the markets through only a few select institutions, all located in New York, are a legacy of a pre-computer world. In contrast, the ECB has more than 500 counterparties from whom they accept bids. Given today's technology, there is no reason that bids cannot be accepted electronically from any well-capitalized member bank. Bids currently are processed and allocated electronically, so there are no technical limitations to the ability to accept and process bids from institutions across the country on a wide range of Treasury securities. Breaking this dependence on a few privileged institutions would ensure that channels remain open when a few institutions find themselves experiencing liquidity problems.

The Need for International Coordination of Monetary, Regulatory, and Supervisory Policies

The current actions of the G-20 leaders as well as the series of coordinated monetary policy efforts by the world's major central banks suggest that interdependent financial markets mean that nations can no longer pursue independent financial policies. As argued earlier, world monetary policies are still out of sync and large institutions are now in position to arbitrage the major central banks in a variant of the Japanese carry trade. Such arbitrage will force policy coordination or else engender significant and potentially disruptive movements in exchange rates and real resources. As for regulation, it now seems clear that the Basel approach is defective, but aside from the approach that the United States has taken through the Federal Deposit Insurance Corporation Improvement Act (FDICIA) of 1991, which admittedly needs substantial fixing, there are few viable alternatives.

Regulatory and Micro Structural Responses and Issues

Several key issues have shown up as a result of how central banks and related government agencies have chosen to respond to the crisis, and they relate primarily to how failed institutions have been handled, the design and structure of deposit insurance guarantees, the need to control regulatory incentives, and the extension of the federal safety net to entities besides banks.[38] Most affected to date have been the United Kingdom and the United States, but some of the same concerns are applicable to the EU as well, where many countries have had to backstop institutions and their deposit insurance systems.[39]

The Need to Unwind Government Ownership

The deep government involvement in the financial system has evolved without an exit strategy and without a vision for the future. Preferred stock has been injected to provide a capital cushion in virtually all of the nation's largest banks and potentially thousands of others as well. That has been done at relatively no cost to existing equity holders except for the granting of warrants, but with no required write-downs of losses against common equity. When, under what circumstances, and at what prices should those warrants be exercised? What are the implications for competition between firms that have exited the capital program or been divested and those that have not and may be the beneficiaries of either implicit or explicit guarantees? The capital injection program also is reportedly being used as a tool to encourage consolidation among firms. What criteria and what vision for financial structure are guiding this policy?

Deposit Insurance Contract and Related Structures

The run on Northern Rock and the subsequent extension of deposit guarantees by the government to deposits in all troubled U.K. institutions resulted from two fundamental problems. The first was the fact that U.K. deposit insurance contract covered 100 percent of only the first £2,000 (about $4,100) and 90 percent of the next £33,000 (about $67,500), which provided for 10 percent coinsurance on deposits over £2,000 for even very small depositors. The second was the lack of a bankruptcy statute that would have permitted authorities to resolve the failure promptly. As it was, the U.K. system relied on its general bankruptcy laws to resolve bank failures, in what can be a lengthy and drawn-out process. Meanwhile, depositors and other customers would face lengthy delays in accessing their funds and borrowers would be denied access to their lines of credit. Faced with a potentially costly inconvenience, it is rational for depositors to with-

---

38. Similar recommendations have also been made by Baily, Elmendorf, and Litan (2008).

39. Eisenbeis and Kaufman (2006, 2008b) have provided extensive discussions of some of these issues, especially those facing the EU should a large, cross-border banking institution experience financial difficulties.

draw their funds at the first whiff of difficulty, despite the fact that their deposits might ultimately be made good by their deposit insurance system.

This is in contrast to the situation in the United States, which not only has more generous coverage but has a well-laid-out process to assure depositors that the failure of an institution will be resolved promptly—usually over a weekend—and that most depositors will have access to their funds by the next business day. Furthermore, under the Federal Deposit Insurance Corporation Improvement Act, problems in an institution are not supposed to fester. FDICIA prescribes a plan of prompt corrective action (PCA) and structured early intervention and resolution (SEIR) that requires supervisors both to intervene before a liquidity problem becomes a solvency problem and, in the unlikely event of a failure, to resolve the problem quickly through recapitalization, sale, or creation of a temporary bridge bank before an institution's net worth goes to zero. Depositors and borrowers thereby have immediate (next-day) access to banking services, making the failure an isolated event rather than a banking system event. However, these provisions have not always worked as intended, as recent experience with IndyMac demonstrates.

An additional consideration has arisen in connection with the rescue of Citigroup by the Federal Reserve and the Treasury. Large depositors, such as those with payroll and other accounts from which regular payments were to be disbursed, reportedly began to transfer funds to other institutions, creating a mini run of large, uninsured depositors. That concern was part of the reason that officials stepped in to provide a capital injection to Citigroup and also a guarantee of its debt obligations up to $306 billion.

Better Failure Resolution Regime

In contrast with the procedures available to U.S. bank regulators to deal with bank and thrift failures, the failure resolution options in both the United Kingdom for Northern Rock and the United States for Bear Stearns, AIG, and Lehman Brothers relied on general bankruptcy statutes, suggesting the need for special failure and resolution regimes for systemically important institutions. The aim of such structures should be to enable responsible authorities to close an institution legally and to avoid the negative externalities associated with failure, which include loss of access to funds and borrowing relationships. The United Kingdom has recently released a second consultative paper laying out a proposal for a detailed framework to reform its failure and resolution process. The proposed "special resolution regime" contains most of the features currently available to U.S. regulators, including provisions for prompt corrective action, the ability to close an institution before it becomes insolvent, the ability to facilitate a takeover or sale, provision of a bridge bank option, the ability to arrange a partial purchase and assumption transaction, and even a temporary nationalization provision.[40] The policy issues for the United States is whether such a regime is necessary for just noncommercial bank primary dealers or also for investment banks, hedge funds, insurance companies, and other types of institutions. In addition, the Federal Reserve and the Treasury have also proposed significant extension of federal regulation and oversight for payment and settlement systems. The nature of public support for payment and settlement systems also is an important concern. Finally, similar issues concerning bank and resolution failure regimes are critical for the EU too. Most EU countries typically rely on general bankruptcy statutes, as does the United Kingdom. Eisenbeis and Kaufman (2005, 2006, 2008b) have discussed in detail the potential problems that the EU will face in resolving a large, cross-border bank failure and some of the problems that arose with the recent rescue of Fortis by authorities in Belgium, the Netherlands, and Luxembourg and the joint nationalization of Dexia SA by Belgium, France, and Luxembourg.

The Need to Control Regulatory Agency Incentives

There have been numerous instances, even under prompt corrective action and structured early intervention and resolution in the United States, that the FDIC has been faced with significant losses in banking failures, despite FDICIA's intention that institutions be closed before their net worth goes to zero. The statute also includes reporting and other requirements when losses occur for additional reporting and evaluation by the agency's inspector general. Despite those requirements, however, losses have occurred; most recently, the failure of IndyMac has been estimated, as noted earlier, to cost the FDIC potentially as much as a third of the value of IndyMac's assets. Kane (1989, 1997, 2001) has highlighted this problem repeatedly, but losses still abound. There have been clear breakdowns in the quality of supervision, especially on the part of the OTS.

Similar incentive problems have been revealed in the detailed forensic investigations in the United Kingdom of the supervision and regulation of Northern Rock. Regulators tend to engage in forbearance when institutions under their supervision get into financial difficulties. Whether that tendency is due to regulatory capture or simply to regulators' desire to gamble that problems will be resolved and not appear as a failure on their watch is an important question.[41]

---

40. See H.M. Treasury (2008a, b)
41. See Kane (2008a, b, and c) for further discussions of the incentive issue.

Given the injection of public capital into most of the major U.S. banks, where FDICIA and its PCA requirements now fit in regulatory and resolution policies is an open question. The U.S. government is now a significant owner-investor in many of the nation's financial institutions, and to close and reorganize them would impose significant losses on taxpayers.

The Need to Limit Leverage

Perhaps the biggest pressing policy problem that the current crisis has brought to the fore is the need to limit leverage. Pervasive dependence on excessive leverage was the problem that created the conditions for the current financial turmoil. Borrowers, especially mortgage borrowers, were highly leveraged, and that was especially true in the subprime and Alt-A markets. In the United States, borrower leverage was not only tolerated but actively encouraged by Congress in the name of increasing homeownership. Derivative instruments depended, in many cases, on highly leveraged positions for their financial viability. Depository institutions had incentives to create highly leveraged conduits and special investment vehicles to get assets off their balance sheets and generate fee income. These so-called bankruptcy-remote schemes relied on legal interpretation but ignored reputational incentives, which de facto meant that their sponsors assumed the leverage of those vehicles when problems occurred. Investment banks were unconstrained by either regulation or the market from becoming highly leveraged. Current bank regulatory policies—especially those in the European Union and the United Kingdom—rely heavily on complex Basel 1 and Basel 2 capital adequacy determinations, which concentrate on the allocation across asset classes and not on overall leverage of institutions. A complete rethinking of the Basel accords is in order, and if the next crisis is to be avoided or at least its effects limited, attention must be directed first and foremost to measuring net worth and limiting leverage.

What to Do with Fannie Mae and Freddie Mac and U.S. Housing Policy?

With Freddie Mac and Fannie Mae under government conservatorship, U.S. taxpayers are now essentially the biggest owner of mortgages. Government involvement raises several issues and questions. Should Freddie and Fannie be reprivatized? Can they be without re-creating the incentive problems that led to their demise? Simply spinning these entities off to resume operations as usual—or attempting to reprivatize them without government guarantees—would merely roll back the clock, because markets would assume that the government would step in again to rescue them again if they got into financial difficulty. Can these firms be liquidated or broken up and, if so, how? Little attention has been paid to the Federal Home Loan Banks, but they played a significant role in lending to financial institutions in general and in particular to providing subsidized support to Countrywide and IndyMac. Dealing with U.S. housing policy requires that the role of these institutions be considered along with that of Freddie Mac and Fannie Mae. Finally, there is the issue of what government ownership of mortgages may imply for the conduct of anti-inflationary monetary policy. At some point the Fed will be required to reverse its course quickly and begin to raise interest rates back toward equilibrium and mop up the liquidity that it has supplied to financial markets. However, to do so will also impose capital losses on the government's holdings of mortgages and other financial assets and at the same time increase their carrying costs. Both imply additional losses and/or costs to taxpayers and may act as a significant deterrent to the independent conduct of monetary policy.

Appendix. *Crisis Events and Regulatory Responses in the European Union, United States, United Kingdom, Switzerland, Japan, and Other Countries*

Country	Date	Condition
United States	12 February 2007	ResMAE files for bankruptcy.
United States	22 February 2007	HSBC fires its first head of U.S. mortgage lending business due to large losses.
United States	12 March 2007	Trading in shares of New Century Financial is suspended due to bankruptcy fears and losses in subprime loans.
United States	13 March 2007	U.S. markets are hit by subprime fears.
United Kingdom	20 March 2007	People's Choice files for bankruptcy protection.
United States	2 April 2007	New Century Financial files for Chapter 11 bankruptcy.
United Kingdom	3 May 2007	U.K. subprime lender Kensington agrees to takeover.
United States	14 June 2007	On June 14, Bear Stearns reports earnings decline for the first time in four quarters on weaker results from its mortgage securities business.
United States	15 June 2007	Bear Stearns suffers big losses on subprime mortgage investments in two hedge funds.
United States	22 June 2007	Bear Stearns reveals that it spent $3.2 billion bailing out two hedge funds due to subprime losses.

(continued)

Appendix. *Crisis Events and Regulatory Responses in the European Union,*
United States, United Kingdom, Switzerland, Japan, and Other Countries (continued)

Country	Date	Condition
United Kingdom	4 July 2007	The U.K.'s Financial Services Authority (FSA) takes action against five subprime lenders for offering loans to people who could not afford them.
United States	17 July 2007	Bear Stearns notifies investors in two hedge funds that little value remains.
United States	20 July 2007	Ben Bernanke, chairman of the board of governors of the U.S. Federal Reserve, indicates that subprime losses might reach $100 billion.
United States	24 July 2007	Subprime losses hit profits at Countrywide.
Germany	30 July 2007	IKB Deutsche Industriebank, a German Bank, is rescued.
United States	31 July 2007	Bear Stearns stops withdrawals from a third hedge fund.
United States	6 August 2007	American Home Mortgage files for bankruptcy.
United States	7 August 2007	Federal Reserve leaves federal funds rate at 5.25 percent.
United States European Union Germany Japan	9 August 2007	Federal Reserve injects funds into markets. The European Central Bank (ECB) pumps a record 95 billion euros into money markets. Bundesbank organizes a meeting to rescue IKB, and Bafin indicates that it is looking into 417.5 billion euros in special funding for Sachsen LB. Bank of Japan injects funds into the market. BNP Paribas freezes withdrawals from three of its hedge funds hit by the U.S. subprime market crisis.
United States	10 August 2007	Federal Reserve notes that banks are experiencing unusual funding needs because of dislocations in money and credit markets and says that it will provide funds as needed. ECB injects additional 61 billion euros into the market.
United States European Union Japan	13 August 2007	Federal Reserve injects more funds into market. ECB provides additional 47.7 billion euros to money markets. Bank of Japan injects more funds. Goldman Sachs provides $43 billion to support a hedge fund.

(continued)

Appendix. *Crisis Events and Regulatory Responses in the European Union, United States, United Kingdom, Switzerland, Japan, and Other Countries* (continued)

Country	Date	Condition
United Kingdom	14 August 2007	Bank of England is alerted to the potential impact of the global credit squeeze on Northern Rock's business in a phone call with officials at the Financial Services Authority and H.M. Treasury.
Germany United States	17 August 2007	Sachsen LB receives bailout from German savings bank association. Federal Reserve cuts the discount rate by half a percentage point, to 5.7 percent, and says it will act as needed to offset adverse effects on the economy arising from disruptions in financial markets.
United Kingdom	21 August 2007	Barclays Bank borrows £314 million from Bank of England's Standing Lending Facility, the first use of the facility during the credit crisis.
United States	23 August 2007	Banks borrow $2 billion from the discount window as Federal Reserve attempts to encourage borrowing. Countrywide gets $2 billion cash injection from Bank of America.
Germany	28 August 2007	To avoid failure, the German regional bank Sachsen Landesbank is sold to Landesbank Baden-Wurttemberg with 17 billion euros in assistance from the government.
United Kingdom	30 August 2007	Barclays Bank borrows £1.6 billion from Bank of England.
Germany	3 September 2007	German regional bank IKB records subprime losses.
United Kingdom	4 September 2007	LIBOR rises to its highest level in almost nine years. The three-month loan rate hits 6.7975 percent, above the Bank of England's emergency lending rate of 6.75 percent, suggesting that banks are reluctant to lend money to each other.
European Union	6 September 2007	ECB injects more cash into markets, bringing the total to 250 billion euros, and leaves the interest rate at 4 percent.
United Kingdom	10 September 2007	Victoria Mortgage Funding becomes the first U.K. mortgage company to fail.
United Kingdom	12 September 2007	Bank of England (BOE) states that it will provide emergency loans to any bank that runs into short-term difficulties as a result of temporary market

(continued)

Appendix. *Crisis Events and Regulatory Responses in the European Union, United States, United Kingdom, Switzerland, Japan, and Other Countries* (continued)

Country	Date	Condition
		conditions. But BOE is to rule out following the lead of the ECB and Federal Reserve in pumping huge sums into the banking system to ease the liquidity drought.
United Kingdom	13 September 2007	Northern Rock asks for and is granted emergency financial support from the Bank of England as lender of last resort.
United Kingdom	14 September 2007	Northern Rock says "extreme conditions" in financial markets forced it to approach the Bank of England for assistance. In a statement, BOE, H.M. Treasury, and FSA say that they believe that Northern Rock is solvent and that the standby funding facility will enable the bank to "fund its operations during the current period of turbulence in financial markets." Meanwhile, lines begin to form outside a number of Northern Rock branches as hundreds of worried savers seek to withdraw their money. The bank's website collapses under the strain, and all its phone lines are jammed.
United Kingdom	15 September 2007	Run on Northern Rock occurs.
United Kingdom	17 September 2007	Crisis surrounding Northern Rock grows as lines at many of its seventy-six branches show no sign of diminishing and the firm's shares plunge a further 40 percent. Chancellor Alistair Darling dramatically agrees that H.M. Treasury will guarantee all deposits held by Northern Rock. Bank of England has been shopping Northern Rock.
United States United Kingdom	18 September 2007	Federal Reserve cuts the federal funds rate by 50 basis points, to 4.75 percent, and cuts the discount rate to 5.25 percent. Bank of England injects £4.4 billion into money markets.
United Kingdom	19 September 2007	The Bank of England says that it will inject £10 billion into the money markets to try to bring down the cost of interbank lending. In another significant development, the range of assets that banks are allowed to use as collateral will be wider than usual,

(continued)

Appendix. *Crisis Events and Regulatory Responses in the European Union, United States, United Kingdom, Switzerland, Japan, and Other Countries* (continued)

Country	Date	Condition
		including mortgage debt. Critics accuse BOE of a U-turn, saying that it should have acted sooner to help Northern Rock.
United Kingdom	22 September 2007	Chancellor Alistair Darling suggests that U.K. government will consider boosting deposit savings guarantee to £100,000.
United Kingdom	26 September 2007	Commercial banks shun Bank of England's rescue fund.
European Union	27 September 2007	ECB indicates that it lent 3.9 billion euros to banks ($5.5 billion) at its penalty rate of 5 percent.
United Kingdom	1 October 2007	Chancellor Alistair Darling announces that the scheme to protect savers with money deposited in U.K. banks is being expanded to guarantee 100 percent of the first £35,000 of savings. He adds that that guarantee is the first stage of a wider reform of the compensation system.
United States	7 October 2007	Citigroup, Merrill Lynch, and UBS report significant write-downs.
United Kingdom	9 October 2007	H.M. Treasury agrees to protect new savings deposited at Northern Rock. The decision extends the guarantee made the previous month, which covered deposits made up to September 19. Bank of England and FSA defend role in Northern Rock crisis.
Japan	15 October 2007	Nomura closes its U.S. mortgage-backed securities business and takes a $621 million hit.
United States	31 October 2007	Federal Reserve cuts the federal funds rate by 25 basis points, to 4.5 percent, and cuts the discount rate to 5 percent.
United States	8 November 2007	Moody's re-estimates the capital adequacy of U.S. monoline insurers and financial guarantors.
United States	15 November 2007	U.S. House of Representatives passes the Predatory Lending and Mortgage Protection Act by a wide majority. Federal Reserve provides $47.25 billion in temporary reserves.
United States	26 November 2007	Federal Reserve promises more than the usual year-end liquidity and says that it will lift limits on how much can be lent to any one bank.

(continued)

Appendix. *Crisis Events and Regulatory Responses in the European Union, United States, United Kingdom, Switzerland, Japan, and Other Countries* (continued)

Country	Date	Condition
United Kingdom	6 December 2007	Bank of England cuts interest rate, the first such cut in response to the financial crisis. ECB keeps rate constant.
United States	11 December 2007	Federal Reserve cuts federal funds rate to 4.25 percent and the discount rate to 4.75 percent.
United States European Union Switzerland United Kingdom Canada	12 December 2007	As part of a global coordinated central bank effort, Federal Reserve establishes the Term Auction Facility (TAF) to provide funds over a longer period to a wider range of banks to meet temporary short-ages of funds. It also establishes foreign exchange swap lines with the ECB and Swiss National Bank (SNB). The arrangements will provide up to $20 billion for the ECB and $4 billion for the SNB. Bank of England and Bank of Canada also an-nounce measure to address short-term funding problems in their markets as well.
Japan United States European Union	13 December 2007	Central banks agree to coordinated action to inject at least $100 billion in short-term interbank credit.
United States	17 December 2007	First TAF auction held.
United States United Kingdom	18 December 2007	Federal Reserve tightens rules on subprime lending. Bank of England makes £10 billion available to U.K. banks to ease credit crunch and lends banks $500 billion.
United States	20 December 2007	Bear Stearns reports first ever quarterly loss.
United States European Union Switzerland	3 January 2008	Federal Reserve raises TAF auction amounts to $30 billion from $20 billion for each of the two auctions in January. The European Central Bank and the Swiss National Bank also offer dollar funds in conjunction with the Fed's auctions.
United Kingdom	4 January 2008	Chancellor Alistair Darling tells the *Financial Times* that he is planning to give the FSA more power to deal with failing banks to avoid another Northern Rock–type crisis. He proposes giving the FSA the

(continued)

Appendix. *Crisis Events and Regulatory Responses in the European Union,
United States, United Kingdom, Switzerland, Japan, and Other Countries* (continued)

Country	Date	Condition
		power to seize and protect customers' cash if their bank gets into financial difficulties.
United States	11 January 2008	Federal Reserve cuts interest rates by half a percentage point, to 3.5 percent, its biggest cut in twenty-five years. Countrywide is bought by Bank of America.
United Kingdom	26 January 2008	The Commons Treasury Committee says that the Financial Services Authority was guilty of a "systematic failure of duty" in the Northern Rock crisis. MPs say that the U.K.'s financial watchdog should have spotted the bank's "reckless" business plan; they also call for the Bank of England to set up a head of financial stability. The FSA says that it has already admitted failings in relation to Northern Rock and insists that it is "addressing" them.
United States	29 January 2008	House of Representatives passes an economic stimulus package with $146 billion in targeted tax relief.
United States	30 January 2008	Federal Reserve cuts interest rate from 3.5 percent to 3 percent.
United States	1 February 2008	Federal Reserve announces that it will continue biweekly TAF auctions in February, holding the amount in each auction steady at $30 billion.
Japan	13 February 2008	Japan's financial watchdog says that Japanese banks had suffered losses of $5.6 billion by the end of 2007, with losses more than doubling in the last three months of the year.
United Kingdom	17 February 2008	The government rejects offers for Northern Rock and takes the bank into public ownership in one of the largest British nationalizations since that of engine maker Rolls-Royce in 1971.
United Kingdom	18 February 2008	Trading in shares in Northern Rock is suspended. Northern Rock is nationalized.
United States	29 February 2008	Federal Reserve announces two TAF auctions of $30 billion each in March. It says that it intends to conduct auctions for as long as necessary to ease pressures in short-term funding markets.
United Kingdom	6 March 2008	Peloton Partners' £1 billion hedge fund collapses.

(continued)

Appendix. *Crisis Events and Regulatory Responses in the European Union, United States, United Kingdom, Switzerland, Japan, and Other Countries* (continued)

Country	Date	Condition
United States	7 March 2008	Federal Reserve says that it will inject $100 billion into the banking system by increasing the size of its two term auctions of short-term funding and start a series of term repurchase transactions with primary dealers expected to be worth another $100 billion.
United States Canada United Kingdom European Union Switzerland	11 March 2008	Federal Reserve broadens the range of acceptable collateral in its securities lending program to include home mortgages. It will provide up to $200 billion to primary dealers for twenty-eight days and accept federal agency home mortgage–backed securities and highly rated private mortgage-backed securities as collateral. The action is coordinated with the Bank of Canada, Bank of England, ECB, and Swiss National Bank. Swap lines with the ECB and SNB are increased to $30 billion and $6 billion.
Japan European Union United States	11 March 2008	Central banks announce $200 billion in new emergency lending.
United States	14 March 2008	Federal Reserve provides emergency funding to Bear Stearns through JPMorgan Chase, the first such move since the Great Depression. Carlyle Capital fails.
United States	16 March 2008	In a surprise move, the Federal Reserve cuts the discount rate that it charges on direct loans to banks and announces a new lending program, the Primary Dealer Credit Facility, to provide credit to other big Wall Street firms. In addition, it increases the maximum maturity of discount rate loans from thirty to ninety days. It takes those actions in concert with a decision to approve special financing to facilitate the purchase of Bear Stearns by JPMorgan Chase.
United States	19 March 2008	Federal regulators finally act to allow Fannie Mae and Freddy Mac to buy more mortgages, easing pressures on the cash-strapped mortgage market.
United States	24 March 2008	Federal Reserve details its role in the amended planned purchase of ailing investment bank Bear Stearns by JPMorgan Chase. It says that it will assume control

(continued)

Appendix. *Crisis Events and Regulatory Responses in the European Union,*
United States, United Kingdom, Switzerland, Japan, and Other Countries (continued)

Country	Date	Condition
		of a portfolio of Bear Stearns assets valued at $30 billion, pledged as security. Any profit from the assets will accrue to the Fed, while JPMorgan will bear the first $1 billion of any losses. Federal Reserve will finance the remaining $29 billion on a non-recourse basis to JPMorgan.
United Kingdom	28 March 2008	The Financial Services Authority admits failures in its supervision of Northern Rock, acknowledging "a lack of adequate oversight and review" by the agency of the troubled bank. The FSA says that it will be overhauling its procedures as a result of the weaknesses identified but says that it should continue to have responsibility for regulating the banking system.
United States	31 March 2008	Treasury announces plan to reform financial regulation in United States.
United States United Kingdom	9 April 2008	Federal Reserve says that it is considering a plan under which the U.S. Treasury would borrow in excess of its requirements and deposit the surplus at the Fed. The central bank also is considering whether to issue debt under the Fed's name and seek authority to immediately pay interest on commercial bank reserves. Bank of England creates Special Liquidity Scheme to permit banks to swap high-quality mortgages for H.M. Treasury bills temporarily.
European Union United States Switzerland	2 May 2008	European Central Bank, Federal Reserve, and Swiss National Bank announce coordinated efforts to enhance market liquidity.
United States	12 July 2008	IndyMac fails and is reopened on July 15.
United States	13 July 2008	Federal Reserve authorizes government-sponsored entities Fannie Mae and Freddie Mac to borrow from its discount window as necessary for emergency funding. Any lending would be collateralized by U.S. government and agency securities. The Fed also agrees to take on a consultative role in setting capital requirements and financial safety and soundness standards for the two companies. U.S. Treasury

(continued)

Appendix. *Crisis Events and Regulatory Responses in the European Union, United States, United Kingdom, Switzerland, Japan, and Other Countries* (continued)

Country	Date	Condition
		proposes injecting equity funds into Freddie and Fannie.
United States	15 July 2008	U.S. Securities and Exchange Commission announces emergency order to curb naked short selling.
United States	23 July 2008	Congress passes housing bill that includes rescue provisions for Freddie Mac and Fannie Mae.
United States	30 July 2008	Federal Reserve extends Primary Dealer Credit Facility (PDCF) and the Term Securities Lending Facility (TSLF) through January 30, 2009. Introduces auctions of options on $50 billion of draws on the TSLF. Adds eighty-four-day Term Auction Facility loans as a complement to twenty-eight-day TAF loans. Increases the Federal Reserve's swap line with the European Central Bank from $50 billion to $55 billion.
United States	7 September 2008	U.S. Treasury and Federal Housing Finance Agency (FHFA) place Freddie Mac and Fannie Mae under conservatorship and replace management. The GSEs will modestly increase portfolios through 2009 and in 2010 will begin to shrink portfolios by 10 percent per year until they reach $250 billion. Treasury will make preferred stock injections as needed to ensure that Freddie and Fannie maintain adequate capital. Treasury establishes a new secured lending facility available to Freddie and Fannie and the Federal Home Loan Banks. Treasury will begin purchase of new mortgage-backed securities.
United States	14 September 2008	The Federal Reserve broadens collateral that can be pledged at the Primary Dealer Credit Facility beyond investment-grade debt securities to match the collateral that can be pledged in the tri-party repo system. The collateral for the Term Securities Lending Facility is expanded to include all investment-grade debt, and TSLF auctions will be conducted every week rather than every two weeks. The Fed also temporarily suspends the prohibition in section 23A of the Federal Reserve Act to permit

(continued)

Appendix. *Crisis Events and Regulatory Responses in the European Union,*
United States, United Kingdom, Switzerland, Japan, and Other Countries (continued)

Country	Date	Condition
		insured depository institutions to provide liquidity to affiliates for assets typically provided in the tri-party repo market until January 30, 2009.
United States	15 September 2008	Lehman Brothers Holdings files for bankruptcy, and Bank of America announces purchase of Merrill Lynch.
United States	16 September 2008	The Federal Reserve authorizes the Federal Reserve Bank of New York to lend up to $85 billion to American International Group (AIG) under section 13(3) of the Federal Reserve Act. The loan term is up to twenty-four months at an interest rate of 850 basis points above the three-month LIBOR. The loan is collateralized by all of AIG's assets including its subsidiaries. The U.S. government will receive 79.9 percent of the equity and the right to veto dividend payments to common and preferred shareholders.
United Kingdom	17 September 2008	Bank of England extends drawdown period for Special Liquidity Scheme. U.S. Treasury issues additional securities, the proceeds to be held at the Federal Reserve to expand the Federal Reserve's balance sheet.
Canada United Kingdom European Union United States Japan Switzerland	18 September 2008	The Bank of Canada, Bank of England, European Central Bank, Federal Reserve, Bank of Japan, and Swiss National Bank will expand dollar swap lines of up to $180 billion, with an additional $55 billion (now to $110 billion total) with the ECB and an increase of $15 billion to $27 billion with the Swiss National Bank. New swap facilities are put in place with the Bank of Canada ($10 billion), the Bank of England ($40 billion), and the Bank of Japan ($60 billion), to be in effect through January 30, 2009. FSA prohibits short selling of financial shares in the U.K.
United States	19 September 2008	U.S. Treasury establishes temporary guarantee program for U.S. money market funds to prevent them from "breaking the buck" for a fee to be paid by the funds using $50 billion from the Exchange Stabilization

(continued)

Appendix. *Crisis Events and Regulatory Responses in the European Union, United States, United Kingdom, Switzerland, Japan, and Other Countries* (continued)

Country	Date	Condition
		Fund. Treasury announces that Freddie Mac and Fannie Mae will expand their purchases of mortgage-backed securities and Treasury will expand its purchases of mortgage-backed securities under the program announced on September 7. Treasury also initiates talks with Congress to establish a fund to purchase troubled mortgages. SEC prohibits short selling in financial shares. The Federal Reserve will extend nonrecourse loans to U.S. banks and bank holding companies to finance the purchase of asset-backed commercial paper from money market mutual funds. Federal Reserve will also purchase from primary dealers federal agency discount notes issued by Freddie Mac, Fannie Mae, and the Federal Home Loan Banks.
Ireland	20 September 2008	Ireland increases deposit insurance limit from 20,000 euros to 100,000 euros.
United States	21 September 2008	Federal Reserve approves applications by Morgan Stanley and Goldman Sachs to become regulated bank holding companies.
United States	22 September 2008	Federal Reserve modifies guidance on the definition and determination of control for purposes of the Bank Holding Company Act to make it more attractive for hedge funds and private equity to inject capital to banks. The Fed also relaxes restriction on equity injections by liberalizing the definition of what constitutes control before a holder becomes subject to the Bank Holding Company Act.
United States	24 September 2008	Federal Reserve expands its swap lines with foreign central banks to include the Reserve Bank of Australia, Danmarks Nationalbank, Norges Bank, and Sveriges Riksbank.
United States	25 September 2008	JPMorgan Chase agrees to buy Washington Mutual, which is about to fail.
United States	26 September 2008	Federal Reserve expands its outstanding swap lines with foreign central banks, increasing the outstanding lines to $290 billion.

(continued)

Appendix. *Crisis Events and Regulatory Responses in the European Union,
United States, United Kingdom, Switzerland, Japan, and Other Countries* (continued)

Country	Date	Condition
United Kingdom United States Belgium The Netherlands Luxembourg	29 September 2008	U.K. nationalizes mortgage lender Bradford and Bingley. Federal Reserve expands the outstanding size of its TAF auctions, puts in place forward auctions, and increases a $330 billion expansion of outstanding swap lines with foreign central banks to a total of $620 billion. House of Representatives votes down Emergency Economic Stabilization Act. Belgium, The Netherlands, and Luxembourg invest 11.2 billion euros in Fortis.
Ireland Belgium France Luxembourg	30 September 2008	Ireland guarantees all retail, commercial, and interbank deposits until September 2010; also covered are certain bonds and other debt instruments. Belgium, France, and Luxembourg nationalize Dexia SA by injecting 6.4 billion euros.
United States	1 October 2008	Senate approves revised version of Emergency Economic Stabilization Act.
United States	2 October 2008	Investor Group rescues GSE Farmer Mac with injection of preferred stock.
United States The Netherlands United Kingdom	3 October 2008	Wells Fargo acquires Wachovia, which was in danger of failing with no financial support (U.S.). U.S. rescue plan for financial markets, the Troubled Asset Relief Program (TARP) is signed into law. Plan authorizes purchases of troubled mortgages and other assets and provides broad authority to recapitalize financial institutions and engage in direct lending. Dutch government acquires Fortis Bank Nederland. FSA raises deposit insurance coverage to £50,000.
Germany Belgium Luxembourg	5 October 2008	Germany guarantees all retail bank deposits. Belgium and Luxembourg arrange a takeover of Fortis NV by BNP Paribas SA.
Germany United States	6 October 2008	Germany rescues Hypo Real Estate. Federal Reserve will begin paying interest on required reserves equal to the average federal funds target rate over the maintenance period less 10 basis points and payment on excess reserves equal to the lowest target rate over the maintenance period less 75 basis

(continued)

Appendix. *Crisis Events and Regulatory Responses in the European Union, United States, United Kingdom, Switzerland, Japan, and Other Countries* (continued)

Country	Date	Condition
		points. The TAF is increased so that a maximum of $900 billion might be outstanding at any one time.
Iceland United States	7 October 2008	Iceland takes control of two institutions, Glitner and Landsbanki. Federal Reserve Board creates the Commercial Paper Funding Facility (CPFF) to provide liquidity to the commercial paper market through direct purchases by issuers of high-quality paper.
United States Canada United Kingdom European Union Sweden Switzerland	8 October 2008	Federal Reserve, Bank of Canada, Bank of England, European Central Bank, Sveriges Riksbank, and Swiss National Bank announce a coordinated cut in their respective policy rates of 50 basis points. U.K. announces plans to recapitalize its banking system. Bank of England will make £200 billion available to banks under its Special Liquidity Scheme. Heritable and Kaupthing deposit business of Kaupthing Singer and Friedlander has been acquired by ING.
United Kingdom	9 October 2008	U.K. to inject capital into several large banks.
United States Germany Spain France Austria	13 October 2008	U.S. plans to inject $125 billion in preferred stock with warrants into nine banking organizations. Germany, Spain, France, and Austria announce plans to recapitalize banks and rescue financial system.
United States United Kingdom European Union Japan Switzerland	13 October 2008	Federal Reserve, Bank of England, European Central Bank, Bank of Japan, and Swiss National Bank will supply unlimited dollar funding in seven-day, twenty-eight-day, and eighty-four-day TAF auctions.
United States Japan	14 October 2008	U.S. announces voluntary capital injection plan. Emergency systemic risk exception is invoked to enable FDIC to guarantee senior debt of all FDIC-insured institutions and bank holding companies. Beginning October 27, Federal Reserve will begin purchasing three-month commercial paper from high-quality issuers. Federal Open Market Committee increases size of swap arrangement with Bank of Japan.

(continued)

Appendix. *Crisis Events and Regulatory Responses in the European Union,
United States, United Kingdom, Switzerland, Japan, and Other Countries* (continued)

Country	Date	Condition
European Union Switzerland	15 October 2008	European Central Bank and Swiss National Bank announce new currency swap arrangements.
United Kingdom United States	16 October 2008	Bank of England replaces its Standing Facilities with Operational Standing Facilities, establishes a Discount Window Facility, and introduces a permanent long-term repo market against a broad array of collateral. Federal Reserve allows bank holding companies to count preferred stock issued to U.S. Treasury as Tier I capital.
United States European Union Denmark	17 October 2008	U.S. banking agencies relax treatment of losses to banks on their holdings of preferred stock of Fannie Mae and Freddie Mac. European Central Bank and Dansmark Bank establish 15 billion euro swap arrangement.
The Netherlands	19 October 2008	Dutch government injects 10 billion euros into ING.
United States	21 October 2008	Federal Reserve creates Money Market Investor Funding Facility.
United States New Zealand	28 October 2008	U.S. establishes temporary swap line of $16 billion with Reserve Bank of New Zealand.
United States Brazil Mexico Korea Singapore	29 October 2008	U.S. establishes temporary swap lines of $30 billion each with Banco Central do Brasil, Banco de Mexico, Bank of Korea, and Monetary Authority of Singapore.
United States	10 November 2008	Federal Reserve and U.S. Treasury increase line of support to AIG to $150 billion.
G-20	16 November 2008	G-20 calls for coordination and articulates principles for financial reform and regulation.
United States	24 November 2008	Citigroup obtains government guarantee of $306 billion of its bad assets; U.S. Treasury injects $20 billion more of preferred stock (bringing its total to $45 billion, plus an additional $7 billion in return for the guarantee) from the TARP; and Citigroup will issue warrants to the Treasury and FDIC for 254 million shares at a strike price of $10.61.
United States	25 November 2008	Federal Reserve announces that it will establish a program to purchase direct obligations of Fannie

(continued)

Appendix. *Crisis Events and Regulatory Responses in the European Union, United States, United Kingdom, Switzerland, Japan, and Other Countries* (continued)

Country	Date	Condition
		Mae, Freddie Mac, Ginnie Mae, and the Federal Home Loan Banks, including not only debt but also MBSs. It will purchase up to $100 billion in agency debt and up to $500 billion in MBSs. Federal Reserve announces that it will create a Term Asset-Backed Securities Loan Facility to lend up to $200 billion on high-quality asset-backed paper based on consumer and small business loans. U.S. Treasury will provide $20 billion in credit protection to the Fed.

Sources: "Subprime Crisis Impact Timeline" (http://en.wikipedia.org/wiki/Subprime_crisis_impact_time line); "Timeline: Northern Rock Bank Crisis," August 5, 2008 (http://news.bbc.co.uk/1/hi/business/7007076.stm); "Countdown to a Crisis," September 25, 2007 (www.guardian.co.uk/business/2007/aug/10/usnews.internationalnews); Timeline: Fed Actions to Boost Liquidity, April 9, 2008 (www.reuters.com/article/businessNews/idUSN0947120920080409?sp=true); "Credit Crisis Timeline," November 20, 2008 (www.creditwritedowns.com/2008/05/credit-crisis-timeline.html).

References

Associated Press. 2007. "ECB Gives Banks Another Cash Injection," August 13.
Atkins, Ralph. 2008. "ECB under Fire for Handling of Downturn," *Financial Times*, August 25.
Baily, Martin, Douglas W. Elmendorf, and Robert E. Litan. 2008. "The Great Credit Squeeze: How It Happened, How to Prevent Another." Discussion Paper (Brookings).
Bank of England. 2008. "Financial Stability Report," October.
———. 2007. "Financial Stability Report," October.
Beams, Nick. 2007. "Credit Claims Another Bank." World Socialist Web Site (www.wsws.org/articles/2007/aug2007/bank-a20.shtml).
Bianco, James. 2008. "The Latest on the Credit Crisis," Special Report, August 14 (Bianco Research).
Boyd, Sebastian. 2007. "BNP Paribas Freezes Funds as Loan Losses Roil Markets (Update 5)." (Bloomberg, August 9).
Buiter, Willem H. 2008a. "Central Banks and Financial Crises." Federal Reserve Bank of Kansas City symposium, "Maintaining Stability in a Changing Financial System," Jackson Hole, Wyoming, August 21–23.
———. 2008b. "Lessons from the North Atlantic Financial Crisis," paper prepared for "The Role of Money Markets," a conference organized by Columbia Business School and the Federal Reserve Bank of New York, May 29–30.

Chailloux, Alexandre, and others. 2008. "Central Bank Response to the 2007–2008 Financial Market Turbulence: Experiences and Lessons Drawn." IMF Working Paper WP/08/210.

Darling, Alistair. 2007. "Statement by the Chancellor of the Exchequer on Financial Markets," September 17 (www.hm-treasury.gov.uk/newsroom_and_speeches/press/2007/press_95_07.cfm).

Dougherty, Carter. 2007. "Europe's Bank Says Financial Turmoil Largely Over," *New York Times*, September 15.

Economist. 2007. "Bankers' Mistrust," August 16.

Eisenbeis, Robert A. 2008. "Primary Dealers and Their Loss Experience," market commentary, Cumberland Advisors (www.cumber.com).

Eisenbeis, Robert A., W. Scott Frame, and Larry D. Wall. 2007. "An Analysis of the Systemic Risks Posed by Fannie Mae and Freddie Mac and an Evaluation of the Policy Options for Reducing Those Risks," *Journal of Financial Services Research* 31: 75–99.

Eisenbeis, Robert A., and George G. Kaufman. 2008a (forthcoming). "Lessons from the Demise of the UK's Northern Rock and the U.S.'s Countrywide and IndyMac." In *Reflections on the Northern Rock Crisis,* edited by David Llewellyn and Franco Bruni. Société Universitaire Européenne de Recherches Financières (SUERF).

———. 2008b. "Cross-Border Banking and Financial Stability in the EU," *Journal of Financial Stability* 4: 168–204.

———. 2006. "Cross-Border Banking: Challenges for the European Union." In *Cross-Border Banking: Regulatory Challenges*, edited by G. Caprio, D. Evanoff, and G. G. Kaufman, pp. 331–48 (Singapore: World Scientific).

———. 2005. "Bank Crisis Resolution and Foreign-Owned Banks," paper prepared for "Banking Crisis Resolution: Theory and Practice," Norges Bank, Oslo, Norway, June 16–17, and published in Federal Reserve Bank of Atlanta, *Economic Review* (fourth quarter): 1–14.

Federal Reserve. 2008. "Federal Reserve Board and Treasury Department Announce Restructuring of Financial Support for AIG," November 10.

Frame, W. Scott, and Lawrence J. White. 2005. "Fussing and Fuming over Fannie and Freddie: How Much Smoke, How Much Fire?" *Journal of Economic Perspectives* 19 (2): 159–84.

———. 2004. "Regulating Housing GSEs: Thoughts on Institutional Structure and Authorities," Federal Reserve Bank of Atlanta, *Economic Review* 89: 87–102.

H.M. Treasury. 2008a. "Financial Stability and Depositor Protection: Special Resolution Regime," July.

———. 2008b. "Financial Stability and Depositor Protection: Further Consultation," July.

Hattori, Masazumi, and Hyun Song Shin. 2007. "The Broad Yen Carry Trade," Discussion Paper 2007-E-19 (Institute for Monetary and Economic Studies, Bank of Japan).

Herring, Richard J. 2008. "The Current Turmoil: The Problem Is Capital, Not Liquidity," paper presented to the Shadow Financial Regulatory Committee, February 10.

Kane, Edward J. 2008a. "Ethical Failures in Regulating and Supervising the Pursuit of Safety-Net Subsidies." Networks Financial Institute Working Paper 2008-WP-12 (http://ssrn.com/abstract=1273616).

———. 2008b. "Who Should Bear Responsibility for Mistakes Made in Assigning Credit Ratings to Securitized Debt?" working paper, Boston College.

———. 2008c. "Regulation and Supervision: An Ethical Perspective," in *Oxford Handbook of Banking*, edited by Allen Berger, Phil Molyneux, and John Wilson (Oxford University Press, forthcoming).

————. 2007. "Incentive Conflict in Central Bank Responses to Sectoral Turmoil in Financial Hub Countries." Working Paper 13593. Cambridge, Mass.: National Bureau of Economic Research.

————. 2001. "Using Deferred Compensation to Strengthen the Ethics of Financial Regulation." *Journal of Banking and Finance* 26, no. 9: 1919–33.

————. 1997. "The Ethical Foundations of Financial Regulation," *Journal of Financial Services Research* 12 (August): 51–74.

————. 1989. "Changing Incentives Facing Financial-Services Regulators." *Journal of Financial Services Research*, 2, 263–72.

King, Mervyn. 2007. "Turmoil in Financial Markets: What Can Central Banks Do?" paper submitted to the Treasury Committee, September.

Meltzer, Alan. 2008. "That 70's Show," *Wall Street Journal*, February 28.

Mollenkamp, Carrick, Edward Taylor, and Ian McDonald. 2007. "Global Scale: How Subprime Mess Ensnared German Bank; IKB Gets a Bailout," *Wall Street Journal*, August 10.

Passmore, Wayne. 2005. "The GSE Implicit Subsidy and the Value of Government Ambiguity." *Real Estate Economics* 33: 465–86.

Passmore, Wayne, Roger Sparks, and Jamie Ingpen. 2002. "GSEs, Mortgage Rates, and the Long-Run Effects of Securitization." *Journal of Real Estate Finance and Economics* 25 (2/3): 215–42.

Taylor, John B. 2009. "The Financial Crisis and the Policy Responses: An Empirical Analysis of What Went Wrong." Working Paper w14631. Cambridge, Mass.: National Bureau of Economic Research (November).

Thompson, Sarah. 2007. "U.K. Stocks Including Smiths Group Advance; Barclays, HBOS Fall." Bloomberg, September 10.

Tobias, Adrian, and Hyun Song Shin. 2007. "Liquidity and Leverage." Working Paper (Federal Reserve Bank of New York and Princeton University) (www.princeton.edu/~hsshin/working.htm).

JOSEPH R. MASON 3

Structuring for Leverage: CPDOs, SIVs, and ARSs

CREATING LESS-RISKY portfolios through diversification is a fairly straight-forward proposition. But while textbooks suggest that leverage can be used to *increase* risk, too, applying leverage is all too cursorily dismissed as being hindered by the practical inability to borrow at the risk-free rate. It is hard to disagree that despite the equity premium puzzle, we rarely see returns dear enough to cover the cost of the additional leverage. Furthermore, there typically are relatively few risk-averse investors who prefer leveraged risk-return combinations, naturally constraining the application of leverage. But in a well-established benign market with low borrowing costs and reduced risk aversion, markets for leveraged positions proliferate.

In the seemingly benign credit environment of the last several years, markets saw low borrowing rates as an opportunity to increase leverage, in effect striving to make investments *more* risky in search of greater marginal yield. Sometimes the pursuit was masked by lowering issuance costs. The effect of both lower issuance costs and lower borrowing rates is the same: increased risk and return. In a benign market, the return is immediately realized while the risk remains latent—until the market turns. That is, until now.

I owe special thanks for constructive comments and criticism to Richard Herring, Robert Litan, Til Schuermann, Robert Eisenbeis, and other participants at the October 2008 Brookings–Tokyo Club–Wharton Conference.

After the fact, we see that risk was masked in two principal ways. First, many highly leveraged instruments were sold on the basis of correlations with underlying collateral rather than the final highly leveraged structure. Auction rate securities (ARSs) were represented as "simple student loan asset-backed securities"; structured investment vehicles (SIVs) as "simple residential mortgage–backed securities (RMBSs); and constant proportion debt obligations (CPDOs) as "simple credit default swaps (CDSs)." Of course, the increased leverage embedded in the structures heightened the credit correlations of the underlying collateral of each, which themselves were only cursorily understood.

Second, market arrangements for the new products were often artificially supported by seller institutions. ARS sellers supported auctions, SIV sellers repatriated debt, and CPDOs sold CDSs to their own sponsor institutions. Of course, when risk is managed through nonfundamental and nonreported means, the correlative properties of such investments will render them explosive; therefore they may fail unexpectedly. Indeed, that is what we have seen.

The rest of this chapter briefly introduces the theory of leveraged returns and risk aversion, a theory that created both supply and demand for leveraged structured products. The following sections describe three applications of structured leverage: SIVs implemented term structure arbitrage to lower funding costs for typical consumer mortgage and other assets at the expense of liquidity risk; ARSs took structured leverage to the extreme, using monthly note auctions to determine rates for even safer underlying student loan collateral; and CPDOs sold credit protection into thin markets, boosting accounting returns as market spreads necessarily declined from increased supply. Of the three asset types, CPDOs are facing steep losses and the market for those structures no longer exists after rating agencies admitted that the statistical models for evaluating the structures were mathematically flawed; SIVs have all been dissolved; and ARSs are being supported by sellers in myriad legal settlements.

Throughout the descriptions are three common themes. First, investment books' dismissal of leverage on the grounds of practical borrowing costs is correct except in a financial bubble. There is no reason that a lender would lend at a risk-free or even appropriately risky rate if the risk premium on the use of funds exceeded borrowing rates enough to enable arbitrage. Second, therefore, the initial increase in leverage has to take place in a benign market environment with a safe underlying collateral or investment type. Third, once the arbitrage is in place and risk has been dismissed, there inevitably comes a push to increase the risk of the underlying collateral or embedded leverage to heighten profits. Of course, when risk manifests—as it inevitably does—dramatic losses follow. But while policymakers ponder the complexity of the current generation of financial instruments, the underlying cause of the crisis is still just leverage.

Review of Financial Literature on Equilibrium Risk Targets

Academic journals contain a voluminous literature on equilibrium risk targets. In portfolio theory, investors choose their own individual risk-return preference. Risk aversion plays a part in that determination, but it is not sufficient to explain risk preferences in total.

The idea is that risk aversion merely shapes the indifference curve of the investor—that is, it makes that curve convex. The fundamental portfolio theory framework is represented in figure 3-1, where the shape of the indifference curve reflects the basic idea that an investor will reach for a greater return only if doing so presents progressively less marginal risk. More or less risk aversion in this framework results in a tighter or more linear representation respectively, with the extreme of the risk-neutral investor being represented by a linear indifference curve; in that case, increased risk is not punished by demanding the characteristic progressively higher marginal returns (even at a de minimus rate).

Figure 3-1, like most standard representations of portfolio choice, suggests that the chosen optimal portfolio lies to the left of the optimal risky portfolio. That is, most investors choose some combination of the optimal risky portfolio and the risk-free asset. But extensions of the theory suggest that leverage can be used to push to the right of the optimal risky portfolio, achieving higher risk-return combinations for investors who have overall higher appetites for risk. Such investors would still be risk averse—the general shape of their indifference curve would remain convex—but the indifference curve would achieve tangency to the right of the optimal risky portfolio.

Standard theory, however, has a hard time justifying the ability to use leverage in the purest sense because the risk-free rate is rarely available to individual borrowers. The standard approach, nonetheless, theoretically accommodates the availability of risk-free borrowing by suggesting that a risky borrowing rate would only rotate the capital allocation line (CAL) clockwise at the point of tangency with the optimal risky portfolio, decreasing—but not removing—the benefits of financial leverage. Still, sufficient spreads between investment returns and borrowing rates may be widely unavailable in the real world and, indeed, they had been difficult to unearth until witnessed under recent market conditions of very low credit premiums that effectively reduced the theoretical rotation of the CAL away from its optimum.

Figure 3-1. *Determining the Investor's Optimal Portfolio*

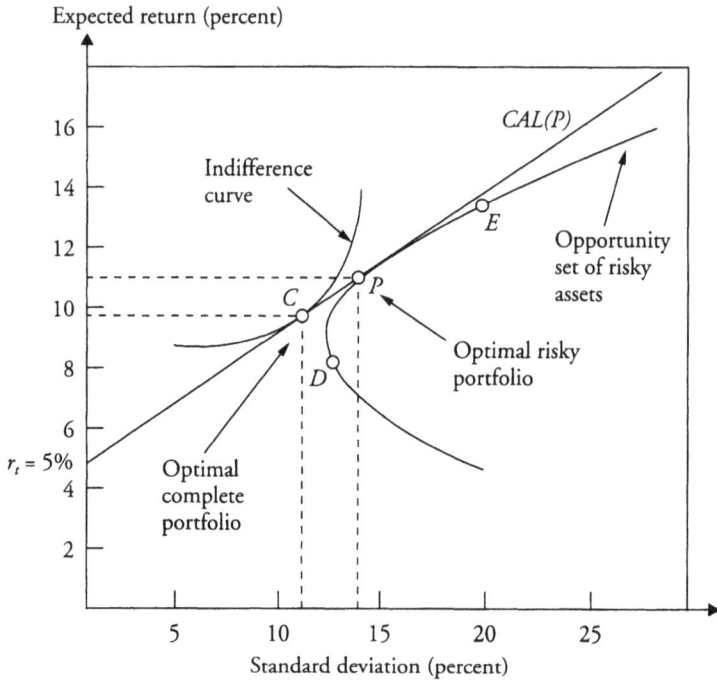

Source: Zvi Bodie, Alex Kane, and Alan J. Marcus, Investments (McGraw-Hill/Irwin, 2007).

But not all leverage is financial. While financial leverage requires a willing lender, structural leverage can be obtained by funding existing collateral investments with financially engineered portfolios of securities to take advantage of term structure, credit, or liquidity mismatches. Structural leverage can be thought of either as new investment opportunities that push the frontier out so that the tangency with the CAL is moved to the right or as nonstandard leverage applied to existing financial products. The choice of characterization depends on whether one considers the resulting structured finance securities to be new financial products in their own right or merely a repackaging of existing financial instruments. Since all financial instruments are already in the optimal risky portfolio, a mere repackaging would be represented as a variant on financial leverage, moving the investor out along the existing CAL from the original and consistent optimal risky portfolio. A new financial instrument, on the other hand, would be represented as a new investment possibility frontier, from which a new optimal risky portfolio emerges.

The choice is more than academic. If we are witnessing a mere shift in financial leverage applied to a consistent optimal risky portfolio, increased risky borrowing rates will effectively delever the system and remove opportunities to the right of the optimal risky portfolio. If, however, we are witnessing the dawn of a new category of financial product, there is no reason to expect that mere increases in risky borrowing rates alone will mitigate today's problems: a new valuation problem will be set before us, and we will need sufficient transparency and adequate modeling techniques in order to put markets right. In truth, the problem probably lies a little bit in both of those influences. In the case of CPDOs, financial leverage was applied to portfolios of new, hard-to-value financial products (CDSs), with the result that the resulting position was both difficult to value and incredibly risk sensitive. In the case of SIVs and ARSs, leverage was attained primarily through fairly typical term structure, credit, and liquidity mismatches.

It would be disingenuous, however, to end this section without a discussion of the new types of risks that have entered into the valuation process. Many of the new financial instruments contain not only elements of opacity, with the result that the underlying cash flows themselves are difficult to gather and estimate—as with pure cash-flow estimation of RMBSs and follow-on mezzanine RMBS collateralized debt obligation (CDO) valuation—but also operational risk, liquidity risk, interacted risks with the seller-servicer, legal contractual risks, and financial structure risk (the risk of just plain bad engineering), which are fundamentally difficult to value. Furthermore, while the "brain-dead" grantor trust basis of many of today's arrangements is thought to impart protection from operational risk, it embeds deleveraging in the contracts in a manner much like that of program trading, which played a significant role in the 1987 crash.

In summary, we have witnessed a shift in investment behavior that can be represented by investor choices on the standard CAL. Whether because of a shift in the underlying investment frontier or merely a reduced cost of leverage on the existing CAL, investors became more comfortable reaching for additional leverage in recent years, whether financial or structural. But while the efficiency gains from some structured finance arrangements may be real, they may simply have been too much for today's financial infrastructure and understanding of risk to bear.

Constant Proportion Debt Obligations

While CPDOs rose to prominence quickly during 2006 and 2007, it seems in hindsight that they may have been suitable to only a very narrow set of market circumstances. CPDOs structure the asset rather than the liability side of the balance sheet. CPDOs offer high fixed coupons, albeit with no upside, so they achieve high-yield bond return characteristics with various strategies to cover undue risk.

Background

Constant proportion debt obligations have a short but illustrious history. They were first launched in 2006 by ABN AMRO and are originated primarily in Europe, although they are sold worldwide. Hence, CPDOs are one of the most recent product innovations in structured credit markets.

Existing CPDO coupons and principal notes have received AAA-ratings from the major rating agencies. Many market observers found those ratings questionable, in light of CPDO premiums of up to 200 basis points.[1] Indeed, in 2008 rating agencies were found to have broadly underestimated CPDO risk, suggesting that actual ratings should have been much lower.

Structure and Leverage

Unlike other recent innovative structured credit products, the term "structured" in the case of CPDOs refers not to the liability side of the issuer but to the asset side. Structuring happens by way of increasing or decreasing the exposure depending on the spread development of the referenced portfolio. Consequently, in most cases there are not the usual equity or mezzanine investors to absorb any losses in the transaction arising from spread widening or actual defaults; it is the sole and hence senior investor in a CPDO who is exposed to the full leverage of the deal.

Initially, a CPDO's only assets are the cash that it holds. The CPDO is obligated to pay investors a fixed coupon during the life of the transaction and to repay principal at maturity, typically ten years. Figure 3-2 shows how the structure works. At inception, there is a natural shortfall between the net asset value (NAV) and the net present value (NPV) of the liabilities. To cover the shortfall, the CPDO shorts (sells coverage on) a CDS index. The index typically represents a synthetic exposure to credit markets so that defaults matter more than recovery rates. The market value of the arrangement is therefore typically driven by the credit default swap premium to be paid for protection on a portfolio of names with credit risk or on a credit index such as iTraxx or CDX.[2] Since the CPDO is the seller, there are no funding constraints.

1. Rama Cont and Katherine Jessen, "Constant Proportion Debt Obligations," Financial Risk International Forum Presentation, March 27–28, 2008 (www.finance-innovation.org/risk08/files/s12_jenssen-slides.pdf).

2. FitchIbca, "First-Generation CPDO: Case Study on Performance and Ratings," April 18, 2007 (www.fitchibca.com).

Figure 3-2. *Basic CPDO Structure*

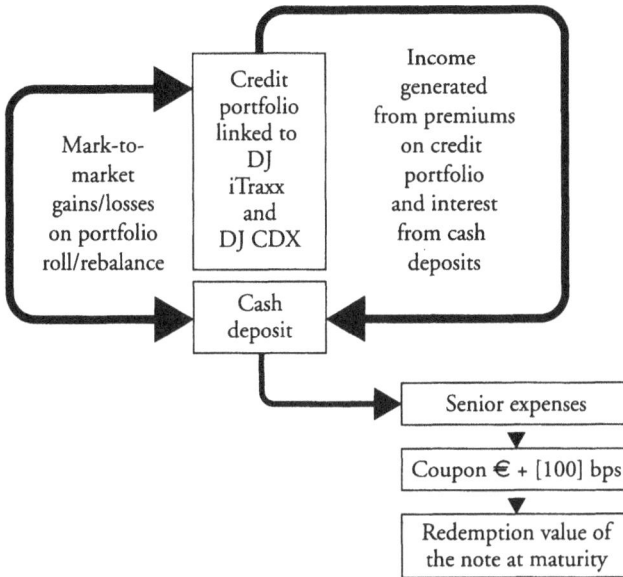

Source: ABN AMRO Surf 100–AAA/AAA CPDO Sales Deck, 2006.

The leverage is adjusted dynamically so that total expected returns from the credit index exposure are sufficient to cover the shortfall. Spread tightening on the CDS leads to mark-to-market gains in a CPDO, thus increasing the NAV and reducing the shortfall. That can lead to lower leverage, in which case leverage is decreased dynamically (hence the "constant proportion" of leverage). Conversely, spread widening on the index leads to higher leverage as NAV cash is used to cover mark-to-market losses. The structure is subject to a leverage cap, with the idea that the cap forms a stop-loss mechanism.[3]

The dynamic leverage in a CPDO is designed to lead to a "cash-in event," which occurs when the value of the assets as measured by the NAV equals the value of future liabilities. At that point, the leverage exposure is unwound and the assets are kept in cash or low-risk collateral until maturity of the transaction, guaranteeing returns for the life of the construct (assuming that the discount rate in the present value calculation remains constant). CPDO notes will default in

3. Ibid.

two cases: one, if over the tenor of the deal the NAV falls by a substantial amount and hits the cash-out trigger, typically set at 10 percent of the initial NAV; two, if at maturity the NAV is not at least equal to the principal.

Prior to 2007, all the CPDO transactions that had been rated by major credit rating agencies sold protection against investment-grade "on the roll" corporate indexes as the underlying risky asset—for example, the Dow Jones CDX and iTraxx credit indexes. There are a number of reasons for the limitation. First, the index composition rolls on a six-month basis to the most liquid investment-grade names, meaning that the transaction exposure to default risk is limited to the six-month straight-to-default risk on investment-grade corporate debt, which is very small. Second, exposure to indexes minimizes the bid-offer spread taken by the structure on the six-month roll—or any rebalancing date—because the indexes reflect the most liquid names traded in the investment-grade space.[4]

The Demise of CPDOs

First-generation CPDOs had a variety of shortcomings. Since the structures use a full fixed-income spread model to estimate portfolio exposure to only default rates, performance and ratings were overly sensitive to even minor changes in the key performance parameters. Furthermore, CPDO leverage contributes further sensitivity to key performance parameters and potential instability in ratings. In addition, scenario analysis through historical back testing showed that many of the more common CPDO structures would probably not have been able to withstand high investment-grade stresses of common market movements. As a result of those limitations, first-generation CPDOs typically did not achieve high (AA or AAA) investment-grade ratings.[5]

ABN AMRO's Surf 100–AAA/AAA CPDO, for instance, was one of the first higher-yielding CPDOs, promising coupons of Euro LIBOR plus 100 basis points. While the reference portfolio for the CDS was stated in offering materials as 50 percent iTraxx Europe and 50 percent DJ CDX.IG, Moody's representation of the CDS reference portfolio, represented in figure 3-3, shows a great deal more complexity. Among the rated credits shown in the figure, nearly 25 percent of the industry distribution of the credits was in the financial institution industry and another 23 percent in consumer products and housing, generally, with more than 60 percent of the exposure in the United States and the United Kingdom.

---

4. Standard & Poor's, "CDO Spotlight: CPDOs Have Arrived in Global Derivatives Market," November 1, 2006 (www2.standardandpoors.com).
5. FitchIbca, "First-Generation CPDO."

Figure 3-3. *CDS Reference Portfolio Ratings Distribution, Moody's*

Percent

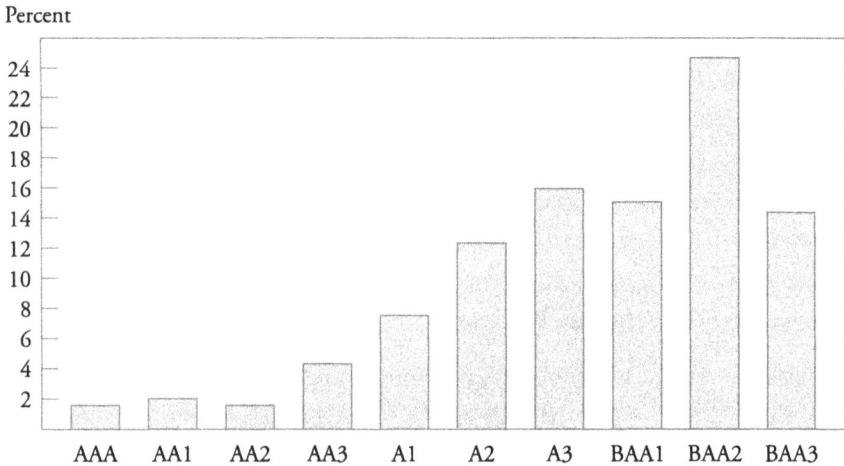

Source: ABN AMRO Surf 100–AAA/AAA CPDO Sales Deck, 2006.

Second-generation CPDOs improved on the shortcomings of the first generation. Second-generation CPDO structures took on a more bespoke CDS portfolio to tailor the leveraged portion to investors' desired returns.[6] As time wore on, CDS portfolios became more and more customized and hence imbalanced. It also appears that some hedge funds were offered vast sums of money to buy the CDSs thrown off by the CPDO underwriting process. CPDOs also seem to have been used to sell CDS coverage to super-senior CDO tranches held by their sponsor investment banks—that is, the same institution sold the CDS funded by the CPDO and bought the CDS to construct the super-senior CDO tranche. In sum, the unfunded CDSs used to construct the CPDOs seem to have skewed the supply of CDSs on some names, which would inherently compress CDS spreads. Of course, as market spreads decline, the CPDOs prosper. Hence, by merely selling protection, a CPDO almost guaranteed its own returns.

Such market conditions were certain to end. Indeed, by February 2008, Bloomberg reported that the ABN AMRO "transactions will unwind at an approximate 90 percent loss to investors" because credit default swaps backing the deals had been "continually increasing over recent weeks."[7] By May 2008, both

6. Standard & Poor's, "CDO Spotlight."
7. Neil Unmack, "CPDO Investors May Lose 90 percent as ABN Funds Unwind," Bloomberg, January 25, 2008.

Moody's and Standard & Poor's reported that they had discovered serious "errors" in their CPDO rating models. Moody's error caused the company to give ratings as much as four levels higher than the structures deserved, although Standard & Poor's did not adjust any ratings as a result of its discoveries. Both firms reported that the flaws were embedded in rating models for more than six months before they were discovered. The flaws were disclosed to the Securities and Exchange Commission (SEC) roughly another six months after they were discovered. Following investigations at both firms, the CPDO market is, for all practical purposes, closed.

Structured Investment Vehicles

SIVs are merely one step beyond asset-backed commercial paper, which itself lies one step beyond commercial paper (CP). ABCP extended the CP paradigm to structured finance collateral, and SIVs built in a more complex funding structure and more complex contractual arrangements. SIVs moved ABCP beyond being a short-term transactional funding mechanism for subprime loans in the process of being securitized to being a funding mechanism in its own right. Of course, the leverage inherent in the arrangement led to a spectacular collapse when the underlying collateral faltered.

Background

SIVs have been around for several decades. Citibank launched Alpha Finance Corporation in 1988 and followed it with Beta Finance Corporation in 1989. In 1995 Gordian Knot set up Sigma Finance Corporation. In May 1996 Singer & Friedlander Capital Markets established Asset Backed Capital Limited; ABC is now managed by Quadrant Capital following a management buyout in 1998. Centauri Corporation, another Citibank vehicle, was established in September 1996. In 1998, the Industrial Bank of Japan (IBJ) set up Ascot Capital Limited and Citibank set up Dorada Corporation and wound down Alpha.

In 1999, four new vehicles were formed: Dresdner Bank set up K2 Corporation; Bank of Montreal established Links Finance Corporation; Citibank opened its fifth vehicle, Five Finance Corporation; and Quadrant Capital established Abacas Investments. In 2000, Ascot Capital was wound down by IBJ in anticipation of the merger of IBJ, Fuji Bank, and the Dai-Ichi Kangyo Bank. Parkland Finance Corporation, Bank of Montreal's second vehicle, was set up in 2001. In 2002, West End Capital Management and Gen Re Securities Limited set up Rathgar Capital Corporation.

By 2007, SIVs were among the highest-growth areas in structured finance, with $370 billion of assets managed across twenty-eight vehicles, ten of which had been launched in 2006 alone. At the height of the market, Moody's rated thirty-six SIVs or SIV hybrids that managed $395 billion in assets.[8]

SIVs became increasingly more sophisticated with the passage of time. While Alpha was set up to operate with fixed leverage, subsequent SIVs developed capital structures that were dynamic with respect to certain factors, including asset ratings, maturity, and concentration. Managers have also focused on a number of other areas, including alternative forms of liquidity, synthetic exposure to risk, and issuance of capital in a variety of currencies, in developing the SIV model.

Typical SIV Structure

SIVs are best understood in relationship to their close cousins, asset-backed commercial paper. Both issue short-term (usually three- to six-month) commercial paper as funding and use the proceeds to invest longer term in various highly rated assets. The longer-term assets pay a coupon rate that is higher than the interest rate on the commercial paper liabilities, providing the necessary return on the arrangement. Both hold similar underlying collateral, typically a mix of highly rated structured finance securities and bank and financial institution securities.

That's where the similarities end. ABCP, like regular commercial paper, has 100 percent liquidity support backing, which ensures that investors are exposed only to credit risk, not market value risk. SIVs, on the other hand, carry only about 5 to 10 percent committed liquidity support; the remaining liquidity support relies on the market value of the collateral assets. Hence, investors are exposed to both market value risk and credit risk.

While SIVs typically hold greater credit enhancement (usually 7 percent) than ABCP, that enhancement adjusts for credit risk, not liquidity risk. Liquidity risk is mitigated by a more diversified funding mix, consisting of junior equity, mid-seniority medium-term notes, and finally senior A1 commercial paper. The basic structure is presented in figure 3-4. The idea is that the equity and medium-term notes absorb the liquidity risk, which, since liquidity shocks are usually short lived, should cover typical temporary market disruptions.

While traditional ABCP was a bridge financing mechanism, funding loans during seasoning until they were moved in roughly quarterly securitizations, SIVs provided permanent financing for the underlying assets. Hence, SIVs issue a mix of short-term and long-term liabilities and purchase assets with the proceeds.

8. Moody's Investors Service, *An Introduction to Structured Investment Vehicles*, January 25, 2002 (www. moodys.com).

Figure 3-4. *Basic SIV Structure*

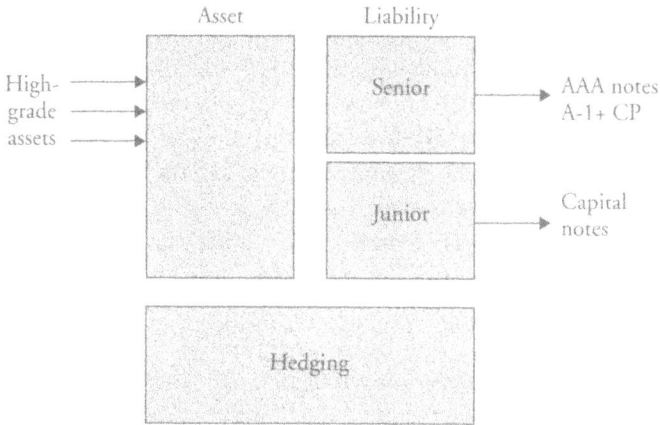

Source: Standard & Poor's, "Structured Investment Vehicle Criteria: New Developments," September 4, 2003.

SIVs therefore engage in maturity transformation through the purchase of long-term assets to support senior short-term liabilities, engendering asset-liability maturity gaps in the range of two to five years.

Because of the inherent risk in the maturity mismatch, the vehicles mark portfolios to market frequently in order to gauge value should it become necessary to delever following an inability to roll liabilities or unexpected downgrades or defaults in the portfolio. Typical triggers can be broken down into three main categories: cash flow tests; portfolio restrictions; and liability constraints. Among the cash flow tests, capital requirements ensure that sufficient credit enhancement is present in the structure at all times; interest rate and foreign exchange tests ensure that the interest rate and foreign exchange swaps continue to hedge asset-liability duration and denomination mismatches; liquidity tests ensure that collateral remains sufficiently liquid to meet investor redemptions on a timely basis; and cash outflow tests ensure that no liability "run" debilitates the liability structure.

Portfolio restrictions ensure that the managed portfolio remains within certain risk tolerance boundaries. Portfolios are restricted in terms of rating quality and counterparty risk (especially for swap transactions). The weighted average life (WAL) of the portfolio is monitored to restrain portfolio maturity mismatch and hence interest rate risk (duration) exposure.

Liability restrictions ensure that the weighted average life of the debt structure also remains within the limits of risk tolerance and that junior note ratings remain

Table 3-1. *SIV Operating States*

State	Portfolio management	Investments	Commercial paper/medium term note issuance
Normal	SIV manager	Yes	Yes
Restricted investment	SIV manager	No	Yes, for refinancing
Restricted funding/ defeasance	SIV manager	No	No
Enforcement	Security trustee/ receiver	No	No

Source: Fitch, "Assessing Potential Exposure of Sponsor Banks," November 2007, p. 2

sufficiently high to keep total liability costs low enough to maintain profitability.[9] Daily marks to market ensure that the cash flow, portfolio restrictions, and liability constraints remain in place and effective through the life of the structure.

Even more unlike ABCP, all those moving parts legally constitute a brain-dead grantor trust operating context, with the result that any deviation can be resolved quickly through either an automatic readjustment of the structure or, if that is not sufficient, an orderly unwind on behalf of investors. Continued trigger breaches will invoke increasingly drastic operating constraints on the structure, as outlined in table 3-1.

Table 3-1 shows that in normal times, SIV managers can increase debt issuance and expand the portfolio to grow the fund (within the brain-dead restrictions set forth earlier). As pressures mount, new liabilities are permitted only for rolling the refinancing and new investments are halted, forcing the fund to stop growing. As pressures deepen, no more refinancing is permitted, forcing the portfolio to run off. Since the shortest maturity liabilities are the senior notes, the provisions form a sort of credit enhancement whereby senior investors are paid today in full and junior noteholders and equity holders are paid later and only in part.

Leverage

Once SIVs became popular, the "SIV-lite" (an SIV collateralized debt obligation) evolved to heighten the risk. SIV-lites are hybrid SIVs that typically invested in U.S. RMBSs. Figure 3-5 illustrates how different SIV-lites were from their (already complex and risky) SIV cousins. As the figure shows, SIVs invested in a relatively broad array of underlying assets—including general financial institution

9. Ibid.

Figure 3-5. *Comparison of SIVs and SIV-lites*

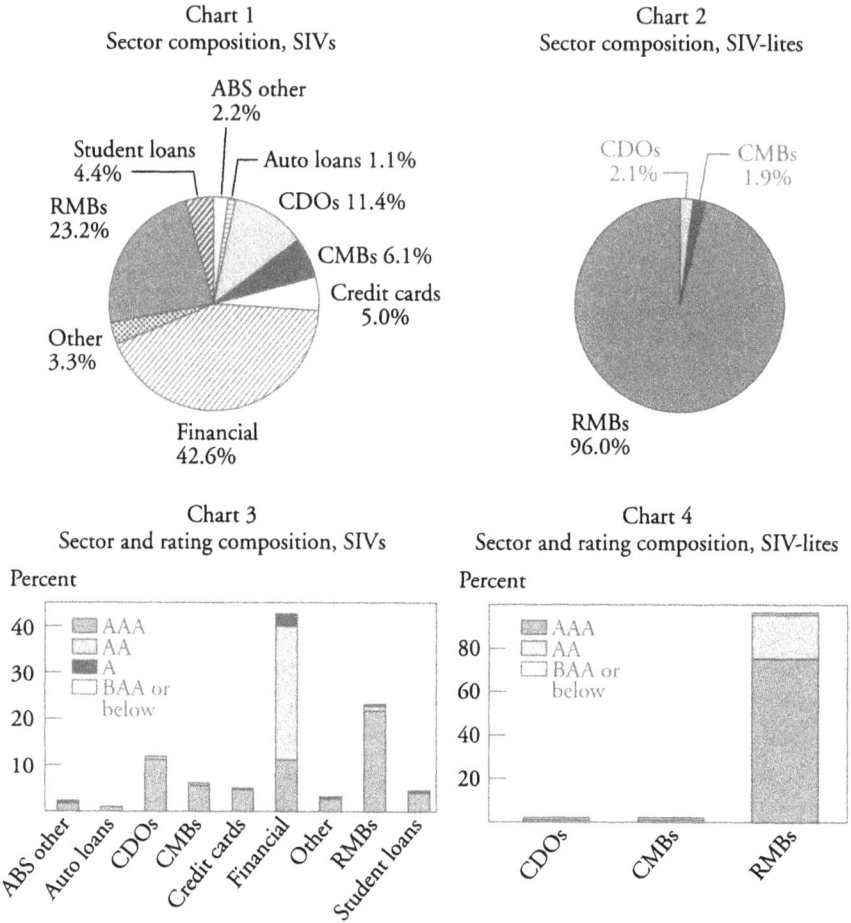

Chart 1
Sector composition, SIVs

ABS other
2.2%

Student loans
4.4%

Auto loans 1.1%

RMBs
23.2%

CDOs 11.4%

CMBs 6.1%

Credit cards
5.0%

Other
3.3%

Financial
42.6%

Chart 2
Sector composition, SIV-lites

CDOs
2.1%

CMBs
1.9%

RMBs
96.0%

Chart 3
Sector and rating composition, SIVs

Percent

40
30
20
10

AAA
AA
A
BAA or
below

ABS other
Auto loans
CDOs
CMBs
Credit cards
Financial
Other
RMBs
Student loans

Chart 4
Sector and rating composition, SIV-lites

Percent

80
60
40
20

AAA
AA
BAA or
below

CDOs
CMBs
RMBs

Source: Moody's, "SIVs: An Oasis of Calm in the Subprime Maelstrom," July 2007.

debt and credit card, commercial mortgage, auto loan, student loan, and residential mortgage securitizations—in addition to various other asset-backed securities and CDOs. The largest concentration of investments is in financial institution debt (42.6 percent); the second-largest is in RMBSs (23.2 percent). Given that financial institution debt already is associated with a diversified portfolio and the SIV holds a fairly diversified portfolio of other investments, the structure would not be expected to have a great deal of remaining diversifiable risk (at least within the financial institution sector).

SIV-lites, on the other hand, held some 96 percent of their investments in a single sector—RMBSs—with only a smattering of commercial mortgage-backed securities and CDOs (around 2 percent apiece). The resulting portfolio is hardly diversified; therefore it is subject to a substantial amount of idiosyncratic risk. Furthermore, SIV portfolios held mostly AAA-rated bonds, with a secondary exposure to AA- and A-rated financial institution debt. While SIVs held a minute exposure to AA-rated RMBS, that sector made up almost 20 percent of SIV-lite exposure. As is now widely acknowledged, SIVs' AA-rated financial institution debt was of a much higher credit quality than the SIV-lites' AA-rated RMBS—that is, "AA" did not always mean "AA"—a factor that was to prove crucial as the sector imploded in mid-2007.

The Demise of Structured Investment Vehicles

The point of the SIV structure is to profit from several types of spreads. The senior-subordinate structure profits from credit spread. The maturity mismatch profits from yield curve spread. The problem with the arrangement is that we typically think of yield curve as being made up of risk-free asset spread, but in August 2007 the underlying assets were anything but risk free. As the value of SIV-lite RMBS holdings deteriorated and credit spreads increased, it became impossible to roll over the short-term senior financing, while the long-term financing remained in place. Hence, the sector toppled from the top down, as senior financing could not be replaced and losses mounted in the junior claims.

Up through the first quarter of 2007, both SIVs and SIV-lites performed well. Figure 3-6 shows that although both sectors were obviously stressed from the deterioration in RMBS valuations, the difficulties that they were experiencing were broadly in line with historical experience. But figure 3-7 shows that in 2007, the value of all major collateral sectors underlying SIVs fell precipitously. In particular, losses were concentrated in nonprime RMBSs, affecting principally SIV-lites. However, losses also accumulated in financial institution debt in general, which also affected regular SIVs. Regular SIVs, however, which also held investments in credit card, commercial mortgage, auto loan, student loan, and residential mortgage securitizations as well as various other asset-backed securities, faced lower losses than SIV-lites. Nonetheless, returns for both SIVs and SIV-lites fell precipitously in the second quarter of 2007, as reflected in figure 3-8.

While ABCP and financial CP issuance declined substantially during the period illustrated in figure 3-8, nonfinancial CP markets were almost completely unmoved. The reduction set in motion a leveraged unwind in the SIV sector as a whole, however, as the collateral impairment triggered contractual terms of SIVs and left them unable to roll senior funding even if markets accepted the paper.

Figure 3-6. *SIV and SIV-lite Net Asset Values, First-Quarter 2002–First-Quarter 2007*

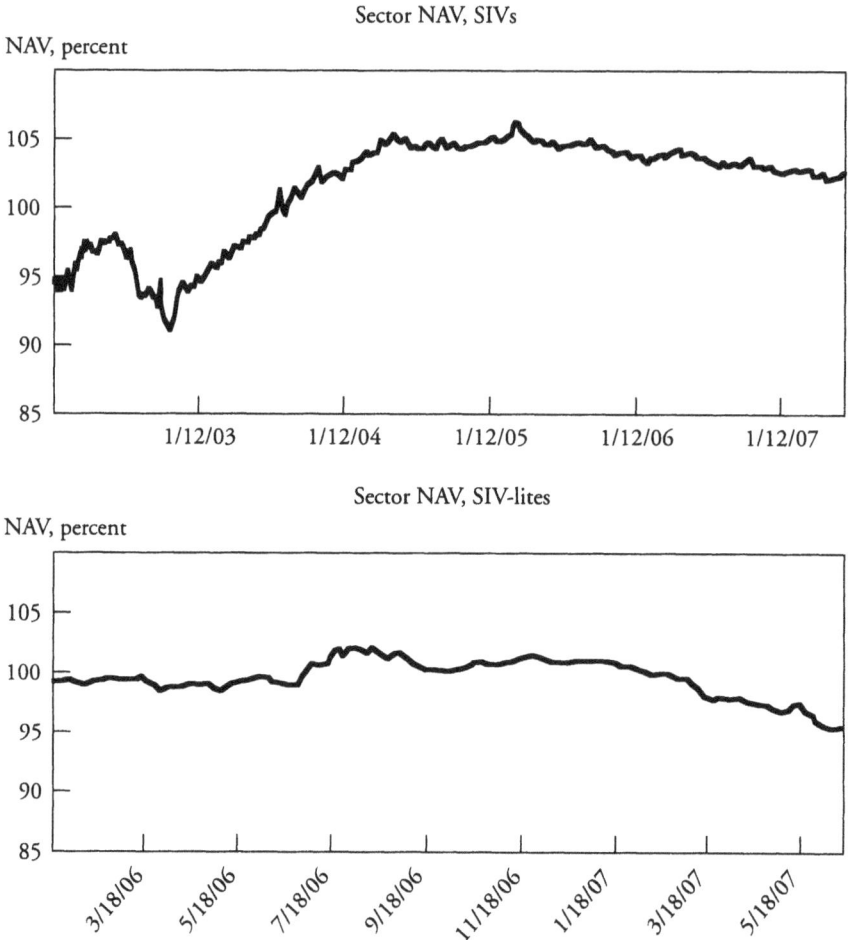

Sector NAV, SIVs

NAV, percent

Sector NAV, SIV-lites

NAV, percent

Source: Moody's, "SIVs: An Oasis of Calm in the Subprime Maelstrom," July 2007.

The increase in CP rates between July and September 2007 therefore reflected only in part the sale of SIV funding for riskier collateral pools, as many of those pools were already prohibited from further issuance by contractual triggers restricting their operation.

When those triggers, similar to the ones illustrated in table 3-1, restricted funding and mandated defeasance, CP funding of SIV liabilities necessarily fell. The decline created the imbalance in liability structures illustrated in table 3-2.

Figure 3-7. *Representative Sector Valuations in mid-2007*

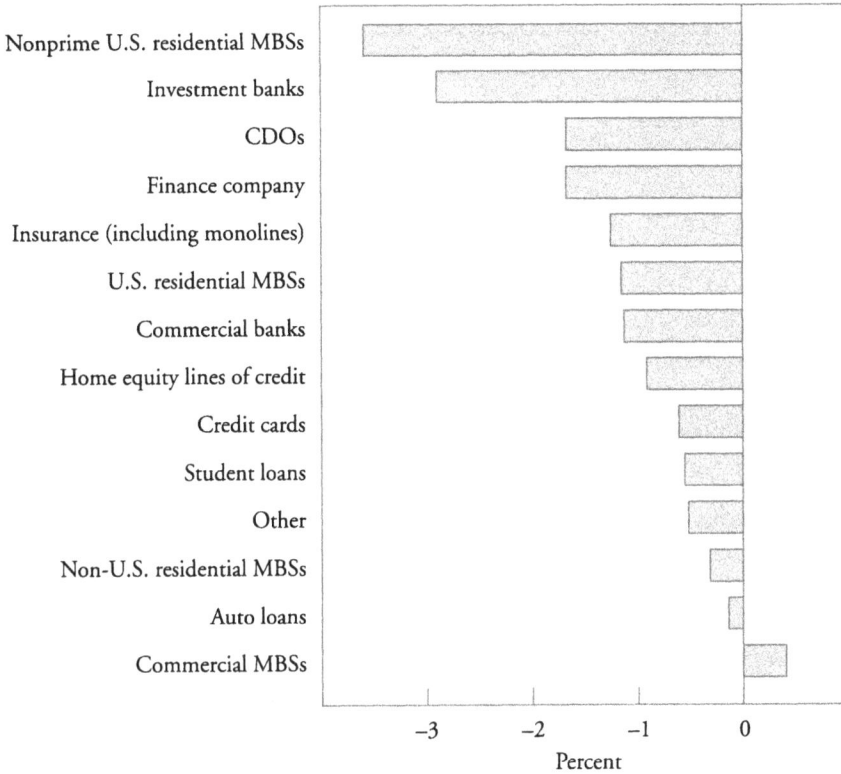

Source: Fitch, "Rating Performance of Structured Investment Vehicles (SIVs) in Times of Diminishing Liquidity for Assets and Liabilities," September 20, 2007, p. 12.

Fitch reports that SIV commercial paper funding composition fell from August 2007 to September 2007 by 6 percent, from 29 percent of SIV liabilities to only 23 percent. At the same time, medium-term notes, the next most junior liability, rose from 62 percent of SIV liabilities to 64 percent and repurchase facilities rose from 2 percent to 6 percent.

Certainly, when SIVs could not roll the short-term funding, the funding composition changed. The important thing to realize, however, is that CP is an "in or out" market, meaning that if an issuer is not prime credit quality, it is excluded from the market. When the issuer is a brain-dead SIV that has been precluded from restructuring its investments by contractual triggers, there is no hope of recovery.

In summary, it is important to ask what kind of risk this is. In a way, it is liquidity risk. But funding liquidity, as well as asset liquidity, was a primary risk as

Figure 3-8. *SIV and SIV-lite Net Asset Values, Third-Quarter 2007*

Price as percent of par

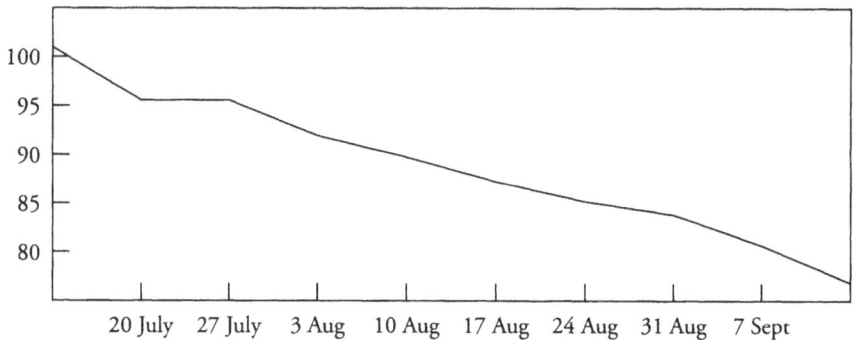

Source: Fitch, "Rating Performance of Structured Investment Vehicles (SIVs) in Times of Diminishing Liquidity for Assets and Liabilities," September 20, 2007, p. 11.

the structure funded long-term assets with short-term liabilities. Such liquidity risk on the liability side is often referred to as roll risk. Market risk manifested itself in the decline in market value of the collateral, threatening solvency of the construct. Some characterize this as cliff risk, since it was largely unanticipated. But seeing the construct in its entirety, the liquidity, roll, market, and solvency risks all manifested themselves interactively to create a rapid and spectacular demise of a financial sector.

Auction Rate Securities

Auction rate securities take the SIV paradigm one step further: they issue short-term (weekly or monthly maturity) debt in auction format to gain the cheapest

Table 3-2. *Composition of Funding in Fitch-Rated SIVs*

Percent

Market	End August 2007	Mid- September 2007	End September 2007
Commercial paper	29	27	23
Medium term note	62	62	64
Capital	7	7	7
Repo facilities	2	3	6

Source: Fitch, "SIVs Rating Performance—Update 1," October 12, 2007.

funding. The scheme completes the term structure arbitrage that SIVs address, but it has a more extreme duration mismatch, more similar to that of commercial bank deposits. As with commercial bank deposit funding, failure is followed by a liability freeze. Without quick recovery in underlying collateral values, the structure is not viable and investors experience both illiquidity and credit losses.

Background

Nearly twenty years ago the ARS market was developed as a simple way of cheaply funding pools of safe municipal bonds. Back then, the large increases in the target federal funds rate to reduce the high inflation of the late 1970s and early 1980s resulted in a dramatic increase in borrowing costs for many institutions. In response to demand for variable-rate and potentially lower-cost financing alternatives, the first ARS was devised by American Express in July 1984,[10] followed by City Federal Savings & Loan, U.S. Steel Corporation, First Boston Corporation, Shearson Lehman, and Lincoln National Corporation in the same year.[11] The first ARS wrapped by bond insurance was U.S. Steel's 1985 issue of money market preferred shares[12] and Mattel's 1987 issue of ARS collateralized by trade receivables.[13] Those deals reportedly sold at prices roughly 200 basis points lower than nonwrapped deals.

Despite the first auction failure, for MCorp in 1987, followed by a couple of failures for the Kroger Company in 1988, ARS markets continued to develop and expand throughout the 1990s and 2000s. Figure 3-9 shows that other types of issuers such as municipalities, closed-end mutual funds, student loan lenders, and even CDOs saw the value in these products, which generally allowed them to finance long-term assets at short-term borrowing rates. By 2007, the ARS market was approaching $300 billion in outstanding securities, held by an array of investors—corporate cash managers, trust departments, municipalities, nonprofits, and private individuals—that sought the safety of sound underlying collateral and reasonable yield.[14]

The securities included an array of taxable and tax-exempt bonds backed by various types of safe collateral. Among those, the most prominent was municipal debt, which made up nearly 50 percent of the market at year-end 2006. Student loans made up 26 percent of the market and closed-end fund (CEF) preferred, 22 percent.

10. "American Express Sets New Preferred Shares," *New York Times*, July 26, 1984.
11. "Shop Talk: New Offering, Old Language," *Wall Street Journal*, November 15, 1984.
12. Ann Monroe, "Money Market Preferred Finds Favor with Debt Issuers since '84 Introduction," *Wall Street Journal*, August 13, 1985.
13. "Mattel Receivables Back Unit's Preferred Stock," *New York Times*, September 18, 1987.
14. Merrill Lynch, "An Introduction to Auction Market Securities," fourth quarter 2006 (New York).

Figure 3-9. *Typical ARS Collateral*

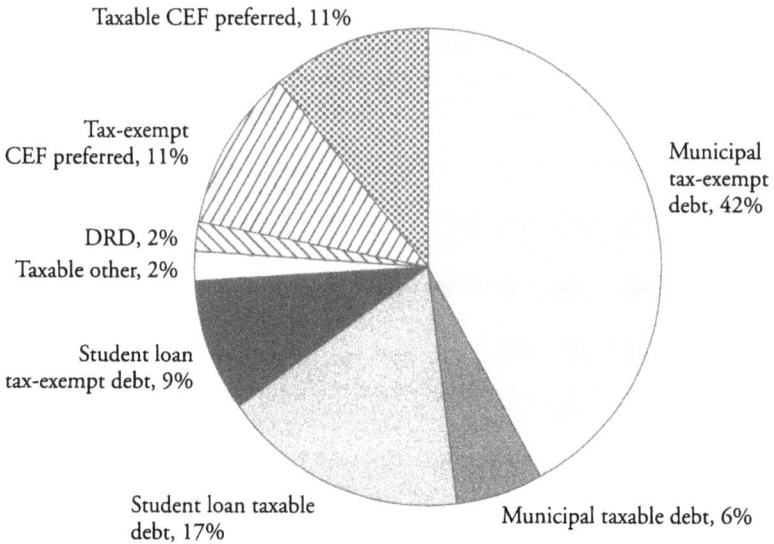

Source: Merrill Lynch, "An Introduction to Auction Market Securities, Fourth Quarter 2006."

Structure

The term "auction rate security" describes a widely disparate array of funding possibilities. Auction rate securities can be equity or debt, taxable or tax-exempt. Rates may reset at intervals of one, seven, twenty-eight, thirty-five, forty-nine, or ninety days. Structures may be overcollateralized internally, stand-alone, or insured. But while a vast array of choices exists, consistent paradigms typically were applied to particular asset classes.

For instance, municipal ARS are sold by states and municipalities for the same funding purposes as conventional municipal debt. The collateral is usually stand-alone, although it may be secured by a municipal bond guarantee. Interest may be taxable or tax-exempt, although—as in the typical municipal bond market—most is tax-exempt. Auction rate cycles in municipal debt may run one, seven, twenty-eight, thirty-five, or ninety days. Bond ratings on municipal auction rate debt typically are very high.

Student loan–backed auction rate debt, one of the most popular securities of the credit crisis, is more like a conventional student loan securitization. The debt is issued by a bankruptcy-remote special purpose entity, established by not-for-profit, for-profit, or state-sponsored originators of student loans. Student loan auction cycles typically are twenty-eight days. Like most securitizations, student loan securitizations are structured on overcollateralized pools that build reserve funds by accumulating excess spread. Different classes of debt may be issued by the structure, forming senior and subordinate claims. But because many student loans are guaranteed by state or federal authorities, the collateral itself is viewed as very safe.

In summary, the auction mechanism is thought to give investors liquidity, in that they can exit by deciding to sell at the next auction. In reality, however, the auctions created illiquidity as investors learned that in the event of a failed auction, it was possible that they would not be able to sell the securities until the next successful auction or final legal maturity.

Leverage

When stressed, the auction mechanism revealed the extreme leverage in the short-funded structure. If there are more sellers than buyers in a given auction, that auction is said to have failed. A failed auction will set a maximum rate as described in the issue's offering document. Since the idea is to remunerate investors for their own loss of term structure yield, the maximum rate often is not that high, representing merely expected market yield until the next auction.

In 2007 Merrill Lynch stated it was "aware of only 13 issuers which have experienced failed auctions since 1984, with only 1 of those experiencing a failed auction since 1993."[15] By 2007, almost 500 "successful" auctions were taking place each day in the sector. But often "successful" was not defined in an especially rigid fashion. An auction could still be successful if the dealer intervened. While few auctions outwardly failed prior to 2008, in reality securities dealers often provided liquidity when auctions might have failed otherwise. Indeed, recent ARS documents disclosed that "an issue's lead dealer, while not obligated to do so and completely at its sole discretion, generally submits a 'support bid' into an auction to ensure the auction is successful." In fact, the "lead dealer may submit a support bid at any rate and that bid may affect the rate set in the auction."[16]

The problem, however, was not that the dealer submitted the bids, per se, but that the dealer, and the dealer alone, knew the true success of the auction, having submitted backup bids without reporting those bids or auction results to investors. In fact, auction rate dealers were sanctioned by the SEC in 2006 for failing to reveal relevant information to investors. Upon concluding an investigation of fifteen firms representing the ARS industry, the SEC reported that "between January 2003 and June 2004, each firm engaged in one or more practices that were not adequately disclosed to investors, which constituted violations of

15. Ibid.
16. Ibid.

the securities laws." The SEC issued a cease-and-desist order to stop these viola-tions. The SEC order notes that while

> the firms were under no obligation to guarantee against a failed auction, investors may not have been aware of the liquidity and credit risks associ-ated with certain securities. By engaging in these practices, the firms vio-lated Section 17(a)(2) of the Securities Act of 1933, which prohibits mate-rial misstatements and omissions in any offer or sale of securities.[17]

However, dealers seem to have interpreted the general disclosure of the possibil-ity of support as sufficient to meet the requirements of the SEC order. As the sit-uation now stands, litigation or further interpretation by the SEC—or both—will determine whether a dealer's approach will suffice.

Demise of Auction Rate Securities

In late 2007 and continuing into early 2008, auctions began to fail, slightly at first and building to complete failure by February 13, 2008 (see figure 3-10). Offi-cially, although there were several auction failures during the second half of 2007, those issues were generally poorly collateralized or had less creditworthy issuers. Through the end of 2007, a few other auction failures occurred, but they were generally believed to be isolated problems.

By late 2007, defaults on subprime mortgages soared and markets began to ques-tion the ability of monoline insurers to support their obligations due to pressures from the RMBS and CDO sectors. As a result, the major rating agencies began to downgrade or review monoline insurer credit ratings. Many of these, such as Ambac, MBIA, FGIC, and XL Capital, had wrapped significant proportions of the auction rate bond market.[18] As investors demanded higher yields than the maximum rate specified in the bond's official documents in order to adjust for the risk, auctions began to fail en masse. Interestingly, the penalty rates for failed auctions sometimes turned out to lie *below* that maximum yield determined by a failed auction, so that some investors actually earned less interest after the failed auction than before.

By February 2008, the auction rate market dried up. More than 1,000 auc-tions failed in three days alone.[19] A Standard & Poor's analyst commented, "I don't think anyone could have predicted in the winter of 2008 the auction rate

17. See "15 Broker-Dealer Firms Settle SEC Charges Involving Violative Practices in the Auction Rate Securities Market," May 31, 2006 (www.sec.gov/news/press/2006/2006-83.htm).

18. *2007 Bond Buyer Yearbook*, Thomson Financial, SourceMedia, Inc.

19. Julie Creswell and Vikas Bajaj, "Municipalities Feel Pinch as Another Debt Market Falters," *New York Times*, February 15, 2008, p. 1.

Figure 3-10. *Auction Rate Failures in February 2008*

Percent

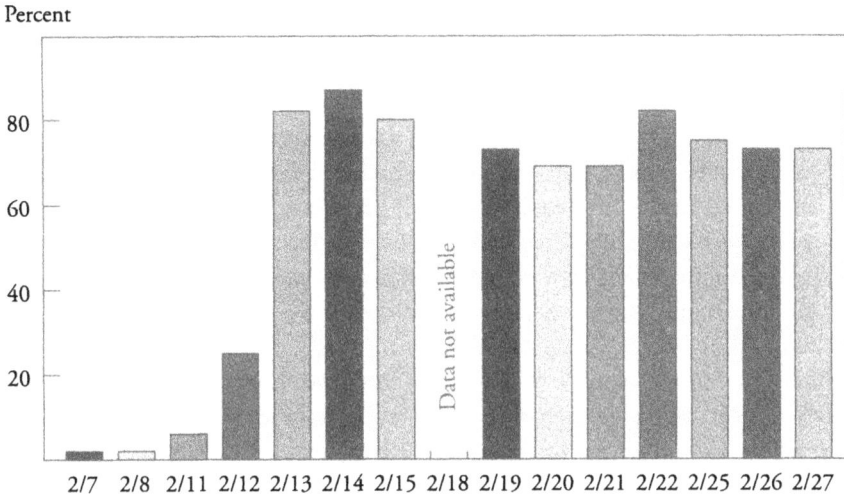

Source: Stephanie Lee, "Auction-Rate Securities: Bidder's Remorse? A Primer" (NERA Economic Consulting, May 6, 2008).

market was going to move away from everybody."[20] But, again, a continuous process existed beneath the seemingly sudden crisis. Unofficially, dealers are now known to have increasingly intervened to prevent failed auctions since roughly the middle of 2007 in order to avoid losing underwriting and auction dealer fees and to allow dealers to sell ARS inventory. The *Wall Street Journal* reported on July 28, 2008, that

> Wall Street firms started raising commissions paid to some brokers at outside dealers who sold securities to clients, an action that might serve as an enticement to them to sell more. On November 2, 2007, for example, Credit Suisse's short-term trading desk sent out an e-mail informing its salespeople that Citigroup was increasing its commissions to outside dealers from 0.15 of a percent of the security sold to 0.20 of a percent on certain of its auction rate securities, according to a person familiar with the e-mail. By the start of January, their commissions on all types of Citigroup's auction rate securities rose to 0.15 of a percent, instead of 0.1, says the person.[21]

20. Dan Fitzpatrick, "Crunch in Bond Market Hits UPMC," *Pittsburg Post-Gazette*, February 20, 2008 (www.post-gazette.com/pg/08051/858719-28.stm).
21. Liz Rappaport, "Auction-Rate Crackdown Widens; UBS Faces New Charges in New York, as Scrutiny of Wall Street's Role Intensifies," *Wall Street Journal*, July 25, 2008, p. A1.

It appears that at the time similar e-mails circulated among many Wall Street firms. It also was at this time that the true nature of the auctions became much more widely known, even inside the industry itself. About this time, the *New York Times* reported that

> experts say that calling these securities auction-oriented is something of a misnomer because real auctions—during which buyers and sellers meet and an interest rate is set based upon their interest—weren't taking place in recent years. Instead, the Wall Street firms in charge of the auctions smoothed the process by bidding with their own capital rather than rustling up thousands of buyers to meet up with sellers every week or so.

The article quoted Joseph S. Fichera, chief executive of Saber Partners, a financial advisory firm, as maintaining that "the investor never knew how many investors there were, how often the brokerage firms were stepping in to make the system work, nor that the broker's support could stop all of a sudden."[22]

On June 5, 2008, the *Bond Buyer* reported that

> Martha Mahan Haines [SEC chief of Office of Municipal Securities] said that one of the biggest problems in the ARS market was its opacity, which may have kept investors from knowing that a small group of broker-dealer firms that bid on the auctions were critical to preventing widespread failures. Even though broker-dealers disclosed that they were bidding on auctions, the extent of their participation was unknown.[23]

On August 15, 2008, the Regional Bond Dealers Association explained the situation in a letter to the SEC as one in which

> lead managers in an ARS transaction exercise an almost complete degree of control over information associated with auctions. Lead managers are the only dealers associated with an ARS that know, for example, the number of bidders at an auction, the individual and aggregate dollar amount of bids, the range of bid prices, whether there are sufficient bids by investors for the auction to succeed, and the clearing rates in successful auctions (before those rates are disclosed to the issuer and investors). The lead manager is also the only party (other than perhaps the auction agent, who is not a principal in

22. "A Long, Cold Cashless Siege," *New York Times*, April 14, 2008.
23. Andrew Ackerman, "Haines Speaks on ARS," *Bond Buyer* 364, no. 32893 (June 5, 2008).

Table 3-3. "Informal Shorthand" Used to Sell Now-Defaulted ARS Deals

Informal shorthand	Description in account statement received later
Athilon Funding	Athilon Cap Corp Sr Cub Deferrable Int
Pivot Funding	Pivot Master Trust AR
Mantoloking Funding	Mantoloking CDO 2006 Ltd.
Pivot Funding Ser. 6	Pivot Master Trust AR
Lakeside Funding	Lakeside CDO Ltd.
South Coast Funding St. Loan	South Coast Funding V Ltd.
Camber Funding St. Loan Ser. 2006-1	Camber 2006-1 Ser. 2
Camber Funding Student Ln Ser. 5	Camber 2006-5 Ser. 06-5
Camber Funding Student Loan Ser. 6	Camber Master Tr Ser. 6

Source: Administrative Office of the U.S. Courts, PACER Service Center (http://pacer.psc. uscourts.gov/).

the transaction) who knows whether the lead manager itself bid for its own account and whether that bid was necessary for the auction's success.[24]

But while lead dealers once knew and had records of such details, key market participants claimed in response to a subpoena issued by the New York attorney general that auction desk records, transcripts, and recordings were destroyed. Hence, we may never know the true extent of auction manipulation in the market.

But the situation was even worse. Two brokers, Eric Butler and Julian Tzolov, who worked in the private client services division of Credit Suisse, became famous in early 2008 for aggressively marketing ARS to investors. One practice in the industry—which has been ascribed to Butler and Tzolov but whose true extent has yet to be revealed—was to use what the industry has alleged to be "informal shorthand" for the names of many deals that were sold to unwitting investors. A brief list of such alleged references is included in table 3-3. By using such shorthand, the industry represented a deal to be standard student loan ARS when in fact it was an auction rate–based mezzanine CDO. The industry referred to "Athilon Funding" when it really meant "Athilon Cap Corp Sr Sub Deferrable Int" securities; to "Lakeside Funding" when it really meant "Lakeside CDO Ltd."; and to "Camber Funding Student Ln. Ser. 5" when it really meant "Camber 2006-5 Ser. 06-5." In summary, as with other financing structures, the leverage that initially was applied to safe collateral grew in magnitude and was eventually applied to riskier assets, with predictable results.

24. See www.regionalbonddealers.com/pdf/RBDA_ARS_Letter_2.pdf, p. 3.

Summary and Conclusions

Throughout the examples of CPDOs, SIVs, and ARSs, we see a trend toward stressing innovative leverage structures with increased risk until they reach the breaking point. The important question is whether these structures represent revolutionary new investment instruments or just new ways of repackaging old investments. Proponents of the view that the structures are new instruments stress that the main problem is the highly difficult task of predicting the performance of innovative structures. Proponents who view the structures as old instruments stress that the problem is merely traditional correlation tightening through yield seeking and leverage, magnified by economic distress. While the reality is somewhere in the middle, the issue will become crucial in the regulatory debate on how to measure and monitor exposures to such instruments on the other side of the credit crisis.

Whatever consensus arises from the outcome of that debate, however, regulators will still have to reckon with the myriad interactions of operational risk, liquidity risk, legal risks, seller-servicer risks, and financial structure risk (the risk of just plain bad engineering) that formed the basis of the leverage as well as the programmatic nature of the brain-dead grantor trust provisions that may have contributed—necessarily or unnecessarily—to the great unwind.

One traditional conclusion, however, remains. While textbook finance teaches us to construct portfolios and structures that are less risky (that is, through diversification), the market is thinking about how to make those constructs more risky when doing so suits investor risk preferences, particularly during a seemingly benign credit environment. Of course, when risk increases, the correlative properties of such investments will render them explosive, so that they may be the first to fail on the other side of the cycle. Hence, from a policy perspective, innovative structures created in periods of relative calm may need to be closely monitored so that their effects can be appropriately contained.

GÜNTER FRANKE
JAN P. KRAHNEN

4

The Future of
Securitization

B Y NOW, THE so-called credit crisis is more than a year old. Over its course, the crisis has caused enormous casualties, forcing large international banks to write off hundreds of billions of dollars. While most of those losses were borne by private investors, namely bank shareholders, the state has had to absorb considerable casualties as well, particularly in the United States, the United Kingdom, and Germany. Bailouts were experienced in Germany (IKB, Sachsen LB), in the United Kingdom (Northern Rock), and most dramatically in the United States (Freddie Mac, Fannie Mae, Bear Stearns, AIG). Finally, a huge $700 billion rescue package was passed in the United States, and various countries in Europe followed with similar state support packages. Accumulated losses of financial intermediaries were estimated at more than $500 billion as of early September 2008 (table 4-1)—an amount equal to about 20 percent of the U.S. budget (3.6 percent of U.S. GDP in 2007 or 18 percent of Germany's 2007 GDP).

We thank the participants of the conference for their very helpful comments, in particular Richard Herring, the discussant, and Peter Wachtell. In addition, Dennis Haensel, Julia Hein, Thomas Weber, Christian Wilde, our coauthors of several relevant background papers, and many other colleagues as well as practitioners from banks and rating agencies provided helpful comments and conversations. We are very grateful to Steffen Seemann for simulating arbitrage transactions. We acknowledge support from Deutsche Forschungsgemeinschaft and from Goethe University's Center for Financial Studies. All errors, of course, are our own.

Table 4-1. *Accumulated Write-Downs by Region*
US$ billions

Region	Total	3Q2008[a]	2Q2008	1Q2008	4Q2007	3Q2007
Worldwide	516.3	18.1	115.1	168.0	167.9	47.2
United States	263.0	18.1	70.3	69.3	75.9	29.4
Europe	229.5	0.0	41.3	89.3	81.3	17.6
Asia	23.9	0.0	3.4	9.4	10.7	0.4

Source: DZ Bank (2008).
a. Preliminary figures.

The epicenter of the crisis lies in the so-called subprime segment of the U.S. housing market, where loan-to-value ratios have risen over time, often exceeding 1. The cooling down of the U.S. real estate market in the first half of 2007, sometimes characterized as the bursting of a housing price bubble, led to write-downs of the banks' loan books. There were two major channels of contagion, one direct, the other more indirect, which shifted loan losses to investors. As for the direct channel of contagion, investors who had held chunks of banks' loan portfolios—for example, in the form of tranches of securitized portfolios—experienced significant write-downs of their financial claims. Investors holding commercial paper were almost universally bailed out by the sponsoring bank or by the state if the former was in distress itself. Examples of loss-taking institutions are Citibank, Merrill Lynch, UBS, and HSBC, among many others (table 4-2).

Then there is the indirect channel of contagion, following from the dramatic rise in credit default swap (CDS) spreads and lending rates in the interbank market, where lending rates reached record levels for an extended period and the inter-

Table 4-2. *Top Five Loss-Taking Institutions*
US$ billions

Firm	Total	3Q2008[a]	2Q2008	1Q2008	4Q2007	3Q2007
Citigroup	55.1	0.5	11.7	19	18.2	5.7
Merrill Lynch	53.4	6.1	9	9.7	18	10.6
UBS	50.2	0	6	19.2	14.4	10.6
HSBC	27.4	0	9.5	4.2	10	3.7
Wachovia	22.7	0.3	13	4.4	3.2	1.8

Source: DZ Bank (2008).
a. Preliminary figures.

Figure 4-1. *Spread between Three-Month LIBOR and Three-Month Treasury Bills*[a]

Percent yield

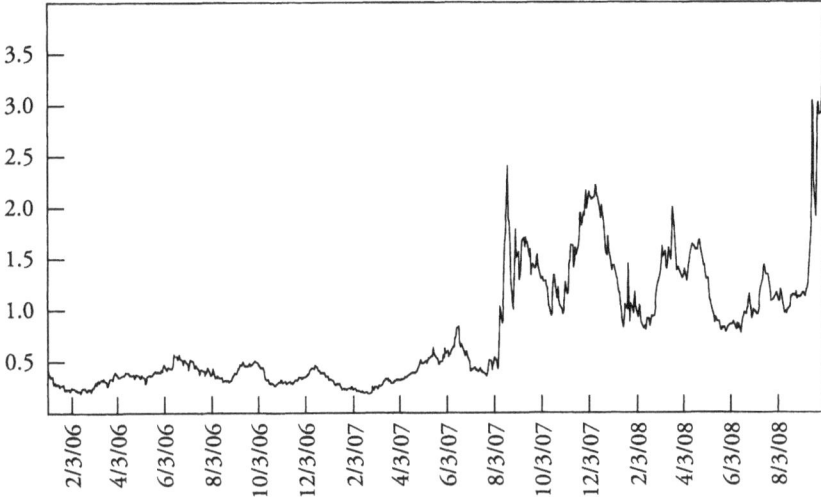

Source: Bloomberg (2008).
a. TED spread, in percent, from third quarter 2005 to third quarter 2008.

bank market became shallow. For some institutions, like Bear Stearns and Northern Rock in March 2008 and Lehman Brothers in September 2008, interbank lending became virtually impossible, and these institutions became illiquid.[1] While Northern Rock was bailed out and Bear Stearns was taken over by JPMorgan Chase with the help of a government subsidy, Lehman Brothers went bankrupt. The indirect channel affected mainly institutions that relied heavily on interbank lending, investment banks in particular. Extremely high levels of LIBOR over risk-free rates (see figure 4-1) and an unprecedentedly small supply of funds in the interbank market forced banks to boost their liquidity reserves. The write-downs of their asset portfolios diminished the banks' equity capital and forced them to raise capital from investors, including sovereign wealth funds.

Furthermore, the breakdown of the interbank market urged central banks, notably the Fed, the Bank of England, and the European Central Bank (ECB), to

1. On a single day, March 13, 2008, the liquid assets of Bear Stearns shrank from $12.5 billion to $2 billion and credit lines were closed.

provide ample access to liquidity for banks. While not being a bailout, the provision of large quantities of central bank lending facilities saved several large banks from becoming illiquid. These central bank interventions were initially intended to be of a short, transitory nature, but such facilities have been extensively used for now more than a year, and there are no signs of a decline in interventions. In the course of providing liquidity assistance, some central banks are said to have taken huge stocks of low-quality collateral on their books.

The broad and extended loss of confidence in the liquidity and solvency of financial institutions, which caused the breakdown of the interbank market, is probably the most distinguishing characteristic of the current financial crisis. It also differentiates this event from many earlier episodes of financial market turmoil, as, for instance, the Asian or the Russian crisis (see Allen and Gale 2007 for a survey).

Given the medley of terrifying headlines that filled the international newspapers during 2008, the call for new and stricter bank supervision rules is anything but surprising. For example, in April 2008, the Financial Stability Forum and the Bank of England proposed regulatory measures to restore the overall confidence of investors in the functioning of the global financial system.[2] After September 15, Black Monday, governments claimed even more strongly that the observed market failure needed to be cured through more regulation related to improving

—prudential oversight of capital, liquidity, and risk management, allowing for countercyclical capital adjustments[3]

—transparency and regulation, facilitating the pricing and ensuring the tradability of complex financial instruments on secondary markets

—the rating process, stipulating different rating scales for structured and nonstructured products

—the sophistication of supervisors with respect to risk control.

In addition, there has been intense discussion on how to avoid the adverse interaction ("downward spiral") between declining asset prices and deteriorating balance sheets that has required equity capital infusions to banks. The International Accounting Standards Board now has relaxed the conditions under which banks are allowed to deviate from marking their assets to market. In addition, banks are permitted to reclassify assets from the trading book to the bank book if

---

2. Financial Stability Forum (2008); Bank of England (2008).
3. See also Kashyap, Rajan, and Stein (2008) on this last point, which emphasizes time-varying capital requirements and state-contingent capital infusions.

the assets are held to maturity. The proposed reform of accounting standards is also intended to lower the suspected pro-cyclicality of the prevailing Basel 2 capital standards, which allegedly is driven by negative spiral effects.[4]

But is tighter regulation reasonable? History teaches us that changes in the regulatory framework are long-lived and very hard to adjust once they are in place. History also suggests that regulatory overreaction often follows financial crises, with Sarbanes-Oxley being a recent example (see Coates 2007). Furthermore, the case for or against a particular regulatory action should be well founded on an economic analysis of the causes and determinants of the current crisis.

Although we agree that the current situation reveals a market failure, we first analyze its causes on the microlevel, by looking at financial intermediaries. Since factual knowledge is lacking, the attribution of causes to what we observe in markets should be followed by detailed empirical checks in the future. Since such checks probably will take years to complete, we present our current understanding now, conceding limited empirical knowledge. We believe that incentives in banks, financial value chains, and rating agencies are at the core of the problem. Incentive misalignment in banks and in financial value chains tends to lower the quality of financial products, thus destabilizing asset valuation. Moreover, incentive misalignment tends to raise the leverage of financial intermediaries. Both effects undermine transparency with respect to asset quality and the risk position of financial intermediaries if ratings turn out to be unreliable. The unreliability of ratings appears to be driven by incentive misalignment within the rating agencies. This cocktail of effects inevitably destabilizes financial markets and the financial system. We therefore argue that incentives need to be changed not only to align the interests of managers and shareholders, but also to give managers incentives to preserve financial stability. These changes can be effective only if there is enough transparency about financial assets and financial intermediaries. Intermediaries providing little transparency about their financial strength endanger financial stability and therefore should be required to provide higher equity capital.

That said, we readily concede that macroeconomic factors, particularly low interest rates, ample liquidity, and the sudden drop in house prices, have contributed

---

4. See Goodhart and Persaud (2008) on this. We do not take up a detailed discussion of accounting standards in this chapter; however, we believe the impact of fair value accounting on the crisis to be grossly exaggerated. Furthermore, departing from fair value principles in the midst of a crisis may increase rather than decrease uncertainty because balance sheets and profit-and-loss (P&L) statements are likely to become even more opaque if fair value is abandoned. We believe opacity to be one of the major reasons for the demise of interbank lending and market illiquidity.

greatly to the severity and the depth of the crisis. We maintain, however, that the fundamental structural cause of the crisis is one of incentive misalignment.

Drawing on recent academic literature, including our own research, we try to provide a consistent description of what has happened in the market for structured finance. Understanding the mechanics of structured finance is essential to understanding why it was possible that so many experts—economists, financial engineers, bankers—were caught by surprise when the crisis hit in the late spring of 2007. We then discuss the actions that we believe are required to correct the problems. More generally, we discuss the promise that securitization holds for the future as well as its limits.

What Happened? A Brief Account

The current crisis has produced large numbers of distressed loans, mortgage-backed loans in particular. That is nothing new; as Reinhart and Rogoff (2008) shows, this type of crisis is recurring and appears to be related to economic downturns following boom phases. We do not ask what drives these repetitive crises; we ask instead what about the current crisis is new, hoping to find constructive approaches to revising the way that assets are securitized.

The historical events leading up to the current crisis have recently been described by several authors. Brunnermeier (2009) and the Bank for International Settlements (2008), for example, give a detailed account of major events leading to the crisis. Along general lines, one may distinguish first a buildup phase and three subsequent waves of devaluation of bank assets. The buildup started roughly in the mid-1990s, when the technique of securitization was gradually applied to a wider range of asset classes, from real estate investments to car loans and credit card debt. Simultaneously, the design of ABS (asset-backed security) transactions became more complex, starting with straightforward issues and culminating in collateralized debt obligation cubed (CDO^3) transactions with hard-to-replicate stochastic properties. Over the entire build-up period, spreads on credit instruments remained stable and relatively low.

Though there were early whistleblowers—for example, the annual reports of the Bank for International Settlements (BIS) since 2006—the first serious signs of a crisis appeared in July 2007, when two of Bear Stearns's hedge funds got into trouble and had to be bailed out by the mother company, the investment bank. Only a few days later, the first wave of devaluations struck the financial industry, accompanied by the first wave of downgraded ratings. The devaluations made refinancing almost impossible for asset-backed commercial paper (ABCP) programs. While there are now write-offs in many parts of the banking industry, the first institution to run into deep trouble was a European bank at the far end of the financing chain, IKB in Germany, followed by Sachsen Landesbank. These two overexposed semi–state-owned institutions had to be bailed out, mostly by the German state and German banks. Soon thereafter, Northern Rock, a British retail mortgage bank that had copied the U.S. subprime lending model, was rescued and nationalized following a run on the bank.

The second phase of the crisis lasted roughly one year, from September 2007 through summer 2008. Banks in the United States, the United Kingdom, Germany, Switzerland, Belgium, and the Netherlands, particularly warehousing banks, were experiencing regular, large, quarterly asset write-downs (tables 4-1 and 4-2), while the interbank market almost completely dried up. Central banks intervened, opening additional discount windows, which grew over time, resulting in ever-larger liquidity infusions. The infusions were accompanied by a rising volume of government paper issues, largely neutralizing the money supply. Simultaneously, investment banks around the world tried to raise additional capital, giving sovereign wealth funds from China and other Asian countries the opportunity to enter the market. However, the speed at which capital was eroding was not matched by the buildup of new capital.

The third phase of the crisis started in summer 2008, when the world's biggest private real estate financiers, Freddie Mac and Fannie Mae, had to be taken over by the U.S. federal government. The resulting additional problems in the interbank market swamped the investment banks, which, one after the other, lost much of their market capitalization before they were either liquidated (Lehmann Brothers) or taken over by a commercial bank (Bear Stearns, Merrill Lynch) or they transformed themselves into commercial banks (Goldman Sachs, Morgan Stanley).

The three phases of the crisis (as of fall 2008) were accompanied by different government reactions. While the regulators did not care much about securitization markets before summer 2007, they responded by selectively rescuing institutions like Bear Stearns, IKB, and Northern Rock. Only in the second phase did they become willing to nationalize institutions, in particular Fannie Mae and Freddie Mac, to stabilize the market. In the third phase, still under way today, governments have come up with a variety of measures, like bank deposit guarantees, interbank loan insurance, the bailout of poorly performing bank assets—such as U.S. Treasury Secretary Henry Paulson's Troubled Asset Relief Program (TARP)—and the provision of equity capital to troubled banks, whether compulsory for all banks (in the United States) or voluntary (in Germany).

The steady intensification of state intervention is one remarkable feature of this crisis. The opaqueness of financial markets and institutions is a second unique feature. Investors obviously retreat from markets when asset or counterparty risk cannot be reasonably estimated. A third remarkable feature is the complete breakdown of interbank markets, which gives central banks a big role to play, effectively substituting for interbank lending.[5]

Why Did It Happen? The Costs and Benefits of Securitization

We used results from the academic literature on contract design to assess the contribution of asset securitization to market efficiency and (investor) welfare, examining both theory and evidence, the latter often scarce. We find that some key assumptions of the textbook securitization model were in effect not met and that the theory was descriptively false. We find four key arguments for a positive contribution of securitization, which require further discussion:

—improved risk allocation: enhancing economy-wide risk sharing through contingent claims (achieving market completion)

—responsible disintermediation: preserving incentives for lenders to monitor obligors in a lending relationship with funding by third parties

—transparency of traded assets: disentangling information-sensitive and information-insensitive assets (creating tradable high-quality claims from a pool of lower-quality, illiquid assets)

—transparency of the risk profile of financial intermediaries engaged in securitization to help to stabilize their funding.

As a corollary to the second and third arguments, we argue that secondary market liquidity of complex financial instruments is directly related to the reliability (accuracy, stability, and validity) of announced asset quality—that is, unbiased rating, which, in turn, is a function of responsible disintermediation.

Risk Transfer and Diversification

Theory tells us that improving worldwide risk allocation and enhancing investor diversification should be major benefits of securitization. By securitizing otherwise nontradable assets, like credit card debt and corporate and consumer loans, the creditor can transfer asset risks to other financial intermediaries and private investors (households). Eventually risks are always borne by private investors, whether risks are intermediated or not. Therefore a bank may retain some risks that, under normal market conditions, are effectively borne by its shareholders.

5. While we focus on crisis prevention in this chapter, we emphasize the formative role of crisis management on future crisis prevention. The high tide of government interventions seen today probably will reshape the incentives of tomorrow's bankers just as much as any forthcoming regulation; it therefore needs to be taken into consideration as well.

However, securitized claims are easier to trade than loan portfolios, just as bonds are easier to trade than loans.

Another benefit of securitization derives from the fact that the underlying asset typically is a portfolio of claims rather than a single claim. Investing in a securitization tranche therefore corresponds to buying a highly diversified claim; no extra effort is needed to diversify individually, at presumably higher transaction costs. This benefit resembles the benefit realized by buying exchange-traded funds instead of a large number of individual stocks.

The available empirical evidence on market growth is consistent with the theoretical benefits mentioned above. Figure 4-2 portrays the strong worldwide growth in securitization issuance until 2008, indicating strong reallocation of default risks. Even though statistics on the allocation of securitization tranches are still almost nonexistent, the available figures on write-downs of bank asset positions give some indication (see tables 4-1 and 4-2).

These write-downs include all bank assets. They are not confined to securitization tranches; they also include loans—in particular, leveraged loans related to mergers and acquisitions. As shown in table 4-1, at the beginning of September 2008, banks worldwide had written off $516 billion, 51 percent of which related to U.S. banks, 45 percent to European banks, and the rest to Asian banks.

These figures indicate that European banks have bought a large share of securitized risks and leveraged loans, consistent with the above theory on the gains of diversification. Previous crises in the U.S. real estate sector were domestic, with little recognition in Europe and outside the United States in general, suggesting that securitization helped the current crisis to spread around the world. Therefore, we conclude that securitization contributed to broad, worldwide dissemination of risk.

The empirical evidence also supports the existence of strong diversification benefits. Usually the loans pooled in a transaction involving residential mortgage–backed securities (RMBSs) add up to a par value of at least $1 billion per transaction. Since a single loan typically does not exceed a par value of $0.5 million, often many more than 2,000 different residential mortgage–backed loans are pooled in a single transaction. The ensuing diversification benefit is very strong even though regional risk or loan-type risk (such as risks of subprime loans versus those of other types of loans) may be strong. Similarly, diversification is very good in credit card, auto loan, and corporate loan securitizations, while it tends to be not as broad in corporate bond transactions.[6]

---

6. In a study of 169 European securitizations of corporate loans and bonds, Franke, Herrmann, and Weber (2007) finds an average Moody's diversity score of 88 for corporate loan securitizations but only 45 for corporate bond securitizations. The diversity score ranges between 1 (no diversification) and 135.

Figure 4-2. *Global Issuance of Asset-Backed Securities*[a]

Global ABS issuance 2007 year to date and 2008 projection

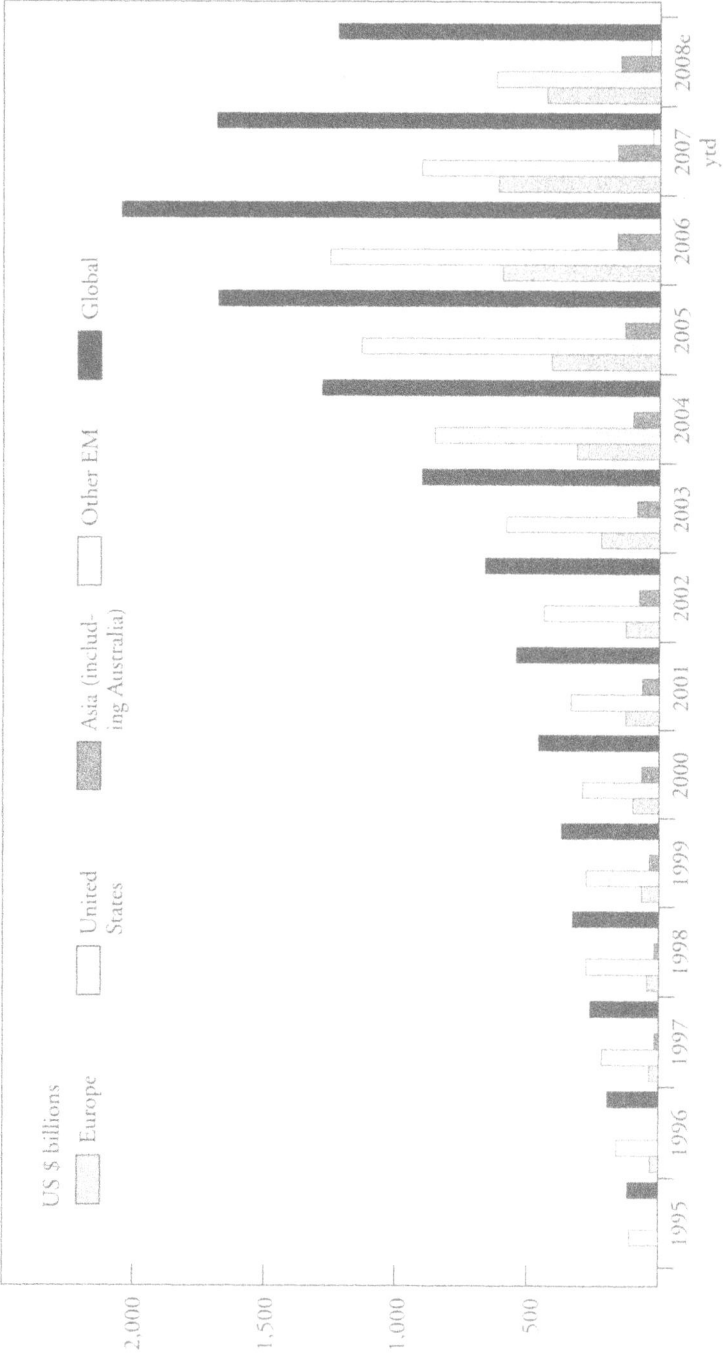

Source: HSBC Global Research (2007).

a. Data include cash ABS publicly announced and rated but not necessarily publicly placed with investors over the past months.

Risk Transfer and Asymmetric Information

The benefits of securitization come at a cost related to the problems implied by information asymmetries. Securitization is a technology that attempts to handle the inherent conflict between efficient decisionmaking and optimal worldwide risk allocation. Efficient decisions are supported if the decisionmaker has to bear all the consequences of his or her decision. That is typical of the bank-based model, in which a bank takes the lending decision and retains the loan on its books until maturity, forgoing benefits from improved risk allocation. In the market-based model, the bank takes the lending decision but transfers the risks to other parties. Thus, risk allocation is improved, but decisionmaking is no longer efficient. The latter follows because, in a world of asymmetric information, the bank inevitably tries to benefit from adverse selection and moral hazard, rendering its decisions second best. Securitization combines the bank- and the market-based models to use their strengths and avoid their weaknesses. However, the empirical evidence so far raises serious questions about the securitization model.

Securitization is one way to use the screening technology of originators without being constrained by their ability to generate funds on their own balance sheet. Therefore, securitization facilitates specialization among financial intermediaries. It may increase the scale of operations of these institutions and, at the same time, broaden the investor base willing to fund their assets directly rather than through bank deposits or bank bonds—and to bear the accompanying risk. To the extent that securitization leads to better risk allocation and to more investors bearing the risks, potential welfare benefits arise.

However, securitization raises agency problems on various levels. First, conflict arises between the originating bank and investors buying securitization tranches. Second, additional conflicts arise if loan origination and servicing is not done by the bank but split into several specialized jobs and delegated to various agents in a value chain. Third, there is an agency problem between bank managers and bank shareholders. Fourth, bank shareholders may be interested in bank policies that benefit them at the expense of financial stability—that is, losses are imposed on third parties.

Two-Tier Agency Relationships: Theory

If all securitization activities are concentrated in one bank, then, apart from borrowers, only the bank and investors are involved. We first address the agency conflict between the bank and investors. Information asymmetries between banks as lenders and tranche investors give rise to adverse selection and moral hazard. This is a typical agency problem. The lending bank grants the loans and transfers the risk of the loans to the investors. The bank has a strong incentive to overstate the quality of the loans in order to buy protection against default losses at lower cost. Investors anticipate that problem and charge higher credit spreads. However, if loan quality deterioration is imperfectly recognized by investors and rating agencies alike, as was the case in the subprime market of 2006, credit spreads on securitization tranches are downward biased. That bias inflates securitization profits and enhances adverse selection as long as the credit spreads on the underlying loans correctly reflect the loan quality. More generally, mispricing in one market creates arbitrage opportunities through risk transfer. Gorton (2008) points to product complexity as another reason for adverse selection. While the seller understands the product, the buyer does not; therefore the buyer may be systematically misled and eventually pay too much.

Besides adverse selection, the bank servicing the loans may be subject to moral hazard. Once default risk is transferred, the bank has little incentive to monitor the obligors or to restructure a loan if necessary to reduce the default risk. From standard agency theory, the conflict between the principal and the agent leads to a second-best contract in which the agent bears more default risk than in a first-best contract. The optimal share of the risk held by the agent is a compromise between optimal incentives and optimal risk allocation; thereby the interests of the principal and the agent are partially aligned.

In securitization transactions, the "magic trick" of incentive alignment is achieved by a contractual device that is very familiar from insurance contracts— the deductible.[7] Of all the issued tranches with different ranks, the lowest-ranked tranche is supposed to be retained by the issuer. That note is called the first loss piece, or the equity tranche. By construction, the first loss piece fully absorbs all default losses up to its notional amount; therefore it pays a very high coupon. In many cases, the first loss piece will have lost a substantial part of its face value before it matures, explaining its widespread characterization as "toxic waste."

In true sale transactions, the equity tranche represents the first loss piece. In synthetic transactions, the junior credit default swap by which the originator buys protection from an investor may contain a threshold and only default losses beyond that threshold are reimbursed by investors. That threshold, then, is the first loss position of the originator unless the originator buys insurance from oth-

---

7. Despite the terminology, the contractual design in structured finance closely resembles designs practiced in the reinsurance industry over centuries. Nonproportional reinsurance in the form of aggregate excess loss leads to payoff patterns similar to those observed in standard ABS transactions. For an early description of reinsurance contracts, see Kopf (1929). Doherty and Smetters (2005) discusses alternative ways and means to align incentives from an insurance perspective. The optimality of deductibles is shown by Arrow (1971).

ers. In addition to the threshold, there may be an unrated tranche, issued by a special-purpose vehicle, which is strictly subordinate to all rated tranches. In this case, the threshold and the unrated tranche together may be considered the first loss piece.

If the bank fully retains the first loss piece, then it retains most of the default risk, since the size of the first loss piece is typically considerably larger than the expected loss of the asset pool (see Franke and Krahnen 2006). That strongly mitigates the aforementioned information asymmetry problems, but it also strongly limits risk transfer and hence is a strong barrier to optimal risk allocation. Agency theory, however, does not require the bank to fully retain the first loss piece. As in insurance contracts, the insured may retain a deductible of, for example, 15 percent of the damage up to a given limit, and that may be sufficient to effectively constrain moral hazard. Similarly, if the bank retains, say, 15 percent of the first loss piece, that may be sufficient to effectively and credibly constrain adverse selection and moral hazard. Whether that is true or not is an empirical issue.

Securitization not only tranches the underlying portfolio into a first loss piece and a more senior remainder of the issue but also splits the rest into several tranches according to strict rules of subordination. The basic technique used in securitization consists of pooling the payment streams of a given asset pool and routing the cash flow to different classes of bonds, called tranches, in order to offer a wide variety of claims of different quality. That enables different groups of investors to buy the claims that fit their needs best. Strict subordination implies, for each payment date, that investors buying part of the lowest tranche, the first loss piece, will receive payments only after all other investors buying senior tranches have satisfied their interest and principal claims in full. Similarly, a mezzanine tranche will receive payments only after all tranches senior to the mezzanine tranche have been fully served, and so on to the highest, most senior tranche, which will be served before all other tranches.

However, the first to be served is the originating bank, which gets fees for arranging and servicing. Often this bank also is the swap counterparty for the special-purpose vehicle, allowing it to collect additional fees hidden in the swap terms. Therefore the originating bank has a first profit position, which is a supersenior position and hence almost risk free. To illustrate the first profit position, consider a true sale transaction. Usually the market value of the underlying portfolio exceeds the par value by 3 to 7 percent, but the par values of all tranches together never exceed the par value of the underlying portfolio. The surplus is translated into the first profit position. The originator may also be able to sell part of the first profit position through net interest margin or interest-only certificates. The first profit position motivates the originator to expand the transaction volume so as to generate higher profits, irrespective of default risk. The super-seniority of the first profit position creates another wedge between the originator and investors.

The properties of pooling and tranching have been analyzed in the security design literature, in particular by Greenbaum and Thakor (1987), Duffie and DeMarzo (1999), Plantin (2003), DeMarzo (2005), and Franke and Krahnen (2006). These studies show that under certain conditions relating to information distribution, risk management capacity, and risk aversion, tranching can emerge as an optimal contractual device to allocate cash flows. In particular, tranching allows for incentive alignment when the underlying assets are subject to moral hazard or adverse selection. Securitization thus should arrive at the optimal trade-off of the costs and benefits of improved risk allocation among the agents in the economy.

As argued above, agency theory tells us that the party affecting through its activities the level of default losses should bear a substantial portion of those losses. Hence the originating bank should retain a substantial part of the first loss piece. Mezzanine tranches often carry below–investment grade ratings because their default probability is substantial. In Plantin (2003), mezzanine tranches are marketed to sophisticated investors—that is, investors with comparatively high monitoring capability—because buyers of mezzanine tranches face a substantial probability of being hit by default losses before the bond matures, implying the need to take over the monitoring task from the holder of the first loss piece. Once the first loss piece is completely absorbed, the mezzanine tranches effectively take over the role of the most junior claim. Since the task of monitoring requires special expertise, mezzanine note holders are likely to be sophisticated investors, like investment banks or hedge funds, effectively shielding senior tranche holders from the cost of incentive misalignment—that is, from a further decrease in asset quality.

This brings us to another hypothesized contribution of securitization to welfare, namely the creation of information-insensitive senior tranches. More precisely, senior tranches are information insensitive in the sense that their payoff strongly depends on macroeconomic tail risk, not idiosyncratic or firm-specific risk.[8] That allows remote investors like households or pension funds to fund the asset pool directly without having to worry about firm-specific information or monitoring of the originating bank. Information-insensitive tranches require no

---

8. On a more general level, securitization may be interpreted as completing the market, since the tranches issued in the process of securitization are nonproportional claims on the underlying risk. Their payoffs depend on macro factors; therefore securitization may be seen as a technique to create state-contingent claims. Investors buy notes carrying predominantly tail risk characteristics. Such securities are called senior bonds, and in today's markets a large fraction of those bonds carry a standardized risk load, rated triple A, signaling a very low expected default probability.

risk management expertise of their buyers and therefore are well suited for remote investors. Information-sensitive tranches, however, should be purchased by sophisticated investors only. This benefit of strict subordination should clearly contribute to the welfare gains achieved by securitization. Therefore, theory predicts substantial first loss piece retention by the originating bank in a typical securitization transaction, while mezzanine tranches are held by sophisticated investors and the most senior tranches are held by remote investors.

Information insensitivity of senior tranches is also of great relevance to the emergence of a secondary market for such instruments. With insensitivity to firm-level information, notes can be traded among investors essentially without recourse to firm-level information and therefore without fear of adverse selection and moral hazard. That reduces the information cost for traders and stabilizes the market value of senior tranches.

In summary, apart from the benefits of improved risk allocation, we find three characteristics of securitization transactions that are potentially relevant to the valuation of these instruments. First, incentive alignment between originator and investor is achieved through an adequate level of recourse, typically through full or partial retention of the equity piece.[9] Second, incentive alignment is further secured by mezzanine investors, since they are potential substitutes for the holders of the equity tranche if portfolio losses reach higher levels. That is why mezzanine tranches are held by sophisticated investors. Third, senior tranches are exposed to systematic tail risk only, making these notes an ideal asset class for non-informed investors like households and pension funds.

Three statements regarding the originating banks can be made. First, securitization allows banks to transfer tail risk from bank balance sheets to investors outside the financial sector, relying on senior tranches. Second, securitization does not lead to unlimited risk transfer, as equity tranches tend to be retained. That is also in the interest of the bank because it reduces its cost of buying protection. Third, transferring part of its loan book to the capital market enables a bank to take new risks. It may even lead to more aggressive risk taking if investors are not aware of it, allowing the bank to benefit from additional adverse selection and moral hazard.

Two-Tier Agency Relationships: Evidence

Eventually risks have to be borne by individuals. In an intermediated world, risks are borne to some extent by the intermediaries, but given the substantial costs of intermediary insolvency, their insolvency risk should be limited. The

---

9. This presupposes that the equity piece is large enough to cover a suitable quintile of the loss distribution. There are functionally equivalent alternatives to equity piece retention, like contractually specified conditional recourse of investors to the originator.

securitization of bank loans is widely seen as one such mechanism, reducing insolvency risk by the transfer of at least part of the loan default risk to other players. Whether securitization achieves that objective depends on various effects. First, to what extent are default risks actually transferred in real-world securitization transactions? Second, does the risk transfer in securitizations reduce or increase the overall risks taken by securitizing banks? Third, does the risk transfer in securitizations undermine the quality of bank lending? Fourth, does risk transfer render risk allocation in financial markets more opaque? The last two questions are dealt with in more detail in the following discussion.

First, we analyze the size and the allocation of the first loss piece (FLP). In a sample of forty European securitization transactions, Franke and Krahnen (2006) finds that in most transactions, the FLP covers a quintile of more than 85 percent of the portfolio loss rate distribution.[10] Of course, that number depends strongly on the ratings assigned to the underlying asset pools as well as on the default correlations assumed in the simulations. Our correlations are similar to those of the rating agencies. Given the high loss absorption by the first loss piece, forcing the originator to fully retain it would largely eliminate any transfer of default risk. But full retention is probably not necessary, as argued above. Nevertheless, we might expect the originator to retain a portion of 15 to 25 percent. If investors know about first loss retention, they can obtain more accurate estimates of default risk and condition their expectations accordingly.

Surprisingly, however, the allocation of risk in securitization transactions is one of the industry's well-guarded secrets. Originating banks never appear to commit in public to retaining a certain fraction of the FLP. Perhaps they consider it important to maintain their freedom to change their position in the FLP over time; perhaps they expect some investors to believe, naively, that they retain a large fraction. They may be afraid, therefore, to disappoint investors by announcing low fractions. On the other hand, anecdotal evidence indicates that smart investors buy rated tranches only if the originator promises to retain some minimum fraction of the FLP. However, in the year before the outbreak of the subprime crisis, anecdotal evidence showed an increasing number of transactions being issued with no retention of the FLP.[11] The opacity regarding the allocation

---

10. For further studies that confirm the extreme riskiness of the first loss piece, see Haensel and Krahnen (2007) and Franke, Herrmann, and Weber (2007). Both studies find that the FLP bears, on average, between 80 and 90 percent of the expected default losses of the securitized portfolios. Those numbers are derived from replicating the loss rate distribution of the underlying asset portfolios, since the allocation of expected losses to individual tranches is not public information. Furthermore, the numbers cannot be used to gauge effective risk transfer, since that depends on whether a tranche is retained by the originator.

11. We have no hard evidence to back up this claim; we rely here on information obtained during private conversations with managers in the industry.

of the FLP is complemented by the opacity regarding the size of the almost risk-free first profit position. Although some servicer fees may be declared in the offering circular, investors know little about the size of the first profit position.

Buyers of the FLP risk presumably are mostly banks and, to a lesser extent, hedge funds and insurance companies.[12] Bank for International Settlements (2008), a study based on surveys conducted by the Basel Institute of leading international banks, notes that equity tranches were acquired predominantly by asset managers, active traders, and institutional investors;[13] retention is not even mentioned in the study. Again, even though the empirical evidence is quite limited, the theoretical prediction that for the most part the originator retains a substantial fraction of the FLP is very likely wrong.

That conjecture regarding FLP risk transfer is supplemented by the opacity concerning the transfer of rated tranches, mezzanine and senior. Originators do not inform the public of their sale of rated tranches, making it difficult for outsiders to estimate the risk of the underlying portfolio kept by the originator on its book. The naive view that the rated tranches are mostly sold to outsiders has been questioned, too. Citibank assumes that most AAA-rated tranches are retained within the banking sector. According to Tett, van Duyn, and Davies (2008), banks bought about 30 percent of the AAA-rated tranches; structured investment vehicles (SIVs) and conduits, about 20 percent; and money market funds, about 25 percent, for a total of 75 percent. The BIS study also argues that over the past few years, issuers increasingly have retained the senior and super-senior tranches. In addition, monoline insurers have taken on a considerable share of senior risk, curtailing risk transfer to remote investors.[14]

Even though the risk of money market funds is, in legal terms, borne by the buyers of those funds, in effect the issuing banks cannot impose substantial losses on them since money market investments are perceived to be almost risk free. And rightly so, since issuers of money market funds typically extend liquidity guarantees on the funds that, in the event of prolonged illiquidity, imply fund buyers hold a put option against the issuer. Therefore banks appear to hold most of the AAA-rated risk.

That conclusion is also supported by the restricted evidence regarding synthetic securitization transactions. Franke, Herrmann, and Weber (2007) finds

---

12. According to the *Credit Derivatives Report* of the British Bankers Association, in the credit default derivatives market of 2006, banks sold 59 percent of the default risk while they bought 44 percent. Hedge funds sold 28 percent and bought 32 percent, and insurance companies sold 6 percent and bought 17 percent (British Bankers Association 2006).
13. Bank for International Settlements (2008, p. 18).
14. Bank for International Settlements (2008, p. 17).

that in synthetic transactions the nonsecuritized AAA-rated portion exceeds 80 percent of the par value of the transaction. Casual talks with bankers indicate that a large part of this nonsecuritized risk is not insured through senior credit default swaps and hence is borne by the originator. That view is somewhat inconsistent with the results reported in Bank for International Settlements (2008) and in Gorton (2008) for Lehman Brothers,[15] which argue that monoline insurers have taken on a considerable share of senior risk. The rationale behind bankers' reluctance to insure the senior risk is probably that the default probability of AAA-rated tranches is so small that buying insurance appears too costly. Also, the low risk weight attached by Basel 2 to AAA tranches does not motivate originating banks to transfer that risk. We therefore conclude that the theoretical prediction that the most senior tranches are held by remote investors is presumably wrong as well.

In summary, it appears that originators sell a large part of the FLP to other banks and to a lesser extent to insurance companies and hedge funds. Furthermore, a significant fraction of the AAA tranches apparently is retained in the banking sector. Both observations obviously run counter to basic assumptions in the securitization model.[16] The proportion of default risk in securitizations retained by the originating banks is not publicly known. We conclude that the observed risk transfer is quite different from what theory (and the common precrisis understanding) predicts. That is why we label the risk transfer story a myth.

Multi-Tier Agency Relationships

So far we have assumed that a financial institution organizes all securitization-related activities in house. However, in reality the industry has outsourced many parts of the financial engineering process in order to reduce production costs and to benefit from the specialized skills and innovations of industry suppliers. Banks also started outsourcing various parts of the production process, as was apparent in subprime lending in the U.S. market. Two-tier agency relationships were thus replaced by multi-tier agency relationships. Ashcroft and Schuermann (2007) discusses in much detail the various parties involved in the securitization of subprime loans. The authors also analyze the various agency problems that arise from the division of banking activities and discuss mechanisms to mitigate those problems.

---

15. Gorton (2008, graph, p. 43).

16. That even clever engineering cannot bypass basic laws of financial gravity is one of the insights gained from the securitization crisis. In commenting on the lessons of the credit turmoil, Joseph Ackerman, CEO of Deutsche Bank, recently said, "We have now learned that what does not work in theory eventually will not work in practice either." See *Euro Finance Week* (Frankfurt), November 17, 2008 (authors' translation).

The parties involved in managing the subprime business form a value chain of highly specialized parties, each having its own interests and its own managers. While the benefits of specialization are indisputable, the agency costs of the value chain are difficult to estimate. The important question is whether a coordination mechanism can be designed for the involved parties to ensure sufficient quality of the overall product. Part of that mechanism is the incentive system.

First, consider the value chain in mortgage lending. In the subprime business, only the originators of mortgage-backed loans and the mortgage brokers cooperating with them are involved in the beginning. Once the loans are contracted, originators are no longer involved, subject to the rule that, within a short time period after contracting, they may have to repurchase loans that were not properly contracted and loans that the debtor fails to pay. Hence originators and mortgage brokers tend to have a short-term perspective. Their rewards depend for the most part on the volume of loans that they contract, not on the long-term performance of the loans. That is reasonable, given that they have little or no influence on the future handling of the loans by other parties.

Thus, loan originators and mortgage brokers demand protection against poor performance by the agents that will be involved at later stages. That in turn implies that hidden long-term characteristics of the loans that are due to the unobservable behavior of the loan originators and mortgage brokers themselves may not matter at all for their reward. Originators and brokers therefore are interested primarily in increasing loan volume, reinforcing adverse quality characteristics.

Another party involved is the warehouse lender that initially funds the loans. It may have some influence on the choice and the activities of the loan originator but not on the choice and the activities of the servicer. Hence, the warehouse lender prefers a reward that is independent of the actions of the servicer.

The servicer of the loans is responsible for collecting interest and principal payments and for making sure that the property on which the mortgage is written is kept in good shape for future action in case of delinquency or default. As pointed out by Ashcroft and Schuermann (2007), the servicer collects servicing fees until default and so has a strong incentive to defer default through restructuring the loan, even though doing so may increase default losses. However, the quality of the servicer may have a strong impact on foreclosure value. Not surprisingly, the loan originator does not want a reward that depends on servicer quality, on which the originator has no influence. Similarly, the servicer has no influence on the choice of loan originator and therefore does not want a reward that depends on the quality of the originator.

The only party involved continuously throughout the securitization process is the arranger, who sets up a special-purpose vehicle (SPV) for securitizing loans and typically manages the SPV. The arranger therefore is in the best position to coordinate and monitor the activities of all parties involved. The SPV buys the loans and securitizes them. Tranches are sold to investors, who usually have little information on the underlying assets and may rely instead on the ratings of rating agencies and the advice of investment managers. While rating agencies are involved long term in the transaction through monitoring and adjusting ratings, for the most part investment managers are involved only at the start of the SPV, when its loan portfolio is assembled. Later on the portfolio may be adjusted again, depending on the advice of the same or other investment managers. While rating agencies and investment managers do not have a financial stake in the transaction, their reputations are at stake.

As pointed out in Ashcroft and Schuermann (2007), the cooperating parties set up rules to safeguard the quality of the transaction; if the rules are violated, then the negligent party may have to pay damages. However, liability is subject to a time horizon. Also, limited liability and low equity capital may restrict any payments by the negligent party. Moreover, it may be difficult to prove negligent behavior. Thus, the negligent party may escape recourse claims, and default losses that could have been avoided by careful behavior may be imposed on other parties, in particular investors. Of course, investors may anticipate negligence and therefore charge a premium. Still, with so many parties being involved, investors are exposed to a high level of operational risk. Effective coordination of those parties appears to be very difficult.

Can these problems be resolved by an incentive system? Standard theory suggests that, in the absence of asymmetric information and agency problems, all parties should share in the overall risk.[17] The share that a party takes increases with its wealth and its influence on overall risk. This simple rule of risk allocation is no longer optimal if parties have different expectations and if they affect overall risk through different activities not fully observable by the other parties.

If, for example, the loan originator has a strong influence on loan quality through its screening activities, then the originator should bear a relatively high share of the risk. But there are two counterarguments. First, the originator has little control of the other parties involved in the transaction. That should reduce its risk share. Second, the parties are involved in the transaction at different points in time. The loan originator is involved only at the beginning and so has no control over the transaction later on; hence, as argued before, the originator desires

---

17. More precisely, if all parties have homogeneous expectations and time additive utility functions belonging to the class of functions with hyperbolic absolute risk aversion with the same exponent, then all parties would buy a share in the overall market risk.

protection from agency behavior of the other parties, for example, by reducing its risk share over time. That is even more efficient if the originator's conduct affects the transaction value early during the life of the transaction, when its risk share is relatively high.

If, however, the consequences become visible only in later years, then its risk share should decline at a slower rate, increasing its exposure to agency problems induced by other parties. Similarly, warehouse lenders are involved with their funding activities only for a short while. Asset managers may be replaced, reducing their time horizon, too. Hence, constant long-term risk sharing of these parties appears inefficient; moreover, long-term risk sharing would require long-term risk management, which is not the core business of the parties. This explains why the various parties do not have long-term financial stakes in the transaction. To some extent the problems might be mitigated through reputation effects, but we are skeptical of that possibility.

Given these difficulties, one way out could be to give the arranger a very prominent role in setting up the transaction—in choosing and monitoring other parties. An incentive for taking a strong role would be a long-term financial stake bearing a substantial part of the default losses—for example, by retaining a substantial part of the first loss piece. But the empirical evidence shows that arrangers are reluctant to retain substantial parts of this piece. In some cases in recent years, as pointed out before, the arrangers sold the first loss piece completely; hence this incentive mechanism clearly failed in those cases.

This discussion raises a general question: how many parties is it desirable to have in the value chain? There is a trade-off between the cost advantage of outsourcing parts of the production process to specialized parties and the corresponding agency costs. The function relating the cost advantage to the number of specialized parties should increase at a declining rate (declining economies of specialization); the function relating the agency cost to the number of specialized parties also should increase. But we do not know whether it increases at a constant, declining, or increasing rate. If n denotes the number of parties, then the number of bilateral agency relationships, $n(n-1)/2$, increases overproportionally; that might indicate that agency costs also rise disproportionately quickly. So far we lack empirical evidence. The view in Ashcroft and Schuermann (2007) that agency problems can be reasonably resolved at each bilateral stage appears quite optimistic. The authors' argument is based in part on reputation cost. Similarly, Gorton (2008) argues that implicit contracts between originators and other involved parties align interests; presumably, he also refers to the reputation mechanism. We doubt the effectiveness of this mechanism, however, given the observed deterioration of the quality of mortgage-backed loans.

Casual observation suggests that some banks have fully separated different stages in the lending process from each other. For example, one German bank has established an internal pricing scheme according to which loan origination is compensated by a flat fee, while all loan cash flows (that is, return and risk) are transferred to a credit risk unit, which sets loan rates and decides whether a particular loan is sold, securitized, or kept on the books. This system leaves the incentive alignment between the originating and the processing units unresolved.

Two implications emerge. First, it does not make sense to maximize benefits from specialization of parties, ignoring agency costs. A viable model of securitization might have just one party for both arranging and servicing; both activities are long term and therefore can be coordinated by one party without giving rise to conflicts of interest due to different time horizons. If some outsourcing of loan origination is unavoidable, then the arranger-servicer also should participate in origination; that would provide the arranger-servicer with updated information on origination that can also be used for more effective monitoring of other originators.

Second, there should be a trade-off between outsourcing activities in a more extended value chain and the retention of default risk by the transaction coordinator. As more activities are outsourced and more problems arise due to information asymmetries, investors' protection against other parties' negligent behavior should become more effective. Therefore, regarding the first loss piece, the arranger should commit to retaining a larger fraction if the value chain is extended. For the arranger, that would clearly imply trading off the risk and return of outsourcing. If the arranger extends the value chain, it benefits from cost savings; at the same time, it has to take a higher share of default risk.

Apart from the difficulty of maintaining comprehensive incentive alignment all along the value chain, another issue regarding nonintegrated (outsourced) business processes is credibility in the market. Effective coordination of the different parties of a value chain appears to be a requirement for financial stability because otherwise some parties may not worry about risks. Excessive risks thus are imposed on other investors, who, in turn, will retreat from the market once they become aware of that fact, possibly causing a market breakdown.

Compensation and Incentives

Risk transfer and conservation of lending relationships are conflicting objectives. This is true in particular with regard to financial assets, where the terminal value is random and sensitive to moral hazard and adverse selection. While the previous discussion focused on agency conflicts between different legal entities, we now discuss agency conflicts between a bank's managers and shareholders in order to identify possible reasons for excessive risk taking, turning to management compensation as a source of conflict. We focus on the sharing of risks by the manager, shareholders, and third parties and on the term structures of payoffs to those parties to show that certain compensation schemes may give bank managers incentives to pursue a high-risk portfolio strategy. That does not necessarily conflict with maximization of shareholder value, but it may endanger financial stability. Therefore, it is not sufficient to look at managers and shareholders; the default probability of a bank, too, is essential as a proxy for the costs imposed on the financial system.

We present four major findings. First, if the bonus is back-end loaded—for example, based on the bank's terminal value—then there is no or only limited conflict of interest between management and shareholders.[18] Yet the probability of bankruptcy may be substantial. Second, if the bonus is front-end loaded—for example, based on the present value of expected profits instead of market values or based on a first profit position—shielding the manager against risk, manager and shareholder preferences clearly differ. Third, if the manager is compensated by a package of base salary, annual bonus, and deferred stock or stock options, his or her optimal risk level depends strongly on the structure of the compensation package. Fourth, the manager has a strong incentive for high bank leverage if the bonus is non-negative and the profit for bonus—the internal profit on which the bonus depends—does not include a penalty for high leverage.

It therefore is essential to supplement the bonus system with a malus component in order to discourage the manager from excessive risk taking, even if shareholders also benefit from such risk taking, because it may endanger financial stability. A malus system needs to be carefully designed so that the manager cannot easily change policy to avoid the malus component while retaining strong risk.

Before presenting a numerical example, we mention that there is a large literature on manager compensation and risk taking. On the theoretical side, Ross (2004) demonstrates that conventional wisdom may be misleading. Ross shows that, for example, the conventional wisdom that stock options motivate the manager to increase business risks may be wrong. Nonlinear compensation structures induce conflicting incentive effects[19] on risk taking, so general statements cannot be made easily (see also Lewellen 2006). On the empirical side, Jin (2002) finds that the level of performance-dependent incentives for CEOs tend to move

---

18. Except for differences in risk aversion, which introduce a departure from optimality.

19. Ross shows that stock options may actually reduce a manager's risk taking. Even though the option protects the manager against downside risk, the option reduces his or her marginal utility in "good" states in which marginal utility is low anyway but does not reduce it in "bad" states in which it is high. Hence, expanding risk so that manager's payoff is reduced (increased) in the bad (good) states may easily *reduce* his or her expected utility.

inversely to systematic and nonsystematic business risk if the CEOs face hedging constraints. Coles, Daniel, and Naveen (2006) finds that higher sensitivity of CEO wealth to stock volatility (vega) induces the CEO to implement riskier business policies; the authors also find a positive impact of business risk on the vega of CEO compensation. A more detailed analysis of dynamic risk taking of hedge fund managers is provided by Hodder and Jackwerth (2007), which shows in a simulation model that hedge fund managers tend to take very high risks when the fund value is close to the high-water mark.

The public discussion on incentives in bank management begins with the observation that today bonus systems are a strong incentive for bank managers and may induce them to take excessive risks. We take a closer look at these systems and explore what can be done to mitigate the problem of excessive risk taking, starting with a few examples taken from annual reports that show that top management often is compensated by a package of a base salary, a cash bonus based on recent profits, and stock options and stock-like claims subject to a minimum holding period. Table 4-3 displays the value of these components as a percentage of the value of the overall compensation for UBS managers in 2006 and 2007 and for Deutsche Bank managers in 2007. While 2006 was a good year for UBS, 2007 was not, which explains the relative increase in base salary. In all three cases, the base salary is rather small and the cash bonus is quite high.

The third component, stock options, serves to align the long-term interests of managers and stockholders. More critical is the second component, cash bonuses, because they provide short-term incentives for managers that may conflict with shareholder value. Any discussion of incentive systems in the financial sector needs to take organizational factors into consideration. Because a bank is managed by a team of managers, one might want to look into team theories. We do not discuss the team aspect here but instead assume a single bank manager.

A Simple Numerical Example of a Loan Portfolio

Because we are looking into potential causes of the subprime crisis, we illustrate our arguments using a loan portfolio as an example of a manager's choices. This example is a deliberately simple one that completely ignores moral hazard and reputation effects; to pinpoint key elements of a potential incentive system, we look just at the manager's initial choice of portfolio. Given a securitization transaction, the manager can choose between loan portfolios of different quality, all with a maturity of seven years. The best portfolio has an AAA rating, the worst one, a B rating. We are not concerned about tranching the portfolio into an equity piece and rated tranches but assume that the bank retains the default risk itself. In the first scenario, the bank has a given amount of money (equity capital)

Table 4-3. *Managers' Compensation Package, UBS and Deutsche Bank, 2006 and 2007*

Percent of compensation

Firm	Base salary	Cash bonus	Stock and stock options
UBS 2006	6	47	47
UBS 2007	22	50	28
Deutsche Bank 2007	13	52	35

Source: UBS's 2006 and 2007 annual reports and Deutsche Bank's 2007 annual report.

to invest. In the second scenario, a leverage option is included, allowing the manager not only to invest the given amount of money but also to borrow money elsewhere and invest the additional amount into an augmented loan portfolio.

SCENARIO I

In the first scenario, the bank has granted 100 loans, each with a par value of $1 million, the same initial rating, and seven years to maturity. The risk-free rate is 3.25 percent per year. The credit spreads for the loans are given in table 4-4, together with the cumulative default probabilities over seven years and the annual net risk premiums. The probabilities are taken from S&P's cumulative loss rate table. In case of default, the loss given default is assumed to be 60 percent. The

Table 4-4. *Default Probabilities, Credit Spreads, and Net Annual Risk Premiums for Loans of Different Ratings*

Percent

Rating	Seven-year cumulative default probability	Credit spread	Annual net risk premium
AAA	0.144	0.75	0.238
AA	0.420	0.85	0.314
A	0.887	0.95	0.374
BBB	3.672	1.45	0.635
BB	13.826	3.45	1.765
B	30.999	7.70	4.543

Source: The cumulative default probabilities are those used by S&P for securitizations. The credit spreads are assumed to correspond to credit spreads for securitization tranches. The annual net risk premium is then derived as the credit spread minus annual transaction costs of 50 basis points and the expected annualized loss. For simplicity, that loss equals the cumulative default probability, divided by 7 and multiplied by (1 − LGD), with LGD (loss given default) = 0.5.

annual net risk premium is defined as the credit spread minus the sum of the annual transaction costs of 50 basis points and the annualized expected default loss.

A loan defaults in year t if its rating changes to D, the default category. Rating transitions are simulated using the S&P transition matrix year by year. The 100 loans are assumed to belong to ten different industries. The correlation coefficient of the annual rating changes of two companies belonging to the same industry is 0.2; if they belong to different industries, it is 0.05.

In the first scenario, the manager decides on loan portfolio quality by selecting the initial rating of the loans. Every year the manager receives a base salary and a bonus, which cannot be negative. The bonus equals the bonus base of the year, multiplied by a given participation rate. The bonus base is defined as the internal profit on which the bonus depends. In this example, the bonus base in year t equals the credit spread earned on the loans that have not defaulted before the beginning of the year minus the loss given default (60 percent) on the loans that default in that year. Thus, the annual transaction cost of 50 basis points is excluded in the bonus base.[20] In each year the certainty equivalent of manager compensation is derived by using a power utility function with relative risk aversion. The total income of the manager is then derived as the date 0 present value of the certainty equivalents in years 1 to 7, using the risk-free rate as the discount rate. In this simple setup, the manager does not bear any outside risks and cannot hedge any income risks. In a complete market, the manager can hedge every risk and performance-related compensation packages therefore have no incentive effect.

The shareholders of the bank invest $100 million initially and receive the terminal portfolio value after seven years, which equals the principal plus interest income (composed of the risk-free rate plus credit spread) on all nondefaulted loans compounded at the risk-free rate to the terminal date, plus the compounded recovery values of all defaulted loans, minus the compounded payments to the manager. For shareholders, the terminal portfolio value is also converted into a certainty equivalent by using a slightly modified power function with a given relative risk aversion. The modification is that shareholders' terminal wealth is composed of the terminal portfolio value plus some given exogenous wealth, for example $50 million. Therefore the risk premium implied by the certainty equivalent is rather small. Finally, the terminal certainty equivalent is discounted to date 0 at the risk-free rate, yielding the shareholder value of the portfolio.[21]

20. The transaction cost could be included, but that would not change the results significantly because the manager is compensated by an increase in base salary.

21. Alternatively, one can use an exogenously given pricing kernel to derive the market value of the portfolio. The results are similar.

Table 4-5. *Manager's Total Income and Shareholder Value for Different Combinations of Base Salary, Profit Participation Rate, and Portfolio Rating*[a]

Variable	Total income of manager (in US$ thousands)				Shareholder value (in US$ millions)			
Base salary	125	35	31	20	125	35	31	20
Participation rate (percent)	1	10	15	20	1	10	15	20
Rating								
AAA	817.1	661.3	851.5	986.4	103.7	103.8	103.6	103.5
AA	821.7	690.6	885.8	**1,007.6**	104.0	104.1	**103.9**	**103.7**
A	825.6	705.3	891.0	964.2	**104.1**	**104.2**	**103.9**	**103.7**
BBB	804.8	722.4	853.1	799.0	104.0	103.9	103.6	103.3
BB	892.7	796.6	837.2	636.5	103.3	102.7	102.1	101.6
B	**979.9**	**977.0**	**990.1**	719.0	102.3	100.9	99.9	98.9

Source: Authors' calculations.

a. Bold figures show the highest total income and highest shareholder value respectively, given the compensation package, for portfolios of various ratings.

Table 4-5 displays the results. The left panel shows the total income of the manager for different loan qualities, assuming a constant relative risk aversion coefficient $\lambda = 2.5$. The right panel shows the shareholder values, assuming the same $\lambda = 2.5$ for the shareholders. They, however, have additional terminal wealth of $50 million, which renders them less risk averse. In order to see the impact of the profit participation rate, we consider four different participation rates, 1 percent, 10 percent, 15 percent, and 20 percent. The base salary will be adjusted to the participation rate so that the total income of the manager is roughly constant.

Given a participation rate of 1 percent and a base salary of $125,000, the manager clearly chooses the poor loan quality B, earning a total income of about $980,000 due to the high annual profit generated with B loans. The manager benefits strongly from those profits because she earns 1 percent of them when defaults are rare but does not suffer negative payments when many defaults occur because profit participation is truncated at zero (the bonus system). Moreover, because a 1 percent bonus imposes little risk on the manager, she does not suffer from a substantial risk premium. The situation is different for shareholders. Shareholder value is roughly the same for all loan qualities. That appears reasonable because credit spreads are market rates. Given the high risk associated with a B-rated portfolio, shareholder value is slightly lower due to imperfect diversification. Shareholder value is highest for the A portfolio.

Up to a participation rate of 15 percent, the manager still prefers the B portfolio; for a participation rate of 20 percent, she prefers AA loans. A high participation rate imposes much risk on the manager, reducing her certainty equivalent substantially, in particular for low-quality loans.[22] Therefore, for any given loan quality, the certainty equivalent of the bonus first increases and then declines with a higher participation rate.

The key implication concerns how the loan quality choice depends on the participation rate. A high participation rate lowers not only shareholder risk, through better loan quality, but also the bankruptcy probability of the bank. If shareholders prefer good loan quality, then they should choose a rather high participation rate.

This finding does not change substantially if shareholders combine a bonus with a small share in the terminal value of the portfolio (TV share), which is equivalent to the extreme form of bonus deferral and similar to stock-based compensation with a long holding period. The reason that the findings are similar is that with no leverage, the probability of bank losses is rather small, so the option feature of the bonus does not really matter. Hence a low (high) participation rate and a small (large) terminal value share have similar effects and induce the manager to choose low- (high-) quality loans. The higher the participation rate and the terminal value share, the better the portfolio quality chosen by the manager.

SCENARIO 2

The story changes fundamentally in the second scenario, in which the manager can also choose the bank's leverage. So far the portfolio had a par value of $100 million, fully financed by equity capital. Now the manager can borrow $100 x million from outside and invest in the portfolio $100 (1 + x)$ million. Hence $(1 + x)$ can be interpreted as the volume of the bank's portfolio in units of $100 million, while x is the leverage of the bank—that is, its debt-equity ratio. With leverage, each loan volume is inflated by the factor $(1 + x)$, holding the credit spread con-

---

22. In disentangling the effects of the participation rate, first consider the call option feature of the bonus. Since the bonus is non-negative, the bonus is a call option on the portfolio payoffs. A call option is more valuable if the underlying risk, represented by vega in most option pricing models, is higher. This effect is also present here. But unlike with option pricing models, in which the pricing kernel is exogenously given, the manager evaluates the risk individually, given her utility function. This means that doubling her income in a given state of nature does not double her utility in that state, because the utility function is strictly concave. In other words, if the participation rate and the underlying risk are high, the endogenous risk premium of the bonus is high as well.

stant (as is typical in buying securitization tranches). For simplicity, the manager is entitled to a base salary plus a bonus but no terminal value share.

We first assume that the interest on bank borrowing charged to the bonus base increases linearly with the borrowed amount—that is, the charged interest rate is constant, independent of the leverage. Then, given the quality of the portfolio and the base salary, the manager will maximize the leverage. The reason is obvious. Leverage implies that the bonus base increases linearly with leverage. Since the bonus can never be negative, the bonus will be multiplied by the factor $(1 + x)$ through leverage. That represents a first-order stochastic dominance improvement of the bonus. Hence, given loan quality, total manager income increases monotonically with leverage. Since the risk premium of the bonus increases disproportionately with leverage[23] and the base salary stays constant, total income increases with leverage at a declining rate. That is visible for poor-quality loans in particular.

The incentive to maximize leverage would be even stronger if leverage did not multiply the par value of each of the 100 loans but multiply instead the number of loans to different obligors in each of the given industries so that the diversification of the loan portfolio improves. That would imply an additional, second-order stochastic dominance improvement, benefiting both the manager and the shareholders. Table 4-6 illustrates the results. The base salary is always $40,000, and the participation rate is 8 percent. The computations are based on a loan portfolio in which the par value of each loan is multiplied by $(1 + x)$.

Given a low portfolio volume, the manager chooses the B-quality loans. High volumes increase the bonus risk. To mitigate that effect, she chooses a better loan quality. For a volume of 15 (that is, a leverage of 14) or more, she prefers AAA loans. More generally, the higher the volume or leverage, the better the loan quality.

This finding is consistent with highly leveraged vehicles like structured investment vehicles and asset-backed commercial paper conduits, which usually are highly leveraged and for the most part hold AAA assets. As the numbers in table 4-6 indicate, the potential for raising income through leverage is impressive.

For shareholders, the effects of leverage are quite different. Shareholder value increases with leverage over a wide range, given high-quality loans. The additional credit spreads outweigh the additional risk, since default risk is low. The situation is different for low-quality loans. High default losses are fully borne by

---

23. Given a positive base salary, the manager displays increasing relative risk aversion with respect to the bonus. Her relative risk aversion approaches λ, so that for high leverage levels her total income increases almost proportionally to leverage.

Table 4-6. *Manager Total Income and Shareholder Value for Different Combinations of Volume and Portfolio Rating*[a]

Variable	Total income of manager (in US$ thousands)				Shareholder value (in US$ millions)			
Base salary			40					
Participation rate (percent)			8					
Volume	1	15	25	35	1	15	25	35
Borrowing rate (percent)	3.25	3.25	3.25	3.25	3.25	3.25	3.25	3.25
Rating								
AAA	605.4	**5,235.2**	**8,345.8**	**11,306.1**	103.9	161.6	202.7	243.8
AA	631.7	4,877.3	7,097,7	8,886.4	104.1	165.6	209.0	**252.1**
A	648.0	3,965.2	5,237.6	6,159.1	**104.2**	**166.6**	**209.8**	252.1
BBB	682.7	2,368.1	2,604.5	2,708.3	104.0	158.4	183.8	202.6
BB	794.1	1,435.3	1,470.6	1,485.7	102.9	112.7	104.7	100.2
B	**994.4**	1,555.9	1,579.7	1,579.7	101.3	76.7	69.7	66.5

Source: Authors' calculations.

a. Volume is (1 + leverage) in units of $100 million. The manager earns a base salary of $40,000; her profit participation rate is 8 percent. The bank always pays 3.25 percent on its debt. Bold figures show the highest total income and highest shareholder value respectively, given volume, for portfolios of various ratings.

shareholders until equity capital is fully absorbed. Those losses increase with leverage, eating up more of the terminal value. That is evident in table 4-6, in particular for B loans. For a volume of 35, shareholder value drops to $66.5 million. Since shareholders have limited liability, the bank may go bankrupt. For moderate loan quality, the bankruptcy probability strongly increases with leverage, thereby affecting financial stability.

If the manager participated in the terminal value, as do shareholders, then leverage would have little effect on the manager's choice. As table 4-6 shows, the shareholders also benefit from high leverage, given excellent portfolio quality; therefore, terminal value participation does not discourage the manager from choosing a high leverage.

What do we learn from this simple model? The good news is that although the manager generally prefers high to low leverage, that preference is strongest with a portfolio of good quality. Shareholders also are happy with that policy. This simple model appears to portray quite well what happened in several banks before the subprime crisis. They bought high-quality tranches of RMBSs using high leverage. The bad news relates to both biased model parameters and biased choice of leverage. First, model results and bank default probability[24] depend heavily on the parameters underlying the simulation. If one assumes a recent history of low default realizations, the temptation is to select simulation parameters that match that history, ignoring the usual long-term swings. That yields misleading model results and renders risk control ineffective.

Second, given a bonus that increases with leverage by first- and/or second-order stochastic dominance, the manager's interest in high leverage is quite strong and that interest is reinforced if the bonus also increases with a super-senior first profit position. High leverage endangers not only bank solvency but also financial stability.

The common argument that risk control driven by shareholder interest implements strict limits to risk taking does not appear to be credible when the parameters used for risk controlling are questioned.[25] That doubt is reinforced by the possibility that shareholders might believe that they also benefit from a higher leverage and therefore are not pursuing strict risk control. Shareholder benefit is even stronger if leverage risk is not fully borne by the shareholders themselves but by third parties.

Therefore, we believe that the current crisis was triggered in part by the strong interest of some managers in high leverage. That may explain why the Swiss Federal Banking Commission proposed stricter limits on banks' leverage as a simple cure. However, we believe that a far more promising route to controlling risk taking is to change the reward system for managers. The bonus component should be supplemented by a malus component so that the manager's interest in taking high risks is clearly mitigated. A malus component need not impose an obligation on the manager to pay in adverse situations; instead, the bonus base could be adjusted to discourage excessive risk taking.

A malus component also could be generated by firing the manager in case of losses. One possibility is to fire the manager when default losses exceed a certain trigger; defining the trigger in the manager's employment contract would make the policy credible. What are the implications? If the manager is fired, her income is unlikely to be zero. First, she may get some severance pay; second, she may get some unemployment compensation; and third, since by law the bank is not allowed to mention her bad performance to potential employers, reputation damages may be small, enabling her to find a job again fairly quickly. In addition, the

24. Especially dangerous is a short-term bank funding policy because creditors may feel strongly exposed to the default risk and refuse further lending.

25. The manager may spend much energy in re-engineering model parameters so as to make her leverage policy appear less risky.

manager might expect to be fired in the event of substantial losses even if her employment contract does not state that she will. Therefore, we are skeptical about the effectiveness of a contractual firing trigger.

A different, possibly more effective malus format consists of adjusting the bonus base for the leverage chosen. We assume that the bonus base is derived using an interest rate for bank borrowing that increases with leverage but is otherwise independent of bank policy. That may appear to conflict with the rational expectations of creditors, but it illustrates a phenomenon typical of liquid asset markets. Management may change bank risk very quickly by trading liquid financial assets, without informing creditors accordingly. Therefore, we assume that the borrowing rate charged to the bonus base depends only on leverage. Since credit spreads paid by banks clearly are lower than credit spreads on securitization tranches, we let the borrowing rate increase rather modestly with leverage. Table 4-7 summarizes the results.

The manager maximizes her total income by choosing AA loans and a volume of 15—that is, a leverage of 14. In this example, the malus imposed on the manager by increasing funding costs is effective; hence, market discipline imposed by credit spreads can function like a malus. In addition, shareholders are quite satisfied. The manager's choice also protects creditors well because AA loans have low default risk and thereby protect financial stability. The strength of the effects depends, of course, on the relationship between the imputed borrowing rate and the bank's leverage. The manager's choice would be similar if she also participates in the terminal value, as does a shareholder. In the example, shareholders would prefer A loans with a volume of 20.

The malus effects would be weakened not only by less sensitivity of the borrowing rate to leverage but also by the manager's attempts to undercut the malus. Managers have more decision parameters than just loan quality and leverage. They can effectively design loans to shift hazard rates from early to later years in order to mitigate the adverse effects of loan defaults. One such method is to prolong loans in case of debtor financial distress, so that the loan does not become delinquent and does not default. Another method is illustrated by the many loans granted in the U.S. subprime market that were sweetened with teaser rates. In the first one or two years, debtors are charged low interest rates, followed by strong step up in interest rates. The effect is not only to provide debtors some relief in the first periods, but also to shift the hazard rates of the loans from early to late years. That effect is illustrated in the appendix.

Regarding management incentives, how the annual profit for bonus is determined is again critical. If, as in the teaser rate example, profits are artificially shifted from the late to the early years, then the certainty equivalents of manager income tend to shift to the early years, too. That fact might render the manager more aggressive. More important, the bonus bases earned in the first years are upward biased because they do not reflect the shift of default risks to later years.

A bonus base scheme should avoid these temporal asymmetries in order to provide undistorted long-term incentives for the manager. More generally, the bonus base should be designed in a forward-looking manner so that expected late-period losses and risks are anticipated on an annualized basis. Otherwise the manager may ride the distorted term structure of bonus bases, rendering malus components ineffective.

The previous examples demonstrate the dangers inherent in various incentive systems. Of course, one might question several assumptions made in these examples. For instance, the manager may be less risk averse, inducing her to take more risks. Or, she might be able to hedge part of the bonus risk, a possibility that might induce her to take even more risk. The qualitative conclusions from these examples appear to be robust even if we change the parameters. Therefore, no further simulation results are presented.

Lessons

What are the lessons to be learned? First, given low leverage, the bonus system with a low participation rate is likely to motivate managers to acquire low-quality financial assets. The reverse is true for a high participation rate. Hence, shareholders can influence the quality of financial assets indirectly through the participation rate.

Second, non-negative bonus payments induce the manager to choose high leverage ratios. Even though high financial leverage usually is associated with high-quality financial assets, the same high leverage increases default risk for shareholders and endangers financial stability. Therefore a bonus-cum-malus system is required, which renders high leverage costly for the manager and should induce managers to have a long-term orientation. Bonus base accounting has to be forward looking, incorporating future expected losses and risks. In addition, the internal control system should make sure that the manager does not undermine the effectiveness of the malus component by making policy adjustments.

The effects of an incentive system depend on the manager's risk attitude and on the investment and financing policies that he or she has available. Moreover, they depend on the bank's internal control system. The effects are therefore difficult to predict for outsiders, which leads to an important conclusion, namely that any outside regulation of bank incentive systems is inappropriate. It might be useful, however, for other market participants interacting with the bank to have

Table 4-7. *Manager Total Income and Shareholder Value for Different Combinations of Volume, Leverage, and Portfolio Rating*[a]

Variable	Total income of manager (in US$ thousands)						Shareholder value (in US$ millions)					
Base salary	40											
Participation rate (percent)	8											
Volume	1	2	10	15	20	25	1	2	10	15	20	25
Borrowing rate (percent)	3.25	3.3	3.36	3.44	3.55	3.75	3.25	3.3	3.38	3.48	3.6	3.75
Rating												
AAA	605.4	891.2	2,913	2,925	**3,065**	2,527	103.9	107.4	135.6	146.9	150.4	135.2
AA	631.7	931.6	**3,008**	**3,284**	1,919	1,813	104.1	108.0	138.3	150.9	155.5	**141.0**
A	648.0	951.1	2,784	3,239	2,834	1,319	**104.2**	**108.2**	**139.2**	**151.8**	**156.3**	140.3
BBB	682.7	936.1	1,875	1,661	1,155	1,149	104.0	108.0	136.0	143.1	138.2	113.1
BB	794.1	990.7	1,310	1,280	1,194	1,132	102.9	106.7	112.1	101.0	87.7	70.4
B	**994.4**	**1,203**	1,482	1,482	1,411	1,344	101.3	104.4	82.2	71.9	64.6	56.5

Source: Authors' calculations.

a. The manager earns a base salary of $40,000; her profit participation rate is 8 percent. The manager cannot be fired. The interest rate paid by the bank increases with volume. Bold figures show the highest total income and highest shareholder value respectively, given volume and leverage, for various portfolios of ratings.

information on the bank's incentive system. That information might improve their understanding of bank risks.

We add a more speculative remark on performance-based compensation regarding the balance between manager income and financial stability. We suspect that managers whose short-term performance has a significant affect on their compensation worry little about the impact of their policies on financial stability. In contrast, managers whose compensation is based on their long-term performance are more concerned about financial stability because they have relatively more to lose through financial turmoil. That effect is likely to be even stronger for managers with a high base salary and low performance-based compensation; in addition, it would be consistent with the view in Osterloh and Frey (2002) that extrinsic motivation crowds out intrinsic motivation.

In other words, we suspect that performance-based compensation reinforces managers' concerns about their income at the expense of public welfare, resulting in financial instability. If one assumes our view to be correct, the compensation package should have a low bonus component, unless it includes a long-term, forward-looking bonus base. Hence it appears that in designing compensation packages, not only should the manager's and shareholders' interests be aligned but also and equally important should the interests of the manager and the public, as reflected in financial stability.

A final remark on compensation and securitization relates to securitization volume. The huge supply of securitization tranches in previous years allowed the manager to acquire loans of any quality in almost unlimited amounts, at constant credit spreads. A similar possibility does not exist in traditional banking. A bank cannot substantially expand its loan business with its own clientele at constant credit spreads; it would have to lower credit spreads or acquire new customers, which usually also requires lower credit spreads, holding default risk constant. That would limit bank expansion and thus risk taking, in contrast to the securitization business.

Observed Effects of Risk Transfer on Loan Quality and Bank Risk Taking

The discussion of incentive problems illustrates a number of threats to the financial system. What is the available empirical evidence?

First, does risk transfer in securitizations undermine the quality of bank lending? There is ample evidence that the lending standards in the U.S. mortgage-backed security (MBS) market have eroded over the past couple of years.[26] The share of subprime loans in overall U.S. MBS lending increased in 2005 and 2006.

26. See, for example, "Fed Shrugged as Subprime Crisis Spread," *New York Times*, December 18, 2007. The article gives an account of many discussions in the Fed regarding mortgage-related lending practices starting in 2000.

It also is likely that the strong increase in U.S. MBS lending would not have been possible without spreading the risks across various parts of the world through securitization, simply because the lending institutions would have run into serious problems with their regulatory capital requirements otherwise. Yet U.S. MBS lending practices cannot simply be generalized to other segments of bank lending. First, in continental Europe, MBS lending has been conservative for the most part over the last few years. Also, credit standards for corporate and private borrowers in Europe have changed somewhat over time, but not significantly.[27] Hence it is difficult to argue that the strong increase in European securitization over the period from 2000 to 2006—which, according to HSBC Global Research (2007), amounted to an average annual growth rate of 40.2 percent, with an issuance volume of about $80 billion in 2000 and about $725 billion in 2006—was based on deterioration of credit standards. Therefore, even if the deterioration of credit standards in the U.S. MBS market was supported by securitization, there is no simple causal link.

Purnanandam (2008) compares mortgage-related write-offs among banks that differ with respect to their involvement in true sale securitizations. The author finds charge-offs to be significantly higher for firms engaged in securitizations and interprets that finding as evidence favoring the hypothesis of loan quality deterioration, a natural consequence of aggressive mortgage lending.

Data limitations have frustrated attempts to estimate the moral hazard effects of MBS securitizations. Keys and others (2008) takes an indirect approach in comparing default rates of loans that, according to the standardized FICO rating, were eligible for a securitization transaction with Fannie Mae and Freddie Mac.[28] After controlling for other possible determining factors, the authors find that loans with a FICO score of above 621 had a default probability that was 20 percent higher (1 percent higher in absolute terms) than FICO-619 loans.[29] The authors explain the difference by the higher likelihood of the FICO-621 loans to be securitized, motivating banks to reduce monitoring of the loans. While the evidence is somewhat indirect—because they cannot show directly that lenders are lenient with borrowers whose loans are securitized—their result is the first widely cited evidence of material incentive problems in securitizations.

Second, regarding financial stability, what matters is not only the impact of securitization on loan quality but also the question of whether securitization

27. The European Central Bank regularly publishes reports on credit standards in its monthly reports.

28. The critical rating below which transfer is ruled out is 620. Thus the study compares loans with a FICO score of 621 to a comparison group with a score of 619.

29. The authors argue that the qualities of firms with FICO scores of 619 and 621 are basically indistinguishable.

makes banks more vulnerable through higher risk taking. Does the risk transfer in securitizations reduce or increase the overall risks taken by securitizing banks?

So far, the existing empirical evidence is not very strong, due to the lack of appropriate studies. The enormous growth in securitizations over the last couple of years is one indicator of a rise in overall risk, since not all the risks have been transferred to outside investors. Worldwide securitization growth rates often exceeded 25 percent over the last years. Some of that growth was also due to arbitrage transactions and therefore does not reflect increased lending. But the numbers do not clearly indicate whether originating banks expand their lending activities because of securitization. Cebenoyan and Strahan (2004) does not find a clear relation between a bank's risk and its securitization activities. Minton, Stulz, and Williamson (2005) looks at bank balance sheet data and finds that securitizing banks tend to buy more protection in the credit derivatives market and also to have low capital ratios. The latter finding is consistent with more risk taking. Franke and Krahnen (2006) analyzes the stock market betas of securitizing banks and finds that they increase with securitization transactions, in particular, with repeated transactions. This finding is consistent with the interpretation that securitizing banks expand their loan portfolios so that the systemic risk of the portfolios increases. According to credit risk models like the model used by the KMV Corporation, the credit risk of a bank should be correlated with stock price movements of borrowers. Hence the market value of a more granular credit portfolio, which also drives bank market value, should be correlated more with the stock market index, leading to higher betas of bank stocks. This finding therefore supports the view that securitizing banks tend to take more credit risk. A related finding is reported in Haensel and Krahnen (2007), suggesting an additional explanation for the rise in systemic risk of banks that securitize their loan book, namely moral hazard. According to that finding, banks with weak balance sheets and poor financial performance are more likely to increase their systematic risk exposure.

To summarize, the process of securitization has led to decomposition of the once-integrated value chain into a string of isolated activities. Those activities should be coordinated in order to avoid moral hazard over the life of the underlying contractual relationship and adverse selection at origination.[30] Effective coordination along the value chain appears hard to implement. The available evidence is still weak, but it clearly suggests a deterioration of the quality of U.S.

---

30. Note that value chain optimization has been a popular project area for bank consultancies like Accenture and Mercer Oliver Wyman, among many others. Given the information technology–driven agenda of these exercises in business process re-engineering, it is at least imaginable that the issue of incentive alignment was largely neglected, leading to the above results.

MBS loans triggered by securitization. The evidence on the effects of securitization on bank risk taking also indicates a positive impact, but more robust tests are needed to establish the relevance of incentive misalignment in securitization transactions to the increase in credit risk.

Ratings and Incentives in Rating Agencies

For remote investors, the quality of structured financial assets is hard to evaluate. When a party is interested in buying protection from others, it is inclined to play down its risks; hence that party's quality assessments typically are not considered credible. In contrast, the quality ratings of the big rating agencies have been regarded with trust by market participants.

As pointed out in the introduction, asset securitization evolved over the 1990s, following the dynamics typical of (financial) innovations (see Ross 1989).[31] Rating agencies played an important role in that process. Riddiough and Chiang (2003) concludes that rating agencies, through the process of standardization, have played "a unique role" in developing and popularizing the market for securitization transactions among investors. As independent experts, agencies evaluated asset portfolios and assigned subordination levels to the tranches with given ratings. Investors apparently trusted such delegated monitoring, acting as if the risk characteristics of securitization tranches were transparent to them. The expertise of major rating agencies and their ability to separate safe, investment-grade assets from risky, non–investment grade assets allowed complex financial instruments, like securitization tranches or CDO^2 notes to be marketed worldwide.

"Investment grade" has become a well-known quality label, even in colloquial language, indicating that a financial instrument carries a low risk of default. Financial instruments with a top rating (AAA) from one of the big agencies are expected to have a very low ex ante default probability. For example, over the past twenty years, the average AAA-rated bond has experienced a one-year default incidence of less than 0.1 percent.[32] For that reason, obtaining an AAA tranche that was as large as possible was a key objective in designing securitization transactions. The flourishing market for AAA tranches relies (or relied) on the credi-

31. As shown in Riddiough and Chiang (2003), a clinical study on the emergence of the structured finance industry, two companies were formative for market development at about the same time (the early 1990s), namely Nomura Securities and Lehman Brothers. The securitization model used by Nomura emphasized a "straightforward" waterfall structure. Due to its simplicity, Nomura became the standard setter for the industry. Lehman, in contrast, was said to focus on complex structured finance products, using lower-quality asset pools. Ironically, at the time of writing, it was apparently Lehman Brothers' own book of structured products, involving protection sold, that eventually brought the firm down.

32. These probabilities are taken from a rating table, which draws on the time series of thousands of bond issues over the past decades.

bility of an independent and reliable rating process. Of course, transparency was only borrowed from the rating agencies, as delegated monitors.

Rating agencies have lost much of their credibility in the current crisis. According to Bank for International Settlements (2008), the dramatic downgrading experienced in October and November 2007 was unheard of among corporate bonds,[33] for which rating migration has followed a fairly stable distribution. The massive wave of downgrades for basically all structured finance asset classes in 2008 has therefore called into question the methodologies used by the agencies to rate such structures. Of the possible reasons for the failure of the rating methodologies, the incentive system in rating agencies is an important one. That belief is supported by witnesses' statements during U.S. congressional hearings held on October 22, 2008, in which former and current managers of rating agencies revealed their perceptions of the ratings crisis.[34]

Before 1970 the rating agencies were paid by investors, who are the recipients and users of ratings. That is in line with standard agency theory: investors demand ratings for their own benefit and therefore should pay to have their interests and those of the rating agencies aligned. After 1970, more and more ratings were solicited by borrowers. That creates a conflict of interest, because borrowers prefer overly optimistic ratings, which can lower their borrowing costs, whereas the rating agencies should produce unbiased ratings, acting on behalf of investors. If borrowers can choose between different agencies, then they can choose the agency that awards the best rating. The standard counterargument claims that rating agencies worry about maintaining their reputation; if they lose that, then neither borrowers nor investors will pay for ratings. The validity of that argument is controversial. It takes a long period of observation to obtain reliable evidence on the quality of ratings or the lack of it. Suppose it takes fifteen years. Most managers in rating agencies will have other responsibilities and positions within the firm or they may have retired by the time any cheating is revealed, so they probably will not have to bear any reputation cost through their income. We therefore are skeptical about the effectiveness of the reputation mechanism. Our skepticism is further reinforced if the management of rating agencies receives large annual bonuses dependent on revenue.

The empirical evidence on compensation and rating activity is mixed. In securitization transactions, agencies were always paid by the arrangers. According to

33. Of the 198 AAA-rated tranches downgraded in this period, the median downgrade was reported to be seven notches, while thirty tranches were downgraded by more than ten notches. Looking at downgrade statistics from 1970 to today, AAA bonds were never downgraded by more than six notches, and even those cases are extremely rare (Bank for International Settlements 2008, p. 22).

34. Fons (2008).

Fons (2008), after 2000 Moody's management focused increasingly on maximizing (short-term) revenues, rather than (long-term) firm value. For structured finance products, agencies handed out client versions of their own rating models, allowing arrangers to game rating standards. According to Raiter (2008), S&P had developed better rating models over the years but never implemented them due to high costs.[35] Also, rating agencies did not subject the loan data provided by investment banks to proper due diligence; they relied instead on the assessment information provided with the data. The excuse was that investment bankers usually had hired specialized firms to perform due diligence. We conjecture that the lax standards can best be explained by an incentive system that awards managers bonuses that depend on fee income.

A related question is whether the rating standards applied by the agencies may have deteriorated over time. While Fons and Raiter support that view, the rating agencies deny it. Blume, Lim, and McKinlay (1998) largely confirms the stability of the rating process for corporate bonds; rather than any loosening of rating standards over time, they find a slight tightening. Their findings are consistent with those of theoretical models of the rating industry, which emphasize credibility and reputation with respect to firm monitoring (see, for instance, Millon and Thakor 1985).[36] A similar study addressing standards of structured finance ratings is not available.

However, in a study of transactions involving commercial mortgage–backed securities (CMBSs), Downing, Stanton, and Wallace (2008) documents that the subordination levels for tranches declined significantly over time. The average subordination level for AAA-rated tranches was about 36 percent in 1996 and declined to less than 15 percent in 2005. Similar declines were reported for AA- and A-rated tranches. The authors argue that some of the decline was driven by the low levels of defaults in recent years, but longer histories showed much higher default rates, suggesting a practice of excessively low subordination levels. That, in turn, is consistent with the view that rating standards in the securitization business have been lowered over time. However, the current chairman and CEO of Moody's, Ray McDaniel, argues that his company began warning about subprime

35. Raiter is a former S&P managing director.
36. More recent studies stress the two-way interaction between rating agencies and firms concerning, for example, capital structure and investment decisions. For example, Kisgen (2006), drawing on the theoretical work by Boot, Milbourn, and Schmeits (2006), shows that firms at risk of losing a particular rating notch try to "improve" their capital structure—that is, to issue less debt relative to equity than they would otherwise. The author concludes that firms make some effort to meet standards set by agencies, which shows that rating downgrades are in fact costly for firms.

market quality back in 2003, and accordingly raised the subordination levels by about 30 percent between 2003 and 2006.[37]

Regarding incentive misalignments, Deven Sharma, the current president of S&P, and McDaniel argue that rating analysts do not get bonuses related to fee income from companies that they rate; therefore, they should have no incentive to lower rating standards.[38] That argument is weak, however. If the managers and rating analysts receive bonus payments depending on the overall revenue of the rating agency, then that promotes an atmosphere of joint revenue maximization, and lowering standards can certainly help to achieve that objective. The argument based on long-term reputation costs may again be dismissed, as above.

We therefore believe that the performance-oriented pay of managers and rating analysts in rating agencies promotes deterioration of rating standards. That hazard can be mitigated by internal measures to safeguard rating standards, but it cannot be ruled out entirely. One self-imposed response might be to restrict performance-oriented pay components in favor of higher fixed salaries. In any case, investors are warned not to accept ratings naively as a reliable sign of quality.

The Transparency Failure

Lack of transparency is often mentioned as one of the main drivers of the asset market and of interbank market illiquidity. Transparency has different meanings in this context, one being transparency about the quality of financial assets, the other being transparency of counterparty risks in the interbank market. We start with the transparency of asset quality.

Transparency of Asset Quality

Before the crisis, asset quality was considered transparent because investors trusted the ratings assigned by the rating agencies. Standard discounted cash flow models were applied based on the ratings and the risk premiums observed in neighboring markets. After the avalanche of downgrades at the end of 2007, confidence in ratings was badly disturbed. Hence, the standard valuation model could not be applied because the necessary data were lacking, and asset valuation became nontransparent.

That lack of transparency relating to tranches is reinforced by three factors, which presumably were unknown to most investors. First, tranching results are very susceptible to the distributional assumptions describing the underlying pool

---

37. McDaniel (2008).
38. Sharma (2008) and McDaniel (2008).

of claims, in particular asset correlations and the moments of the portfolio loss rate distribution.[39] Second, AAA tranches and corporate bonds of the same rating quality possess very different sensitivities to macro risk factors, as illustrated in Krahnen and Wilde (2008). Given the same default probability for tranches and bonds—for example, 1 percent for a maturity of ten years—macro factor sensitivity is much stronger for the tranche than for the bond. That is due to the strong diversification in AAA tranches, making them more sensitive than bonds to macro factor deterioration.

Such differences in sensitivities were not widely known, and they certainly were not reported to the outside investor.[40] Even experts in the industry saw hardly any need to add caveats to the use of well-known bond ratings in assessing the default risk of tranches from a securitization transaction.

Third, a first-order stochastic dominance deterioration of the loss rate distribution raises the expected loss of the first loss piece and of the AAA tranche. That is relevant for our analysis because a key piece of information, typically not reported to outside investors, may have a strong impact on both the actual portfolio loss rate as well as the loss rate expected by the market. That critical piece of information is the originator's retention of the FLP, because of its likely effect on management incentives.[41] As stated above, despite all efforts by analysts and researchers, there exists no overview of first loss piece allocation. Perhaps financial institutions have not yet recognized the signaling potential that a revelation of equity retention could have on the market.[42]

It is therefore necessary to have information on the retention decision if one wishes to estimate the default risk of an asset portfolio and securitization tranches. Rating agencies may have some knowledge about the whereabouts of equity pieces, but apparently they have not made use of the information. Furthermore, it appears that the retention question typically was not discussed among model builders, as they probably felt it to be irrelevant for their estimations.[43] Since

---

39. See Krahnen and Wilde (2008); Franke and Hein (2008).

40. Gibson (2004) presents a detailed description of the pooling and tranching methodology used by the major agencies.

41. A more complete presentation of this argument will have to lay out the value-enhancing effect of long-term relationships, accompanied by risk underwriting and therefore long-term incentive alignment concerning initial screening, intensive monitoring, and proper bailout incentives (see Brunner and Krahnen 2008).

42. In an ECB conference on financial market statistics in 2006, the need for detailed information on equity piece allocation was discussed and proposals for implementation were presented as a novel idea; see Haensel, Krahnen, and Wilde (2006).

43. Despite many attempts by both authors to address this topic in workshops with practitioners, mostly financial engineers, and in industry gatherings since 2004, the question never elicited a serious response or debate. Another sign of complete negligence vis-à-vis the incentive issue relates to the techni-

models rely on historical loan portfolio data in validating ratings, the models used by the agencies may fail to recognize the importance of first loss piece retention.

The issue of opaqueness of effective risk allocation has been addressed by several studies, for example, Gorton (2008) and Brunnermeier (2009). Their authors point at the complexity of the pooling and tranching methodology and the difficulty of seeing through the many layers of CDOs and conduits and other financial institutions. However, they do not address the retention decision, which we believe to be at the core of the problem.[44]

To summarize, we find transparency about financial assets, securitization tranches in particular, to be very poor, notably following the breakdown of confidence in ratings, which resulted in lack of the data needed for valuing securitization tranches. It therefore is not surprising that the issue of opacity was seriously discussed only after mid-2007, perhaps because many investors had become aware of incentive misalignments by that time.[45]

Transparency of Counterparty Risks

In 2008, several investment banks collapsed almost overnight, even though their Tier 1 and Tier 2 capital ratios were clearly above the levels required by Basel 2. Speculators' short selling of stocks of these banks proved very profitable; subsequently, short selling was restricted in many countries. That raises the question of why the banks apparently could not regain market confidence and survive. Our explanation relies on a lack of transparency concerning counterparty risks. Even though banks publish quarterly accounts, the reports provide only limited insight into a bank's risk position; even fellow banks will find it hard to evaluate the risk exposure of their peers. For example, consider the value-at-risk figures that had been disclosed by banks in the years before the onset of the crisis. Those numbers were said to be in the low three-digit US$ millions, even for large international banks—

---

cal manuals published by the rating agencies that explain their modeling techniques. While the manuals do not specify all the details, presumably to avoid duplication of techniques by rivals and customers, we could not find any hint of the sort of retention-related agency problems that we address.

44. Note that opaqueness relating to the location of senior tranches, mentioned in Gorton (2008), will have little if any repercussions on the underlying asset value. Hence senior tranche opaqueness will have less dramatic consequences than junior tranche opaqueness. Interestingly, it is apparently easier to obtain information on the allocation of senior tranches. See the table "Estimated Holdings of AAA CDO Tranches" in Gorton (2008, p. 43), which shows a breakdown of holdings by type of buyer. Similar tables for junior tranches do not exist.

45. In a speech on the subprime lending market given on May 17, 2007, Ben Bernanke concluded: "In sum, some misalignment of incentives, together with a highly competitive lending environment and, perhaps, the fact that industry experience with subprime mortgage lending is relatively short, likely compromised the quality of underwriting" (Bernanke 2007).

small numbers compared with the figures for the subsequent write-downs in 2007 and 2008.

We argue that the nontransparency of the quality of financial assets translates into nontransparency of the balance sheets of the financial intermediaries holding the assets. Consider the models used by banks for determining write-downs of their financial assets. The high level of write-downs shown by many international financial institutions over the 2007–08 period may be due to the fall of secondary market prices. However, it may also be due to bank reporting policy, independent of market price movements. Finally, lack of transparency of bank risk is also a consequence of risk fungibility. Banks can alter their risk position very quickly by using financial assets, financial derivatives in particular. Since most of the time derivatives can be traded with little impact on liquidity, such transactions are especially easy to carry out.

These arguments explain why bank risks are difficult to evaluate from the out-side; they also explain why risk reporting of banks is an important topic on the current policy agenda. The obvious implication of the risk evaluation challenge pertains to evaluation of counterparty risk. Another implication is that a bank cannot easily invalidate adverse rumors about its solvency, rendering itself vulnerable to speculative attacks.

Here we see another "private good, public bad" problem. Bank managers consider information about "their" bank risk to be valuable private information and therefore are reluctant to disclose it to the public. At the same time, financial markets cannot work properly without sufficient information on bank risks; hence that information has the character of a public good. By not disclosing the information, managers try to free ride on financial stability—that is, they hope that they can extract all the benefits from trading in financial markets without making the contributions necessary to the proper functioning of the markets.

Liquidity

The preceding arguments relate closely to loss of market liquidity, which has been widely documented.[46] Liquidity loss is observed in financial asset markets as well as in the interbank market. Market microstructure research has emphasized the importance of information on trading and pricing of financial assets. Glosten and Milgrom (1985), among other studies, has argued that transaction costs on asset markets, reflecting liquidity, increase with asymmetry of information among market participants. The stronger the information asymmetries, the higher the

---

46. See Allen and Carletti (2008) and Brunnermeier (2009) on the enormous loss in liquidity emanating from the CDO market and then spreading to neighboring markets with similar opacity characteristics.

bid-ask spread required by market makers to insure themselves against a bad trade with an informed party.

By a similar argument, the ask price for an asset will be inversely related to the degree of asset opacity. The term "opacity" describes the extent to which a buyer, using available information, is able to asses the "true" cash flow distribution of an asset and thus its riskiness. Caballero and Krishnamurthy (2008) models these opaque situations as Knightian uncertainty, in which probabilities are unknown. Buyers may then follow min-max strategies in these situations, focusing on the extreme scenario. Thus, with high levels of opacity, prices may drop significantly.

Hence, the liquidity (or rather illiquidity) of an asset can be related to the information regime. As argued previously, transparency about securitization tranches is impaired by lack of information on the agency problems in the value chain. Equally, transparency impairment results from a lack of information on FLP retention and on the quality and stability of agency ratings. Apparently, before the onset of the crisis, that lack of information was not felt to be critical by investors. When investors became aware of the transparency failure, asset market liquidity collapsed. Furthermore, the opacity of asset values may translate into opacity of financial intermediaries trading those assets (see also Adrian and Shin 2007). Given this and the lack of reliable reporting of bank risk, the interbank market largely disappeared as well.

We therefore believe that the liquidity loss in secondary markets for notes, bonds, and commercial paper as well as the shutdown of the interbank market is not a natural disaster caused by a sudden decline of U.S. house prices nor is it the consequence of euphoria and fear in asset markets. Rather, it is, at least in part, an implication of externalities imposed on financial market stability by financial intermediaries that used securitization technology without regard to the stability of the quality of underlying assets.

The Future of Securitization

Taking a helicopter view of today's financial market turmoil, one is inevitably reminded of an old economic tale, the tragedy of the commons. The term originally was coined by Gerrit Hardin in his seminal article in *Science*, in which he recounts the story of the demise of community grazing land open to all residents of a township.[47] The upshot is, of course, that individuals pursuing their self-interest may exert external effects in the form of overgrazing, ultimately destroying the common resource.

---

47. Hardin (1968).

The crisis that we are now witnessing has some analogous characteristics. Financial stability may be seen as a commons, undermined by the overleveraging of standard banking activities, the erosion of real estate loan quality, and the design of complex financial instruments. Market liquidity eroded to the point of complete market disruption, and prices fell to levels unimaginable at the time of issue.

Still, looking down from the helicopter, we now realize that misaligned incentives on the micro level—that is, the pursuit of individual happiness on the firm level—can lead to complete opacity on the macro level, eliminating vital market functionalities, namely pricing efficiency, market depth, and liquidity. Of course, deficiencies on the micro level are not universal. A large number of financial intermediaries maintained a prudent policy over the last years. But others, including some large players, did not. That caused the contagion, which first affected those players but then undermined confidence in the financial system on a large scale, with far-reaching effects.

As we have tried to show, this crisis is a "rational crisis." It is not the result of irrational exuberance of any sort, nor is it the consequence of euphoria and fear, as some observers have argued (see Greenspan 2008). We have identified weaknesses and violations of rules of prudent financial engineering that may be called the root cause of the immense degradation of asset value over the period from the middle of 2007 to the end of 2008. These violations also have contributed to the significant drying up of market liquidity in several of the most popular financial instruments of the last decade, like CDOs, commercial paper, and ABSs in general.

We thus deliver a structural explanation of why the crisis was to be expected, given the incentives of market participants and the inadequacy of the current rules of the game. These structural faults refer mainly to the design of securitization transactions, which in turn determine the subsequent decisionmaking of banks, firms, and households. Consider incentive-compatible engineering. The tranching of asset portfolios, which is the key construction element of these transactions, did not (or not sufficiently) take into consideration the externality that a loan sale exerts on loan quality, both ex ante and ex post. Since incentive alignment can minimize that externality, one would have expected investors to ask for ample information describing incentive arrangements in these transactions. But nothing of that sort happened; nor did the issuers inform the market or the rating agencies publicly address the question of incentive compatibility.[48]

---

48. However, industry experts acknowledge that large institutional investors typically have forced originators to retain the first loss before investing in these products.

As a result, the market was flooded with financial instruments whose underlying quality was doomed to deteriorate over time. The degradation of asset quality came as a surprise to most individual and institutional investors, whose trust in agency ratings was badly damaged. Investors responded rationally by shutting down the market.

However, a question remains: why did financial engineers and managers pursue a strategy that created externalities in the first place? We have offered our view, but we acknowledge the existence of other explanations that produce similar predictions. Research may eventually tell the full story. One plausible explanation starts with an individual manager using securitization to maximize his or her wealth. The ensuing transfer of long-term assets from the balance sheet to investors in the market allows reaping almost risk-free profits at the time of issue but weakens long-term incentives.

To see how, consider a set of assets held on the balance sheet, producing a stream of profits over time. The very same set of assets securitized and sold in the market will earn the originator an almost risk-free first profit position. If the originator fully sells the FLP, then he or she is left with a position that is almost equivalent to a gain on sale. Thus, securitization allows for front-end loading of the transaction, although it would have produced more back-end loaded profits if retained on the balance sheet.

If bank management is motivated by some profit-sharing bonus, we predict that bank managers will be interested in asset securitization simply because it may increase their income without imposing any commensurate risk premium—the risk in the form of increased default probabilities is borne for the most part by shareholders and third parties in case of bank insolvency. In other words, the incentive to expand securitizations was reinforced by the fact that the management payoff was cashed out as a bonus well before the externality was felt in the profit-and-loss statements of the bank. In addition, profit sharing through bonuses without an appropriate malus reflecting downside risk may have invited managers to increase bank risks, since managers could appropriate returns privately while the added risks were borne largely by shareholders and third parties.[49]

Who, then, is to blame? We claim that, apart from the lack of a malus component in compensation, internal accounting rules for deriving bonus bases were not designed for the "hybrid" world of modern banking that has emerged over the past ten years. To date, there is no explicit accounting for future losses and risks in profit-and-loss statements. Thus, by marketing information-sensitive assets, financial intermediaries could realize and distribute profits that otherwise would

49. Of course, a malus can be imposed by giving the manager a share in the terminal value at date zero.

accrue only in later years and only under favorable ("normal") circumstances. The intertemporal transfer of earnings (to the present time) partially explains the enormous interest of investment bankers in these transactions, and it also explains why such transactions simultaneously tended to undermine the real value of the underlying portfolios.[50]

We now turn to the policy options, taking our structural explanation of the crisis as the foundation for policymaking. Since we see negative externalities at work, there is indeed a case for policy intervention. The aim is to internalize to the extent possible the externalities found in the markets.

Securitization 2.0

If we go back a few years, we encounter another financial crisis that has shaped our understanding of equity markets. Around the year 2000, the so-called dotcom bubble, a drastic fall in stock prices of mostly young technology firms, wiped out the wealth of many equity investors. Preceding the crisis was a long and enormous rise in market valuation for high-tech firms, which eventually proved to be unsustainable. Of particular importance in these markets were web-oriented business models. In hindsight, it is clear that many of the firms did not have a sustainable business model.

Only a few years later, the market is embracing a number of successful firms that are built on very similar web-based business models, but these firms are said to cope much better with the difficulties of generating earnings on the otherwise free, open-access Internet. The amended business models often are subsumed under the heading "Web 2.0" to indicate their advanced degree of sophistication (O'Reilly 2007). But in fact, the now-successful enterprises have profited from the dotcom bubble as an important learning experience.

In quite a similar fashion we expect securitization to face a strong future—after it digests the lessons of the current credit crisis. That is why we look for the minimum government intervention required to ensure that those lessons have an effect in the markets. Our recommendations fall into three broad categories, which we refer to as incentive-related, transparency-related on the microlevel, and transparency-related on the macrolevel.

Incentive Alignment and Compensation

As explained, the lack of public information on the status of incentive alignment along the securitization value chain is probably the single most important

---

50. Ralf Ewert alluded to the Enron and Worldcom cases, which display quite similar features, notably concerning the use of earnings preponement. See Benston and Hartgraves (2002).

reason for the recent investor strike.[51] That insight, however, does not imply that the arrangers should be forced to retain a specified fraction of the issue, as suggested in a recent legislative proposal of the European Parliament. It does not even imply that arrangers ought to retain any part of the issue, provided that investors know that they don't.

The analysis suggests instead that for each issue, the market needs to know precisely what incentives the agents in the value chain have to safeguard loan quality. In particular, it is important to communicate the extent to which the arranger and other agents retain the first loss piece. Regardless of whether an investor is a monitoring specialist like the local commercial bank or a banking amateur like a pension fund, once the investor knows how the first loss piece is allocated, it should be able to understand the risk implications. We claim therefore that public information about incentive alignment, by issuer, will lead the market to sort it out and to establish different prices that reflect incentive alignment or the lack thereof. That implies that differences in incentive alignment become visible in a separating instead of a pooling equilibrium.

Once prices reflect individual qualities, opacity is diminished, as is necessary for liquid asset markets. With transparency regarding the holding of the first loss piece, arrangers will internalize the effects of selling the equity piece, and we predict that substantial first loss piece retention will be the model of choice whenever the underlying assets are highly information sensitive.[52] In other words, investors will buy tranches only if there is effective retention of the first loss piece.

In practice, retention alone will not be sufficient for "comprehensive incentive alignment," as we have explained. However, that information can be amended by a more comprehensive measure of incentive alignment throughout the securitization value chain that could be produced and continuously monitored by independent information providers. Whether or not auditing firms and rating agencies are independent probably depends on their business model. Ideally, the market reaction to this information would induce the arranger to reshape the value chain so as to mitigate incentive problems. We therefore expect to see some re-intermediation.

Our suggestion emphasizes public information on incentive alignment in order to give it the prominence it deserves, which is mostly lacking in today's ABS markets. We are confident that the industry will quickly develop reasonable standards that allow internalizing incentive alignment in valuation models.

---

51. The term "investor strike" refers to the refusal of private and institutional investors and banks to buy securitization tranches.

52. "Information-sensitive" in this context refers to underlying assets that are prone to adverse selection and moral hazard.

We argue that front-end loading in securitization transactions is one reason why performance-oriented remuneration generates perverse incentives; here "perverse" means without proper regard to the implications for the longer-term quality of the underlying assets. Compensation systems provide strong incentives for transactions that allow for large gains on sale, for example, through first profit positions.[53] Risks imposed on others tend to be ignored. Moreover, the incentives stemming from annual bonuses depend on the accounting of the bonus base, which, in turn, is closely related to accounting method. If the profit in early years does not correctly anticipate losses and risks, then the present value of manager bonuses will be overstated because it includes risk premiums for subsequent years. Accountants need to develop models that take those risks into account properly. If managers do not face downside risk—for example, through a malus—we should not be surprised to find them selecting high rates of bank leverage. A malus needs to be built into the compensation model, shifting profits into the future so that the manager bears more of the risk.

If one looks for remedies against departures from incentive-compatible back-end loaded compensation, there is not much room for the regulator. The only instrument available to encourage incentive harmonization is, once again, transparency. Let investors know what compensation a deal produces and they will learn how to sort out the major incentive problems. Furthermore, once the market differentiates between deals according to the design of their incentives, there will be competitive pressure in the financial industry to install appropriate compensation systems.

Once again, independent information providers are candidates for the task of producing information about compensation-related incentive alignment, regularly updating that information, and communicating it to the market. Rating agencies have demonstrated in the past that even coarse information systems, like bond rating schemes, can fulfill that task quite well. While we see a positive role for the regulator in getting such a reporting system started, we see no role in designing the compensation system.

Rating

While we appreciate the improved access to statistical data, particularly for research purposes, that is not the kind of transparency required to liquefy ABS markets. As argued before, the key providers of information to investors in these

---

53. In addition, the accounting for retained tranches—in particular, the equity tranche—poses serious problems. These tranches are booked at fair values. Since there is no active market for them, management has discretion to select a value. In effect, management can select, within certain boundaries, the size of the gain to be booked into the income statement. See for example Dechow, Myers, and Shakespeare (2007) and

markets are rating agencies,[54] which have a strong record of judging default risk of corporate bonds but were not adequately prepared to handle asset-backed securities.

Proposals to regulate the rating industry abound. A major concern is the conflict of interest between investors and rating agencies, which are paid by the bond issuers. We are not in a position to present entirely new proposals. However, we see a major problem in the compensation system of rating agencies, which includes strong performance-related components. Performance cannot be measured easily by the quality of ratings because quality becomes visible only after a long time. Currently performance with respect to compensation is typically measured by the fee income of the agencies, creating a substantial conflict with rating quality. Hence, the compensation of employees of rating agencies should be independent of agency fee income. Compensation that is less dependent on performance might be viewed by investors as a sign of quality.

Is regulation required? We see a positive role for regulation in principle, although one that is perhaps very different in substance from what we have seen in the literature or the political arena. More precisely, we are skeptical about having regulatory bodies regulate any technical detail of the rating method or requiring a rating agency to make its methodology public. Agencies should be free to develop their own methodology, just as they have successfully done in the case of corporate bond ratings.

Regarding transparency of rating agencies, we see three areas on which a regulatory body might publish data. First, regarding the short term, investors should know to what extent rating agencies carry out first-hand due diligence as part of the rating process. The reported lack of any proper due diligence in the case of MBS transactions is a sign of serious incentive misalignment that presumably facilitates the lowering of credit standards. Second, the regulatory body should assess the implications of the incentives used by the rating agencies in developing their compensation systems. Third, regarding the long term, regulatory bodies could publish information on performance. Rating performance refers to the validity of rating assignments—that is, the accuracy with which the announced default probability predicts default. There is a set of common accuracy statistics. In theory, accuracy determines the economic value of agency ratings. Solid rating requires a precise and long-lived database of assigned ratings and observed defaults and an independent body to warehouse and analyze the

---

Karaoglu (2005). There is some evidence in the empirical accounting literature that earnings management in gains-on-sale transactions is indeed an issue; see, for instance, Dechow and Shakespeare (2006).

54. Because rating information reports broad rating notches only and does not provide continuous updates, it is coarse and slow, but it nevertheless is relevant for remote investors.

data. That also includes the difficult task of reliably estimating default correlations in asset portfolios or, even more complicated, in copula parameters. Otherwise, tranching of portfolios cannot be viable. Today, investors rely on performance statistics disclosed by the agencies themselves, which may be biased due
to conflicts of interest.

Reducing Opacity:
Differential Capital Charges and Comprehensive Exposure Survey

While our previous recommendations addressed opacity in incentives and asset
quality, the following recommendations address opacity in banks and risk exposure of the banking sector. Bank managers have strong incentives to hide information on financial assets and on the risks of their institutions. That leads to
opacity on the macro level and impairs liquidity of asset markets and of the interbank market—that is, it generates negative externalities. Capital regulation can be
used to encourage financial institutions to increase transparency; one way is
through capital charges that are inversely related to transparency. Requiring banks
to hold equity against opacity in addition to holding capital against risk-weighted
assets would be an innovation in capital regulation. It explicitly addresses incentive problems at the bank level through capital requirements. Note that such a
regulatory extension need not imply an increase in overall capital charges. If, for
example, an average capital charge of 8 percent is desired, the differential charges
may range from 6 percent for very transparent banks to a charge of 10 percent for
institutions with low transparency.[55] Differential charges signal to banks that
more transparency pays off, stabilizing financial markets at the same time. We
have no recommendations on how to construct an opacity index for banks. That
is not an easy job, and is as difficult as bank risk reporting.

Another transparency issue that we have not addressed so far refers to sector-specific information, in particular information on the exposure of the banking sector
to particular risks. A single bank may be strongly exposed to some (idiosyncratic)
risks without endangering financial stability if those risks materialize. If, however,
the banking sector is systematically exposed, then such risks may easily destabilize
the financial system as a whole. Therefore, sector-specific information can act as an
early warning device, encouraging banks to be careful when underwriting those
risks.[56] Central banks and supervisors should be able to map out the allocation and
distribution of risk exposures in financial markets. That clearly is not done today,

---

55. How to determine the incentive alignment score is still an open question; we do not go into any
details here.
56. It might also have the opposite effect if bank managers herd—that is, select highly correlated risks.

and some research effort is needed to develop concepts and tools for drawing what one may call an international risk map.

In many ways, that is what the BIS has attempted to do over the past few years. No doubt, BIS reports will become more recognized after this crisis, as they pointed out the weaknesses of the once-celebrated risk-transfer market as early as 2005. Comprehensive risk reporting has to look at the large financial institutions, including entities that so far have managed to avoid the reporting obligations demanded by regulatory bodies, like hedge funds, or institutions domiciled in off-shore financial centers. The comprehensive risk survey that we envisage is a periodic rather than a continuous exercise, with the objective of providing an early warning system for market participants and regulators alike.

The early warning mechanism can be strengthened further by setting up an international credit register that aggregates liabilities on the debtor level. If the scope of such a credit register is defined to encompass financial institutions as well, for the first time supervisors will have a database that allows them to evaluate systemic risk.[57]

Summing up: Proposed Regulatory Measures

Building on our analysis of how misaligned incentives at the bank level can bring down the entire financial market if many banks use such incentives, we propose five regulatory measures whose objective is to restructure the now-defunct asset and interbank markets:

—First, require transparency with respect to tranche allocation in all ABS transactions, especially concerning first loss pieces.

—Second, ensure transparency regarding the use of front- and back-end loaded compensation systems, including a balance between bonus and malus components. A methodology has to be developed to measure transparency, and independent information providers should publish the information when it becomes available.

—Third, make information on the compensation system of rating agencies publicly available. Moreover, validate the information content of agency ratings for corporate bonds and for securitization tranches by credible and independent institutions, such as supervisory bodies and auditors.

—Fourth, impose opacity-related capital charges in addition to risk-related charges in order to regulate banks. Again, the metric for capturing degrees of opacity still has to be developed, but we are confident that it is possible to do so.

57. There also may be indirect measures of systemic risk, like the correlations of bank stock prices with a market index, as suggested in Haensel, Krahnen, and Wilde (2006).

—Fifth, aggregate the risk exposures of financial institutions across countries and over time and report them in order to provide a complete picture of the sector exposure (a global risk map).

These five rules for greater transparency and soundness are less severe than many of the ambitious regulatory proposals that are being discussed in the public domain today. Our main reservation regarding these proposals is that often they are not sufficiently backed by theory or empirical research and that dysfunctional proposals are hard to correct. An example is a recent legislative proposal of the European Parliament requiring banks to retain 10 percent flat of every securitized transaction. The German government went even further, demanding 20 percent retention on all asset-backed securitizations. However, forced retention cannot be derived from theory. Conversely, the X percent-retention rule actually invites banks to bypass its intended effects and to game the loss rate distribution. We believe that investors can learn, so that it should be sufficient to force banks to publicly disclose their retention decision.

In concluding we point out that currently there are two camps in the debate. One stresses the hypothesis that the credit crisis that we are witnessing today was caused by an exogenous liquidity or solvency shock, with prices diverging from fundamental values, and employs limits-to-arbitrage arguments to rationalize the enduring fall in prices. In contrast, the second camp claims that the credit crisis is all about incentives—or rather, about misaligned incentives and the ensuing lack of transparency. We clearly belong to the second camp. We advocate transparency in order to stimulate investor reactions, which in turn induce institutions to adopt prudent incentive systems.

References

Adrian T., and H. S. Shin. 2007. "Liquidity and Leverage." Discussion paper. Federal Reserve Bank of New York and Princeton University, Bendheim Center for Finance.

Allen F., and E. Carletti. 2008. "The Role of Liquidity in Financial Crises." 2008 Jackson Hole Symposium. August 21–23, Jackson Hole, Wyoming, sponsored by the Federal Reserve Bank of Kansas City.

Allen F., and D. Gale. 2007. *Understanding Financial Crises*. Oxford University Press.

Arrow, K. J. 1971. Control in Large Organizations: Essays in the Theory of Risk-Bearing. Markham Publishing Co.

Ashcroft, A. B., and T. Schuermann. 2007. Understanding the Securitization of Subprime Mortgage Credit. Federal Reserve Bank of New York.

Bank for International Settlements. 2008. Credit Risk Transfer: Developments from 2005 to 2007.

Bank of England. 2008. *Financial Stability Report 23*.

Benston, G. J., and Al L. Hartgraves. 2002. "Enron: What Happened and What We Can Learn from It." *Journal of Accounting and Public Policy* 21: 105–27.

Bernanke, B. S. 2007. "The Subprime Mortgage Market." Speech delivered at the 43rd Annual Conference on Bank Structure and Competition, Federal Reserve Bank of Chicago, May 17, 2007 (www.federalreserve.gov/boarddocs/speeches/2007/20070517/default.htm).

Bloomberg. 2008. Investment Tools. 3Y-Chart TEDSP:INI (www.bloomberg.com/apps/cbuilder?ticker1=.TEDSP%3AIND).

Blume, M. E., F. Lim, and A. C. McKinlay. 1998. "The Declining Credit Quality of U.S. Corporate Debt: Myth or Reality?" *Journal of Finance* 53: 1389–413.

Boot, A. W. A., T. T. Milbourn, and A. Schmeits. 2006. "Credit Ratings as Coordination Mechanisms." *Review of Financial Studies* 19 (1): 81–118.

British Bankers Association. 2006. *Credit Derivatives Report.* September (www.bba.org.uk/content/1/c4/76/71/Credit_derivative_report_2006_exec_summary.pdf).

Brunner, A., and J. P. Krahnen. 2008. "Multiple Lenders and Corporate Distress: Evidence on Debt Restructuring." *Review of Economic Studies* 75 (2): 415–42.

Brunnermeier, M. 2009. "Deciphering the 2007–08 Liquidity and Credit Crunch," *Journal of Economic Perspectives* 23 (1): 77–100.

Caballero, R., and A. Krishnamurthy. 2008. "Collective Risk Management in a Flight to Quality Episode." *Journal of Finance* 48: 2195–230.

Cebenoyan, A. S., and P. E. Strahan. 2004. "Risk Management, Capital Structure, and Lending at Banks." *Journal of Banking and Finance* 28: 19–43.

Coates, J. C. 2007. "The Goals and Promise of the Sarbanes-Oxley Act." *Journal of Economic Perspectives* 21 (1): 91–116.

Coles, J. L., N. D. Daniel, and L. Naveen. 2006. "Managerial Incentives and Risk Taking." *Journal of Financial Economics* 79: 431–68.

Dechow, P. M., and C. Shakespeare. 2006. "Do Managers Time Securitization Transactions to Obtain Accounting Benefits?" Working paper, University of California at Berkeley, Haas School of Business, and University of Michigan, Stephen M. Ross School of Business.

Dechow, P. M., L. A. Myers, and C. Shakespeare. 2007. "Fair Value Accounting and Gains from Asset Securitizations: A Convenient Earnings Management Tool with Compensation Side-Benefits." Working paper, University of California at Berkeley, Haas School of Business, and University of Michigan, Stephen M. Ross School of Business.

DeMarzo, P. 2005. "The Pooling and Tranching of Securities: A Model of Informed Intermediation." *Review of Financial Studies* 18: 1–35.

Doherty, N. A., and K. Smetters. 2005. "Moral Hazard in Reinsurance Markets." *Journal of Risk and Insurance* 72 (3): 375–91.

Downing, C., R. Stanton, and N. Wallace. 2008. "Volatility, Mortgage Default, and CMBS Subordination." Working paper. University of California at Berkeley.

Duffie, D., and P. de Marzo. 1999. "A Liquidity-Based Model of Security Design." *Econometrica* 67: 65–99.

DZ Bank. 2008. *Der gordische Knoten* [The Gordian Knot]. Research publication. September 19.

Financial Stability Forum. 2008. *Report of the Financial Stability Forum on Enhancing Market and Institutional Resilience.*

Fons, J. S. 2008. *Credit Rating Agencies and the Financial Crisis.* Written testimony before the U.S. House Committee on Oversight and Government Reform, 110 Cong., October 22.

Franke, G., and J. P. Krahnen. 2006. "Default Risk Sharing between Banks and Markets: The Contribution of Collateralized Debt Obligations. In *The Risks of Financial Institutions*, edited by M. Carey and R. Stulz, pp. 603–34. Cambridge, Mass.: National Bureau of Economic Research.

Franke, G., M. Herrmann, and T. Weber. 2007. "Information Asymmetries and Securitization Design." Working paper. University of Konstanz.

Franke, G., and J. Hein. 2008. "Securitization of Mezzanine Capital in Germany." *Financial Markets and Portfolio Management* 22: 219–40.

Gibson, M. 2004. "Understanding the Risk of Synthetic CDOs," Finance and Economics Discussion Series. Federal Reserve Board.

Glosten, L., and P. Milgrom. 1985. "Bid, Ask, and Transaction Prices in a Specialist Market with Heterogeneously Informed Agents." *Journal of Financial Economics* 14 (1): 71–100.

Goodhart, C., and A. Persaud. 2008. "How to Avoid the Next Crash." *Financial Times*, January, 20.

Gorton, G. 2008. "The Panic of 2007." 2008 Jackson Hole Symposium. August 21–23, Jackson Hole, Wyoming, sponsored by the Federal Reserve Bank of Kansas City.

Greenbaum, S., and A. Thakor. 1987. "Bank Funding Modes." *Journal of Banking and Finance* 11: 379–401.

Greenspan, A. 2008. "We Will Never Have a Perfect Model of Risk." *Financial Times*, March 16 (www.ft.com/cms/s/0/edbdbcf6-f360-11dc-b6bc-0000779fd2ac.html?nclick check=1).

Haensel, D., and J. P. Krahnen. 2007. "Does Credit Securitization Reduce Bank Risk? Evidence from the European CDO Market." Working paper. Goethe-University Frankfurt.

Haensel, D., J. P. Krahnen, and C. Wilde. 2006. "Monitoring Risk Transfer in Capital Markets: Statistical Implications." Paper prepared for *Financial Statistics for a Global Economy*, Third ECB Conference on Statistics. May 4–5, Frankfurt.

Hardin, G. 1968. "The Tragedy of the Commons." *Science* 162: 1243.

Hodder, J., and J. Jackwerth. 2007. "Incentive Contracts and Hedge Fund Management." *Journal of Financial and Quantitative Analysis* 42: 811–26.

HSBC Global Research. 2007. "Global ABS and Covered Bonds 2008." December 20, p. 7 (www.hsbc.research.com).

Jin, L. 2002. "CEO Compensation, Diversification, and Incentives." *Journal of Financial Economics* 66: 29–63.

Karaoglu, N. E. 2005. "Regulatory Capital and Earnings Management in Banks: The Case of Loan Sales and Securitizations." Working Paper 2005-05. Federal Deposit Insurance Corporation Center for Financial Research.

Kashyap, A. K., R. G. Rajan, and J. C. Stein. 2008. "Rethinking Capital Regulation." Conference draft. University of Chicago and Harvard University.

Keys, B. J., and others. 2008. "Securitization and Screening: Evidence from Subprime Mortgage–Backed Securities." Working paper. London Business School.

Kisgen, D. J. 2006. "Credit Ratings and Capital Structure." *Journal of Finance* 61 (3): 1035–72.

Kopf, E. W. 1929. "Notes on the Origin and Development of Reinsurance." *Proceedings of the Casualty Actuarial Society* 16: 33–34.

Krahnen, J. P., and C. Wilde. 2008. "Risk Transfer with CDOs." Working paper. Goethe-University Frankfurt.

Lewellen, K. 2006. "Financing Decisions When Managers Are Risk Averse." *Journal of Financial Economics* 82 (3): 551–89.

McDaniel, R. 2008. *Credit Rating Agencies and the Financial Crisis.* Written testimony before the U.S. House Committee on Oversight and Government Reform, 110 Cong., October 22.

Millon, M., and A. Thakor. 1985. "Moral Hazard and Information Sharing: A Model of Financial Information-Gathering Agencies." *Journal of Finance* 40 (5): 1403–22.

Minton, B., R. Stulz, and R. Williamson. 2005. "How Much Do Banks Use Credit Derivatives to Reduce Risk? Working paper. Ohio State University.

O'Reilly, T. 2007. "What Is Web 2.0? Design Patterns and Business Models for the Next Generation of Software," *Communications and Strategies* 65: 17–37.

Osterloh, M., and B. Frey. 2002. "Does Pay for Performance Really Motivate Employees?" In *Business Performance Measurement*, edited by A. Noely, pp. 107–22. Cambridge University Press.

Plantin, G. 2003. "Tranching." Working paper. London School of Economics.

Purnanandam, A. 2008. "Originate-to-Distribute Model and the Subprime Mortgage Crisis." University of Michigan.

Raiter, F. 2008. *Credit Rating Agencies and the Financial Crisis.* Written testimony before the U.S. House Committee on Oversight and Government Reform, 110 Cong., October 22.

Reinhart, C., and K. Rogoff. 2008. "Is the 2007 U.S. Subprime Crisis So Different? An International Historical Perspective." *American Economic Review* 98: 339–44.

Riddiough, T., and R. Chiang. 2003. "Commercial Mortgage–Backed Securities: An exploration into Agency, Innovation, Information, and Learning in Financial Markets." Working paper. University of Wisconsin.

Ross, S. A. 2004. "Compensation, Incentives, and the Duality of Risk Aversion and Riskiness." *Journal of Finance* 59 (1): 207–25.

———. 1989. "Institutional Markets, Financial Marketing, and Financial Innovation." *Journal of Finance* 44 (3): 541–56.

Sharma, D. 2008. *Credit Rating Agencies and the Financial Crisis.* Written testimony before the U.S. House Committee on Oversight and Government Reform, 110 Cong., October 22.

Tett, Gillian, Aline van Duyn, and Paul J. Davies. 2008. "A Re-emerging Market? Bankers Are Seeking Simpler Ways to Sell on Debt."*Financial Times*, June 30, p. 9.

JENNIFER E. BETHEL
ALLEN FERRELL
GANG HU

5

Legal and Economic Issues in Litigation Arising from the 2007–08 Credit Crisis

T HE CREDIT CRISIS is the foremost economic issue facing the United States today. With housing prices high and interest rates low through 2006, millions of households with weak credit histories purchased new homes or refinanced existing ones, using subprime residential mortgage loans, many with adjustable interest rates. Investment banks securitized those loans into residential mortgage–backed securities (RMBSs) and collateralized debt obligations (CDOs), selling risk-differentiated tranches to investors. With the rise of interest rates and the decline in housing prices beginning in 2007, as many as 2 million homeowners have faced or are facing interest rate resets that will increase mortgage payments by as much as 30 percent. Many homeowners have negative equity. Some have already defaulted, whereas others will default in the future. Those defaults and foreclosures have driven down the value of many RMBSs and CDOs. Losses on these securities and their derivative effects are being felt by banks, investors, loan originators, credit appraisers, underwriters, bond rating agencies, bond insurers,

The authors have benefited from discussions with Ralph Ferrara, Paul Ferrillo, Tamar Frankel, Hal Scott, Steve Shavell, Erik Sirri, Laura Stiglin, David Sugarman, and the participants at many seminars and presentations of the paper, including the Harvard Law School Law and Economics Workshop and the Brookings–Tokyo Club–Wharton conference "Prudent Lending Restored: Securitization after the 2007 Mortgage Securities Meltdown." We appreciate research assistance from AK, Eric Chan, Wallace de Witt, and Johnson Elugbadebo. Allen Ferrell is grateful to the John M. Olin Center in Law, Economics, and Business at Harvard Law School for financial support.

and others. Having written down and continuing to write down assets, banks are now facing liquidity, solvency, and funding issues. Counterparty risk is high, and lending markets, including the markets for leveraged loans, auction rate securities, commercial mortgages, student loans, and others, have seized up. In this chapter we explore some of the causes and consequences of the 2007–08 credit crisis and its impact on various market participants. We investigate the risks that can arise from innovations in finance and technology and losses that are uniquely related to correlated events in loan markets.

The credit crisis is not solely an economic phenomenon but a legal one as well. It is widely believed that the substantial decrease in the value of asset-backed securities held by commercial and investment banks and other purchasers will generate substantial, perhaps even unprecedented levels of litigation. The facts so far are sobering. In 2007 filings of class action suits involving securities rose dramatically; the increase was even higher in 2008. The threat of private litigation (along with its settlement cost) has been heightened by recent revelations that the FBI is investigating accounting practices and pricing of securities in several major banks, while civil investigations already are under way by the U.S. Securities and Exchange Commission (SEC) and state attorneys general. These government investigations are important not only in their own right, but also because they may reveal information that may fuel further private class action litigation.

The litigation wave includes the filing of rule 10b-5 class action lawsuits against an extensive list of major financial firms, including Citigroup, Merrill Lynch, Morgan Stanley, and UBS as well as against a number of mortgage originators, such as Coast Financial Holdings, Countrywide Financial Corporation, IMPAC Mortgage Holdings, New Century Financial, Thornburg Mortgage, and Washington Mutual. Predictably, ERISA class action litigation has been filed against a number of firms, including many of the major financial institutions. Tellingly, State Street Corporation, which is facing multiple ERISA lawsuits concerning the operation of some of its funds, set aside a reserve of $618 million in the fourth quarter of 2007 to cover legal exposure.

Appendix 5A provides a summary of the securities class action lawsuits filed between February 8, 2007, and November 15, 2008, against investment banks, mortgage originators, bond insurers, and credit rating agencies arising from losses resulting from the credit crisis. Using information from Bloomberg,[1] the table summarizes the alleged legal basis for liability,[2] the filing date of the complaint,

1. We are grateful to Bloomberg for providing complaints from courthouse records that were not available electronically. We also double-checked our list of class action litigation against the records maintained by the Stanford Securities Class Action Clearinghouse.

2. Rule 10b-5 of the Exchange Act of 1934; section 11 and section 12(a)(2) of the Securities Act of 1933.

Table 5-1. *MBS Underwriters in 2007 and Write-Downs Related to Subprime Loans as of August 27, 2008*

Rank	Book runner	Number of offerings	Market share (percent)	Proceeds amount + overallot- ment sold in U.S. ($ millions)	Announced write-down ($ millions)
1	Lehman Brothers	120	10.80	100,109	8,200
2	Bear Stearns	128	9.90	91,696	3,200
3	Morgan Stanley	92	8.20	75,627	14,400
4	J. P. Morgan	95	7.90	73,214	14,300
5	Credit Suisse	109	7.50	69,503	10,400
6	Banc of America Securities	101	6.80	62,776	21,200
7	Deutsche Bank	85	6.20	57,337	10,600
8	Royal Bank of Scotland Group	74	5.80	53,352	14,600
9	Merrill Lynch	81	5.20	48,407	51,800
10	Goldman Sachs	60	5.10	47,696	3,800
11	Citigroup	95	5.00	46,754	55,100
12	UBS	74	4.30	39,832	44,200

Source: Yalman Onaran and Dave Pierson, "Banks' Subprime Market-Related Losses Reach $506 Billion," Bloomberg, August 27, 2008 (www.bloomberg.com).

and the class period if the action is based on rule 10b-5. In total, the table covers 251 securities class action lawsuits (a number of the complaints are partially duplicative) against ninety-five companies. Much of the litigation is directly related to the extensive asset write-downs taken by banks. Table 5-1 summarizes the credit crisis–related asset write-downs taken through August 27, 2008, by the largest underwriters of mortgage-backed securities (MBSs) in 2007.

However, appendix 5A surely underestimates—and most likely substantially underestimates—the extent and impact of likely litigation. We anticipate three significant additional sources of litigation: litigation against companies other than those directly involved in the structured finance market that nevertheless suffered losses due to MBS and CDO exposure; non–class action litigation brought by MBS and CDO purchasers (such as money market mutual funds) and investment banks; and government action against various participants in the structured finance process (with agencies like the SEC having greater subpoena powers than private parties and the ability to pursue parties based on aiding-and-abetting theories). An example of the first type of litigation would be litigation brought against and by operating companies that invested corporate cash in securities whose value was tied to pools of mortgages and that suffered substantial losses as a result. The second category of litigation includes litigation brought by banks against mortgage originators (a subsidiary of Deutsche Bank reportedly has already filed fifteen lawsuits against mortgage originators for violations of repurchase agreements); registered MBS purchasers bringing section 11 and section 12(a)(2) claims against MBS underwriters for misleading statements in offerings; and disputes between different CDO tranche holders regarding the distribution of assets of liquidating CDOs. The third category includes a variety of civil and criminal investigations by state and federal entities, including pending investigations of "due diligence firms," which are responsible for verifying the underwriting quality of securitized assets.

An example of the extensive litigation arising from losses from mortgage exposure is the situation of Luminent Mortgage Capital, a real estate investment trust (REIT) that purchased MBSs. Luminent is suing Merrill Lynch (and various Merrill Lynch subsidiaries and affiliates) for alleged misrepresentations with respect to the sale of junior MBS tranches. Luminent is also suing HSBC Holdings for allegedly improperly placing too low a value on nine subprime mortgages that a subsidiary of Luminent posted as collateral. In turn, Luminent Mortgage Capital has had five rule 10b-5 class action lawsuits filed against it for making false statements as well as a countersuit filed by HSBC Holdings for breach of contract. There is speculation that Luminent may be subject to ERISA lawsuits as well. Luminent is just one of many players in the RMBS and CDO marketplace.

Of course at this point in the credit crisis, the losses suffered by a wide range of actors extend well beyond the value of securities tied to mortgages, including declines in the value of leveraged loans (which actually exhibited signs of stress in early 2007), auction rate securities, and commercial mortgages, among other instruments. It nevertheless remains true that the most significant source of losses in the financial sector—and in particular the losses underlying many of the writedowns announced by the commercial and investment banks to date—is poor mortgage performance.

In the remainder of this chapter we describe the process by which mortgage loans are originated and securitized and discuss the role of various participants in the mortgage securitization market. We also discuss the causes and consequences of the current credit crisis, with a focus on mortgage lending, and explore reasons why market participants may have underestimated the risks. We present some original data analysis in the course of our discussion, including information on MBS tranche structure and the number of MBS bookrunners.

We then review the legal issues facing market participants, focusing on the causes of actions available to MBS and CDO purchasers and three principles of securities law that we believe will play an important role in the class action litigation filed against banks, mortgage originators, and others. Those principles are "no fraud by hindsight"; "truth on the market"; and "loss causation." Last, we summarize our findings.

Residential Mortgage–Backed Securities and Collateralized Debt Obligations

The United States has one of the highest rates of homeownership in the world, and it has risen in recent years, from 64.0 percent in 1994 to 68.8 percent in 2006.[3] That increase was facilitated in part by aggressive lending standards that allowed people from a broad economic spectrum to own homes and by the use of mortgage securitization, which increased mortgage capital and broadly distributed the risk of loans. Mortgage-backed securities are debt obligations whose cash flows are backed by the principal and interest payments of pools of mortgage loans, most commonly on residential property. The process by which loans are originated, securitized, and sold to investors is depicted in figure 5-1.

Homeowners and Loan Originators

The road to homeownership typically depends on the availability of financing. Lenders establish underwriting guidelines, evaluate prospective homeowners' credit, and make loans. Having done so, lenders generally hold only a fraction of the loans that they originate in their own portfolios. Most are sold to the secondary market, where they are pooled and become the assets underlying RMBSs.

Individuals with strong credit histories qualify for traditional mortgages, whereas those with weak histories—which may include payment delinquencies and possibly more severe problems, such as charge-offs, judgments, and bankruptcies—qualify for subprime loans. Subprime borrowers may also display reduced repayment capacity as measured by credit scores and debt-to-income ratios, or they may have incomplete credit histories. As can be seen in figure 5-2, subprime mortgages are an important part of the overall mortgage market, and the share of subprime mortgages in total mortgage originations rose over time. In 2001, 8.6 percent ($190 billion) of the more than $2.2 trillion in mortgages originated was from subprime

3. Bureau of the Census (www.census.gov/hhes/www/housing/hvs/historic/index.html).

Figure 5-1. *Mortgage Origination and Mortgage-Backed Securitization*

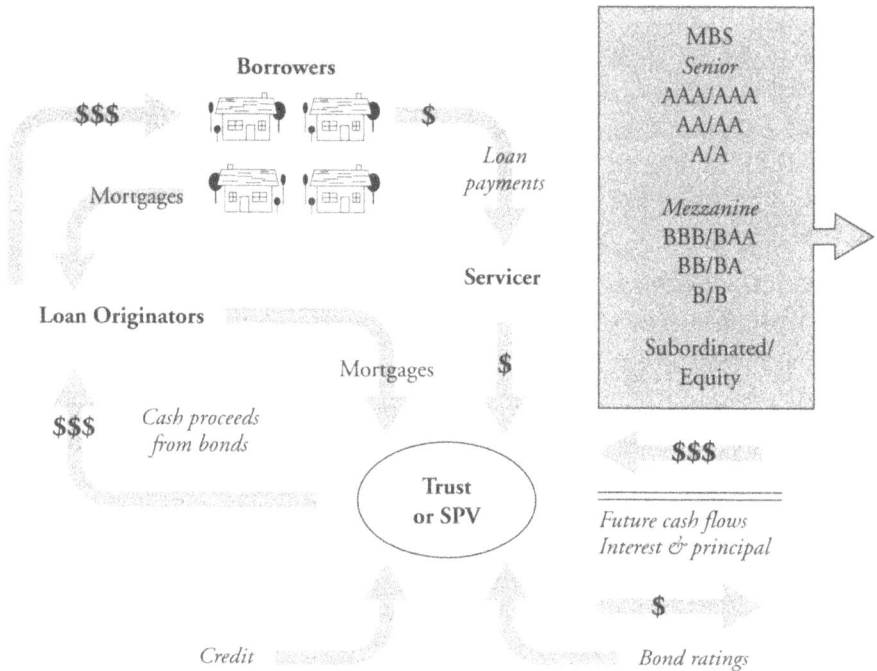

mortgages. The percentage rose to 20 percent by 2005, when originations of subprime mortgages were valued at more than $600 billion.

Most of the later-vintage subprime mortgage loans were ARMs (adjustable rate mortgages), interest-only mortgage loans (IOMs), and negatively amortizing mortgage loans (NegAmMs) rather than fixed-rate mortgage loans (FRMs). Many of the loans are "2/28" and "3/27" hybrid ARMs. A typical 2/28 hybrid ARM has a low fixed interest rate and mortgage payment (teaser) during the initial two-year period. After two years, the interest rate is reset every six months for the next twenty-eight years based on an interest rate benchmark, such as the London Interbank Offered Rate (LIBOR). Payments are often much higher when they are reset at the end of the initial fixed-rate period.

Most subprime loans are originated by mortgage banks and brokers rather than by commercial banks or other depository institutions. Mortgage banks originate subprime residential mortgage loans and then sell them to banks, whereas mortgage brokers originate subprime residential mortgage loans on behalf of

Figure 5-2. *Mortgage Originations, 2001–06*

Billions of dollars

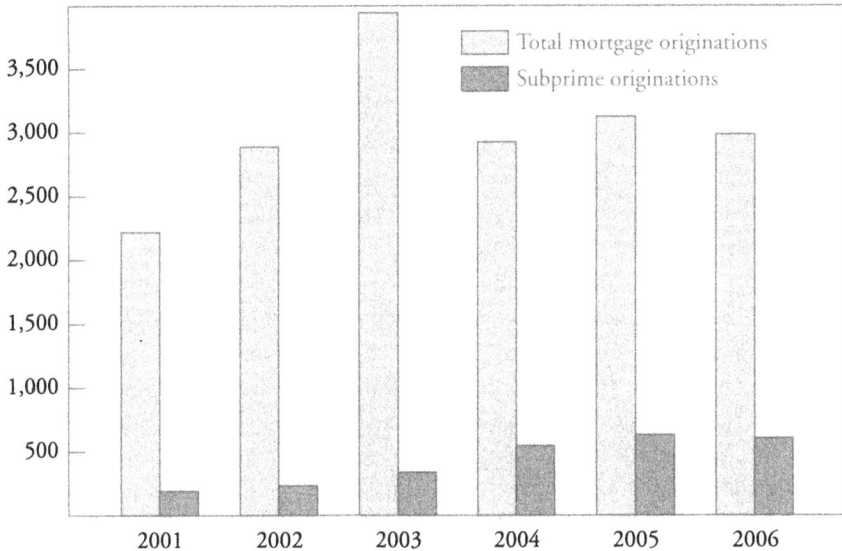

Sources: *The Subprime Lending Crisis: The Economic Impact on Wealth, Property Values, and Tax Revenues and How We Got Here*, report and recommendations by the majority staff of the Joint Economic Committee of the U.S. Congress, October 27, 2007; data are from "Top Subprime Mortgage Market Players and Key Data for 2006," *Mortgage Market Statistical Annual 2007* (Bethesda, Md.: Inside Mortgage Finance Publications, 2007), p. 19.

banks. Independent mortgage companies sell loans for securitization to other financial service firms. Banks and thrifts, which are more highly regulated than mortgage banks and brokers, deal primarily in lower-priced prime mortgages, selling to government-sponsored enterprises (GSEs) such as Fannie Mae and Freddie Mac, which securitize conventional conforming loans.[4] Over the past decade, the market shares for loan originators have changed dramatically. Originations moved out of banks and thrifts to mortgage banks, brokers, and independent mortgage companies. At the same time, the market consolidated: as of 1990, the top twenty-five originators accounted for approximately 28 percent of the industry's roughly $500 billion in loans, whereas in 2005 the market share of the top twenty-five originators rose to approximately 85 percent of the industry total of $3.1 trillion.[5]

4. Apgar, Bendimerad, and Essene (2007, p. 6).
5. Ibid.

Issuers

MBS sponsors or originators purchase mortgage loans from loan originators, assemble them into asset pools, and structure them into MBSs. After a large-enough portfolio of mortgages is pooled, it is sold to a special purpose vehicle (SPV), which issues the MBS. The SPV is formed for the specific purpose of funding the loans; once the loans are transferred to the issuer, there is usually no recourse to originators (putting aside repurchase agreements, discussed later). The issuer is "bankruptcy remote," meaning that if an originator goes bankrupt, the assets of the SPV cannot be distributed to the originator's creditors.

The SPV issues securities to fund the purchase of the loans. Securities are generally split into tranches differentiated by maturity and credit risk. Tranches are categorized as either senior, mezzanine, or subordinated/equity, according to the degree of credit risk. If homeowners default or mortgages otherwise underperform, scheduled payments to senior tranches take priority over payments to mezzanine tranches, and scheduled payments to mezzanine tranches take priority over those to subordinated/equity tranches. Senior and mezzanine tranches typically are rated, with the former receiving ratings of AA to AAA (investment grade) and the latter receiving ratings of A to BBB. The ratings reflect both the credit quality of the underlying collateral as well as the cash flow protection provided by the subordinated tranches. In recent years, senior MBS tranches have represented more than 85 percent of the value of a typical pool, whereas mezzanine pieces have accounted for around 10 percent and have been used primarily in CDOs.[6] The most junior class (often called the equity class) has the highest credit risk and accounts for about 5 percent of the value in the pool. In some cases, the equity class receives no coupon, getting instead the residual cash flows (if any) after all the other classes are paid. There may also be a special class of securities that absorbs early mortgage repayments, which are an important source of credit risk. Because early repayments are passed on to this class, the other tranches' investors receive more predictable cash flows. Often sponsors or MBS originators retain the equity.

Because SPV structures, as described above, pool assets and issue MBSs, they arguably fit the broad definition of "investment company" in the Investment Company Act of 1940. As such, they would be subject to the act's extensive requirements.[7] However, those requirements are widely viewed (including by SEC staff) as being inconsistent with the normal operations of SPVs; hence, vir-

6. Steven Drucker (Renaissance Technologies) and Christopher Mayer (Columbia Business School and National Bureau of Economic Research), "Inside Information and Market Making in Secondary Mortgage Markets," working paper, January 6, 2008.

7. See sections 3(a)(1)(A) and 3(a)(1)(C) of the Investment Company Act of 1940.

tually all SPVs are structured so as to be exempt from the act. The primary exemption relied on is rule 3a-7 of the Investment Company Act, which provides an exemption if an SPV issues fixed-income securities that, at the time of sale, are rated in one of the four-highest categories of investment quality from a "nationally recognized statistical rating organization" (typically S&P, Moody's, or Fitch). Pursuit of that exemption is one reason why it is important for an SPV's securities to be structured so that they receive the necessary investment-grade rating.

The SPV has a trustee whose primary role is to hold loan documents and distribute payments from the loan servicer to the bondholders. Although trustees typically are given broad authority with respect to certain aspects of loans under pooling and servicing agreements, they may delegate that authority to servicers.

Between 2001 and 2007, the size of the MBS market grew dramatically, peaking at more than $2.7 trillion in 2003. The percentage of subprime mortgages securitized (based on dollar values) rose from a low of 50.4 percent in 2001 to 81 percent in 2006.[8] Using data from Securities Data Corporation, we find that MBS volume transferred from agency to non-agency sponsors between 2001 and 2007. Panels A and B of figure 5-3 indicate that the volume of agency-sponsored MBSs, in terms of both number of deals and principal amount, peaked in 2003 and that virtually all of it was registered and publicly traded. In contrast, private label (non-agency) MBS volume was at its highest level in 2005, and private label equity line-of-credit securitization peaked in 2006. Although the private label rule 144A market was much smaller than the private label registered market, it too was robust throughout the period, with private label sponsored rule 144A MBS volume peaking in 2005 and private label rule 144A equity-line-of-credit securitization at its highest level in 2006.

The biggest sponsors of private label MBSs in 2007 were either commercial or investment banks. As shown in table 5-1, the MBS industry in 2007 was relatively concentrated, with most deals being structured by one of the top-twenty sponsors. Each of the top-five sponsors structured at least 7 percent of the market.

The riskier tranches of MBSs may be packaged into CDOs.[9] Like MBSs, CDOs have a sponsoring organization, such as a commercial or investment bank. A CDO's sponsor establishes an SPV that issues securities, typically multiple

8. *The Subprime Lending Crisis: The Economic Impact on Wealth, Property Values, and Tax Revenues and How We Got Here*, report and recommendations by the majority staff of the Joint Economic Committee of the U.S. Congress, October 27, 2007; data are from "Top Subprime Mortgage Market Players and Key Data for 2006," *Mortgage Market Statistical Annual 2007* (Bethesda, Md.: Inside Mortgage Finance Publications, 2007), p. 19.

9. According to the Securities Industry and Financial Markets Association, aggregate global CDO issuance totaled $157 billion in 2004, $272 billion in 2005, and $549 billion in 2006 (www.sifma.org/research/pdf/SIFMA_CDOIssuanceData2007q2.pdf).

Figure 5-3. *MBS Issuance Trends, 1996–2007*

Panel A. Number of deals

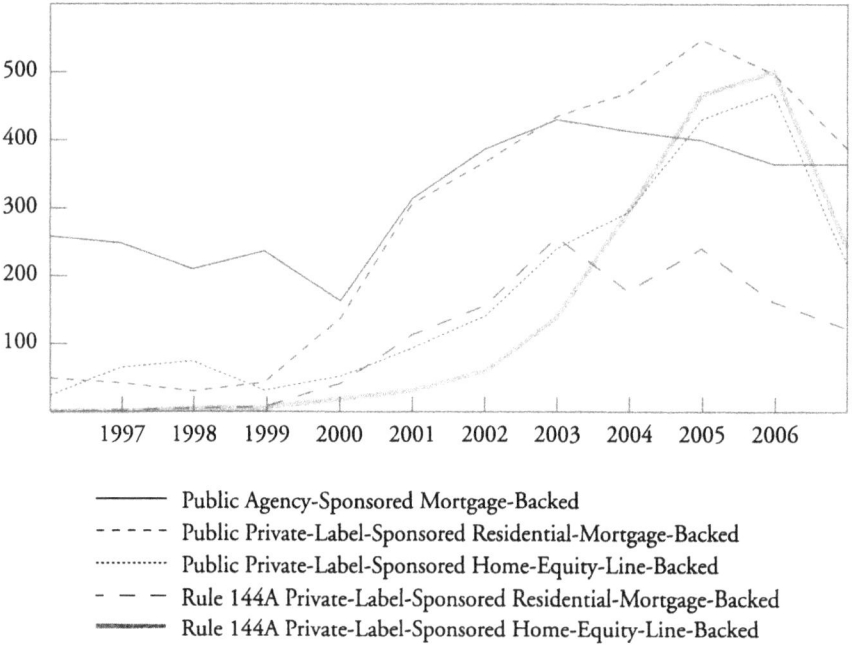

—————— Public Agency-Sponsored Mortgage-Backed
– – – – – Public Private-Label-Sponsored Residential-Mortgage-Backed
············· Public Private-Label-Sponsored Home-Equity-Line-Backed
– – – Rule 144A Private-Label-Sponsored Residential-Mortgage-Backed
▬▬▬▬ Rule 144A Private-Label-Sponsored Home-Equity-Line-Backed

Panel B. Total principal amount

Billions of dollars

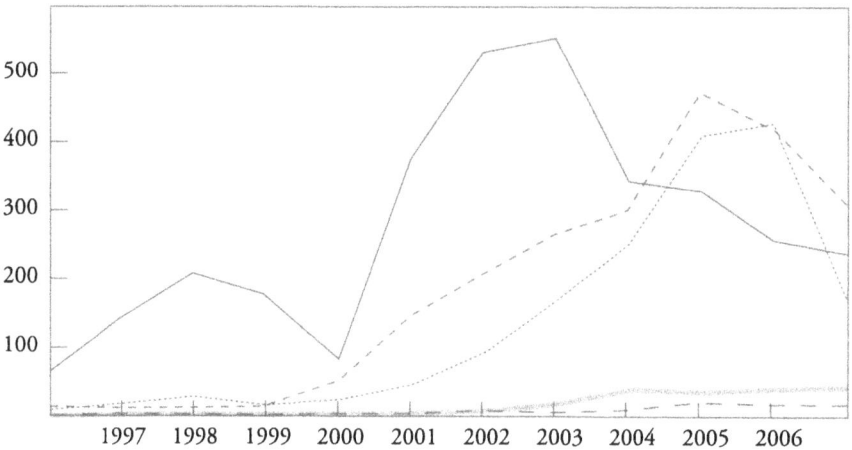

Source: Data are from SDC Platinum (http://thomsonreuters.com/products_services/financial/sdc).

tranches differentiated by maturity and credit risk, to raise money to invest in financial assets. Most of the debt that finances the purchase of CDO assets is floating-rate, off-LIBOR debt and can include short-term debt, such as commercial paper, often called asset-backed commercial paper (ABCP). ABCP is also issued against conduits that hold various CDO tranches, often the most senior ones. ABCP's maturity is quite short, running anywhere from one to 270 days, and generally is much shorter than the maturity of the underlying assets of the CDO or conduit. That difference can create problems if the CDO or conduit holding CDO tranches has trouble refinancing or rolling over the commercial paper. Consequently, CDOs and conduits typically contract with standby liquidity providers that guarantee liquidity for a fee. CDO sponsors often retain senior tranches for investment purposes. Like the market for RMBSs, the market for CDOs has grown dramatically over the past ten years, as has the ABCP market.[10] Growth slowed significantly in 2007, however, when housing prices fell, loan delinquencies rose, foreclosures increased, and the performance of recent-vintage RMBSs declined.[11]

Many CDOs, although not all, are actively managed, which entails the ongoing purchase and sale of assets. For instance, many CDO agreements with investors merely outline the type of assets that can be purchased and impose various restrictions on when assets can be bought or sold. The party entrusted with managing a CDO's assets (subject to those restrictions) is the collateral manager. The limitations imposed often are a function of the conditions under which the CDO must operate to maintain favorable credit ratings for its various tranches from rating agencies. Even if a collateral manager does not have the authority to trade CDO assets on an on-going basis, many CDOs raise funds before the purchase of assets (the so-called "ramp-up" period). With respect to a CDO's uninvested funds, the collateral manager has the obligation to invest those funds in a manner consistent with the CDO's asset strategy. In some ways, actively managed CDOs resemble hedge funds in that the purchasers of CDO interests are financially sophisticated investors rather than retail buyers.

CDOs often are designed to meet specific investor needs. Investors can specify the desired maturity and credit risk characteristics of securities, which results in more highly tailored but less liquid securities than might otherwise be available. The time necessary to confer with investors tends to preclude CDOs from being publicly tradable on registered exchanges or markets. Investors must therefore rely on dealers to execute trades.

---

10. Lucas, Goodman, and Fabozzi (2006).
11. Maller and Antonoff (2008, p. S6, col. 1).

Collateral Appraisers

MBS sponsors and underwriters typically hire firms known as collateral appraisers or due diligence firms to review and verify the quality of loans sold to SPVs. They evaluate the credit and collateral risks of loans in the pool and verify the information provided by loan originators to MBS sponsors, including a borrower's identity, place of residence, and employment status. They typically review details of the note, mortgage riders, title, and mortgage insurance and may include a property appraisal as well as a review of the loan originator's property and closing procedures. The information verified by collateral appraisers is at the heart of much of the mortgage litigation. Collateral appraisers in 2007 included Clayton Holdings, First American, LandAmerica Financial Group, and Stewart Information Services Corporation.

Sources of Credit Enhancement

MBSs and CDOs typically are credit enhanced, meaning that their credit risk is managed so that it is lower than the credit risk of the asset pool. Credit enhancement is designed to absorb all or a portion of credit losses, thereby increasing the likelihood that investors receive their contractual cash flows and raising the securities' credit ratings. Credit enhancement can either be internal or external. Internal sources of credit enhancement include but are not limited to providing for "excess" interest; including a spread or reserve account that guarantees that funds remaining after payment of expenses—such as principal and interest payments, charge-offs, and other fees—are available for use if the SPV's expenses are later greater than its income; overcollateralizing pool assets; and structuring transactions to include subordinated classes of securities that absorb cash flow shortfalls. CDOs are structured so that the cash flows from the assets are sufficient to cover the interest and principal payments of tranches with prescribed levels of certainty. Those levels are based on the par value of the assets in the CDO that are not in default relative to the par value of a given tranche's securities. CDOs can also establish advance rates that limit the debt that can be borrowed against particular assets. CDOs value assets regularly to ensure that asset values and cash flows are adequate. If there is a shortfall, a CDO must either sell the assets and distribute the proceeds or the equityholders must contribute cash to prevent the CDO from liquidating.

External sources of credit enhancement include third-party letters of credit, repurchase agreements that require loan originators to buy back from SPVs loans that become seriously delinquent or go into foreclosure within a specified time,

Table 5-2. *Insurers of U.S. Mortgage-Related Issues, 2006–07*

	2006		2007	
Insurer	Issuance ($ millions)	Market share (percent)	Issuance ($ millions)	Market share (percent)
MBIA	9,250.4	18.9	10,694.7	28.3
Ambac	10,815.0	22.1	7,474.3	19.8
FSA	6,428.4	13.1	7,175.5	19.0
XL Capital	6,146.4	12.6	4,184.0	11.1
FGIC	14,278.7	29.2	3,984.3	10.5
Assured Guaranty	513.0	1.0	3,644.5	9.6
CIFG	1,473.1	3.0	651.9	1.7
Total	48,905.0	100.0	37,809.2	100.0

Source: *Asset-Backed Weekly Update*, January 18, 2008 (www.abalert.com/).

and bond insurance. It is worth noting that standby liquidity arrangements for CDOs and ABCP conduits do not provide insurance against credit risk per se but instead provide insurance against liquidity risk—that is, the risk of not being able to roll over commercial paper.

Bond insurance, a commitment by an insurance company to make contractual payments if an issuer of a bond cannot meet its financial obligations, has been an important source of credit enhancement. Historically, bond insurers insured primarily municipal bonds, but they entered the structured finance market in the 1990s. By 2006, insurers wrote $606 billion of new coverage, with a net par value of insurance outstanding of $2.4 trillion by the end of the year.[12] The largest insurers of structured finance products in 2007 were MBIA Insurance Corporation, Ambac Assurance Corporation, and Financial Security Assurance, a subsidiary of the Belgian-French bank Dexia. Table 5-2 summarizes the insurance written on 2006 and 2007 MBS issuances, broken down by bond insurer.

Credit Rating Agencies

Credit rating agencies, such as Standard & Poor's, Moody's, and Fitch, assess the creditworthiness of obligors with respect to specific financial obligations. The agencies take into consideration the cash flow risk of the underlying assets and the creditworthiness of guarantors, insurers, or other forms of credit enhancement on

12. "Credit FAQ: The Interaction of Bond Insurance and Credit Ratings," Standard & Poor's, December 19, 2007 (www2.standardandpoors.com/portal/site/sp/en/us/page.article/3,1,1,0,1148450123839.html).

the obligation.[13] In at least some instances, credit rating agencies review due diligence firms' reports or summaries of reports when evaluating credit risk.

Investors

Hedge funds, corporations, banks, life insurers, pension funds, mutual funds, and wealthy individuals buy RMBSs and CDOs. In certain instances, institutional bond buyers are subject to legal limitations that permit them to buy only investment-grade or AAA-rated debt. For ERISA fiduciaries, who must "use care, skill, prudence, and diligence" in the course of investing plan assets, purchasing unrated RMBSs and CDOs runs the legal risk that the instruments may be deemed imprudent.[14] ERISA exempts CDOs, however, if CDO tranches are deemed "debt" for purposes of ERISA (and if several other requirements are satisfied). One basis for arguing for the debt status of a CDO tranche—and hence an ERISA exemption—is that the tranche is investment grade. If an SPV issues securities that are deemed to be "equity," then the mortgages will as a general matter be deemed part of the "plan assets." The legal result is that a bank deemed to be an ERISA fiduciary cannot act as sponsor of the SPV, as doing so would arguably constitute a "self-dealing" transaction, prohibited by ERISA. One way for a bank to avoid the "equity" label and thereby remove a potential bar to acting as sponsor of an SPV is to obtain an investment-grade rating on the securities. Another ERISA exemption commonly used by CDOs is to argue that no more than 25 percent of the CDO's equity has been purchased by ERISA plans (in conjunction with certain specified benefit plans). Interestingly, the issue of ERISA coverage usually does not come up in the context of MBS purchases because Department of Labor regulations exempt from ERISA requirements SPVs whose mortgage-backed securities are registered under the Securities Act of 1933.[15]

The advent of investment-grade MBSs and CDOs dramatically changed the investment opportunities for pension funds. Before their introduction, pension funds were largely precluded from investing either directly or indirectly in real estate. Investment-grade MBSs and CDOs have allowed pension funds to include real estate exposure in their portfolios while limiting credit risk (although the availability of CDOs is still somewhat restricted, given the use of the less-than-25-percent test by some CDOs). The securitization of mortgage loans permitted real estate investments to be classified as passive rather than active investments and to be considered traditional rather than alternative investments.[16]

13. Ibid.
14. 29 U.S.C. 1104(a)(1)(B).
15. See Frankel (2006, p.184) for a discussion of these regulations.
16. Maller and Antonoff (2008, p. S6, col. 1).

Servicers

Servicers are hired to collect mortgage payments from borrowers and pass the payments, less fees (including guarantee and trustee fees), through to trustees, who then pass payments on to MBS investors. Servicers can affect the cash flows to investors because servicers control collection policies, which influence the proceeds collected, the charge-offs, and the recoveries on loans. Any income remaining after payments and expenses is usually accumulated in reserve or spread accounts or returned to sellers. Often a loan originator is also the servicer, because servicers need expertise that is similar to that required for loan origination. If the loan originator is the servicer, it has highly attuned financial incentives to ensure that loans are repaid to the SPV and cash flows are subsequently distributed to investors. The due diligence firms, pursuant to item 1122(d) of Regulation AB, often attest to the procedures created to ensure compliance with the terms of servicing agreements in MBS registration statements.

Crisis in the Mortgage Lending Market

From 1997 to the middle of 2006, nominal U.S. housing prices rose by an average of 7.5 percent a year, whereas real U.S. housing prices increased by an average of 5 percent a year.[17] As shown in figure 5-4, the annual rate at which housing prices increased accelerated from 2001 through 2005. Rising housing prices and the availability of ARMs persuaded many potential homeowners with marginal incomes, limited net worth, and poor credit histories to buy or refinance homes. In some instances, buyers, knowing that they could not service loans from their income, still bought homes, anticipating that they could quickly flip them for a profit or refinance with accumulated equity. The demand for home financing by borrowers with weak credit histories and mortgage originators' vision of earning additional fees by expanding the pool of borrowers resulted in some originators lowering their underwriting standards. As shown in table 5-3, the share of subprime loans originated for borrowers for whom employment, income, or other credit-related information was not verified (low- or no-documentation loans) increased from 28 percent in 2001 to more than 50 percent in 2006, and borrowers' total debt payments rose relative to income. At the same time, the share of ARM loans originated on which borrowers paid interest only (no principal) as a percentage of subprime loans increased from zero to more than 22 percent. ARMs' share of the subprime market increased from about 73 percent to more than 91 percent.

---

17. S&P/Case-Shiller Home Price Indices (www.macromarkets.com/csi_housing/sp_caseshiller.asp).

Figure 5-4. *Real and Nominal Housing Prices and Population, 1997–2007*

Real and nominal home price indices ($ thousands)   U.S. population (millions)

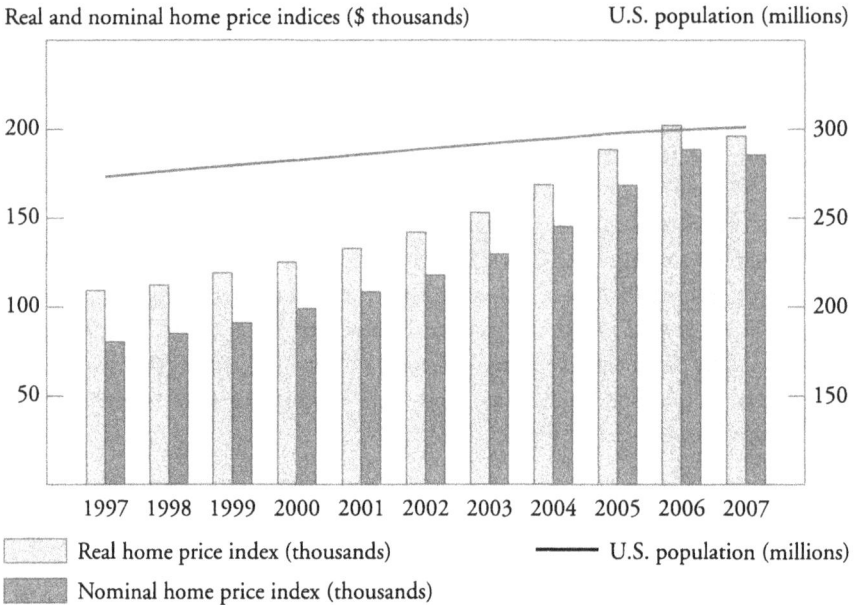

Real home price index (thousands)   ——— U.S. population (millions)

Nominal home price index (thousands)

Source: S&P/Case-Shiller Home Price Indices (www.macromarkets.com/csi_housing/sp_case shiller.asp).

Evidence is now mounting that at least some mortgage bankers and brokers may have submitted false appraisals and financial information to qualify otherwise unqualified buyers for subprime mortgage loans. Others purportedly did not document or verify subprime mortgagers' income, net worth, and credit history. According to an analysis by Fitch of a small sample of early defaults from its 2006 Fitch-rated subprime RMBSs, as much as one-quarter of the underperformance of the 2006 vintage of subprime RMBSs may have resulted from inadequate underwriting and fraud.[18] The Fitch report concludes that there was "apparent fraud in the form of occupancy misrepresentation; poor or a lack of underwriting relating to suspicious items on credit reports; incorrect calculation of debt-to-income ratios; poor underwriting of 'stated' income loans for reasonability; and substantial numbers of first-time homebuyers with questionable credit/income."[19] Base-

18. *The Impact of Poor Underwriting Practices and Fraud in Subprime RMBS Performance*, Fitch Ratings Ltd., November 28, 2007 (www.americansecuritization.com/uploadedFiles/Fitch_Originators_1128.pdf).
    19. Ibid.

Table 5-3. *Underwriting Standards in Subprime Home Purchase Loans, 2001–06*
Percent

Year	Low- or no-doc share	Debt payments/ income ratio	Loan/ value ratio	ARM share	Interest- only share
2001	28.5	39.7	84.0	73.8	0.0
2002	38.6	40.1	84.4	80.0	2.3
2003	42.8	40.5	86.1	80.1	8.6
2004	45.2	41.2	84.9	89.4	27.2
2005	50.7	41.8	83.2	93.3	37.8
2006	50.8	42.4	83.4	91.3	22.8

Source: Freddie Mac, obtained from the International Monetary Fund (www.imf.org/external/pubs/ft/fmu/eng/2007/charts.pdf).

Point Analytics, a fraud analysis and consulting firm, found results consistent with Fitch's findings. BasePoint analyzed more than 3 million loans originated between 1997 and 2006 (the majority during the 2005–06 period), including 16,000 non-performing loans that had evidence of fraudulent misrepresentation in the original applications. BasePoint's research found that as much as 70 percent of mortgages on which borrowers had early payment defaults contained fraudulent misrepresentations on applications.[20] The New York attorney general's office is investigating loan originators' appraisals and has filed suit against real estate appraiser First American Corporation and its subsidiary eAppraiseIt for allegedly colluding with Washington Mutual, a loan originator, to inflate appraisal values.[21]

The due diligence firms that review and verify loan information and loan origination policies and procedures are the gatekeepers; they are supposed to detect loan origination fraud and lax underwriting standards. Several of these firms are currently under investigation by the state attorneys general in New York and Connecticut and by the SEC. Linked to those investigations are allegations that some MBS sponsors may have ignored or withheld information about the credit risks of mortgage pools and even may have pressured due diligence firms to overlook credit issues on loans. Government officials are investigating whether MBS

20. *Broker Facilitated Fraud: The Impact on Mortgage Lenders*, BasePoint Analytics, 2006 (www.basepointanalytics.com/mortgagewhitepapers.shtml).
21. *The People of the State of New York* v. *First American Corporation and First American Eappraiseit* (Supreme Court of the State of New York, County of New York).

and CDO sponsors failed to disclose information to credit rating agencies and investors about high-risk loans, known as "exceptions," that failed to meet credit standards. Deutsche Bank, for instance, underwrote $1.5 billion of New Century mortgages in 2006 that included a number of exception loans. According to the *New York Times*, those loans suffered unusually high numbers of defaults and delinquencies.[22] The number of loans reviewed by due diligence firms fell from about 30 percent in 2000 to 5 percent in 2005.[23] Even for the loans reviewed, due diligence firms encountered obvious challenges, given that many loans lacked standard documentation or, indeed, any documentation. In assessing such practices, one must bear in mind that RMBS originators almost certainly purchased exception loans at discounts to face value and, in turn, sold them at discounted prices to SPVs. At issue is whether the discounted prices were a reasonable reflection of the ex ante probability of losses from defaults and foreclosures.

By mid-2006, housing prices began to decline nationally, dropping by about 1.5 percent between 2006 and 2007. Although that decline seems small, some markets were hit harder than others. Home sales fell as well, as shown in figure 5-5. Interest rates increased, and more than 2 million homeowners faced interest rate resets on their mortgages by February 2008.[24] Mortgage payments increased by as much as 30 percent of earlier payments,[25] and many homeowners could not afford them. In the past when housing prices rose, ARM borrowers sold or refinanced their homes to pay off loans before they reset to unaffordable rates. But given flat or declining housing prices, homeowners' options dwindled, and many became delinquent in their payments or defaulted. Using data from the Mortgage Bankers Association, the Government Accountability Office (GAO) found that ARMs experienced relatively steeper increases in default and foreclosure rates than did fixed-rate mortgages and accounted for a disproportionate share of the increase in the number of loans in default and foreclosure.[26] Fitch also found that the delinquency and foreclosure rates of subprime ARMs increased sharply and expects those rates to continue to rise.[27]

22. Vikas Bajaj and Jenny Anderson, "Inquiry Focuses on Withholding of Data on Loans," *New York Times*, January 12, 2008, p. A1.

23. Ibid.

24. C. Cagan, *Mortgage Payment Reset: The Issue and the Impact*, First American CoreLogic, 2007, pp. 42–43, estimates that 2.17 million subprime ARMs will have their first reset between 2007 and 2009 (www.facorelogic.com/uploadedFiles/Newsroom/Studies_and_Briefs/Studies/20070048MortgagePaymentResetStudy_FINAL.pdf).

25. Ibid.

26. *The Subprime Lending Crisis*; data are from "Top Subprime Mortgage Market Players and Key Data for 2006," p. 19.

27. *The Impact of Poor Underwriting Practices and Fraud in Subprime RMBS Performance*, Fitch Ratings, November 28, 2007 (www.americansecuritization.com/uploadedFiles/Fitch_Originators_1128.pdf).

Figure 5-5. *Houses for Sale and Median Housing Prices, 1997–2007*

Median housing price ($ thousands)   Houses for sale (thousands)

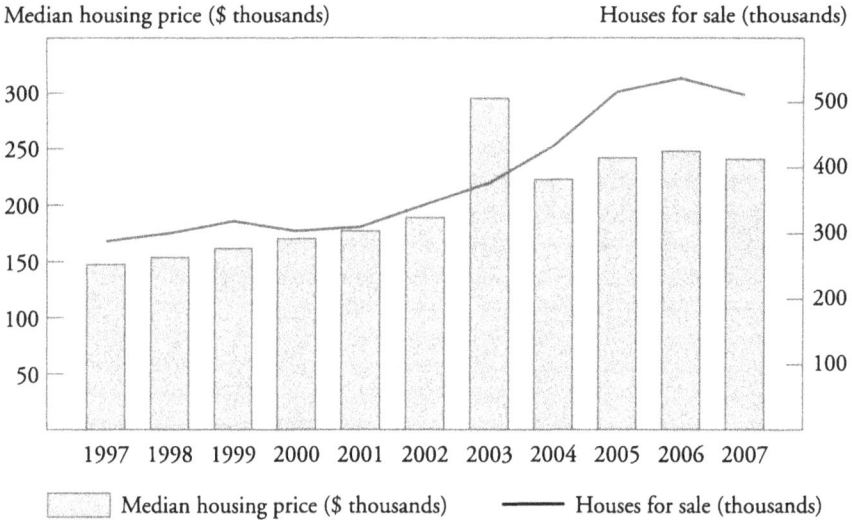

Source: Bureau of the Census (www.census.gov/hhes/www/housing/hvs/historic/index.html).

Whereas many of the problem subprime loans are ARMs, there are non-ARM subprime borrowers who also are at high risk of default. Using data on both ARM and non-ARM subprime mortgages originated between 1998 and the first three quarters of 2006, Schloemer and colleagues estimate cumulative foreclosures of 2.2 million, with losses to homeowners of $164 billion.[28] That estimate is probably low, given that housing prices have declined more than the authors may have assumed. Using data from the Mortgage Bankers Association and Moody's, the GAO estimates defaults and forecloses to be rising overall, with the largest share being subprime loans: subprimes constitute less than 15 percent of loans serviced but about 66 percent of the overall increase in the number of mortgages in default and foreclosure from the second quarter of 2005 through the second quarter of 2007.[29]

By late 2006, banks had reduced their purchases of subprime mortgages for SPVs and some banks and larger mortgage lenders tried to enforce repurchase agreements from previous deals, requiring loan originators to buy back troubled

28. Schloemer and others (2006).

29. *Home Mortgage Defaults and Foreclosures: Recent Trends and Associated Economic and Market Developments,* Briefing Report GAO-08-78R, briefing to the Committee on Financial Services, House of Representatives, October 10, 2007.

mortgages originated in 2005 and 2006.[30] Because loan originators tended to be thinly capitalized, many faced financial distress. By the end of 2007, more than twenty-five subprime mortgage originators, including New Century Financial Corporation and American Home Mortgage Investment, had filed for bankruptcy. Bank of America announced that it would buy Countrywide Financial, which had fallen on hard times. Ameriquest Mortgage Company stopped taking mortgage applications and has numerous lawsuits pending. A number of originators are under investigation for fraud, predatory lending practices, and other illegal acts.

Over the summer of 2007, unanticipated delinquency and default rates on subprime residential mortgages caused market participants to re-evaluate the credit risk inherent in subprime RMBSs and CDOs.[31] The ABX Home Equity Index for the lowest non-equity credit rating (BBB–), a widely used indicator of investors' estimation of the risk of funding subprime mortgage loans through secondary markets, fell from 97.47 in January 2007 to 31.96 in August 2007.[32] Moody's and other credit rating agencies began downgrading RMBSs and CDOs. For example, by September 2007, Moody's had downgraded subprime mortgage-backed securities valued at around $25 billion, or roughly 5 percent of the $460 billion in subprime MBSs that it had rated in 2006. In comparison, Moody's had downgraded only 2.1 percent by dollar volume in the subprime RMBS sector for the 2002–06 period and only 1 percent by dollar volume for all RMBSs.[33]

In the face of such downgrades, financial institutions had to write down mortgage-related and other assets whose values were impaired. As documented in table 5-1, the biggest underwriters in 2007 reported huge losses tied to mortgages and other assets. In February 2008, UBS analyst Philip Finch reported that

30. Carrick Mollenkamp, James R. Hagerty, and Randall Smith, "Banks Go On Subprime Offensive: HSBC, Others Try to Force Struggling Smaller Players to Buy Back Their Loans," *Wall Street Journal,* March 13, 2007, p. A3.

31. Michael Kanef, group managing director, Moody's Investors Service, "The Role and Impact of Credit Rating Agencies on the Subprime Credit Markets," testimony before the U.S. Senate Committee on Banking, Housing, and Urban Affairs, 110th Cong., 2nd sess., September 26, 2007.

32. The ABX tracks the performance of a basket of credit default swaps based on U.S. subprime home mortgages. Every six months, a new series is issued to track the twenty largest current deals. Thus, over time, the ABX Index covers a number of vintage-based series. Each series includes five credit rating–based tranches (AAA, AA, A, BBB, and BBB–). In using the ABX index, one must keep in mind how the index is constructed and its limitations. For example, by its nature, it does not reflect the various waterfall features inherent in CDO tranche structures.

33. Michael Kanef, group managing director, Moody's Investors Service, "The Role and Impact of Credit Rating Agencies on the Subprime Credit Markets," testimony before the U.S. Senate Committee on Banking, Housing, and Urban Affairs, 110th Cong., 2nd sess., September 26, 2007.

"write-downs for collateralized debt obligations and mortgage-related losses already total $150 billion. That may rise by a further $120 billion for CDOs, $50 billion for structured investment vehicles, $18 billion for commercial MBS, and $15 billion for leveraged buyouts."[34] By August 2008, asset write-downs and credit losses at more than 100 of the world's biggest banks and securities firms had ballooned to $506.1 billion.[35] Losses were being recognized by a broad range of financial firms on assets that were not related to subprime loans. Banks wrote down Alt-A and prime MBSs, ABCP, syndicated loans, consumer loans, and many other types of securities.

To respond to asset write-downs, many financial firms needed to raise capital to meet regulatory capital requirements. By late August 2008, 100 of the world's biggest banks and securities firms had raised $352.6 billion in capital.[36] As an alternative or additional measure, firms needed to sell assets, especially unwanted inventories of mortgage-related assets. Bank inventories of mortgage-related debt typically includes debt that banks have only because they have not yet sold it to an SPV or because it is a remnant of an already completed securitization; debt that is part of an SPV that is consolidated on the banks' balance sheet for some reason; and debt that is held as a result of proprietary trading. Because so many financial institutions were trying to raise capital and sell mortgage-related assets, the market for those assets was glutted and highly illiquid. As a result, firms faced steep discounts on asset prices and in many instances market prices were not readily available. The problem was further compounded because many institutional investors were trying to sell downgraded assets too. ERISA restrictions, other legal requirements, and their own stated investing criteria preclude institutions from holding non–investment grade securities. Hedge funds and mutual funds had to sell assets to meet investor redemptions. The selling in turn caused bond values to fall even further, resulting in additional write-downs by investors and financial institutions.

Those write-downs and deep-discount asset sales raised fears among market participants about the creditworthiness of a number of financial institutions, which resulted in runs on some of them. Whereas in the Great Depression, depositors of commercial banks withdrew their deposits, here providers of capital withdrew secured and unsecured funding from banks. The result has been a

34. Poppy Trowbridge, "Banks at Risk from $203 Billion Write-Downs, Says UBS," Bloomberg, February 15, 2008 (www.bloomberg.com).

35. Yalman Onaran and Dave Pierson, "Banks' Subprime Market-Related Losses Reach $506 Billion," Bloomberg, August 27, 2008 (www.bloomberg.com).

36. Ibid.

massive reorganization of the financial services industry. In March 2008, JPMorgan Chase acquired Bear Stearns. In September, Bank of America bought Merrill Lynch. Market pressures the same month forced Morgan Stanley and Goldman Sachs to become commercial bank holding companies, and on September 15, 2008, Lehman Brothers announced that it would file for bankruptcy protection. Commercial and other banks have not been immune to market pressures either. IndyMac Bancorp was taken into federal receivership. Washington Mutual, Wachovia, and numerous other banks merged or were taken over. The U.S. government seized control of Fannie Mae and Freddie Mac,[37] signed a definitive agreement with AIG to provide financial support, and bought preferred shares in a number of banks.[38] What began as a problem in the United States spread overseas. Governments around the world are issuing credit guarantees and buying equity in financial institutions.

Since the end of 2007, bond insurers also have suffered. The top seven insurers "enhance the credit of some $2 trillion worth of debt securities held by investment banks, pension funds, mutual funds, and other investors around the globe."[39] By fall 2008, many of the bond insurers' financial strength ratings had been lowered. Without an AAA rating, issuers are unlikely to use these firms to insure securities, further undermining the insurers' financial well-being. As bond insurers' credit ratings fall, so too will the ratings of insured securities. If securities' ratings fall far enough, pension funds and other investors that are required to hold highly rated securities may need to sell them, creating an even larger glut in the market and further downward price pressure. This cycle could mean yet additional write-downs for investors and banks.

37. Under the plan, the Treasury will receive $1 billion of senior preferred stock, with warrants representing ownership stakes of 79.9 percent of Fannie Mae and Freddie Mac. The Treasury can purchase up to $100 billion of a special class of stock in each company as needed to maintain a positive net worth. It also will provide secured short-term funding to Fannie Mae, Freddie Mac, and twelve federal Home Loan Banks and purchase mortgage-backed debt in the open market. The government will receive annual interest of 10 percent on its stake. The Federal Housing Finance Agency will take over Fannie and Freddie under a so-called conservatorship, replacing their chief executives and eliminating their dividends. As a condition for assistance, Fannie Mae and Freddie Mac have to reduce their holdings of mortgages and securities backed by home loans. Each firm's portfolio "shall not exceed $850 billion as of Dec. 31, 2009, and shall decline by 10 percent per year until it reaches $250 billion," the Treasury said. Fannie's portfolio was $758 billion at the end of July, and Freddie's was $798 billion.

38. As part of the deal, AIG will issue a series of convertible participating serial preferred stock to a trust that will hold the new securities for the benefit of the Treasury. The preferred stock will get 79.9 percent of any dividends paid on AIG's common stock and will give the government almost 79.9 percent of the voting power. The securities then will be converted to common stock at a special shareholders' meeting.

39. Tomoeh Murakami Tse, "Insurer of Bonds Loses Top Rating," *Washington Post*, January 19, 2008, p. D01.

What Went Wrong?

The question, then, is this: how could the credit crisis have happened? At the end of 2008, there were perhaps more hypotheses than answers, and a full analysis obviously is far beyond the scope of this chapter.[40] The answer will likely involve, in part, market participants' experience or lack thereof with the securitization of a relatively new class of assets—subprime mortgage products that previously had not been originated and that perhaps had been built on unanticipated declining loan underwriting standards. The credit risk of the pools of mortgages that included subprime loans, especially hybrid ARMs, were different from the credit risk of mortgage pools previously securitized. It appears that borrowers may have been qualified to borrow money on the basis of the low teaser rates for the early years of loans rather than the higher rates for later years. Loan originators may have waived minimum down payments, reducing homeowners' equity. In addition, the mix of mortgages underwritten, which included a higher percentage of ARMs than in the past, had greater exposure to key risks, including interest rate and housing price risks, than mortgage pools in the past. Between 2001 and 2006, the number of subprime mortgages increased and the share of ARMs in total subprime MBSs rose from 60.8 percent to 74 percent.[41] Those changes, coupled with lower underwriting standards, may not have been fully appreciated by market participants. The market had limited experience in understanding the credit risks of such loans and their high representation in mortgage securitizations was new to the industry.

Other risks, created by changing origination and appraisal policies, may also have contributed to the unpredictability of the performance of various pools of mortgages under different market conditions. For example, loan originations shifted away from depository institutions to mortgage brokers and firms specializing in loan originations. Those originators, in contrast to banks and thrifts, tended to have more focused financial incentives, including fees and yield spread premiums, to close as many loans as possible at terms favorable to lenders.[42] Other structural changes in the residential mortgage origination industry may have contributed to lower credit standards and permitted fraudulent loan underwriting.

40. Steven L. Schwarcz, "Protecting Financial Markets: Lessons from the Subprime Mortgage Meltdown," Duke Law School Legal Studies Paper 175, November 2007 (http://ssrn.com/abstract=1056241).

41. Sandra Thompson, director of the Division of Supervision and Consumer Protection, Federal Deposit Insurance Corporation, statement on "Mortgage Market Turmoil: Causes and Consequences," testimony before the U.S. Senate Committee on Banking, Housing, and Urban Affairs, March 22, 2007.

42. *Broker Facilitated Fraud: The Impact on Mortgage Lenders*, BasePoint Analytics, 2006.

Mason and Rosner note the impact of increasingly automated valuation and underwriting systems.[43]

The issues raised by such changes may have been masked. Low interest rates in the economy, low teaser rates on ARMs that did not reset to higher levels until years later, and high housing prices through mid-2006 staved off loan delinquencies and foreclosures.[44] According to Fitch managing director Diane Penndel, "during the rapidly rising home price environment of the past few years, the ability of the borrower to refinance or quickly re-sell the property before the loan defaulting masked the true risk of these products and the presence of misrepresentation and fraud." So although loan quality declined between 2001 and 2006, loan performance did not immediately deteriorate. In fact, aggregate delinquency and foreclosure rates for subprime loans *declined* during 2001–05.[45] Similarly, subprime mortgages originated during 2001–05 performed *better* than those originated in 2000.[46] The strong credit performance of subprime loans between 2001 and 2005 may have resulted in MBS ratings being too high, in hindsight. Calomiris argues that because subprime loan products were relatively novel, later vintages (2005–06) of MBSs and CDOs with subprime collateral were rated on the basis of subprime loan defaults and losses from earlier vintages (2001–03).[47] That period was unusual, because although the economy was in a mild recession, housing prices boomed. Of course, housing prices eventually flattened out and began to fall. Interest rates rose, and teaser rates began resetting to higher levels. Noticeably higher delinquency rates appeared for loans originated in 2006 and 2007, revealing borrowers' financial weaknesses.

The answer also may involve in part the experience or lack thereof of market participants with RMBSs and CDOs that had somewhat different structures and were more complex and less transparent than in the past. RMBSs, for example, changed dramatically over time. In addition to holding more complex collateral, private label RMBS deals, as shown in figure 5-6, increased in average size over time, peaking in 2005. That increase was accompanied by an increased likelihood of multiple bookrunners, which arose as a way to better share the risk and distribution challenges of larger deals. At the same time, the average number of

---

43. Joseph R. Mason (LeBow College of Business, Drexel University) and Joshua Rosner (Graham Fisher & Company), "How Resilient Are Mortgage-Backed Securities to Collateralized Debt Obligation Market Disruptions?" working paper, February 15, 2007.

44. Yuliya Demyanyk and Otto Van Hemert, "Understanding the Subprime Mortgage Crisis," working paper, August 19, 2008 (http://ssrn.com/abstract=1020396).

45. *The Subprime Lending Crisis.*

46. Ibid.

47. Charles W. Calomiris (Columbia Business School and National Bureau of Economic Research), "The Subprime Turmoil: What's Old, What's New, and What's Next," working paper, August 20, 2008.

tranches for those transactions decreased from a high of 11.9 in 1999 to 2.18 at the peak of the market in 2005. Not surprisingly, the main tranche of private label MBS offerings in 1999 constituted 20 percent of total offering principal, whereas it was 91 percent in 2005. Similar patterns exist for agency-sponsored RMBSs and rule 144A deals. The reduced complexity of the structure of MBSs was in part a response to the development of highly customizable CDOs. Previous RMBSs catered to the needs of investors for tailor-made duration and risk exposures. With the rise of CDOs, RMBSs were no longer the only way to fulfill that demand. In contrast to RMBSs, CDOs have more tranches than ever before; those tranches are increasingly complex and may include, for example, interest-only and principal-only strips and other difficult-to-value securities.[48] In addition, the credit risk of the underlying assets is relatively opaque to market participants, who are several times removed from the actual loan underwriting and verification process. By purchasing securities that distribute and redistribute risk broadly, investors must rely on information produced and verified by third parties, who in turn rely on information produced further down the chain. A compromise in quality at any point in the chain can result in unanticipated risks for market participants further up the chain. CDOs especially have experienced substantial changes in the last eight years in terms of asset distribution and transaction structure.[49] Although it is tempting to point a finger at MBS originators as the culprits, it is difficult to believe that they would have chosen to keep securities on their books that would later be written down by more than $500 billion if they had understood and appreciated the inherent risks.

The market appears to have not fully anticipated the probability or effect of correlated market events or the very small probability of an extremely negative outcome. So, for example, SPVs wrote repurchase agreements to protect against mortgage fraud and defaults. That protection is of limited value, however, if many repurchase agreements are exercised and loan originators seek bankruptcy protection. Similarly, securities were insured against shortfalls of cash flow, but such guarantees are not very useful if the credit ratings of insurers are downgraded or if they go bankrupt. Consistent with this thesis, Mason and Rosner suggest that credit rating models may underestimate the correlation of defaults and hence understate risk.[50] In turn, market participants appear to have not fully appreciated

48. Mason and Rosner, "How Resilient Are Mortgage-Backed Securities?"

49. Jian Hu (Moody's Investors Service), "Assessing the Credit Risk of CDOs Backed by Structured Finance Securities: Rating Analysts' Challenges and Solutions," August 31, 2007 (http://ssrn.com/abstract =1011184).

50. Joseph R. Mason (LeBow College of Business and Drexel University) and Joshua Rosner (Graham Fisher and Company), "Where Did the Risk Go? How Misapplied Bond Ratings Cause Mortgage-Backed Securities and Collateralized Debt Obligations Market Disruptions," working paper, May 2007.

Figure 5-6. *Changes in Mortgage-Backed Securities, 1996–2007*

Panel A. Average deal size in millions of dollars

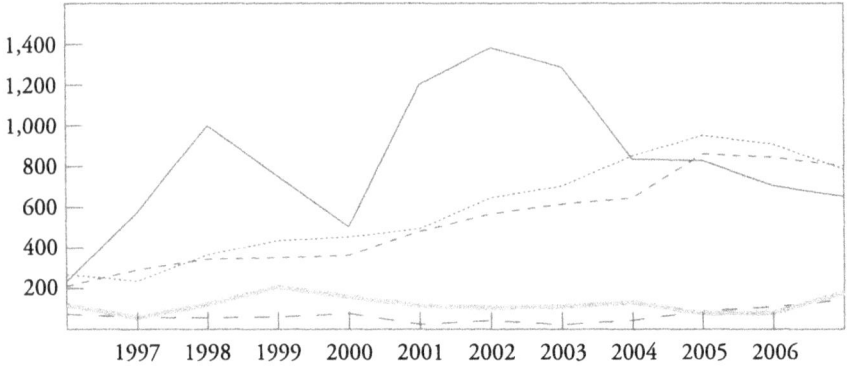

Panel B. Percentage of deals with multiple bookrunners

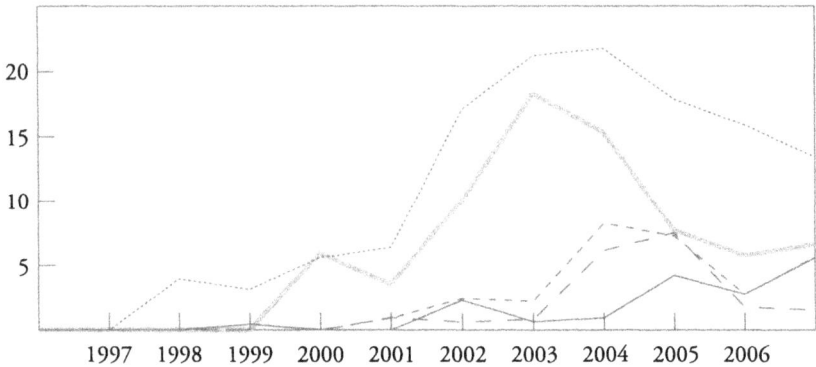

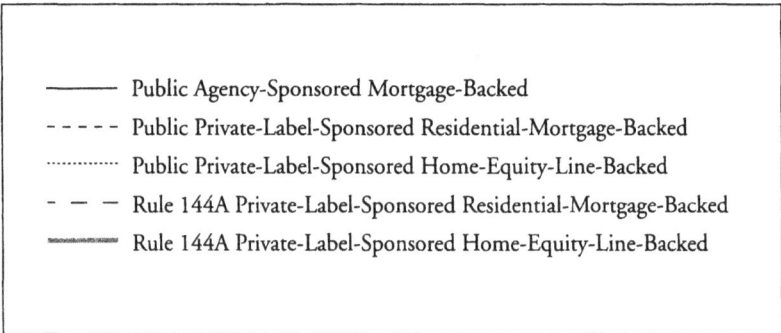

————— Public Agency-Sponsored Mortgage-Backed

- - - - - Public Private-Label-Sponsored Residential-Mortgage-Backed

.... Public Private-Label-Sponsored Home-Equity-Line-Backed

— — — Rule 144A Private-Label-Sponsored Residential-Mortgage-Backed

▬▬▬▬ Rule 144A Private-Label-Sponsored Home-Equity-Line-Backed

(continued)

Figure 5-6. *Changes in Mortgage-Backed Securities, 1996–2007* (Continued)

Panel C. Average number of bookrunners

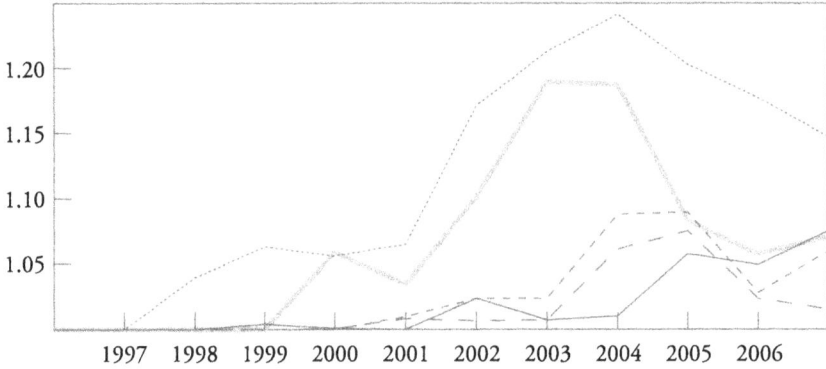

Panel D. Average number of tranches

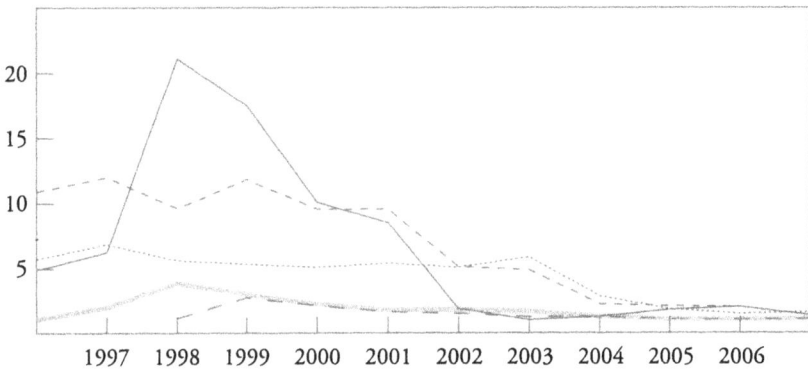

Panel E. Average percentage of main tranche principal

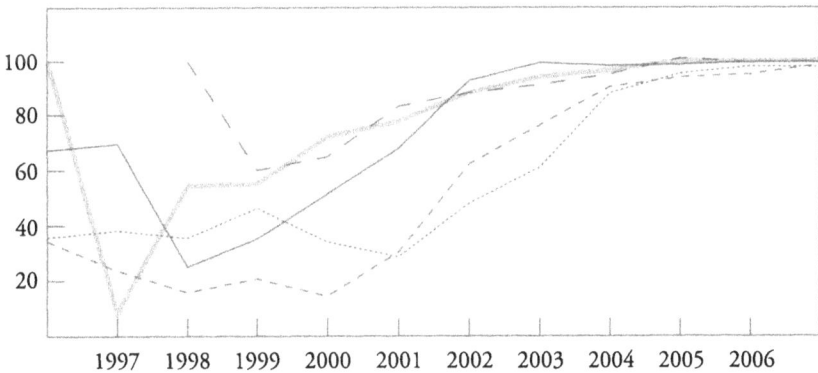

Source: Data are from SDC Platinum (http://thomsonreuters.com/products_services/financial/sdc).

the probability of bond insurer downgrades or their impact on investor purchases and sales of securities and the subsequent effect on market liquidity and bond prices. Firms also suffered because asset sales were highly correlated, resulting in excess supply and low prices. Another potential source of correlation appears to have been in the structuring of CDOs' tranches to garner investment-grade ratings. Once a relatively novel CDO's senior tranche is structured so as to receive an investment-grade rating from the credit rating agencies, other CDOs tend to mimic that structure.[51] If that structure has some risk that rating agencies do not fully recognize or if some information is not disclosed to or understood by investors or rating agencies, the same weakness or deficiency will likely be repeated by a large number of CDOs. That herding may result in correlated downgrades later. Those types of correlations, whereby a small error aggregates up to a substantial problem, can result in what is now known as a "black swan." According to Nassim Taleb, the author of *The Black Swan*, finance is an area that is dominated by black swans—rare events that have extreme impacts that can be and usually are explained away after the fact. "The tools we have in quantitative finance do not work in what I call the 'Black Swan' domain . . . people underestimate the impact of infrequent occurrences. Just as it was assumed that all swans were white until the first black species was spotted in Australia during the 17th century, historical analysis is an inadequate way to judge risk."

Related to the failure of the market to fully anticipate the probability or effect of correlated market events is the market's apparent lack of appreciation of certain types of funding risk for banks. Most banks rely on short-term secured borrowing to finance certain assets; they then use those assets as collateral. If the value of the assets, which in this instance included MBSs and derivative positions, falls, banks receive margin calls, and they may need to raise cash to meet their financial obligations and regulatory requirements. Historically they would have sold assets or raised debt or equity. In the severely stressed market of 2008, however, numerous financial institutions were selling assets, resulting in a market glut and plummeting prices. The lower prices set off rounds of write-downs and the further need to raise cash and delever. Gorton and Allen and Carletti argue that Financial Accounting Standards Board Statement (FASB) 157 exacerbated the problem, because firms had to value assets for accounting purposes at market prices that were lower than cash flow and risk characteristics would otherwise suggest were appropriate.[52] The problem was also made worse by heightened counterparty risk. Market participants did not know which banks were finan-

51. Peter Tufano (1989).

52. See Gary Gorton (Yale School of Management and National Bureau of Economic Research), "The Panic of 2007," working paper, 2008, and Franklin Allen (University of Pennsylvania) and Elena Carletti

cially weak and so refused to lend more generally. Even banks with collateral were denied loans, as lenders feared that they would not be able to monetize collateral if borrowers failed. With the value of assets impaired, few buyers in the market, and the capital markets effectively shut down, firms had few options for raising cash and some began to experience financial distress.

Perhaps the starkest examples are Bear Stearns and Goldman Sachs. During the week of March 10, 2008, rumors about liquidity problems at Bear Stearns began spreading in the market. Lenders and counterparties, fearing that the firm might not be able to meet its financial obligations, began denying not only "unsecured financing, but short-term secured financing as well, even when the firm's collateral consisted of agency securities with a market value in excess of the funds to be borrowed. Counterparties would not provide securities lending services and clearing services. Prime brokerage clients moved their cash balances elsewhere."[53] The firm began to experience a liquidity shortfall, even though it met and exceeded regulatory net capital, capital, and liquidity standards. To put the run on Bear Stearns's funding in perspective, the firm had more than $18 billion in liquidity on Monday, March 10, 2008.[54] By Tuesday, March 11, its liquidity pool declined to $11.5 billion. On Wednesday, March 12, its liquidity pool actually increased by $900 million, for a total of $12.4 billion. On Thursday, March 13, however, the firm's liquidity pool fell sharply and continued to fall on Friday,[55] until Bear Stearns had no choice but to be acquired by JPMorgan Chase at a fire-sale price or to fail altogether. The holding company's capital ratio was 13.5 percent on February 29, 2008, which far exceeded the threshold of 10 percent established by the Federal Reserve Board (Federal Reserve) for being "well capitalized."[56] Its ratio never fell below 10 percent during the week of March 10. Until Friday, March 14, Bear Stearns's short-term credit ratings were investment grade.[57]

Even more surprising was the funding run on Goldman Sachs, which had minimal asset write-downs or issues with bad MBSs and CDOs. To avoid being

---

(University of Frankfurt and European University Institute), "The Role of Liquidity in Financial Crises," working paper, 2008.

53. Christopher Cox, chairman of the SEC, "Turmoil in U.S. Credit Markets: Examining the Recent Actions of Federal Financial Regulators," statement before the U.S. Senate Committee on Banking, Housing and Urban Affairs, 110 Cong., 1st sess., April 3, 2008.

54. "Chairman Cox Letter to Basel Committee in Support of New Guidance on Liquidity Management," SEC, March 20, 2008 (www.sec.gov/news/press/2008/2008-48.htm).

55. "Answers to Frequently Asked Investor Questions Regarding the Bear Stearns Companies, Inc.," SEC, March 18, 2008 (www.sec.gov/news/press/2008/2008-46.htm).

56. "Chairman Cox Letter to Basel Committee in Support of New Guidance on Liquidity Management."

57. Mark Pittman and Caroline Salas, "Bear Stearns Has Credit Ratings Slashed after Bailout," Bloomberg, March 14, 2008 (www.bloomberg.com).

acquired to mitigate funding issues, it was forced to convert to a commercial bank holding company regulated by the Federal Reserve. A few days before Goldman Sachs applied to be a commercial bank, it reported positive earnings for the quarter and $102 billion in liquidity, and its stock price was around $133 per share.[58] Even Goldman Sachs, however, could not withstand funding pressures. Ultimately it sought access to the insured deposits of a commercial bank and the Federal Reserve's expansive discount window as an alternative to secured borrowing as a basis for its funding model.

In the wake of the credit crisis, we now know that a funding strategy—one embraced by an entire industry for many years—can work well when few institutions are financially distressed but can break down when markets are stressed overall.[59] We also now know that a lack of confidence in a bank's creditworthiness can cause such a run on its secured funding that it can fail, even though its capital exceeds the Federal Reserve's standard for being well capitalized[60] and its liquidity exceeds SEC recommendations. Even given adherence to regulatory standards, a number of investment and commercial banks experienced financial distress during this period, with investment banks generally faring worse early on than commercial banks. Investment banks generally held a greater portion of their assets for trading purposes than commercial banks. Because FASB 157 requires firms to mark the value of traded assets to market, investment banks were forced to revalue more of their assets sooner than most commercial banks. Unlike commercial banks, which fund themselves at least in part with "sticky" federally insured deposits and which have access to Fed funds, investment banks relied heavily on unsecured and secured funding that until recently was not guar-

58. Goldman Sachs Group, Inc., Third Quarter Results, Form 8-K, September 16, 2008 (www.sec.gov/Archives/edgar/data/886982/000095012308011074/y71185e8vk.htm).

59. See Anil K. Kashyap (University of Chicago and National Bureau of Economic Research), Raghuram G. Rajan (University of Chicago and National Bureau of Economic Research), and Jeremy C. Stein (Harvard University and National Bureau of Economic Research), "Rethinking Capital Regulation," working paper, 2008, for the argument that the cycle could be broken if firms were able to buy capital insurance.

60. Capital is the difference between a firm's assets and liabilities. "It is important to realize capital is not synonymous with liquidity. A firm can be highly capitalized, that is, can have more assets than liabilities, but can have liquidity problems if the assets cannot quickly be sold for cash or alternative sources of liquidity, including credit, obtained to meet other demands. Whereas the ability of a securities firm to withstand market, credit, and other types of stress events is linked to the amount of capital the firm possesses, the firm also needs sufficient liquid assets, such as cash and U.S. Treasury securities, to meet its financial obligations as they arise. Accordingly, large securities firms must maintain a minimum level of liquidity in the holding company. This liquidity is intended to address pressing needs for funds across the firm. This liquidity consists of cash and highly liquid securities for the parent company to use without restriction." "Answers to Frequently Asked Investor Questions Regarding the Bear Stearns Companies, Inc.," press release, SEC (www.sec.gov/news/press/2008/2008-46.htm).

anteed by the Federal Reserve and that we now know can disappear within hours.

The question, then, is whether the market could reasonably have anticipated that investment banks could face such a dramatic funding crisis. Critics have asserted that gross leverage (assets divided by stockholders' equity) was high over the period.[61] Measuring leverage for financial service firms, however, is more complex than for industrial firms, and gross leverage is rarely used. Instead leverage is nearly always measured by using globally accepted Basel standards.[62] Under the Basel 2 standard, the capital ratio of regulatory capital to risk-weighted assets is the reciprocal of a leverage ratio. But, unlike gross leverage measures, the Basel standard incorporates the impact of off–balance sheet positions, especially over-the-counter (OTC) derivatives, and differences in the riskiness of assets (it weights high-risk positions more than low-risk positions). The largest investment banks were "required to maintain an overall Basel capital ratio of not less than the Federal Reserve's ten percent 'well-capitalized' standard for bank holding companies"[63] and to maintain tentative net capital of at least $1 billion and net capital of at least $500 million.[64] Firms also had to meet a holding company liquidity standard that was designed to allow them to survive at least one year without access to unsecured funding under the assumption that secured funding for liquid assets would be available.[65] The liquidity requirements, like those of other international and domestic regulators contemplating similar issues, did not anticipate the complete unwillingness of lenders to provide financing collateralized by high-quality assets (such as Treasuries or agency securities) or the failure of committed secured lending facilities.[66] According to a May 2008 report of the International Organization of Securities Commissions (IOSCO), firms' problems arose because "the inability to obtain secured or unsecured debt financing, difficulty in obtaining funds from a subsidiary,

61. See, for example, Kara Scannell, "SEC Faulted for Missing Red Flags at Bear Stearns," *Wall Street Journal*, September 27–28, 2008, p. A3.

62. "The Basel Committee on Banking Supervision (Basel Committee) seeks to improve the quality of banking supervision worldwide, in part by developing broad supervisory standards. The Basel Committee consists of central bank and regulatory officials from 13 member countries: Belgium, Canada, France, Germany, Italy, Japan, Luxembourg, the Netherlands, Spain, Sweden, Switzerland, United Kingdom, and United States. The Basel Committee's supervisory standards are also often adopted by nonmember countries." Government Accountability Office (2007).

63. Securities and Exchange Commission (2008, p. 8).

64. "SEC Holding Company Supervision with Respect to Capital Standards and Liquidity Planning," SEC, March 7, 2007 (www.sec.gov/divisions/marketreg/hcliquidity.htm). Tentative capital is net capital before deductions for market and credit risk. SEC (2008, p. 11).

65. SEC (2008, p. 4).

66. Cox, "Turmoil in U.S. Credit Markets: Examining the Recent Actions of Federal Financial Regulators."

incapability to sell assets or redeem financial instruments and outflows of cash or capital harm a firm's liquidity. These situations become difficult for firms to control as ABSs, CDOs, or other structured products often do not have a liquid market. The situation is exacerbated when many firms are in the market at the same time."[67] Before the collapse of Bear Stearns and Lehman and the financial difficulties faced by the other investment bank holding companies, it would have been difficult if not impossible for market participants to anticipate the inadequacy of the international standards for holding company capital adequacy and liquidity that were relied on by both commercial and investment banks. Similarly, it would have been difficult if not impossible to understand the flaw in the fundamental assumption in the funding models of most investment banks and many commercial banks—that is, that secured lending that needs to be refinanced frequently will be available, even when markets are stressed.[68]

Legal Issues Raised by Credit Crisis Losses

Needless to say, a number of different parties have been adversely affected by the losses resulting from the decline in the value of financial instruments—particularly instruments tied to the value of mortgages—and they are bringing or are likely to bring legal claims seeking to recover some of those losses. We begin by discussing some of the possible claims by CDO and MBS purchasers, then examine some of the issues facing plaintiffs bringing the various class action lawsuits (appendix 5A). Plaintiffs will have to successfully navigate three basic principles of securities law to defend their claims: there can be no "fraud by hindsight"; there can be no actionable disclosure deficiency with respect to information that the market knew (the "truth on the market" defense); and plaintiffs must prove loss causation for their claimed damages. The application of those principles is necessarily informed by the evolving nature of the securitization market in the years immediately before the credit crisis.

Obviously, it is impossible to cover the entire spectrum of the types of claims that will be brought by different parties as a result of the current financial crisis. Perhaps most notably, we will not specifically discuss various legal issues raised by exposure due to credit default swaps, the derivative actions that have been filed against firms under state law, or claims arising out of losses suffered by mutual fund investors and purchasers of auction rate securities. The exclusion of such

---

67. Technical Committee of the International Organization of Securities Commissions (2008, p. 14).
68. See Brunnermeier (2009).

claims is not to say that some of them will not also raise some of the issues that we discuss, such as the requirement that plaintiffs establish loss causation.

Claims by CDO Purchasers

To understand the fallout from the credit crisis and the legal claims that it has generated, it is important to recognize that many of the losses suffered by investors, particularly the commercial and investment banks, are due to CDO exposure. More specifically, the CDO exposures of the commercial and investment banks often arose from either retaining the highest-rated CDO tranches, often with credit default swap protection (the so-called super-senior securities) or purchasing commercial paper issued by ABCP conduits that held super-senior securities. Banks' purchases of ABCP typically were triggered by either contractual obligations as standby liquidity providers or concern for maintaining their reputations in the commercial paper market.

For instance, consider the source of the losses for UBS and Merrill Lynch, two firms with among the highest amounts of asset write-downs. On February 14, 2008, UBS announced approximately $18.7 billion in losses for its full-year 2007 results. Approximately 50 percent of those losses were due to UBS's super-senior positions, and another 16 percent arose from its CDO warehouse positions acquired through its CDO origination and underwriting business.[69] On October 24, 2007, Merrill Lynch disclosed $7.9 billion in write-downs, including $5.6 billion in super-senior CDO losses.[70] On January 17, 2008, the firm announced further write-downs of $11.5 billion for its CDO positions, and in July 2008, it sold a $30.6 billion gross notional amount of U.S. super-senior CDOs for $6.7 billion. Those securities were valued at $11.1 billion before the sale. Super-senior CDO exposures wrecked havoc at other banks as well.[71]

From the standpoint of both litigation and regulatory policy, it is critically important to bear in mind that CDO securities were sold almost exclusively in rule 144A offerings. As a result, CDO purchasers were not retail investors but rather very large, financially sophisticated investors. For an offering to be exempt under rule 144A, purchasers (and, indeed, the offerees) must be "qualified institutional

69. The UBS Shareholder Report on UBS's Write-Downs, 2008 (www.ubs.com/1/ShowMedia/investors/shareholderreport?contentId=140333&name=080418ShareholderReport.pdf).

70. The Merrill Lynch, October 24, 2007, 8-K (http://ir.ml.com/sec.cfm?DocType=Current&Year=2007).

71. See, for example, Morgan Stanley's 2008 10-K (filed January 29, 2008), in which it attributed most of its $9.4 billion loss to super-senior CDOs (www.sec.gov/Archives/edgar/data/895421/000119312 509013429/d10k.htm).

buyers" (QIBs), which include pension plans, hedge funds, and banks. Hedge funds, in particular, are reported to have been major purchasers of CDOs, including the riskier CDO tranches that constituted, in effect, leveraged positions in mortgages. Commercial and investment banks tended to purchase super-senior CDO securities or retained CDO warehouse positions as part of their origination and underwriting businesses. The credit rating agencies, viewing the situation ex post, underestimated the risk of many of those securities. Relative to the errors in rating MBSs, the errors were large. The result has been credit rating downgrades and substantial losses for investors.

The fact that CDO interests are issued pursuant to rule 144A means that simply because there is no registration statement, CDO purchasers will not be able to bring section 11 claims under the Securities Act of 1933 against the issuers or sponsors of CDOs. Nor can CDO purchasers bring section 12(a)(2) actions under the Securities Act of 1933 for misleading disclosures in communications made during the CDO sales process. Under the Supreme Court's decision in *Gustafson* v. *Alloyd Co.*, communications made in private offerings (such as rule 144A offerings) are not "by means of a prospectus or oral communication," which is a necessary prerequisite to having a cause of action under section 12(a)(2).[72]

Another implication of the fact that the CDO market is a rule 144A market, besides the unavailability of the most attractive causes of action under the Securities Act of 1933, is its implication for regulatory policy going forward. A number of commentators, including the Counterparty Risk Management Policy Group, have called for higher standards for investor sophistication before investors are qualified to purchase a "financially risky complex product."[73] However, the need for such a revision is called into question by the fact that CDO purchasers have long satisfied the most demanding investor sophistication requirements known to securities regulation.

Much of the litigation involving CDOs will involve contractual claims. It is unclear at this point how fruitful the CDO "subscription agreement," pursuant to which purchasers agree to buy CDO interests, will be as a source of contractual claims because such agreements often had relatively little in the way of explicit representations or warranties. A more important source of contractual claims will likely be the CDO indenture agreement (most of which are governed by either New York or British contract law), which governs the collection and distribution of CDO funds among various CDO tranches. A CDO trustee is the party responsible under indenture agreements for ensuring compliance with the terms of the

72. *Gustafson* v. *Alloyd Co.*, 513 U.S. 561 (1995).
73. *Containing Systematic Risk: The Road to Reform*, Report of the Counterparty Risk Management Policy Group III, August 6, 2008 (www.crmpolicygroup.org/docs/CRMPG-III.pdf).

agreement. Table 5-4 documents the identity of CDO trustees for 2006 through the first half of 2008.[74] It is quite possible that the holders of the more junior or mezzanine tranches, perhaps hedge funds that wish to limit their losses, will argue that under the terms of the indenture agreement, some of the CDO proceeds belong to them—an interpretation that the holders of the more senior CDO tranches obviously will resist. Indeed such "tranche warfare" litigation is already well under way. For instance, Deutsche Bank, as trustee of a CDO indenture agreement, has sought judicial resolution of a dispute between various CDO tranche holders over how CDO proceeds should be distributed.[75] The disputes will arise when, according to the terms of a CDO indenture agreement, there is a "default" that potentially triggers an obligation on the part of the trustee to distribute to the CDO tranche holders whatever assets are held by the CDO. Appendix 5B documents the CDOs that were on the path to liquidation as of May 30, 2008, whereas table 5-5 documents CDO sponsors by number of CDO defaults as of January 18, 2008.[76] Contractual disputes are likely to be complex, given that the provisions governing the distribution of CDO funds can be quite intricate due to the waterfall structures that typically are in place and the fact that more than one document often purports to contain provisions relevant to such distributions. One possible source of elucidation of the parties' intended meaning of the various waterfall provisions governing the distribution of CDO proceeds is the computer simulations, generated under various scenarios or assumptions, of the returns that, hypothetically, holders of various CDO tranches would enjoy. Such computer simulations are typically provided to QIBs during the marketing of CDOs.

There is yet another potential source of litigation by CDO purchasers—claims against CDO collateral managers. This type of litigation has already occurred in the United Kingdom. One case, for instance, involved HSL Nordbank, which had invested in investment-grade tranches of a CDO called Corvus for which Barclays Capital was the collateral manager (Barclays also sponsored and marketed Corvus). HSL Nordbank claimed that as a result of the original assets of Corvus having been sold and replaced with poorly performing assets, its investment was rendered largely worthless. HSL Nordbank brought a number of claims against Barclays, including claims that Barclays had not adequately disclosed the

74. The table is based on data presented in *Asset-Backed Weekly Update*, November 15, 2008 (www. abalert.com/). We are grateful to *Asset-Backed Weekly* for providing us with a free subscription to their publication.

75. See, for example, the complaint filed in *Deutsche Bank Trust Company* v. *Lacrosse Financial Products LLC*, Supreme Court of the State of New York, County of New York, December 3, 2007 (http://securities. stanford.edu/).

76. The tables are based on data presented in *Asset-Backed Weekly Update*, January 18, 2008 (www. abalert.com/) and from *UBS CDO Research*, May 30, 2008.

Table 5-4. Trustees for CDOs Issued Worldwide, 2006 through First Half of 2008

Trustee	2008 (first half)			2007			2006		
	Issuance ($ millions)	Number of deals	Market share (percent)	Issuance ($ millions)	Number of deals	Market share (percent)	Issuance ($ millions)	Number of deals	Market share (percent)
Bank of New York	15,493.6	25	30.9	96,562.5	162	23.5	66,162.5	155	13.8
Deutsche Bank	7,801.1	27	15.5	61,313.1	126	14.9	50,486.7	136	10.5
LaSalle Bank	7,516.5	6	15.0	99,474.9	127	24.2	104,469.6	164	21.7
State Street	3,162.0	6	6.3	3,330.0	4	0.8	0.0	0	0.0
Ahorro y Titulizacion	2,493.8	1	5.0						
Citibank	2,041.5	4	4.1	10,590.7	19	2.6	2,986.1	6	0.6
Stichting Security	1,895.1	3	3.8						
Titulizacion de Activos	1,577.9	1	3.1	3,108.4	2	0.8	0.0	0	0.0
Mizuho Trust	941.0	1	1.9	139.9	1	0.0	758.9	1	0.2
Fortis Bank	752.3	1	1.5						
HSBC Bank	716.2	4	1.4	7,328.4	33	1.8	6,367.1	30	1.3
BNP Paribas	602.3	1	1.2	4,653.3	11	1.1	4,897.6	9	1.0
Deloitte & Touche	413.2	2	0.8	921.8	2	0.2	642.4	2	0.1
U.S. Bank	296.4	2	0.6	16,883.3	41	4.1	28,149.9	65	5.9
Wells Fargo				61,613.6	88	15.0	61,997.5	77	12.9
Investors Bank & Trust				5,739.7	9	1.4	7,709.9	15	1.6
Ernst & Young				2,728.1	1	0.7	1,147.5	2	0.2
Law Debenture Trust				1,809.5	12	0.4	7,525.6	43	1.6
Wilmington Trust				1,718.4	4	0.4	0.0	0	0.0
GestiCaixa				1,523.1	1	0.4	384.2	1	0.1
Europea de Titulizacion				1,194.8	1	0.3	0.0	0	0.0
First Commercial Bank				309.3	1	0.1	432.0	1	0.1
Capita IRG Trustees				303.5	1	0.1	316.7	1	0.1
Bank of Nova Scotia				125.0	1	0.0	0.0	0	0.0
Others	3,762.6	15	7.5	29,448.9	58	7.2	136,142.7	350	28.3
Total	50,196.7	100	100.0	410,820.2	705	100.0	480,576.9	1,058	100.0

Source: Asset-Backed Weekly Update, November 15, 2008 (www.abalert.com/).

Table 5-5. CDO Sponsors by Number of Defaults as of January 18, 2008

Collateral manager	Defaulted issuance ($ millions)	Number of deals
Cohen & Co.	6,361.9	4
Tricadia (Mariner Investment)	6,268.2	5
Vertical Capital	5,209.2	4
Vanderbilt (Pioneer Investments)	4,985.5	3
BlackRock	4,583.5	1
Harding Advisory	4,557.7	5
State Street Global	4,369.7	3
GSC Group	4,145.5	4
ACA Securities	3,959.6	4
Church Tavern Advisors	3,175.5	2

Source: *Asset-Backed Weekly Update* (January 18, 2008) (www.abalert.com/).

risks of purchasing the CDO interests, that Barclays had breached its duty of care in the management of Corvus as collateral manager, and finally, that Barclays had inflated the value of the CDO's assets in reports to Corvus investors. The HSL Nordbank lawsuit settled prior to judicial resolution.

What form are the types of claims brought by HSL Nordbank likely to take in the United States? With respect to claims concerning actions by CDO collateral managers—such as that collateral managers improperly substituted poorly per-forming assets for existing CDO assets—one possible approach would be to argue that a collateral manager is an ERISA fiduciary with respect to CDO pension plan purchasers. From the litigation filed so far, it appears plaintiffs will aggres-sively deploy the concept of ERISA fiduciary. Assuming that a collateral manager of a CDO is deemed to be an ERISA fiduciary with respect to the CDO invest-ments of pension plan funds, the collateral manager will arguably owe a duty of care and loyalty to the pension funds in the course of exercising its discretion in making investment decisions. Claims of a breach of a fiduciary duty would likely include claims of improper substitution of subpar performing assets for existing CDO assets (as was alleged in the HSL Nordbank case). Potential ERISA duty of loyalty claims, to which ERISA fiduciaries also are subject, could be brought based on transactions between CDOs and affiliates of CDO sponsors, assuming that the CDO sponsors and collateral managers are one and the same. Being involved in transactions with CDOs, such as by being the counterparty to certain types of derivative transactions entered into by the CDOs, is potentially quite lucrative for sponsoring institutions.

Not surprisingly, whether the collateral manager is in fact an ERISA fiduciary will turn on whether an exemption from ERISA is applicable. ERISA exempts CDOs when CDO tranches are deemed "debt" for purposes of ERISA (in conjunction with several other requirements being satisfied). One basis for arguing for the debt status of a CDO tranche—and hence an ERISA exemption—is that the tranche is rated investment grade. One question that this type of argument will raise is the effect of recent credit rating downgrades of a large number of CDO tranches to below–investment grade status. Another claim to exemption from ERISA commonly used by CDOs is the argument that no more than 25 percent of a CDO's equity has been purchased by ERISA plans (in conjunction with certain specified benefit plans). Interestingly, the issue of ERISA coverage usually does not come up in the context of MBS purchases because Department of Labor regulations exempt from ERISA those SPVs whose MBSs are registered under the Securities Act of 1933.[77]

Another interesting source of potential litigation with respect to CDO purchases is the claim that the pricing of CDO assets or interests therein was inflated relative to the "true" value of the assets or interests. Even if a CDO purchase agreement does not contain representations or warranties, there might well be a contractual obligation to provide pricing information on an on-going basis that could give rise to a contractual claim. A related legal basis for bringing a pricing claim is found in a long line of cases that have held that, absent adequate disclosure, when the price charged an investor bears no reasonable relation to the "prevailing price," it operates as a fraud on purchasers under rule 10b-5.[78] Such pricing claims are likely to be challenging to prove, in part because of the lack of comprehensive data on comparable CDO structures and performance that could help inform an analysis of the appropriateness of a valuation in any particular set of circumstances. For instance, whereas Bloomberg has comprehensive coverage of the MBS market (as well as the ABS market in general), it offers very little transaction or pricing information on CDOs. Other standard sources of financial data also lack comprehensive pricing data on CDOs.

Besides the difficulty of obtaining CDO information, two additional issues could loom large in the context of valuation claims. First, as the earlier discussion of CDOs emphasized, many CDOs are structured to cater to the needs and preferences of targeted investors, with the result that there is substantial heterogeneity across CDOs. That customization makes pricing comparisons across CDOs quite challenging, even when data are available. Second, if CDO purchasers

---

77. See Frankel (2006, p. 184) for a discussion of these regulations.

78. See Allen Ferrell, *The Law and Finance of Broker-Dealer Markups* (FINRA-commissioned study) discussing this line of cases.

received adequate disclosure, then it would be difficult to claim that there was fraudulent conduct in the valuation of a CDO.

Claims by MBS Purchasers

Although the most dramatic losses occurred for purchasers of CDOs, MBS credit ratings also were downgraded and investors suffered significant losses. Litigation brought by major purchasers of MBS already is under way.[79] One possible basis for a claim, given that the vast bulk of MBSs are registered, is a false or misleading registration statement, giving rise to section 11 liability. The issuer of the security, the SPV sponsor, underwriters, and auditors all will be subject to potential section 11 liability (with all but the issuer having due diligence defenses). With respect to other communications made during the registered offering process, misleading statements can give rise to section 12(a)(2) liability. And, of course, such misstatements would be subject to rule 10b-5 liability, although such a cause of action would have to survive the difficult hurdle of demonstrating scienter. Finally, there are a number of possible state causes of action, including breach of contract, fraud, and negligent misrepresentation, that might be brought by MBS purchasers.

What actions are likely candidates for being characterized as misleading disclosures in the registration statement or offering documents for registered MBSs? MBS purchasers could pursue potentially any of the four following actions, each of which relates in some way to the underwriting quality of the underlying mortgages themselves:

—outright fraud with respect to mortgage origination documents, rendering statements made in the offering process false

—inadequate disclosure of underwriting standards for the underlying mortgages

—misrepresentation of the extent to which exceptions were made to underwriting standards

—pricing of the various MBS tranches.

The presence of these disclosure issues in registration statements, including fraud in mortgage origination, will prove problematic for SPVs because there is no section 11 due diligence defense for issuers. Presumably, however, purchasers are more interested in suing the bank responsible for establishing, marketing, and underwriting the SPV and the MBSs in question.

One interesting issue that will arise in the context of litigation is the circumstances in which misstatements will be deemed "material," a requirement for

---

79. See, for example, *Luminent Mortgage Capital Inc.* v. *Merrill Lynch* (Eastern District Court of Pennsylvania).

bringing action under section 11, section 12(a)(2), rule 10b-5, and most related claims under state law. For instance, to what extent should the determination of the materiality of a misrepresentation turn on the hedging strategy of an MBS purchaser? Consider, for example, an MBS purchaser who buys the most junior tranches of an MBS as well as the MBS tranche that is entitled only to prepayment penalties collected when homeowners pay off mortgages early. One possible rationale for such a strategy is that the prepayment tranche serves as a hedge for the junior MBS tranches. As prepayments and hence prepayment penalties increase, the value of the prepayment tranche should rise, whereas the value of the junior MBS tranche should fall because fewer interest payments will be paid. The converse also is true: a reduction in prepayments should increase the value of the junior MBS tranches, but at the expense of the prepayment tranche. In such a context, is a misrepresentation about the likely incidence of prepayment material? Does the fact that the risk of prepayment is at least partially hedged make it less likely that such a misrepresentation will be deemed material? An analogous issue will arise in the context of a claim that there was mispricing due to a false statement that prepayments were likely to be substantial, because an inflated price for the prepayment tranche would arguably imply an offsetting underpricing of the junior tranche.

With respect to all four disclosure issues, the role of the due diligence firm looms as a potentially critical issue in litigation being brought against various actors in the structured finance arena. The information about the quality of the underlying mortgages that due diligence firms provided to those actors could be the subject of extensive litigation for a number of reasons. First, the provision or even availability of information to banks acting as underwriters for MBSs will arguably affect the availability of section 11 due diligence defenses with respect to material misstatements in MBS registration statements. In this regard, plaintiffs are likely to point to the decision in *In re Worldcom, Inc. Securities Litigation*, wherein the court concluded that the defendants had not established a due diligence defense due to "red flags" that should have put the section 11 defendants on notice that Worldcom's accounting was inaccurate.[80] Second, the provision of information on the underwriting quality of the mortgages will arguably speak to the availability of a "reasonable care" defense (the defendants did not know and in the exercise of reasonable care could not have known) with respect to section 12(a)(2) lawsuits brought by MBS purchasers. Third, such information might be used in actions proceeding under state law, such as breach of contract and negligent misrepresentation claims.

---

80. *In re Worldcom, Inc. Securities Litigation*, 346 F.Supp. 2d 628 (S.D.N.Y. 2004). The key issue here will be what constitutes a "red flag" that calls for further investigation before a due diligence defense will be viable. The discussion in *In re Worldcom* is quite sparse on this critical issue.

In short, it is quite likely that plaintiffs, in attempting to establish liability for various disclosure deficiencies, will try to use information uncovered by ongoing federal and state investigations. For example, the New York and Connecticut attorneys general as well as the SEC are investigating what due diligence firms knew about mortgage underwriting quality and the extent to which that information was shared with the banks sponsoring SPVs and underwriting MBSs. It has been reported that the FBI also is investigating issues relating to the quality of loan underwriting standards. As of the writing of this chapter, it was still unclear what revelations, if any, those investigations will produce.

Claims against the Investment Banks: Three Basic Principles of U.S. Securities Law

Although the litigation by purchasers of CDOs and MBSs is noteworthy, by far the most important litigation likely to arise from the credit crisis is class action litigation against publicly traded companies. In particular, the rule 10b-5 class action litigation that has been filed against the commercial and investment banks and mortgage originators as well as the associated follow-on ERISA litigation is substantial (see summary in appendix 5A). Of course, the litigation extends well beyond financial firms, with rule 10b-5 class action, section 11, and ERISA complaints being filed against nonfinancial firms as well.

Plaintiffs undoubtedly will argue that the information provided by the banks sponsoring MBS special purpose vehicles and underwriting MBSs or sponsoring CDOs establishes scienter, one of the main hurdles in bringing rule 10b-5 actions. Plaintiffs will claim that banks knew that the MBS and CDO interests held on their own books were worth significantly less than reported and that that information was both material and not adequately disclosed in 10-Ks and other disclosure documents. Similarly, plaintiffs will argue that the "contingent losses" faced by banks as a result of bringing SPV or SIV (structured investment vehicle) assets onto their books or purchasing ABCP were both large and understood by the banks. The ERISA litigation filed against the banks and mortgage originators claims that when acting in the role of fiduciary with respect to ERISA-covered plans, they breached their fiduciary duties by purchasing (or making available) imprudent investments on behalf of ERISA plans.

We believe, however, that plaintiffs that bring rule 10b-5 class action lawsuits will face substantial challenges. Given that the burden of proof is on the plaintiffs to establish the elements of their cause of action and damages, we will focus on areas where that burden is potentially the most difficult to satisfy. For purposes of providing an overview, we identify three basic principles of the securities laws that plaintiffs will have to successfully navigate. Of course, such an abbreviated discussion cannot and is not intended to fully cover the range of issues that are likely to be raised in this litigation.

No Fraud by Hindsight

The basic distinction between reasonable ex ante expectations and ex post losses is fundamental to finance theory and has long been reflected in the U.S. securities laws. That distinction will go to the core of many of the alleged actionable deficiencies with respect to disclosures by banks and mortgage originators to their security holders. It is also likely to prove quite important in the litigation brought by MBS and CDO purchasers. In our judgment, an important stumbling block for a number of the claims being brought will be whether plaintiffs have a cause for action in the failure of certain market participants to provide detailed disclosures concerning the implications of an event—the first national fall in housing prices since World War II, in conjunction with a dramatic and increasingly global credit crisis—from which those participants themselves suffered huge losses. More specifically, the class periods of many of the rule 10b-5, section 11, and ERISA class action lawsuits begin in 2006 or even earlier, as shown in appendix 5A. The timing raises the important question of whether the credit crisis was foreseeable in 2006 or before.[81]

Judge Henry Friendly pithily captured the distinction between ex ante expectations and ex post losses in *Denny* v. *Barber*, when he explained that there can be "no fraud by hindsight."[82] Judge Friendly made that observation in the course of rejecting a claim that Chase Manhattan Bank had engaged in fraud as evidenced, according to the plaintiffs, by inadequate disclosure of the bank's participation in making risky loans that eventually resulted in the bank suffering significant losses. More recently, in *Olkey* v. *Hyperion 1999 Term Trust*, the Second Circuit Court considered a claim by investors in a closed-end fund that held MBSs that the fund should face liability under sections 11 and 12(a)(2) of the Securities Act of 1933 and rule 10b-5.[83] The investors claimed, among other things, that there was misrepresentation in the fund prospectuses because the prospectuses failed to disclose the risky nature of the underlying MBS portfolio. They also claimed that the fund failed to disclose the potential size of losses if there was an adverse movement in interest rates. Needless to say, the investors in the closed-end fund suffered sub-

81. The complaints filed to date typically assert that the losses were foreseeable, but with little in the way of substantiation, at least at this time. See, for example, *Coulter* v. *Morgan Stanley* Class Action Complaint: "Despite the fact that Morgan Stanley was able to anticipate the losses from its exposure to subprime mortgage investments as far back as 2006, it failed to take any action to protect the Plans' participants from these foreseeable losses" (paragraph 103).
82. *Denny* v. *Barber*, 576 F.2d 465 (2d Cir. 1978).
83. *Olkey* v. *Hyperion 1999 Term Trust*, 98 F.3d 2 (2d Cir. 1996).

stantial losses when interest rates changed. In rejecting their claims, the court noted that the plaintiffs "claim that another set of investment choices should have been made, based upon a different conception of what interest rates would do. . . . This is only to say in *hindsight* that the managers of [other] funds turned out to be more skillful in their predictions" [emphasis added].

In other words, the presence of disclosure failures and the materiality thereof must be assessed in light of what was knowable at the time of the disclosure without the benefit of 20/20 hindsight, even if substantial losses occur ex post. The Second Circuit Court recently emphasized yet again the importance of what was knowable at the time of the alleged disclosure deficiency in *Teamsters Local 445 Freight Division Pension Fund* v. *Dynex Capital*.[84] The court stressed that to establish a disclosure deficiency as a result of the loss of value of bonds (securitized by homes), the plaintiffs must, among other things, be able to point to contemporaneous materials indicating that such undisclosed losses were occurring.

The case law of other circuit courts is in line with the Second Circuit Court's ex ante approach toward considering disclosure adequacy. For instance, in *Ford Motor Company Securities Litigation*, the Sixth Circuit Court explained that there is a duty to disclose the potential hazards of a product and future potential regulatory action only if such eventualities are "substantially certain" at the time the purported duty arises.[85] On a similar note, *In re K-Tel Int'l, Inc. Securities Litigation*, the Eighth Circuit Court conditioned the duty to disclose the impact of a future occurrence on the ability to "reasonably estimate[]" that occurrence.[86]

A number of pieces of evidence will speak to what was foreseeable at different points in time, some of which have already been discussed here, such as the profound changes in the RMBS and CDO markets in recent years. One way to consider this issue is to look at banks' reported value-at-risk (VaR) estimates, a metric widely used by banks immediately before the credit crisis to measure the risk inherent in at least some of their financial positions. Did those estimates predict, even in a rough way, the size of subsequent asset write-downs or which firms were most exposed if credit markets tightened? Based on the VaR figures disclosed in banks' 10-Ks from 2006 (summarized in table 5-6), the answer appears to be a resounding "no." Table 5-6 indicates that Goldman Sachs had the second-highest reported VaR for 2006, a figure that is itself an underestimation given that Goldman Sachs reports a VaR estimate solely for its trading portfolio, not a firm-wide VaR (a figure that UBS, the bank with the highest reported VaR, does report). Toward the

84. *Teamsters Local 445 Freight Division Pension Fund* v. *Dynex Capital*, 2008 U.S. App. LEXIS 13449 (2d Cir., June 26, 2008).
85. *Ford Motor Company Securities Litigation*, 381 F.3d 563 (6th Cir. 2004).
86. *In re K-Tel Int'l, Inc. Securities Litigation*, 300 F.3d 881, 893 (8th Cir. 2002).

Table 5-6. *Value at Risk, 2004–07*[a]
Millions of dollars

Firm	2004	2005	2006	2007
Bank of America[b,e]	44.1	41.8	41.3	---
Bear Stearns[c,d]	14.8	21.4	28.8	69.3
Citigroup[b,e]	116.0	93.0	106.0	---
Credit Suisse[b,e]	55.1	66.2	73.0	---
Deutsche Bank[b,e]	89.8	82.7	101.5	---
Goldman Sachs[c,e]	67.0	83.0	119.0	134.0
J. P. Morgan[b,e]	78.0	108.0	104.0	---
Lehman Brothers[c,e]	29.6	38.4	54.0	124.0
Merrill Lynch[c,e]	34.0	38.0	52.0	---
Morgan Stanley[c,d]	94.0	61.0	89.0	83.0
UBS[b,d]	103.4	124.7	132.8	---
Wachovia[b,e]	21.0	18.0	30.0	---

Source: Securities and Exchange Commission, 2006 10-K annual reports (www.sec.gov).

a. VaR statistics as reported in the 10-K or 20-F (in the case of foreign firms) of the respective firms. Note that firms use different assumptions in computing their value at risk. Some annual reports were not yet available for 2007.

b. Represents a 99 percent confidence interval, one-day holding period.

c. Represents a 95 percent confidence interval, one-day holding period.

d. Aggregate (trading and nontrading portfolio) VaR.

e. Trading portfolio VaR.

other end of the spectrum, the third-lowest reported VaR estimate was that of Merrill Lynch, whose VaR was less than half that of Goldman Sachs. Of course, Merrill Lynch has had among the highest asset write-downs, whereas Goldman Sachs has fared comparatively better so far. The correlation between banks' reported VaRs for 2006, the year immediately before the credit crisis, and their asset write-downs as of August 27, 2008 (summarized in table 5-1) is a meager 0.2. The average ratio of asset write-downs as of August 20, 2008, to VaRs reported for 2006 is 291.

Besides the predictability of credit crisis losses at different points in time, a more micro issue also speaks to what was reasonably knowable before the credit crisis began. The ability to model different scenarios for asset-backed securities depends heavily on having information regarding the historical performance of the underlying collateral. As a result, the level of knowledge concerning possible scenarios increases over time relative to what was known or knowable at the time that an SPV was created and interests therein sold to investors. A commonly held view among those who structure asset-backed securities is that one needs at least two years of historical information about asset performance, preferably through different economic conditions, to predict future performance accurately in different scenarios. In the case of MBSs and CDOs that own MBSs, the relevant information is the historical information for *that* type of mortgage pool or MBS. This observation is potentially important because most of the MBSs and CDOs that suffered substantial losses were created in the two years immediately before the credit crisis began or were exposed to mortgages and other assets originated in the same two-year period.

In short, plaintiffs will have to establish that there were false or misleading material disclosures or a violation of the duty to disclose material information, not merely observe that they suffered extensive economic losses.

Truth-on-the-Market Defense

Another important issue that will be germane to many of the securities claims being filed is what the market knew and when it knew it. With respect to macroeconomic issues, such as the current or future state of the economy, interest rates, or the national housing market, it is quite implausible that bank sponsors of SPVs and CDOs and underwriters of MBSs had any knowledge concerning these matters that was not also known to the market at large. Indeed, it is unclear what basis one could use to establish that participants in the structured finance market had private knowledge of information such as the national default rate on subprime mortgages, which directly, immediately, and sometimes substantially affected the values of certain MBS and CDO tranches.

In a situation in which the market is as informed as a defendant regarding a particular issue, then the truth-on-the-market doctrine in securities law will provide an opportunity for defendants to argue that any misrepresentation or violation of a duty to disclose information, assuming that there was one, was not material and hence not actionable, whether the cause of action is section 11, section 12(a)(2), or rule 10b-5. As the Second Circuit Court succinctly summarized this doctrine in *Ganino* v. *Citizen Utilities Co.*, "a misrepresentation is immaterial if the information is already known to the market because the misrepresentation cannot then defraud the market."[87] Consider, for example, a claim that a bank knew (because a due diligence firm informed the bank that the underwriting quality of some mortgages was questionable) that the true value of a pool of mortgages held in an SPV or on its own books was lower than that publicly reported in the offering materials or in the bank's disclosures to the market. If the underwriting quality for the specific type of mortgage in question (for example, 2006

---

87. *Ganino* v. *Citizen Utilities Co.*, 228 F.3d 154, 167 (2000).

refinancing no-documentation mortgages originated by mortgage brokers) is impaired on a marketwide basis (and not just for the mortgage pool in question), then it becomes debatable whether the information on underwriting quality held by the bank was any different from that known by the market based on existing marketwide information. In other words, the issue will be the extent to which the information allegedly held by the bank would have changed market expectations had the market learned the information directly from the bank. As always, the burden of establishing that such a change in market expectations would have occurred—and hence that the disclosed information is arguably "material"—is placed on the plaintiff.

Even assuming that a bank had private information that the underwriting quality of the mortgages held by an SPV or retained on its own books directly or through a CDO exposure was inferior to the typical underwriting quality of the universe of mortgages (holding constant the other attributes of the mortgage pool that were publicly disclosed), what the market knew and when it knew is nevertheless still legally relevant. The relevant private information known by the bank would be the difference between the information known by the bank about the underwriting quality of the particular pool of mortgages in question and the information known by the market at large. In that connection, it is worth noting that large and diversified pools of mortgages or MBSs, all else being equal, may tend to be representative of mortgages economy wide. As such, the average underwriting quality of the pool is likely to be similar to the quality of mortgages at large.

The truth-on-the-market doctrine also will be potentially relevant to claims that there was inadequate disclosure of financial exposure to off–balance sheet losses. Even assuming an obligation to disclose such information, the question will remain whether nondisclosures were material or whether the market was already aware of potential exposure. Putting aside whether a firm adequately disclosed such information in its SEC filings (10-K, 10-Q, 8-K), three considerations potentially speak to the market's knowledge of off–balance sheet exposure or the lack thereof.

First, the purchasers of CDO tranches and ABCP issued by conduits holding CDO securities were large institutional investors that were likely aware of the details of certain off–balance sheet arrangements, including sources of credit enhancement and the terms of liquidity guarantees by banks.[88] In fact, such arrangements typically are described in offering circulars and term sheets, as many potential purchasers simply refuse to buy such securities without liquidity guarantees. Potential investors' knowledge could constitute an important mechanism

88. Gorton and Souleles (2006).

by which information relating to off–balance sheet exposure would have reached the market and been impounded in security prices. How one might establish or disprove that hypothesis econometrically will be an important issue in litigation. It is worth pointing out that plaintiffs, in bringing the rule 10b-5 class action lawsuits summarized in appendix 5A, claim that the market is "semi-strong efficient"—that is, that the security prices of defendants reflected all readily available information. That argument is required to establish reliance on a classwide basis under the "fraud on the market" doctrine, but it raises the specter of a successful truth-on-the-market argument regarding the nonmateriality of off–balance sheet exposure if information about it was readily available.

Second, there are at least two important sources of disclosures besides firms' periodic reports under the Securities Exchange Act and in offering circulars: MBS registration statements and commercial banks' quarterly form Y-9C disclosures. Registration statements, which provide detailed information on the underlying collateral (including information on the underwriting quality on the pool of mortgages for MBSs), are readily accessible for all publicly traded MBSs. Table 5-7 summarizes some of the information disclosed in the registration statements of two representative Banc of America MBS deals; one from 2001 and another from 2006. The summaries reveal three things that appear to be true more generally for most MBS registration statements during that period. First, the quality of the MBS disclosures appears to increase over time; that is, more information was disclosed in 2006 than 2001. The difference may simply be a function of the SEC's promulgation in 2004, after a number of years of study and consultation, of Regulation AB, which mandated certain disclosures for asset-backed securities, including MBSs. Second, extensive deal characteristics, including the attributes of mortgage pools, were clearly disclosed in both 2001 and 2006. Third, the quality of mortgages that were securitized appears to have declined over time. Specifically, the average time until interest rates first adjusted declined substantially from 2001 to 2006, interest rate ceilings rose, loan-to-value ratios increased, and the geographic concentrations of assets fell.

Besides the MBS registration statements, commercial bank holding companies, such as JPMorgan Chase, Citigroup, and Bank of America, have to file form Y-9C quarterly (among other forms) with the Federal Reserve. Form Y-9C is the required consolidated financial statement for bank holding companies with consolidated assets of $500 million or more. Of particular relevance is schedule HC-S, which provides detailed information on the securitization activities of banks—information that typically is more specific than that available from SEC filings. For instance, schedule HC-S provides information on ABCP conduits, including "unused commitments to provide liquidity to conduit structures" broken down by conduits

Table 5-7. *Summary of Some Information Disclosed in Two Banc of America MBS Issuances from 2001 and 2006*

Information	Issue date 6/27/01		Issue date 4/15/06	
	Range or total	*Weighted average*	*Range or total*	*Weighted average*
Unpaid principal balance	$276,063 to $1,000,000	$490,115	$430,400 to $2,864,000	$714,114
Interest rates (percent)	5.250 to 7.625	6.90	5.125 to 7.250	6.22
Rate ceiling (percent)	10.250 to 12.625	11.90	11.125 to 13.250	12.22
Months to first adjustment date	58 to 60 months	59 months	5 to 36 months	35 months
Remaining terms to stated maturity	119 to 360 months	359 months	359 to 360 months	359 months
Original term	120 to 360 months	360 months	360 months	--
Loan age	0 to 2 months	1 month	0 to 1 month	1 month
Original loan-to-value ratio	8.29 to 95.00	67.94	40.91 to 95.00	73.91
Debt-to-income ratio			13.80 to 61.00	39.27
Credit scores			642 to 810	749
Latest maturity date	July 1, 2031	--	March 1, 2036	--
Percent of interest-only mortgage loans		30.47		80.31
Percent of "alternative" underwriting guideline mortgage loans		2.57	--	--
Percent of mortgage loans secured by investor properties			--	
Percent of leasehold mortgages			0.00	--
Geographic concentration of mortgaged properties in excess of 5 percent of the aggregate unpaid principal balance				
Maximum single zip code concentration (percent)	1.99		8.02	

sponsored by the bank and conduits sponsored by unrelated institutions. For example, JPMorgan Chase disclosed $2.68 billion in sponsored unused ABCP conduit liquidity guarantees outstanding and another $99 million in unsponsored conduits for the second quarter of 2007, which ended June 30. In terms of balance sheet assets, schedule HC-B requires banks to disclose MBS holdings, including collateralized mortgage obligations.

Third, the academic literature generally concludes that off–balance sheet exposures, including transfers of financial assets in securitizations, are "priced" by the market (see the literature survey in Schipper and Yohn 2007).[89] For example, Niu and Richardson document that off–balance sheet debt relating to securitization has the same risk relevance to a firm's stock—the stock's capital asset pricing model (CAPM) beta—as on–balance sheet debt. In other words, the market prices the implicit put option conferred by the off–balance sheet debt issued in the course of securitizations—that is, investors' ability to force a firm, either as a result of contract or reputational concerns, to purchase off–balance sheet debt.[90] Consistent with those findings, Landsman, Peasnell, and Shakespeare report that analysts treat securitizations as secured borrowing in much the same way that analysts view securitized assets and liabilities as belonging to sponsoring banks.[91] Lim, Mann, and Mihov document that the market impounds off–balance sheet financing of operating leases into corporate debt yields, despite limited disclosure by firms of such arrangements.[92] Of course, whether the market knew and priced certain information will ultimately turn on the specific factual circumstances at question in the litigation.

Loss Causation

In the wake of the Supreme Court's 2005 decision in *Dura Pharmaceuticals* v. *Broudo*, the issue of loss causation has become increasingly important in securities class action litigation.[93] Loss causation requires plaintiffs to prove in a rule 10b-5 action that the losses that they seek to recover were "caused" by misconduct

89. Schipper and Yohn (2007).

90. Flora Niu (School of Business and Economics, Wilfrid Laurier University) and Gordon D. Richardson (Joseph L. Rotman School of Management, University of Toronto), "Earnings Quality, Off–Balance Sheet Risk, and the Financial-Components Approach to Accounting for Transfers of Financial Assets," Social Science Research Network, 2004 (http://ssrn.com/abstract=628261).

91. Wayne R. Landsman (University of North Carolina at Chapel Hill), Ken V. Peasnell (Lancaster University), and Catherine Shakespeare (Ross School of Business, University of Michigan), "Are Asset Securitizations Sales or Loans?" research paper, August 2006 (http://ssrn.com/abstract=924560).

92. See Steve Lim, Steven Mann, and Vassil Mihov (all affiliated with the M. J. Neeley School of Business, Texas Christian University), "Market Evaluation of Off–Balance Sheet Financing: You Can Run but You Can't Hide," working paper, 2003.

93. *Dura Pharmaceuticals* v. *Broudo*, 544 U.S. 336.

that ran afoul of rule 10b-5 and not by marketwide declines. Perhaps the most notable loss causation decision is the Fifth Circuit Court's opinion in *Oscar Private Equity Investments* v. *Allegiance Telecom, Inc.* that loss causation must be established before classwide reliance can be presumed under a fraud-on-the-market theory *at the class certification stage*.[94] In a section 11 suit, loss causation is also an important issue, although the burden of proof is on the defendant.

Loss causation is likely to be a challenging litigation issue for plaintiffs, because market prices, especially of financial sector securities, declined overall. Perhaps the most dramatic evidence of a marketwide break can be seen in the so-called "TED spread," which is the difference between the three-month LIBOR (in dollars) and the three-month U.S. Treasury bill rate. This spread is often interpreted as the risk premium banks demand for lending money to other banks, as LIBOR is the rate for unsecured interbank lending in the London wholesale money market and the Treasury bill rate is viewed as a proxy for the risk-free rate of return. As shown in figure 5-7, the most dramatic market break in the TED spread occurred on August 9, 2007,[95] although some commentators perceived signs of distress emerging as early as July 2007, when several Bear Stearns hedge funds ran into trouble. The spread has been elevated ever since. Other spreads, such as the difference between the rates of thirty-year agency debt and thirty-year Treasury bonds, exhibited an even sharper break in July than the TED spread.[96] It bears emphasizing that the most relevant spread for valuing securities will depend on the instruments in question. For instance, super-seniors, which were the source of substantial losses for banks, were not downgraded by rating agencies until mid-October 2007.[97]

There is an important and ongoing academic debate on what caused the increases in spreads over time. Some financial economists interpret the jump in the TED spread as a sign that banks perceived an increase in borrower default risk (counterparty risk), even though the counterparties in the LIBOR wholesale

94. *Oscar Private Equity Investments* v. *Allegiance Telecom, Inc.*, 2007 U.S. App. LEXIS 11525 (May 16, 2007).

95. On August 9, 2007, the European Central Bank and the Federal Reserve injected money into the banking system because of concerns over credit market conditions. On the same day, BNP Paribas reported that it was suspending the calculation of net asset value as well as subscriptions/redemptions for three of its funds; the *Wall Street Journal* reported that the North American Equity Opportunities hedge fund, backed by Goldman Sachs, was in trouble; IKB Deutsche Industrie Bank AG reported substantial subprime losses; and Toll Brothers announced a 21 percent reduction in preliminary revenue for the third quarter and refused to provide future guidance.

96. Brunnermeier (2009).

97. Mark Pittman, "Moody's Downgrades $33.4 Billion of Subprime Bonds," Bloomberg, October 11, 2007 (www.bloomberg.com).

Figure 5-7. *Three-Month US$ LIBOR–Three-Month Treasury Bill Spread*

Percent yield

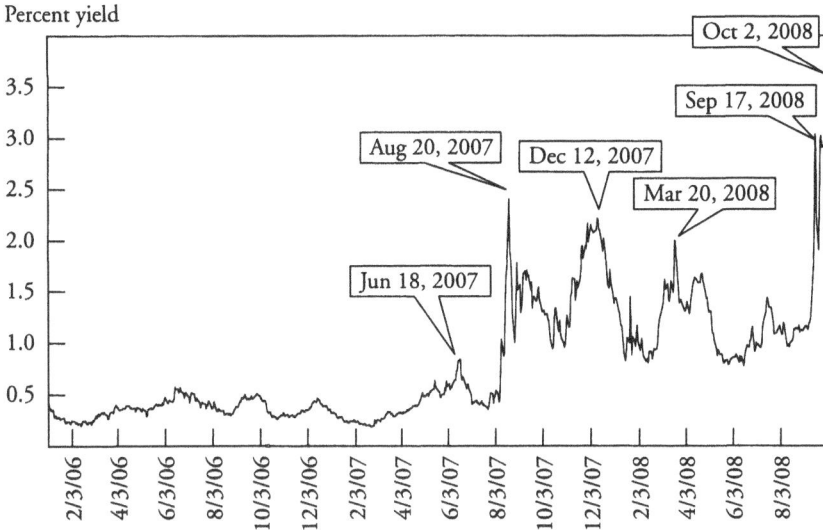

Source: Federal Reserve Bank of Saint Louis (http://research.stlouisfed.org/fred2/data/DTB3.txt) and British Bankers' Association (www.bba.org.uk/bba/jsp/polopoly.jsp?d=141&a=627).

money market are among the largest, most well-established banks.[98] Others, however, believe that the spread widened because cash-constrained banks have been unwilling to lend (liquidity risk).[99] Regardless of the answer, the important legal point is that increases in spreads appear to have resulted from marketwide factors. That conclusion is important because losses arising from the decline in the market value of MBS and CDOs that resulted from marketwide increases in counterparty and liquidity risk will have a difficult time being traced to misconduct by individual firms that is actionable under rule 10b-5.

Even if an institution fails in its legal duty to disclose the full details of potential exposure, including under extreme market conditions, the relevance of such

98. The contributing banks for the LIBOR rate (US$) in 2007 were Bank of America, Bank of Tokyo–Mitsubishi UFJ, Barclays Bank, Citibank, Credit Suisse, Deutsche Bank, HBOS, HSBC, JPMorgan Chase, Lloyds TSB Bank, Rabobank, Royal Bank of Canada, Norinchukin Bank, Royal Bank of Scotland Group, UBS, and WestLB.

99. John B. Taylor (Stanford University) and John C. Williams (Federal Reserve Bank of San Francisco), "A Black Swan in the Money Market," Working Paper W13943 (Cambridge, Mass.: National Bureau of Economic Research, April 2008) (http://ssrn.com/abstract=1121734).

disclosure will likely be a function of the market conditions that existed at the time. This argument is directly related to the doctrine of loss causation, if one interprets loss causation as existing only when a "corrective disclosure" reveals actionable misconduct to the market and thereby dissipates "inflation" present in a stock's price. In turn, "inflation" in rule 10b-5 litigation typically refers to the extent to which a stock traded above the price that it would have but for the actionable misconduct. If such a disclosure—say, at the beginning of 2006—of a firm's full potential exposure would not have changed the firm's stock price, then loss causation will fail to exist as there simply would be no such inflation present in the stock price that could have been dissipated by a corrective disclosure. Interestingly, these market concerns, at least as evidenced by rate spreads such as the TED spread, were essentially absent in 2006. In short, the relevance of various types of disclosures can well be a function of market conditions.

Some plaintiffs claim that banks and other market participants could reasonably have known the extent of their trading partners' counterparty risk and thus avoided losses. The challenge for plaintiffs, however, will be to show that a single institution could have known such information. Consider, for example, one of the most exposed investments, the lower tranches of MBS issued against subprime mortgages. Those tranches often were repackaged into CDOs, which were repackaged yet again into other CDO structures. SPVs issuing the MBSs and CDOs hedged the credit risk by entering into transactions, such as credit default swaps, with third parties. The investors in each of the above interests were varied, and some traded the instruments in the secondary markets. It therefore may have been impossible for any single entity to know who was exposed to subprime losses. Indeed, it was precisely the most exposed interests, the lower tranches, that saw the most repackaging and whose risk was least transparent. Not surprisingly, a common observation is that rule 144A CDO global notes, the typical form in which CDO tranches are issued, are difficult to track. Indeed, some CDO purchasers used confidentiality agreements to prohibit CDO collateral managers from knowing their identities.

ERISA Litigation

Appendix 5A indicates that credit crisis–related ERISA complaints have already been filed against numerous companies, including Citigroup, MBIA, Merrill Lynch, Morgan Stanley, and State Street. The potential sums involved in these lawsuits should not be underestimated. For instance, in one of the ERISA complaints filed against Fremont General Corporation, the complaint states that the ERISA "breaches have caused the [ERISA] plans to lose over 164 million dollars of retirement savings."[100] The Citigroup ERISA complaint alleges that the losses from the ERISA violations were "over $1 billion."[101] In many ERISA complaints, not surprisingly given the early stage of the litigation, the allegations concerning damages are quite vague. For instance, one of the ERISA complaints filed against State Street states merely that State Street's alleged ERISA violations caused "hundreds of millions of dollars of losses."[102]

The ERISA litigation represents an important component of the subprime litigation, as ERISA provides plaintiffs important legal advantages over the securities laws. First, plaintiffs do not need to establish scienter, as is the case under rule 10b-5. Rather, liability is based on the defendant's breach of its fiduciary duty. Second, the damages resulting from a breach of fiduciary duty under ERISA have tended to be quite generous, at least as reflected in the terms on which ERISA lawsuits were settled before the *Dura Pharmaceuticals* decision.

The Fiduciary Breach

Virtually all the ERISA complaints filed to date against the banks and mortgage originators claim that the companies' executives and administrators who oversaw the retirement plans—and who allegedly therefore were ERISA fiduciaries—knew or should have known that the companies faced substantial losses. They therefore should have disclosed that information to plan participants or should have refused to purchase the securities in the first place.

Several interesting issues will arise with respect to such claims, besides the obvious issue once again of whether the credit crisis was foreseeable. One issue will be whether the courts will transform ERISA into a third general securities disclosure statute complementing or substituting for the detailed disclosure regimes established in the Securities Act of 1933 and the Exchange Act of 1934. The issue arises because many of the ERISA complaints allege that company executives and administrators had a duty to disclose information about potential losses facing firms to plan participants. At the end of the day, however, if ERISA fiduciaries had such a duty, surely it would have extended to all investors, plan participants or not. It is simply not tenable or consistent with other aspects of U.S. securities laws to have such a duty extend to only a subset of investors.

A second interesting issue is how to think about what plan participants' situations would have been but for the purported ERISA violation. Presumably an

100. *Johannesson* v. *Fremont General Corporation* Complaint, p. 4 (http://securities.stanford.edu/).

101. *Rappold* v. *Citigroup* Complaint (http://securities.stanford.edu/).

102. See *Unisystems, Inc.* v. *State Street Bank and Trust Company* Complaint (http://securities.stanford.edu/).

announcement by an ERISA fiduciary that a firm faced substantial losses would have resulted in a lower stock price. If not, it is difficult to see how the information would have been material. The ERISA fiduciary would not have had a duty to disclose it. But that logic has an interesting implication for damages resulting from such violations. In such cases, ERISA fiduciaries' failure to disclose adverse information would not have *caused* the losses suffered by plan participants with respect to the securities that they held at the time the breach of the duty to disclose but rather merely *delayed* it, because the information eventually came out.

Loss Causation in ERISA Litigation

Plaintiffs bringing ERISA actions have long relied on the Second Circuit Court's 1985 opinion in *Bierwirth* v. *Donovan* to argue that damages should be calculated on the basis of the best-performing fund available in the plan.[103] In times of market decline, such a fund might well be a money market mutual fund. That approach can effectively render an ERISA fiduciary an insurer against general declines in the stock market.

The ERISA statute itself merely states that the ERISA fiduciary shall "make good to such plan any losses to the plan resulting from each such breach."[104] The Supreme Court's decision in 2005 in *Dura Pharmaceuticals* explained that losses due to market and industry-wide developments will not result in damages if such damages are not caused by actionable misconduct by the defendant (in *Dura Pharmaceuticals* the misconduct was actionable under rule 10b-5). Applying the same reasoning to ERISA damages, one could argue that market and industry-wide declines are not the "result" of a breach of fiduciary duty. Such an argument, given the important implication that it might have for the extent of the damages available under ERISA, will be hotly contested. The issues involved in resolving such a debate are quite complex, including consideration of the proper interpretation of the *Bierwirth* opinion, the continued validity of *Bierwirth* in light of *Dura Pharmaceuticals*, and the notion of "causation" in the common law of trust that has been used by courts in the course of interpreting the ERISA statute.

The Rating Agencies

Many commentators have blamed the rating agencies, principally Moody's, Standard & Poor's, and Fitch, for investor losses. Both Moody's and McGraw-Hill, the parent company of Standard & Poor's, are facing rule 10b-5 class action lawsuits. This litigation raises some interesting issues. The crux of plaintiffs' claims is that

103. *Bierwirth v. Donovan*, 754 F.2d 1049.
104. 29 U.S.C. 1109 (2000).

the rating agencies "assigned excessively high ratings to bonds backed by risky sub-prime mortgages."[105] The challenges facing plaintiffs here are two-fold: specifying the precise meaning of "excessively high" and establishing why "excessively high" ratings, so defined, "inflated" the stock prices of the rating agencies to the detriment of their security holders. As to the first issue, if the ratings criteria for MBSs and CDOs were publicly available, it will be difficult to maintain that ratings based on the criteria were too "high," irrespective of how one judges the criteria themselves. A rating arguably has no meaning without reference to the criteria that generated it. Given that rating criteria are generally acknowledged to be broadly known and can be independently assessed by third parties, the source of the fraud is difficult to locate. As to the second issue, even if one stipulates that the ratings were "high" by reference to some metric other than the stated criteria themselves, it will still be necessary to show that such "high" ratings inflated rating agencies' stock prices. Even if one were to assume, for purposes of discussion, that unduly "high" ratings were generated to ensure repeat business from MBS and CDO issuers (and putting aside the fact that issuers had very few choices for ratings), the mere fact that business practices might be questionable does not establish that a stock price did not reflect the true value of the business so conducted.

Some commentators have suggested that rating agencies should be deemed "underwriters" of the MBS and CDO tranches that they rated for purposes of the Securities Act of 1933 and hence subject to section 11 liability. Such a conclusion seems unlikely for two reasons. First and perhaps most fundamentally, many of the losses as well as the controversy over the quality of ratings have arisen with respect to CDOs. These securities, however, are issued pursuant to rule 144A rather than registered. It is therefore legally impossible, by definition, for rating agencies to be deemed section 11 underwriters. Second, rating agencies are not paid for the success of offerings but for their rating services. Rating agencies do not purchase rated tranches with a view toward resale. As a result, it is unlikely that rating agencies will be deemed "underwriters," at least as that term has long been understood in the context of the Securities Act of 1933.

Conclusions

Two of the strengths of the U.S. capital market are its ability to innovate and to spread risk widely among investors. The recent past has highlighted, however, that successful innovation and risk spreading are predicated on the ability of sophisticated market participants to rely on information conveyed across the

---

105. See, for example, *Teamsters Local 282 Pension Trust Fund* v. *Moody's Corporation* Complaint.

chain of participants that originate, appraise, and service collateral and under-write, manage, insure, rate, and sell securities. When information cannot be or is not conveyed or when a market participant acts in such a way as to undermine the integrity of the chain, the chain can be compromised and losses may be incurred.

Over the next few years, litigation among market participants may serve to identify weak links in that chain. Alternatively, the litigation may serve to high-light where the market may have underappreciated certain risks or failed to antic-ipate particular circumstances. That distinction is one with which current liti-gants undoubtedly will have to struggle.

Appendix 5A. *Summary of Securities Class Action Lawsuits as of November 15, 2008*

Firm	Date	Case	Cause of action	Class period
ACA Capital Holdings	1/11/08	*Rose v. ACA Capital Holdings Inc.*	10b-5/Section 11 & 12(a)(2)	11/2/06 – 11/20/07
	11/21/07	*Blackmoss Investments Inc. v. ACA Capital Holdings, Inc.*	Section 11 & 12(a)(2)	11/10/06 – 11/10/06
Accredited Home Lenders	6/25/07	Consolidated various actions against Accredited Home Lenders	10b-5/section 11 & 12(a)(2)	11/1/05 – 3/12/07
Ambac Financial Group	8/25/08	Consolidated various actions against Ambac Financial Group	10b-5/section 11 & 12(a)(2)	10/25/06 – 4/22/08
Amer. Home Mort. Investment	3/19/08	Consolidated various actions against American Home Mortgage Investment	10b-5/section 11 & 12(a)(2)	6/19/05 – 8/6/07
Amer. International Group	10/09/08	*Carroll v. American International Group, Inc.*	Section 11 & 12(a)(2)	12/11/07 – 12/11/07
	5/21/08	*Jacksonville Police and Fire Pension Fund v. American International Group, Inc.*	10b-5	5/11/07 – 5/9/08
Bankatlantic Bancorp	12/12/07	Consolidated various actions against Bankatlantic Bancorp, Inc.	10b-5	11/9/05 – 10/25/07
BankUnited Financial Corp.	9/16/08	*Waterford Township Employees Retirement System v. BankUnited Fin. Corp.*	10b-5	9/16/08 – 6/18/08
Beazer Homes	4/30/07	*Miller v. Beazer Homes*	ERISA	12/31/05 – 3/29/07
	8/08/07	Consolidated various actions against Beazer Homes	10b-5	1/27/05 – 5/12/08
Canadian Imp. Bank of Comm.	9/19/08	*Plumbers/Steamfitters Pension Fund v. Canadian Imperial Bank of Commerce*	10b-5	5/31/07 – 5/28/08
Care Investment Trust	9/18/07	*Briarwood Investments Inc. et al. v. Care Investment Trust Inc.*	Section 11	6/22/07 – 6/22/07
CBRE Realty Finance	7/29/08	*Philip Hutchinson v. CBRE Realty Finance, Inc.*	Section 11 & 12(a)(2)	9/29/06 – 8/06/07
Centerline Holding	7/07/08	Consolidated various actions against Centerline Holding Company	10b-5	3/12/07 – 12/28/02

(continued)

Appendix 5A. *Summary of Securities Class Action Lawsuits as of November 15, 2008 (continued)*

Firm	Date	Case	Cause of action	Class period
CIT Group	7/25/08	*Plumbers, Pipefitters, and Apprentices Pension Fund v. CIT Group, Inc.*	10b-5	4/18/07 – 3/05/08
Citigroup Global Markets	7/9/08	Consolidated various actions against MAT Five LLC	Section 12(a)(2)	12/18/06 – 12/18/06
Citigroup Mort. Loan Trust	4/07/08	*City of Ann Arbor Retirement System v. Citigroup Mortgage Loan Trust Inc.*	Section 11	12/12/06 – 12/12/06
Citigroup	8/20/08	Consolidated various actions against Citigroup, Inc.	10b-5	N/A
	11/16/07	*Rappold v. Citigroup*	ERISA	1/1/07 – present
Coast Financial Holdings	8/24/07	Consolidated various actions against Coast Financial Holdings	Section 11 & 10b-5	1/21/05 – 1/22/07
Compucredit Corp.	10/22/08	Waterford Township Employees Retirement System	10b-5	11/06/06 – 06/09/08
Countrywide	1/16/08	*Snyder v. Countrywide Financial Corporation*	California state law	
Financial Corp.	4/11/08	Consolidated various actions against Countrywide	10b-5/Section 11 & 12(a)(2)	3/12/04 – 3/07/08
	10/30/07	*Argent Classic Convertible Arbitrage Fund v. Countrywide Financial Corp.*	10b-5	5/16/07 – 11/21/07
	10/12/07	*Saratoga Advantage Trust v. Countrywide Financial Corporation*		
Credit Suisse Group	6/23/08	*Cornwell v. Credit Suisse Group*	10b-5	4/24/04 – 8/9/07
			10b-5	2/15/07 – 4/14/08
Downey Financial Corp.	9/30/08	Consolidated various actions against Downey Financial Corporation	10b-5	10/16/06 – 3/14/08
Etrade Financial	11/21/07	*Ferenc v. Etrade Financial Corporation*	10b-5	4/20/06 – 11/9/07
	11/16/07	*Davidson v. Etrade Financial Corporation*	10b-5	12/14/06 – 11/9/07
	10/12/07	*Boston v. Etrade Financial Corporation*	10b-5	12/14/06 – 9/25/07
	10/2/07	*Freudenberg v. Etrade Financial Corporation*	10b-5	12/14/06 – 9/25/07
Evergreen Investment Mgmt.	6/23/08	*Keefe v. Evergreen Investment Management Co.*	Section 11 & 12(a)(2)	6/23/05 – 6/23/08
Fcstone Group	7/16/08	*Luman v. Paul G. Anderson*	10b-5	4/10/08 – 7/9/08

Company	Date	Case	Claim	Period
Federal Home Loan Mortgage	8/15/08	Kuriakose v. Federal Home Loan Mortgage Company	10b-5	11/21/07 – 8/05/08
Federal National Mortgage Association	9/23/08	Mark v. Goldman Sachs & Co.	Section 12 (a)(2)	11/29/07 – 11/29/07
	9/8/08	Genovese v. Ashley	10b-5	11/16/07 – 9/5/08
	10/8/08	Schweitzer v. Merrill Lynch, Pierce, Fenner & Smith, Inc.	10b-5	12/11/07 – 9/5/08
	9/16/08	Crisafi v. Merrill Lynch, Pierce, Fenner & Smith Inc.	10b-5	5/13/08 – 9/06/08
	11/10/08	Fed. Nat. Mort. Association ERISA Litigation	ERISA	4/17/07 – present
Fidelity Mgmt & Research	6/5/08	Zametkin v. Fidelity Management & Research Company	Section 11 & 12(a)(2)	6/5/05 – 6/5/08
Fifth Third Bancorp	6/20/08	The Esche Fund v. Fifth Third Bancorp	10b-5/Section 11	10/19/07 – 6/17/08
	8/12/08	McGee v. Fifth Third Bancorp	Section 11 & 12(a)(2)	11/26/07 – 6/6/08
First American Corp.	6/23/08	Berks County Employees' Retirement Fund v. First American Corporation	10b-5	4/26/06 – 11/6/07
First Home Builders	10/19/07	Sewell v. First Home Builders	10b-5/Section 12(a)(2)	9/1/03 – 12/31/05
First Horizon National Corp.	5/09/08	Sims v. First Horizon National Corporation	ERISA	5/01/02 – 4/28/08
First Trust Portfolios	9/12/08	Gosselin v. First Trust Portfolios, L.P.	10b-5/section 11 & 12(a)(2)	7/26/05 – 7/7/08
Fortis	10/22/08	Copeland v. Fortis	10b-5	1/28/08 – 10/6/08
Franklin Bank Corp.	6/6/08	Roucher Trust v. Franklin Bank Corporation	10b-5	10/29/07 – 5/1/08
Fremont General Corp	6/12/08	Antencio v. Fremont General Corporation	10b-5	7/28/05 – 8/10/07
	9/21/07	Matheus v. Fremont General Corporation	10b-5	5/9/06 – 2/27/07
	9/19/07	Miller v. Fremont General Corporation	10b-5	5/9/06 – 2/27/07
	9/4/07	Al-Beitawi v. Fremont General Corporation	10b-5	5/9/06 – 2/27/07
	4/24/07	McCoy v. Fremont General Corporation	ERISA	1/1/03 – present
	5/29/07	Sullivan v. Fremont General Corporation	ERISA	1/1/05 – present
	5/25/07	Salas v. Fremont General Corporation	ERISA	12/31/05 – present
	5/15/07	Johannesson v. Fremont General Corporation	ERISA	1/1/05 – present
	5/15/07	Anderson v. Fremont General Corporation	ERISA	5/9/06 – 3/5/07
General Electric	7/30/08	Coyne v. General Electric Company	10b-5	3/12/08 – 4/10/08

(continued)

Appendix 5A. *Summary of Securities Class Action Lawsuits as of November 15, 2008* (continued)

Firm	Date	Case	Cause of action	Class period
Harborview Mort. Loan Trust	6/2/08	*New Jersey Carpenters Vacation Fund v. HarborView Mortgage Trust*	Section 11 & 12(a)(2)	4/26/06 – 10/3/06
Home Equity Mort. Trust 2006-5	6/23/08	*New Jersey Carpenters Vacation Fund v. Home Equity Mortgage Trust*	Section 11 & 12(a)(2)	10/30/06 – 10/30/06
Homebanc Corp.	11/30/07	*Kadel v. Homebanc Corp*	10b-5/Section 11 & 12(a)(2)	3/7/06 – 8/3/07
	1/4/08	*Harbour v. Flood*	10b-5	9/26/05 – 8/3/07
Homebank Corp.	12/17/07	*Cleuley v. Flood*	10b-5	9/26/05 – 8/3/07
Hovnanian Enterprises	9/14/07	*Mankofsky v. Sorsby*	10b-5	12/8/05 – 8/13/07
Huntington Banc.	1/18/08	*Vecchio v. Huntington Bancshares Inc.*	10b-5	7/20/07 – 11/16/07
	12/19/07	*Ellman v. Huntington Bancshares Inc.*	10b-5	7/20/07 – 11/16/07
	2/25/08	*Cedarleaf and Moening v. Huntington Bancshares Inc.*	ERISA	7/01/07 – present
	5/7/08	*Tom v. Huntington Bancshares Inc.*	Section 11 & 12(a)(2)	11/16/07 – 5/7/08
Impac Mortgage Holdings	10/27/08	Consolidated various claims against Impac Mortgage Holdings Inc.	10b-5	5/10/06 – 8/15/07
	12/17/07	*Page v. Impac Mortgage Holdings, Inc.*	ERISA	N/A
Indymac Financial	6/6/08	Consolidated various against IndyMac Bancorp Inc.	10b-5	1/26/06 – 1/25/07
	6/11/08	*Folsom v. IndyMac Bancorp, Inc.*	10b-5	6/16/07 – 5/12/08
Istar Financial Inc.	4/14/08	*Citiline Holdings Inc. v. iStar Financial Inc.*	Section 11 & 12(a)(2)	12/13/07 – 12/13/07
JP Morgan Acceptance Corp.	3/26/08	*Plumbers'/Pipefitters' Trust v. J. P. Morgan Acceptance Corporation*	Section 11	1/1/06 – 3/31/07
Kkr Financial Holdings	8/7/08	*Charter Township of Clinton Retirement v. KKR Financial Holdings, LLC*	Section 11	5/4/07 – 5/4/07
Lehman Brothers Holding	2/22/08	*Reese v. O'Meara*	10b-5	9/13/06 – 7/30/07
	9/24/08	*Fogel Capital Management v. Fuld*	Section 11	2/5/08 – 2/5/08
Levitt Corp.	9/3/08	Consolidated various claims against Levitt Corporation	10b-5	1/31/07 – 8/14/07

Company	Date	Case	Claim	Class Period
Luminent Mortgage Cap	2/15/08	Consolidated various claims against Luminent Mortgage	10b-5	6/25/07 – 8/6/07
MBIA	10/17/08	Consolidated various claims against MBIA Inc.	10b-5	7/02/07 – 1/9/08
Merrill Lynch	5/21/08	Consolidated various claims against Merrill Lynch & Co.	10b-5/Section 11 & 12(a)(2)	2/26/07 – 10/23/07
	10/22/08	Louisiana Sheriff's Pension Fund v. Merrill Lynch & Co.	Section 11 & 12(a)(2)	3/21/08 – 3/21/08
	11/13/07	Estey v. Merrill Lynch	ERISA	2/26/07 – present
MGIC Investment Corp.	5/12/08	Wayne County Employees' Retirement System v. MGIC Investment Corp.	10b-5	2/06/07 – 2/12/08
Moneygram International	10/3/08	Consolidated various claims against MoneyGram International Inc.	10b-5	1/24/07 – 1/14/08
Moody's Corp.	6/27/08	Consolidated various claims against Moody's Corp.	10b-5	2/23/06 – 10/24/07
Morgan Asset Management	2/5/08	Hartman v. Morgan Asset Management Inc.	Section 11 & 12(a)(2)	12/06/06 – 11/07/07
	12/21/07	Willis v. Morgan Asset Management Inc.	Section 11 & 12(a)(2)	N/A
	12/6/07	Atkinson v. Morgan Asset Management Inc.	Section 11 & 12(a)(2)	12/06/04 – 10/03/07
	3/31/08	Hamby v. Morgan Asset Management Inc.	ERISA	11/04/06 – 1/30/08
	4/04/08	DeJoseph v. Morgan Asset Management Inc.	10b-5	12/08/06 – 12/05/07
Morgan Stanley	12/2/07	Siefkin v. Morgan Stanley	ERISA	8/9/06 – present
	1/18/08	Major v. Morgan Stanley	ERISA	12/11/05 – present
	12/28/07	Coulter v. Morgan Stanley	ERISA	1/1/07 – present
	2/12/08	McClure v. Lynch	10b-5	7/10/07 – 11/7/07
Municipal Mort. & Equity	1/30/08	Geimis v. Municiapl Mortgage & Equity, LLC	10b-5	1/30/03 – 1/28/08
National City Corp.	1/24/08	Casey v. National City Corporation	10b-5	4/30/07 – 1/2/08
	5/20/08	Parker and Enns v. National City Corporation	Section 11 & 12(a)(2)	12/1/06 – 12/1/06
	1/10/08	National City Corp. ERISA Litigation	ERISA	N/A
Netbank Inc.	9/19/07	Adcock v. Netbank, Inc. et al.	10b-5	5/1/06 – 9/17/07
New Century Financial	3/24/08	Consolidated various claims against New Century Financial	10b-5/Section 11 & 12(a)(2)	5/05/05 – 3/13/07
NextWave Wireless	9/16/08	Lifschitz v. NextWave Wireless	10b-5	3/30/07 – 8/07/08

(continued)

Appendix 5A. *Summary of Securities Class Action Lawsuits as of November 15, 2008* (continued)

Firm	Date	Case	Cause of action	Class period
Nomura Asset Acct. Corp.	6/30/08	*Plumbers' Union Pension Fund v. Nomura Asset Acceptance Corporation*	Section 11 & 12(a)(2)	7/1/05 – 11/30/06
Novastar Financial	10/19/07	*Novastar Financial Securities litigation*	10b-5	5/4/06 – 2/20/07
Opteum Inc.	9/29/08	*Consolidated various complaints against Opteum*	10b-5/section 11 & 12(a)(2)	11/3/05 – 5/10/07
Perini Corporation	8/20/08	*Isham v. Perini Corporation*	10b-5	11/2/06 – 1/17/08
PFF Bancorp	8/12/08	*Perez v. PFF Bancorp*	ERISA	N/A
Premium Connections	5/5/08	*Aldridge v. Premium Connections, Inc.*	10b-5/Section 12(a)(2)	N/A
Radian Group	9/11/07	*Maslar v. Radian Group*	10b-5	1/23/07–7/31/07
	8/15/07	*Cortese v. Radian Group*	10b-5	1/23/07 – 7/31/07
Regions Financial Corp.	3/14/08	*Williams v. Regions Financial Corporation*	ERISA	11/04/06 – present
RAIT Financial Trust	8/21/07	*Reynolds v. RAIT Financial Trust*	10b-5	6/8/06 – 7/3/07
	8/16/07	*Salkowitz v. RAIT Financial Trust*	10b-5/Section 11 & 12(a)(2)	5/13/06 – 7/31/07
	8/1/07	*A1 Credit v. RAIT Financial Trust*	10b-5/Section 11 & 12(a)(2)	1/10/07 – 7/31/07
Residential Accredit Loans	10/14/08	*New Jersey Carpenters Health Fund v. RALI Series 2006-QO1 Trust*	Section 11 & 12(a)(2)	1/26/06 – 2/26/07
Sallie Mae	1/31/08	*Burch v. SLM Corporation ("Sallie Mae")*	10b-5	1/18/07–1/3/08
Security Capital Assur.	4/24/08	*Consolidated various claims against Security Capital Assurance Ltd.*	10b-5/Section 11 & 12(a)(2)	3/15/07 – 3/17/08
Societe Generale	10/17/08	*Various consolidated claims against Societe Generale*	10b-5	8/01/05 – 1/25/08
Sovereign Bancorp	4/28/08	*Wentworth v. Sovereign Bancorp, Inc.*	ERISA	1/1/05 – 4/28/08
State Street	12/7/07	*Merrimack Mutual v. State Street*	ERISA	1/1/07 – 10/5/07
	12/7/07	*Unisystems v. State Street*	ERISA	1/1/07 – 10/5/07
	10/24/07	*Nashua v. State Street*	ERISA	1/1/07 – present
	9/11/08	*Plumbers and Steamfitters Union Fund v. State Street Corporation*	Section 11 & 12(a)(2)	9/11/05 – 9/11/08
	6/30/08	*Yu v. State Street Corporation*	Section 11 & 12(a)(2)	6/30/05 – 6/30/08

Company	Date	Case	Claim	Class period
Swiss Reinsurance Company	9/10/08	Plumbers Union Local Pension Fund v. Swiss Reinsurance Company	10b-5	3/1/07 – 11/19/07
Tarragon Corporation	9/11/07	Judelson v. Tarragon	10b-5	1/5/05 – 8/9/07
The Bear Stearns Companies	3/17/08	Eastside Holdings Inc. v. The Bear Stearns Companies Inc.	10b-5	12/14/06 – 3/14/08
	3/17/08	Howard v. The Bear Stearns Companies Inc.	ERISA	12/14/06 – 3/14/08
	3/18/08	Becherv v. The Bear Stearns Companies Inc.	10b-5	12/14/06 – 3/14/08
	3/25/08	Greek Orthodox Archdiocese Foundation v. The Bear Stearns Companies Inc.	10b-5	3/12/06 – 3/14/08
	6/2/08	Bransbourg v. The Bear Stearns Companies Inc.	10b-5	12/14/06 – 3/14/08
The Blackstone Group	10/27/08	Various consolidated actions against the Blackstone Group	Section 11 & 12(a)(2)	6/25/07 – 6/25/07
The Charles Schwab Corp.	10/2/08	Various consolidated actions against the Charles Schwab Corporation	Section 11 & 12(a)(2)	3/17/05 – 3/17/08
The First Marblehead Corp.	4/10/08	Keller v. The First Marblehead Corporation	10b-5	8/10/06 – 4/7/08
	4/18/08	Byrne v. The First Marblehead Corporation	10b-5	8/10/06 – 4/7/08
	5/12/08	Largent v. The First Marblehead Corporation	10b-5	8/10/06 – 4/7/08
The McGraw-Hill Companies	8/17/07	Reese v. Babash	10b-5	7/25/06 – 8/15/07
The PMI Group	9/04/08	Various consolidated complaints against The PMI Group, Inc.	10b-5	11/02/06 – 3/03/08
The Reserve Primary Fund	9/18/08	Miller v. The Primary Fund	Section 11 & 12(a)(2)	9/28/07 – 9/16/08
	11/07/08	Pogozelki v. The Primary Fund	10b-5/Section 11 & 12(a)(2)	9/28/07 – 9/16/08
Thornburg Mortgage	10/9/07	Snydman v. Thornburg Mortgage	10b-5	10/6/05 – 8/20/07
	9/24/07	Sedlmyer v. Thornburg Mortgage	10b-5	10/6/05 – 8/17/07
	9/20/07	Smith v. Thornburg Mortgage	10b-5	4/19/07 – 8/14/07
	9/7/07	Gonsalves v. Thornburg Mortgage	10b-5	4/19/07 – 8/14/07
	8/21/07	Slater v. Thornburg Mortgage	10b-5	10/6/05 – 8/17/07
Toll Brothers	4/16/07	Lowrey v. Toll Brothers	10b-5	12/9/04 – 11/8/05

(continued)

Appendix 5A. *Summary of Securities Class Action Lawsuits as of November 15, 2008* (continued)

Firm	Date	Case	Cause of action	Class period
UBS AG	1/29/08	Garber v. UBS AG	10b-5	2/13/06 – 12/11/07
	12/11/07	Wesner v. UBS AG	10b-5	3/13/07 – 12/11/07
UBS Financial Services	11/06/08	Gott v. UBS Financial Services Inc.	Section 11 & 12(a)(2)	5/30/06 – 9/18/08
Wachovia Corp.	6/06/08	Bristol County Retirement System v. Wachovia Corporation	10b-5	5/08/06 – 4/11/08
	7/07/08	Lipetz v. Wachovia Corporation	10b-5	5/08/06 – 4/11/08
	2/29/08	Miller v. Wachovia Corporation	Section 11 & 12(a)(2)	5/01/07 – 5/01/07
	6/09/08	Wachovia Corp. ERISA Litigation	ERISA	1/01/06 – present
Washington Mutual	12/20/07	Garber v. Washington Mutual	10b-5	4/18/06 – 12/10/07
	11/5/07	Abrams et al. v. Washington Mutual	10b-5	10/18/06 – 11/11/07
	11/5/07	Koesterer v. Washington Mutual	10b-5	7/19/06 – 10/31/07
	11/7/07	Nelson v. Washington Mutual	10b-5	4/18/06 – 11/1/07
WSB Financial Group	4/11/08	Consolidated various complaints against WSB Financial Group	Section 11 & 12(a)(2)	12/21/06 – 12/21/06

Source: Complaints obtained from Bloomberg.

Appendix 5B. *CDO Liquidations as of May 30, 2008*

Name	EOD date	Collateral manager	Original balance ($ millions)	Type	Vintage
Liquidated					
Adams Square Funding I	10/18/07	Credit Suisse Alternative Capital	500	Sub Mezz	2006
Ansley Park ABS CDO	11/6/07	SunTrust Capital Markets	600	Sub Mezz	2006
ARCA Funding 2006-II	2/21/08	TCW Asset Management	700	Sub Mezz	2006
BFC Silverton CDO	11/13/07	Braddock Financial Corporation	750	Sub Mezz	2006
Carina CDO	10/26/07	State Street Global Advisors	1,500	Sub Mezz	2006
Corona Borealis CDO	2/1/08	New York Life Investment Mgmt.	1,500	Sub Mezz	2007
Diogenes CDO III	12/11/07	State Street Global Advisors	800		2007
Durant CDO 2007-1	1/23/08	SCM Advisors	400		2007
Hamilton Gardens CDO II	3/5/08	Rabobank International	400		2007
IMAC CDO 2007-2	1/18/08	Ivy Asset Management Corp.	500	Mezz	2007
Kefton CDO I	2/12/08	Terwin Money Management	670	Sub Mezz	2006
Markov CDO I	11/16/07	State Street Global Advisors	2,000	Mid	2007
Mystic Point CDO	12/11/07	Fortis Investment Management	500	Sub Mezz	2006
Pampelonne CDO I	11/9/07	Vertical Capital	1,250		2006
Pampelonne CDO II	11/9/07	Vertical Capital	2,000		2007
PASA Funding 2007	2/22/08	AllianceBernstein	3,000		2007
TABS 2006-5	11/1/07	Tricadia CDO Management	1,500	Sub Mezz	2006
TABS 2007-7	11/9/07	Tricadia CDO Management	2,250	CDO[2]	2007
Vertical ABS CDO 2007-1	10/19/07	Vertical Capital	1,500	Sub Mezz	2007
Visage CDO 2006-2	12/24/07	TCW Asset Management	400	Sub HG	2007

(continued)

Appendix 5B. *CDO Liquidations as of May 30, 2008* (continued)

Name	EOD date	Collateral manager	Original balance ($ millions)	Type	Vintage
Notice of liquidation					
6th Avenue Funding 2006-1	2/29/08	6th Avenue Investment Mgmt. Co.	825	Sub HG	2006
ACA ABS 2007-2	10/18/07	ACA Management	750	Sub Mezz	2007
Brooklyn SF CDO	2/25/08	Deutsche Investment Mgmt.	1,000	Sub HG	2006
Camber 6	3/3/08	Cambridge Place Collateral Mgmt.	750	Sub Mezz	2006
Careel Bay CDO	2/11/08	Allegiance Advisors	750	Sub Mezz	2007
Cherry Creek CDO I	4/15/08	Surge Capital Management	300	Sub Mezz	2006
Draco 2007-1	2/13/08	Declaration Mgmt. & Research	2,000	Mezz	2007
Gulf Stream-Atl. CDO 2007-1	2/7/08	Gulf Stream Structured Advisors	500	Sub Mezz	2007
Halyard CDO I	2/8/08	Solent Capital	750	Sub Mezz	2006
Hartshorne CDO I	11/9/07	ZAIS Group	1,000	Mezz	2007
IXIS ABS CDO 2	2/1/08	IXIS Securities North America	502	Sub Mezz	2006
Kleros Real Estate CDO III	2/5/08	Strategos Capital Management	1,000	Sub Mid	2006
Lancer Funding II	2/5/08	ACA Management	1,000	Sub Mezz	2007
Neo CDO 2007-1	11/16/07	Harding Advisory	300	Mezz	2007
Octans I CDO	12/18/07	Harding Advisory	1,500	Sub Mezz	2006
Timberwolf I	4/3/08	Greywolf Capital Management	1,000	Sub Mezz	2007
Tricadia CDO 2007-8	3/10/08	Tricadia CDO Management	501	Sub Mezz	2007
Visage CDO 2006-1	11/20/07	TCW Asset Management	400	Sub Mezz	2006
Notice of acceleration					
ACA ABS 2006-1	3/5/08	ACA Management	750	Sub Mezz	2006
ACA ABS 2006-2	11/5/07	ACA Management	750	Sub Mezz	2006
Armitage ABS CDO	12/4/07	Vanderbilt Capital Advisors	3,000	Sub HG	2007
Auriga CDO	2/13/08	250 Capital	1,500	Sub Mezz	2006

Bernoulli High Grade CDO II	3/4/08	Babcock & Brown Securities	1,500		2007
Bonifacius CDO	1/24/08	Collineo Asset Management	2,500		2007
Broderick CDO 2006-2	2/27/08	Seneca Capital Management	1,600	Sub Mid	2006
Broderick CDO 2007-3	11/14/07	Seneca Capital Management	1,500	Sub HG	2007
Brookville CDO I	2/19/08	Petra Capital Management	500		2007
Cairn Mezz ABS CDO II	2/4/08	Cairn Financial Products	750	Sub Mezz	2006
Cairn Mezz ABS CDO III	4/25/08	Cairn Financial Products	1,000	Sub Mezz	2007
Cairn Mezz ABS CDO IV	2/27/08	Cairn Financial Products	500	Mezz	2007
Camber 7	3/12/08	Cambridge Place Collateral Mgmt.	900	Sub Mezz	2007
Cetus ABS CDO 2006-1	4/10/08	GSC Partners	1,000	Sub Mezz	2006
Cetus ABS CDO 2006-2	3/12/08	GSC Partners	1,000	Sub Mezz	2006
Cetus ABS CDO 2006-3	12/7/07	GSC Partners	1,250	Sub Mezz	2006
Cetus ABS CDO 2006-4	11/5/07	GSC Partners	1,500	Sub Mezz	2006
Cherry Creek CDO II	11/14/07	Surge Capital Management	500	Sub Mezz	2007
Diversey Harbor ABS CDO	12/27/07	Vanderbilt Capital Advisors	750	Sub HG	2006
Duke Funding XII	3/28/08	Duke Funding Management	750	Sub Mezz	2006
E*Trade ABS CDO VI	12/17/07	E*Trade Global Asset Management	750	Mezz	2007
FAB US 2006-1	4/2/08	Gulf International Bank (UK)	3,000		2006
Faxtor HG 2007-1	2/28/08	Faxtor Securities B.V.	1,500		2007
Fort Denison Funding	12/13/07	Basis Capital Securitisation	1,500	Sub Mezz	2007
Fourth Street Funding	3/12/08	NIR Capital Management	2,500		2007
G Square Finance 2006-2	5/6/08	Wharton Asset Mgmt. Bermuda	1,600	Sub Mid	2006
GSC ABS CDO 2006-3g	2/1/08	GSC Partners	1,500	Sub Mid	2007
GSC ABS CDO 2006-4u	10/31/07	GSC Partners	500	Sub Mezz	2006
SC CDO 2007-1r	11/5/07	GSC Partners	750	Sub Mezz	2007
Highridge ABS CDO I	11/27/07	ZS Structured Credit Capital Mgmt.	1,000	Sub HG	2007
Highridge ABS CDO II	4/3/08	ZS Structured Credit Capital Mgmt.	500		2007
Independence V CDO	2/29/08	Declaration Mgmt. & Research	900	Sub Mezz	2004

(continued)

Appendix 5B. *CDO Liquidations as of May 30, 2008* (continued)

Name	EOD date	Collateral manager	Original balance ($ millions)	Type	Vintage
Independence VII CDO	4/9/08	Declaration Mgmt. & Research	1,000	Sub Mezz	2006
Ivy Lane CDO	3/26/08	Princeton Advisory Group	1,000	Sub Mezz	2006
Jupiter High-Grade CDO V	11/2/07	Harding Advisory	1,250	HG	2007
Jupiter High-Grade CDO VII	11/30/07	Harding Advisory	1,500	HG	2007
Lacerta ABS CDO 2006-1	2/7/08	Unknown	500	Sub Mezz	2006
Libra CDO	4/30/08	Lehman Brothers Asset Mgmt.	2,500	Sub Mezz	2006
Millstone IV CDO	11/30/07	Church Tavern Advisors	2,250	HG	2007
MKP CBO VI	11/15/07	MKP Capital Management	420	Sub Mezz	2006
Montrose Harbor CDO I	11/29/07	Vanderbilt Capital Advisors	400	Sub Mezz	2006
Mugello ABS CDO 2006-1	2/6/08	Unknown	1,250	Sub Mezz	2006
Neptune CDO IV	1/4/08	Chotin Fund Management	500	Sub Mezz	2007
Nordic Valley 2007-1 CDO	12/18/07	250 Capital	500	Sub Mezz	2007
Norma CDO I	3/10/08	NIR Capital Management	1,000	Sub Mezz	2007
NovaStar ABS CDO I	2/4/08	NovaStar Asset Management Co.	1,600	Sub Mezz	2007
Octans III CDO	12/4/07	Harding Advisory	750	Sub Mezz	2006
Orion 2006-2	11/6/07	NIBC Credit Management	750	Mezz	2006
Palmer ABS CDO 2007-1	3/6/08	GSC Partners	1,500	HG	2007
Pinnacle Peak CDO I	1/17/08	Koch Global Capital	1,000		2007
Pinnacle Point Funding II	12/13/07	Blackrock Financial Management	600	Sub Mezz	2007
Pyxis ABS CDO 2007-1	2/1/08	Putnam Advisory Co.	600		2007
Ridgeway Court Funding I	1/25/08	Credit Suisse Alternative Capital	500	Sub Mezz	2006
Rockbound CDO I	12/6/07	Brigade Capital Management	1,500		2007
Sagittarius CDO I	11/6/07	Structured Asset Investors	1,500		2007
Scorpius CDO	2/12/08	Strategos Capital Management	2,000	Sub Mezz	2006

Deal	Date	Manager	Rating	Year	Amount
Sherwood Funding III	10/19/07	Church Tavern Advisors	Sub HG	2007	1,500
STACK 2007-1	12/17/07	TCW Asset Management	HY	2007	2,200
Stillwater ABS CDO 2006-1	4/14/08	Long Lake Partners		2006	297
Stockton CDO	2/22/08	Princeton Advisory Group	HY	2007	900
Tenorite CDO I	2/7/08	Blackrock Financial Management	Sub Mezz	2007	1,000
Tourmaline CDO I	4/3/08	Blackrock Financial Management	Sub Mezz	2005	750
Tricadia CDO 2006-7	11/20/07	Tricadia CDO Management	Sub Mezz	2007	500
Volans Funding 2007-1	1/8/08	VERO Capital Management	Sub Mezz	2007	1,100
Wadsworth CDO	2/26/08	Hartford Investment Mgmt. Co.	Sub HG	2006	1,200
Webster CDO I	10/18/07	Vanderbilt Capital Advisors	Sub HG	2006	1,000
Western Springs CDO	2/7/08	Deerfield Capital Management	HG	2007	500
Retracted					
Citius II Funding	2/7/08	Aladdin Capital Management	Prime HG	2006	2,000
Event of default					
888 Tactical Fund	12/13/07	Harding Advisory		2007	1,000
Aardvark ABS CDO 2007-1	1/2/08	Harbourview Asset Mgmt. Corp.		2007	1,500
ACA ABS 2007-1	11/15/07	ACA Management	Sub Mezz	2007	1,500
ACA Aquarius 2006-1	5/13/08	ACA Management	Sub Mezz	2006	2,000
Acacia Option ARM 1 CDO	5/16/08	Redwood Asset Management	Mid	2007	500
Adams Square Funding II	2/14/08	Credit Suisse Alternative Capital	Sub Mezz	2007	1,000
Alpha Mezz CDO 2007-1	4/30/08	Countrywide Alt. Asset Mgmt.	Sub Mezz	2007	500
ARCA Funding 2006-I	3/27/08	Unknown	Sub Mezz	2006	710
ART CDO 2006-1	2/1/08	Allianz Risk Transfer	Sub HG	2006	1,000
Aventine Hill CDO I	2/6/08	FSI Capital		2007	750
Bantry Bay CDO I	12/3/07	Investec Bank	Mezz	2007	241
BelleHaven ABSCDO 2006-1	4/14/08	NIBC Credit Management	Sub HG	2006	1,996
Biltmore CDO 2007-1	2/7/08	ING Clarion Capital		2007	1,000

(continued)

Appendix 5B. *CDO Liquidations as of May 30, 2008* (continued)

Name	EOD date	Collateral manager	Original balance ($ millions)	Type	Vintage
Brigantine HG Funding	4/14/08	Delaware Asset Advisers	2,000	Sub HG	2006
Cairn HG ABS CDO II	2/29/08	Cairn Financial Products	896	Sub Mid	2006
Citation HG ABS CDO I	3/13/08	Highland Financial Holdings Group	1,100	Sub HG	2007
Class V Funding I	5/12/08	CSFB Alternative Capital	200	Sub Mezz	2005
Class V Funding II	1/22/08	Credit Suisse Alternative Capital	300	CDO² Mezz	2006
Class V Funding III	11/19/07	Credit Suisse Alternative Capital	1,000		2007
Costa Bella CDO	4/24/08	PIMCO	500	Sub Mezz	2006
Delphinus	1/4/08	Delaware Asset Advisers	1,600		2007
Duke Funding XIII	5/5/08	Duke Funding Management	1,800	Mezz.	2007
E*Trade ABS CDO IV	5/7/08	E*Trade Global Asset Management	300	Sub Mezz	2005
ESP Funding I	2/28/08	Elliott Structured Products	1,000	Sub HG	2006
Fiorente Funding	3/18/08	VERO Capital Management	850		2006
Forge ABS HG CDO I	1/30/08	Forge ABS	1,500		2007
Furlong Synth. ABSCDO 2006-1	4/15/08	Invesco	500	Sub Mezz	2006
G Square Finance 2007-1	3/5/08	Wharton Asset Mgmt. Bermuda	1,700	Sub Mid	2007
Gemstone CDO VII	4/15/08	HBK Investments	1,101	Sub Mezz	2007
Glacier Funding CDO IV	4/15/08	Terwin Money Management	400	Sub Mezz	2006
HG Struct. Credit CDO 2007-1	2/27/08	Bear Stearns Asset Management	4,000		2007
HSPI Diversified CDO Fund I	5/12/08	Halcyon Securitized Products	600	CDO² Mezz	2006
HSPI Diversified CDO Fund II	5/1/08	Halcyon Securitized Products	700		2007
Hudson HG Funding 2006-1	5/5/08	Unknown	1,500	Sub HG	2006
Independence VI CDO	5/5/08	Declaration Mgmt. & Research	950	Sub Mezz	2005
Kleros Preferred Funding III	1/4/08	Strategos Capital Management	2,000	Sub Mid	2006
Kleros Preferred Funding IV	12/14/07	Strategos Capital Management	2,000	Sub Mid	2006

Deal	Date	Manager	Amount	Type	Year
Kleros Preferred Funding IX	4/11/08	Strategos Capital Management	2,000		2007
Kleros Preferred Funding V	12/19/07	Strategos Capital Management	1,200	Sub Mid	2007
Kleros Preferred Funding VI	12/14/07	Strategos Capital Management	3,000	Sub Mid	2007
Kleros Preferred Funding VII	2/8/08	Strategos Capital Management	1,500		2007
Kleros Real Estate CDO I	4/29/08	Strategos Capital Management	1,000	Sub Mid	2006
Kleros Real Estate CDO II	4/7/08	Strategos Capital Management	1,000	Sub Mid	2006
Laguna Seca Funding I	4/8/08	GSC Partners	500	Mezz	2007
Libertas Preferred Funding II	5/16/08	Strategos Capital Management	500	Sub Mezz	2007
Liberty Harbour II CDO	5/12/08	250 Capital	3,350		2007
Lochsong	5/19/08	Unknown	1,200	Sub HG	2006
Longport Funding III	2/11/08	Delaware Asset Advisers	750	Sub Mezz	2007
Longridge ABS CDO I	4/2/08	ZS Structured Credit Capital Mgmt.	500	Sub Mezz	2006
Longridge ABS CDO II	2/13/08	ZS Structured Credit Capital Mgmt.	500	Sub Mezz	2007
Longshore CDO Funding 2007-3	2/8/08	Structured Asset Investors	1,300		2007
Longstreet CDO I	4/22/08	J.P. Morgan Investment Mgmt.	500	Sub Mezz	2006
Maxim High Grade CDO I	4/14/08	Maxim Capital Management	2,000	Sub HG	2006
Maxim High Grade CDO II	4/14/08	Maxim Capital Management	2,000	Sub HG	2007
McKinley Funding III	12/11/07	Vertical Capital	1,510	Sub Mid	2006
MKP Vela CBO	5/1/08	MKP Capital Management	1,500	Sub Mezz	2006
Mulberry Street CDO II	4/28/08	Clinton Group	700	Sub Mezz	2003
Neptune CDO V	11/9/07	Chotin Fund Management	350		2007
Newbury Street CDO	3/6/08	MFS Investment Management	2,000		2007
Octans II CDO	5/8/08	Harding Advisory	1,500	Sub Mezz	2006
Octorion I CDO	2/8/08	Harding Advisory	1,000	Sub Mezz	2007
Pacific Pinnacle CDO	2/4/08	Blackrock Financial Mgmt.	1,000	Sub Mezz	2007
Plettenberg Bay CDO	3/6/08	Investec Bank	500	Sub Mezz	2007
Preston CDO I	2/12/08	J.P. Morgan AM	350	HY	2007
Raffles Place Funding II	4/4/08	UOB Asset Management	1,000		2006

(continued)

233

Appendix 5B. *CDO Liquidations as of May 30, 2008* (continued)

Name	EOD date	Collateral manager	Original balance ($ millions)	Type	Vintage
Ridgeway Court Funding II	1/15/08	Credit Suisse Alternative Capital	3,000		2007
Rockville CDO I	4/17/08	Petra Capital Management	1,200	Sub Mezz	2006
Silver Marlin ABS CDO I	2/22/08	Sailfish Struct. Investment Mgmt.	1,250		2007
Singa Funding	3/11/08	Lion Capital Management	1,000	Sub Mezz	2006
Sorin Real Estate CDO 2007-6	5/12/08	Sorin Capital Management	550	Mezz	2007
Squared CDO 2007-1	1/18/08	GSC Partners	1,100	Sub Mezz	2007
Static Residential CDO 2006-C	4/18/08	Unknown	750	CDO^2	2006
Straits Global ABS CDO I	5/7/08	Declaration Mgmt. & Research	400	Sub HY	2004
SF Advisors ABS CDO III	4/18/08	Structured Finance Advisors	275	Sub Mezz	2002
Summer Street 2007-1	2/1/08	GE Asset Management	400		2007
TABS 2005-4	3/19/08	Tricadia CDO Management	400	Sub Mezz	2006
TABS 2006-6	11/16/07	Tricadia CDO Management	1,500	Sub HG	2006
Tahoma CDO I	3/25/08	Bear Stearns Asset Management	1,000	CDO^2	2006
Tahoma CDO III	2/25/08	Bear Stearns Asset Management	350	Sub Mezz	2007
Tallships Funding	4/4/08	Bear Stearns Asset Management	1,500	Mezz	2006
Tasman CDO	3/17/08	Credaris	300		2007
Tazlina Funding CDO I	4/23/08	Terwin Money Management	1,500		2006
Tazlina Funding CDO II	5/19/08	Terwin Money Management	1,500	Mezz	2007
Topanga CDO II	4/15/08	Metropolitan West Asset Mgmt.	1,000	Sub HG	2006
Tourmaline CDO II	3/31/08	Blackrock Financial Management	1,000	Sub Mezz	2006
Tourmaline CDO III	3/31/08	Blackrock Financial Management	1,500	Sub HY	2007
Vertical ABS CDO 2007-2	2/14/08	Vertical Capital	737	Sub Mezz	2007

Source: UBS CDO Research, proprietary data, May 30, 2008 (underlying data from Standard & Poor's and trustee reports).

References

Apgar, William, Amal Bendimerad, and Ren S. Essene. 2007. *Mortgage Market Channels and Fair Lending: An Analysis of HMDA Data.* Joint Center for Housing Studies, Harvard University, April 25.

Brunnermeier, Markus K. 2009. "Deciphering the 2007–08 Liquidity and Credit Crunch." *Journal of Economic Perspectives* 23 (1): 77–100.

Frankel, Tamar. 2006. *Securitization,* 2nd ed. Fathom Publishing.

Gorton, Gary, and Nicholas S. Souleles. 2006. "Special Purpose Vehicles and Securitization," in *The Risks of Financial Institutions,* edited by Rene Stulz and Mark Carey. University of Chicago Press.

Government Accountability Office. 2007. "Bank Regulators Need to Improve Transparency and Overcome Impediments to Finalizing the Proposed Basel II Framework," Report 07-253, February 15.

Lucas, Douglas J., Laurie S. Goodman, and Frank J. Fabozzi. 2006. *Collateralized Debt Obligations.* Hoboken, N.J.: John Wiley and Sons.

Maller, Brant, and Rick Antonoff. 2008. "Spillover Effect from Subprime Collapse; News; As Legislation and Liability Get Sorted Out, Modern Real Estate Lending Process Faces a Big Test." *New York Law Journal* 239 (9).

Securities and Exchange Commission, Office of Inspector General, Office of Audits. 2008. *SEC's Oversight of Bear Stearns and Related Entities: The Consolidated Supervised Entity Program,* Report 446-A, September 25, p. 8.

Schipper, Katherine, and Teri Lombardi Yohn. 2007. "Standard-Setting Issues and Academic Research Related to the Accounting for Financial Asset Transfers." *Accounting Horizons* 21 (4): 59–80.

Schloemer, Ellen, and others. 2006. *Losing Ground: Foreclosures in the Subprime Market and Their Cost to Homeowners.* Center for Responsible Lending (www.responsiblelending.org/issues/mortgage/research/page.jsp?itemID=31217189).

Technical Committee of the International Organization of Securities Commissions. 2008. *Report of the Task Force on the SubPrime Crisis: Final Report* (www.iasplus.com/iosco/0805 ioscosubprimereport.pdf).

Tufano, Peter. 1989. "Financial Innovation and First Mover Advantages." *Journal of Financial Economics* 25 (2): 213–40.

JACK GUTTENTAG
IGOR ROITBURG

6

Mortgage Payment Insurance and the Future of the Housing Finance System

I N THIS CHAPTER we argue that a systemic weakness in the way that the mortgage finance system deals with default risk has contributed greatly to the current mortgage crisis. That weakness is the prevailing system of risk-based interest rate pricing—the practice of charging higher interest rates on mortgage loans that are perceived to be riskier than the best ("prime") loans. With few exceptions, interest rate risk-based premium dollars that are not needed to cover current losses are realized as income by investors. Because they are not reserved, they are unavailable to meet abnormally large losses when such losses occur. That makes the system more vulnerable to episodes of high rates of default.

In addition, because interest rate risk-based premiums reflect the return that investors require to compensate for the danger of "going broke," they are substantially higher than premiums based on long-run actuarial loss experience. The borrowing cost to less-than-prime borrowers is higher than justified by expected losses. Yet in the absence of reserving, interest rate risk premiums are never high enough to meet the losses that occur in a crunch, such as the one that we are in now.

A better way to manage mortgage default risk is through a new type of mortgage insurance called mortgage payment insurance (MPI). Under MPI, the insurer would guarantee timely payments to investors after a borrower defaults. If the default is not corrected, payments from the insurer continue until the foreclosure process is completed. At that point the investor is reimbursed for the unpaid balance plus foreclosure costs up to an agreed-on cap similar to the cap on traditional mortgage insurance. Caps on insurance coverage can be adjusted to equate expected losses with those on prime loans.

Under MPI, interest rates would not vary with default risk. Instead, borrowers would pay mortgage insurance premiums based on default risk. Unlike interest rate risk premiums, insurance premiums would be reserved for ten years and available to pay for abnormally large losses if and when they occur, reducing the vulnerability of the system to future shocks. Also, unlike interest rate risk premiums, insurance premiums would reflect long-run actuarial loss experience, thereby reducing the overall financing cost to most borrowers. In addition, with MPI the party underwriting the risk—the private mortgage insurer (PMI)—owns the risk, eliminating an agency problem that weakens the system.

Although MPI provides greater coverage, it will actually cost insurers (and by extension, borrowers) little more than the strictly collateral risk coverage that they provide now and in many cases it will cost less. Insuring against cash flow risk and collateral risk in combination is incredibly efficient because all of the payments that the insurer advances in its role as cash flow insurer reduce dollar for dollar the ultimate amount that it must pay at foreclosure. Further, the enhanced protection against loss that MPI provides to investors lowers interest rates, and lower rates reduce losses to both investors and insurers on loans that go to foreclosure. Despite the greater protection provided by MPI, the rate plus insurance premium paid by less-than-prime borrowers would be substantially lower than the rate plus insurance premium under the current system of interest rate risk-based pricing.

To make MPI work, however, the secondary market must price loans carrying MPI at prime; in 2008, that meant the government-sponsored enterprises (GSEs) Fannie Mae and Freddie Mac. These agencies should support MPI because it will sharply reduce the systemic vulnerability of the housing finance system. MPI extends the process of reserving against future default losses and concentrates the risk of default in the hands of those who underwrite the risk. Since the agencies cannot separate their own fortunes from those of the system, they have a vital stake in how the system evolves in the future. Further, MPI aligns the interest of the agencies with those of borrowers. In addition, MPI would eliminate the need for risk-based pricing by the agencies, which creates needless controversy. All risk-based pricing would be done by PMIs.

While this chapter focuses on the mortgage insurance industry, the core principle of MPI—"transaction-based reserving"(TBR)—has much wider applicability. With TBR, a portion of the risk premium on every transaction must be reserved and cannot be withdrawn except in exigent circumstances. In contrast to capital requirements, TBR is largely immune to cyclical swings in investor sentiment. Under existing requirements, during periods of euphoria when lenders are prone to making riskier loans, they can do so without increasing their required capital by shifting to riskier assets within the defined asset categories. However, with TBR, because riskier assets carry higher premiums, such a shift would result automatically in larger allocations to reserves.

Mortgage Default Risk

Investors in mortgages face two kinds of risk from borrowers who default. Collateral risk is the risk that the investor who forecloses on a loan and sells the property will fail to recover the unpaid balance of the loan plus the foreclosure costs. On loans with small down payments, on which the collateral risk is the highest, private mortgage insurance is available to protect investors. Investors also face cash flow risk. While they ultimately may be made whole from their collateral and mortgage insurance, until that happens a loan in default is a nonperforming asset—it is not generating any income and cannot be sold except at a substantial loss. No insurance is now available against cash flow risk on individual mortgages.

Borrower Payments for Default Risk

Borrowers are charged for default risk in two ways. The first and larger charge is to impose a risk premium in the interest rate. The risk premium is a rate increment above that charged on a "prime" transaction, which carries the lowest risk. The greater the perceived risk, the larger the premium. As mentioned, a weakness of the interest rate risk premium system is that, with few exceptions, risk premium dollars that are not needed to cover current losses are realized as income by investors. They are not reserved and therefore are not available to meet future losses—a serious limitation because losses tend to bunch. For example, interest rate risk premiums collected on loans originated in 2000 had very low losses because of the marked appreciation in house prices in subsequent years. Most of the risk premiums collected on those loans became investor income. In contrast, loans originated in 2006 had large losses but none of the excess premiums from the 2000 vintage were available to help meet those losses.

Another weakness of the interest rate risk premium system is that premiums are based not on long-run actuarial loss experience but on the return that investors require to compensate for the risk of going broke. Such premiums are substantially higher than premiums based on actuarial experience. Furthermore, interest rate risk-based premiums as well as underwriting requirements can change markedly over short periods—for example, easing during periods of euphoria such as 2000–05 and then sharply reversing course when market sentiment changes, as in 2006–08.

The second method of charging borrowers for default risk is to charge a mortgage insurance premium. Borrowers may be required to purchase mortgage insurance if their down payment on a home purchase or their equity in a refinance is less than 20 percent. In contrast to interest rate risk premiums, more than half of the mortgage insurance premiums collected from borrowers are placed in reserve accounts. The reserves that accumulate during long periods when losses are small are available when a foreclosure crunch comes, as has happened now.

The reserving process requires mortgage insurance companies to view expected losses over a long time horizon. While premium structures change over time, such changes are based on revised estimates of losses over long periods rather than on short-term swings in market sentiment. Furthermore, the premiums arising out of the reserving process are significantly lower than those charged when there is no reserving.

The upshot is that a mortgage system in which borrower payments for risk are reserved is more stable and the average premium paid by borrowers is much lower than one in which borrower payments are divided between current losses and income. Unfortunately, for every risk-based dollar paid by borrowers that is subject to reserving, borrowers pay ten or more risk-based dollars that are not subject to reserving.

Introducing Mortgage Payment Insurance

Traditional mortgage insurance (TMI) on individual mortgages is insurance against collateral risk. It usually comes into play after foreclosure, when the insurer pays for any shortfall (up to an agreed-on cap) between the net proceeds of the property sale and the loan balance (including accrued interest) plus expenses. Our proposed mortgage payment insurance covers both collateral risk and cash flow risk. Under MPI, the insurer would guarantee timely receipt of the payments, so that from the investor's perspective the loan remains in good standing when the borrower defaults. That constitutes the cash flow insurance part of the policy.

If the default is not corrected, the payments continue until the foreclosure process is completed, at which point the investor is reimbursed under the collateral risk insurance part of the policy. Any cure payments would go to the insurer to reimburse it for the advances made. To avoid the risk of loan servicers allowing MPI payments to run on indefinitely, PMIs would limit the period that the servicer has to foreclose. The maximum period would depend on typical foreclosure timelines and would vary by state.

The insurance premiums covering both types of risk would vary from loan to loan, but because the insurer assumes the default risk there would be no interest rate risk premiums. All borrowers would pay the prime interest rate on the type of mortgage that they select. That assumes that the insurer's credit is not in question and that the coverage cap is adjusted to the level required by investors to provide prime pricing.

Cost of MPI versus TMI

It is natural to assume that because MPI covers both cash flow risk and collateral risk, the required mortgage insurance premiums would be substantially larger than those on TMI. In fact, more often than not they are smaller, and when they are larger, they are not much larger. That astounding fact stems from two sources. The first is that insuring against cash flow risk and collateral risk in combination is incredibly efficient. All of the payments that the insurer advances in its role as cash flow insurer are simply prepayments—dollar for dollar—of the ultimate amount that they must pay at foreclosure in their role of collateral risk insurer.[1] The only net loss to the insurer is the interest opportunity cost on the funds advanced, which turns out to be small. The second reason that MPI premiums are so small is that by assuming all the default risk instead of just part of it, MPI eliminates interest rate risk premiums, and lower rates reduce losses on loans that default. A lower rate means more rapid amortization and therefore a lower balance, and it also means smaller accruals of unpaid interest.

We illustrate with an example based on wholesale price quotes covering two loans on November 27, 2007, when the market was less unsettled than it is today. The loans were the same except for a few critical differences that made one of them prime and the other Alt-A. The features of the loans are shown in table 6-1. The prime loan was made to purchase a home as a primary residence with full documentation, whereas the Alt-A loan was made to take cash out by refinancing an investment property with no documentation. The Alt-A loan carried a rate that was 3.875 percent higher and a mortgage insurance premium that was 0.62 percent higher. We assumed that the Alt-A loan went into default, followed by foreclosure, and calculated losses with a TMI policy. We then used the same default/foreclosure scenario to calculate the losses on an MPI policy with the interest rate reduced to 6 percent, the prime rate in our example. We found that the total losses were $21,111 lower with MPI (see table 6-2 for details). Both insurer and investor share in that loss reduction. The insurer's cap (maximum loss exposure) is reduced by $4,473, while the investor's losses are reduced by $16,638.

---

1. Payments consist of interest plus principal. Interest payments reduce dollar for dollar the accrued interest for which the insurer is liable, while principal payments reduce dollar for dollar the outstanding balance.

Table 6-1. *Characteristics of Prime and Alt-A Loans*[a]

Loan characteristic	Prime loan	Alt-A loan
Price/value (dollars)	444,444	444,444
Loan (dollars) / LTV ratio(percent)	400,000 / 90	400,000 / 90
TMI coverage (percent)	25	25
Borrower FICO	700	700
Property type	Single-family	Single-family
Occupancy	Primary residence	Investment
Loan purpose	Purchase	Cash-out refinance
Documentation	Full	None
Loan rate (percent)	6.000	9.875
TMI premium (percent)	0.67	1.29

Source: Authors' illustration.

a. Loan is thirty-year fixed-rate loan, the property is in California, and the lock period is thirty days. Rates are wholesale at zero points as of November 21, 2007; the insurance premiums are from the MGIC Rate Finder at that time. Note that rate risk and mortgage insurance premiums have both risen since the table was prepared in November 2007. In attempting to update the table, we found that the Alt-A loan was no longer being priced, by the market or by MGIC. See the discussion in text ("Excessive Interest Rate Risk Premiums").

Table 6-2. *Breakdown of Cost Savings on MPI at 6 Percent Relative to TMI at 9.875 Percent*[a]

Costs and savings	Amount (dollars)
Incremental costs	
Payment advances, default to foreclosure	28,778
Interest cost of payment advances to insurer	805
Total	29,583
Cost savings	
Interest charges due at foreclosure	39,025
Larger borrower equity at default	5,327
Larger borrower equity at foreclosure	5,537
Interest gained on payment advances by investor	805
Total	50,694
Net savings on MPI	21,111

Source: Authors' illustration.

a. It is assumed that the loan defaults after twenty-four months; that it takes twelve months after default to foreclose and another nine months after foreclosure to sell the property to a third-party purchaser; that house value at disposition is 20 percent less than at origination; that loss on cash flow advances is 6 percent; and that foreclosure expenses are based on those developed by HUD in *Providing Alternatives to Mortgage Foreclosure: A Report to Congress*, March 1996.

Table 6-3. *Loss Reductions on MPI as a Function of Interest Rate Reduction*

	Loss reduction from using MPI rather than TMI		
Interest rate reduction (percent)	Total loss reduction in dollars (percent)	Loss reduction to insurer in dollars	Loss reduction to investor in dollars
3.875	21,111 (12.2)	4,473	16,638
3.000	16,648 (9.9)	3,357	13,291
2.000	11,368 (6.9)	2,037	9,331
1.000	5,876 (3.7)	664	5,212
0.500	3,043 (2.0)	–44	3,087
0.000	151 (0.0)	–767	918

Source: Authors' illustration.

Our example involved a relatively large rate reduction. Smaller rate reductions generate smaller savings, as shown in table 6-3. The costs in table 6-3 are calculated in the same way as those in table 6-2, except that the interest rate on the Alt-A loan—and therefore the rate reduction associated with MPI—takes different values. If there is no interest rate reduction, MPI costs the insurer more than TMI—but not much more—and the investor always incurs a smaller loss with MPI.

Excessive Interest Rate Risk Premiums

Note that in moving from the prime loan to the Alt-A loan, the TMI premium rose by only 0.62 percent while the interest rate premium rose by 3.875 percent.[2] The increase in the risk premium charged by the lender was more than six times larger than the increase charged by the insurer, despite the fact that the increase in risk exposure was substantially higher for the insurer because the insurer is in the first loss position.

Extending our model, loss to the insurer occurs if the property value *appreciates* by less than 30 percent, whereas loss to the investor does not occur unless the property value *declines* by more than 2.5 percent! The property value has to decline by 35 percent before the investor's loss equals the insurer's loss. In other words, both the incidence and severity of loss are expected to be greater for the insurer than the investor, yet the incremental charge by the investor is more than six times larger than the incremental charge by the insurer.

---

2. This actually understates the interest rate increase because the 9.875 percent rate is wholesale and does not include the retail markup, which on riskier loans includes an "opportunistic pricing premium"—some would call it a "predatory pricing premium." That premium would largely disappear if the borrower's payment for default risk was embedded in the insurance premium.

If one assumes that the mortgage insurance premium accurately reflects the losses expected over a long time horizon, the interest rate risk premium is grossly excessive. Interest rate risk premiums are excessive mainly because they are not reserved and depend on investor sentiment, which is heavily influenced by current market conditions, not on long-term actuarial loss experience. When losses escalate, as they did during 2007–08, the prevailing view is that the interest rate risk premiums charged borrowers in prior years must have been too small, which results in marked price adjustments. Interest rate risk premiums are now substantially larger than they were earlier, and the eligibility cutoff—the point at which loans become unavailable at any price—occur at lower values of risk variables.

This reaction by the market is understandable and perhaps unavoidable in the current environment. But relative to what they would be in a reserving environment, interest rate risk premiums are grossly excessive. In a system in which insurers offer MPI and all borrowers pay the prime rate, the interest rate plus the MPI insurance premium paid by nonprime borrowers would be substantially smaller than the interest rate plus the TMI insurance premium that they pay now.

A Gaming Analogy

Imagine a world in which all home mortgages are placed in securities, of which there are two types. Both promise to pay investors the prime rate but protect them in different ways. On a rate risk premium (RRP) security, borrowers pay interest rate risk premiums, which are placed in a reserve fund. Each security has its own fund, which cannot be commingled with any other. The RRP security holder thus is protected only by the reserve fund for that security. On an MPI security, borrowers pay insurance premiums to an insurer, who places an MPI policy on every mortgage in the pool. The MPI security holder thus is protected by the total capital and reserves of the insurer.

Make the following assumptions: Every security faces a market environment that is determined by a single twirl of a roulette wheel, which has fifteen slots, fourteen of them blue and one red. If blue comes up, as it will 93.3 percent of the time, the environment is one in which house prices increase and credit losses to investors amount to one-tenth of 1 percent of loan balances. If red comes up, as it will 6.7 percent of the time, the environment will be one in which house prices decline and credit losses will be 6 percent of loan balances.

In this world, the insurer will assume that it will experience fourteen rising markets for every one declining market. The reserve needed by the insurers to cover losses of 0.10 percent on 93.3 percent of the loans that they insure and losses of 6 percent on 6.7 percent of them is about 0.50 percent. Their premium will be about twice that, or 1 percent. The investor is protected when the market declines and losses jump because the insurer has the reserves needed to meet the claims.

Investors in an RRP security, on the other hand, are protected only by the reserve established for that particular security. For the investor to accept a 1 percent risk premium (comparable to the insurance premium on the MPI security), he would have to diversify across many RRP securities over time and avoid paying taxes on the risk premiums in excess of losses on all low-loss securities. Since that is not feasible, the risk premium would have to exceed 1 percent, probably by a considerable margin.[3]

Full protection for the investor in RRP securities requires a risk premium reserve of 6 percent *on every security*. However, because any risk premium above 1 percent would be profitable 93.3 percent of the time, the market will settle somewhere between 1 percent and 6 percent, depending on investor attitudes toward the risk of very high losses that might put them out of business. Borrowers will pay more on the RRP security, and when the roulette wheel comes up red, the risk premium reserve still will not be adequate to cover the losses.

This gaming analogy illustrates very well why interest rate risk premiums are both too large and too small. They are too large in the sense that most of the time they far exceed what is needed to meet losses, and they are too small in the sense that they are inadequate to meet losses when a default crunch does occur.

Fixing the System with MPI

With MPI, financing costs to nonprime borrowers would be substantially lower. Furthermore, the system would be much less vulnerable to default crises such as the one we are in now.

Lower Costs to Borrowers. Mortgage insurers assume almost 100 percent of the default risk under an MPI policy. A very small amount remains because of the cap on insurer liability.[4] Assuming that the cap is adjusted to meet investor requirements, the only material risk remaining to the investor is the risk that the insurer itself will fail. Assuming that risk is nil, interest rate risk premiums disappear. Borrowers would pay different mortgage insurance premiums, but they would all pay the prime interest rate. MPI would cost insurers little more and in many

---

3. A more complete model would distinguish the investor and security issuer, with the latter positioned to pocket a major part of the excess premiums on the low-loss securities while allowing investors to take most of the loss on the high-loss security.

4. On MPI, the targeted expected loss on the nonprime loan will be the same as that on the prime loan. Because the incidence of default will be higher on the nonprime loan, the severity of loss must be correspondingly lower. That is accomplished by setting a higher insurance coverage ratio on the nonprime loan.

cases less than their traditional limited insurance. Hence, the total financing cost to borrowers would drop, with the cost imposed on riskier borrowers dropping the most.

The case in tables 6-1 through 6-3 illustrates how large the savings can be. Assuming the TMI insurance premium of 1.29 percent in table 6-1 is properly priced to meet losses under that policy, it is more than adequate to meet the lower losses under an MPI policy. Hence, the 3.875 percent rate premium, which investors require when they are protected only by TMI, is redundant if they have MPI. Further, with all borrowers eligible for mortgage insurance paying prime rates, the potential for predatory practices would be sharply reduced. Elimination of risk-based pricing would eliminate opportunistic pricing of mortgages at the point of sale, which is one of the most important sources of abuse. In addition, borrowers would have an important ally in the mortgage insurers, who have a financial interest in seeing that borrowers are not overcharged.[5] Higher rates mean greater risk exposure for the insurer. Insurers would have the clout and information needed to protect borrowers because insurer/lender relations would shift to a more level playing field.

Since the private mortgage insurance industry began, it has been beholden to lenders because lenders select the insurers to whom they refer borrowers. With MPI, lenders and insurers (and by extension, borrowers) would be on a more equal footing because borrowers could go to insurers knowing that MPI is a de facto loan approval that will allow them to borrow at the prime rate.

Elimination of a Critical Agency Problem. One of the features of the existing housing finance system that has been much commented on in discussions of the current crisis is that the parties making risk decisions are not the parties that end up assuming the risk. That creates what economists term an "agency" problem, in which one party (the agent) is supposed to act in the interest of another (the principal), even though their interests are not the same. Various techniques have been developed to ensure that the actions of the agent are consistent with the interests of the principal. For example, when loan originators sell loans, the purchaser often has the right to sell them back if they do not meet the purchaser's requirements. The problem is that those mechanisms do not always work the way that they are supposed to—and during a period of euphoria in the market, such as that

---

5. Although the interest rate has an important effect on insurer losses, insurers have never recognized that in their premium structures. One executive explained that to us by saying that the premium-setting process began back in the days when rate dispersion was very small. However, the companies did not use FICO scores in premium setting in the early days either, but they use them now. A more plausible explanation is that basing premiums on the rate would mean that upward rate adjustments would mean an upward insurance premium adjustment, which lenders would not appreciate.

experienced during 2000–05, they may not work at all. MPI eliminates the agency problem in connection with default risk. The PMI underwrites the loan, and the PMI assumes all or virtually all of the risk.

Reduced Systemic Vulnerability. With default risk covered by MPI rather than by a combination of TMI and rate risk premiums, vulnerability to financial crises would be substantially reduced. Today, only TMI premiums are placed in reserve accounts to protect against future losses. With minor exceptions, interest rate risk premiums that are not needed to meet current losses become investor income. With MPI replacing rate risk premiums, the process of reserving for contingencies would be extended to cover all default risk, not just part of the collateral risk. Reserves available to meet losses might be ten times larger, as a rough order of magnitude.

In addition, risk underwriting would shift into more dependable hands. Mortgage insurance companies already offer underwriting to lenders as a service, but with MPI they would do it for all loans except those that did not qualify for MPI. In setting underwriting requirements, lenders and investment banks have a short-run orientation that can lead to sharp swings in how liberal or restrictive the requirements are. They become excessively liberal when market sentiment is euphoric, as it was during 2000–05, and then excessively tight when pessimism reigns, as is the case now. As noted, that tendency is encouraged by their ability to pass along most default risk to the next party in the chain. Insurers, in contrast, have a long-term orientation because they remain on the hook for a loan until it is repaid or the insurance is terminated. In addition, by keeping defaulted mortgages performing until they are paid off, MPI would block the contagious erosion of investor confidence that stems from mounting increases in the number of non-performing loans. That has been a central feature of the current crisis.

MPI Requires Secondary Market Support

MPI will not come about without support from either Fannie Mae or Freddie Mac. For it to work, loans with MPI must be priced at prime plus a competitive retail markup. Without a secondary-market buyer paying prime, lenders will undervalue MPI for an indefinite period, and neither borrowers nor insurers will receive the benefits that they deserve.

If agencies are willing to price a prime loan at 6 percent with TMI, they should be willing to take a riskier loan at 6 percent if it carries MPI and if the insurer's credit is beyond reproach. The insurer's credit is better than that of the prime borrower. Further, in the event of a default, the payments will continue to be made on the riskier loan but not on the prime loan. While the riskier loan will have a

higher incidence of default, in the event of default the loss to the investor with
MPI is lower. How those factors balance out is not clear, but if there is any added
risk, the coverage can be adjusted to shift it to the insurer, with the borrower paying for it in a higher insurance premium. Any such adjustment would not mate-
rially reduce the borrower's cost saving. Moreover, there are other advantages of
MPI to the agencies:

Reduction in Systemic Vulnerability. If there is one lesson that the agencies
should have learned from the current crisis, it is that they cannot separate their
own fortunes from those of the housing finance system as a whole. They have a
vital stake in how the system evolves in the future, and being an active participant
in the process is in their own self-interest.

Elimination of Risk-Based Pricing. With MPI, all risk-based pricing would be
done by PMIs. The agencies would have to stipulate only the amount of insurance coverage required. Community groups adamantly oppose risk-based pricing
by Fannie Mae and Freddie Mac, so eliminating it removes a source of needless
controversy.

Stabilizing the PMIs. MPI will open a new source of profitable business for existing private mortgage insurers, increasing their chances of surviving the crisis. The
more premium income that they can generate, the greater their chances. Existing
PMIs are currently in a "hunker-down" mode, husbanding their reserves and tightening their underwriting requirements, and they are strongly disinclined to initiate
new programs. That mindset is counterproductive and increases the likelihood that
some of the PMIs will fail. They need a new mindset. The agencies could encourage (or even require) them to view MPI as a way out of their difficulties because
lower borrowing costs will stimulate demand, increasing their premium income.

Alignment of Agency and Borrower Interests. Perhaps the most important reason
for Fannie Mae and Freddie Mac to support MPI is that it would align the agencies' interests with those of borrowers. As already noted, MPI would reduce the
financing costs of most borrowers, the potential for predatory practices would be
sharply reduced, and borrowers would have an important ally in mortgage insurers, who have a financial interest in seeing that borrowers are not overcharged.
That would help the agencies rebuild their political capital.

Concluding Comment: The Reserving Principle

While this chapter focuses on the mortgage insurance industry, the core principle
of MPI, transaction-based reserving, has much wider applicability. With TBR, a
portion of the risk premium on every transaction must be reserved and cannot be
withdrawn except in exigent circumstances. TBR is an approach to regulating the

safety and soundness of financial institutions generally. It can be viewed as an alternative (or perhaps a supplement) to capital requirements. As applied to a depository, the required allocation to a contingency reserve would be, say, 50 percent of the portion of any charge that is risk-based. If a prime mortgage was priced at 6 percent and zero points, for example, the reserve allocation for a 7 percent, 2-point mortgage would be 0.50 percent plus 1 point. Of course, income allocated to reserves would not be taxed until it was withdrawn ten years later.

The great advantage of TBR is that a shift to riskier loans during periods of euphoria automatically generates larger reserve allocations because riskier loans carry higher risk premiums. Hence, TBR is largely immune to cyclical swings in investor sentiment. That is in contrast to capital requirements, which allow lenders to increase their risk exposure without any increase in required capital by replacing less risky assets with more risky assets within any given asset class defined by the regulator. Another advantage of TBR is that it has universal applicability and does not leave destabilizing innovations uncovered. When so-called credit default swaps appeared, for example, the TBR regulator would immediately have realized that the premium was 100 percent risk based, and sellers would have been obliged to reserve 50 percent of their premium income. The bottom line is that every financial institution is, at least in part, in the insurance business and therefore ought to be regulated as such.

EIICHI SEKINE
KEI KODACHI
TETSUYA KAMIYAMA

7

The Development
and Future of
Securitization in Asia

THE GLOBAL FALLOUT from the subprime mortgage crisis in the United
States has fueled debate about the advantages and disadvantages of securitization. Our view, however, is that it would be more constructive to identify and
remedy any shortcomings in the securitization process in order to make the most
of its inherent advantages than to question its very existence.

The debate about securitization in the United States has raised a wide range of
issues. In this chapter, however, we focus on only two such issues: those concerning securitized products and those concerning the business process and those
involved in it. At the heart of the problem with securitized products, in our view,
is the difficulty that investors face in understanding the contents of the packaging—the underlying assets. That is the case with products such as residential
mortgage–backed securities (RMBSs) in particular, in which the underlying assets
are numerous and have no credit rating.

One problem as far as the business process is concerned is that posed by the
"originate to distribute" model. Generally speaking, the people who originate loans
in the United States are not the same as those who distribute securitized products.
That and the fact that such products usually also contain a high-risk tranche means
that there is little incentive for either originators or distributors to manage the
risks posed by the underlying assets. Other issues that have been raised include
whether credit ratings are adequate (as rating agencies have not always been quick

to spot risks) and whether it is proper that ratings, which originally were intended purely as a reference for investors, have ended up becoming a must.

That raises the question of whether such problems are part and parcel of securitization or can be overcome—just as other problems have been in many of the crises that financial and capital markets have faced over the years—if those involved can put their heads together and devise an approach that allows society to continue to benefit from the advantages that securitization offers. We hope that by analyzing the development and future of securitization in Asia, where the market for securitized products is still in its infancy compared with the U.S. market, we can find some answers to these questions.

The concept of securitization is another item that Asia has imported from the United States. Our main aim in this chapter is to answer the question of whether in the future Asian securitized products are likely to pose problems similar to those in the United States or whether such problems are likely to be avoided because the methods and styles adopted in Asia are different from those in the United States even if the basic concept is the same.

Development and Future of Asian Bond Markets

In our view, securitization has an even more important role to play in Asia than in Europe and the United States because Asian bond markets are still underdeveloped and Asian companies still depend heavily on banks for their funds. In the following discussion we consider those factors and how they relate to securitization.

Asian bond markets—especially the corporate bond markets, where companies raise funds—are underdeveloped. Table 7-1 shows that although Asian bond markets have grown in size, they are still small compared with those in the United States and Japan as well as in terms of their own GDP.

Asia's need for bigger and more sophisticated bond markets became apparent following the Asian currency crisis of 1997. The problem was a "double mismatch"—of both currency and maturity—when the local savings that European and U.S. banks had recycled in the region on a short-term basis were invested in long-term projects but then suddenly "repatriated" when the Thai baht collapsed. The response of the finance ministers of ASEAN (Association of Southeast Asian Nations), Japan, China, and South Korea (ASEAN + 3) was to propose an "Asian Bond Markets Initiative" (ABMI) as a means of recycling those savings within the region as local currency.

From the outset, securitization was considered an important part of the initiative. In the press release that followed their meeting in Manila in August 2003,

Table 7-1. *Size of Asian Bond Markets*

| | 1997 | | 2004 | |
Nation	Outstanding amount (dollars, billions)	Percent of GDP	Outstanding amount (dollars, billions)	Percent of GDP
China	116.4	12.9	483.3	24.9
Indonesia	4.5	1.9	57.7	22.7
Korea	130.3	25.1	568.3	83.2
Malaysia	57.0	57.0	106.6	90.0
Philippines	18.5	22.3	25.0	28.8
Thailand	10.7	7.1	66.5	41.1
Hong Kong	45.8	25.9	76.8	46.3
Singapore	23.7	24.7	78.6	73.1
Japan	4,433.6	97.6	8,866.7	197.7
United States (for comparison)	12,656.9	62.9	19,186.6	161.6

Source: Asian Development Bank; Asian Bonds Online (http://asianbondsonline.adb.org/regional/regional.php); World Bank.

the ASEAN + 3 finance ministers announced, among other things, the creation of markets for asset-backed securities (ABSs), including collateralized debt obligations (CDOs), and the establishment of a working group to create new securitized debt instruments. The aim of the working group was to consider measures to encourage the securitization of bond issues and the issuance of bonds denominated in a number of local currencies to create a more diversified bond market in the region. Among the other working groups that were set up following that meeting was a working group on credit guarantee mechanisms and one on local and regional rating agencies.

The working group set up to create new securitized debt instruments spent some time studying the possibility of issuing asset-backed securities denominated in an Asian currency basket as well as measures to encourage an Asian medium-term note program. One of the results of the initiative was the issuance of a ¥7.7 billion collateralized bond obligation (CBO) backed by yen-denominated bonds issued by a group of forty-six Korean small and medium enterprises (SMEs) in 2004.[1]

---

1. The CBO consisted of senior and subordinated tranches. The senior tranche was guaranteed by Industrial Bank of Korea (IBK) and Japan Bank for International Cooperation (JBIC), while the subordinated tranche was underwritten by Korea's Small Business Corporation.

The new ASEAN+3 ABMI Roadmap announced in May 2008 focuses on four main areas:
—promoting the issuance of bonds denominated in local currencies
—encouraging the demand for local currency–denominated bonds
—improving the regulatory framework for bond markets
—improving related infrastructure for bond markets.

We see the roadmap as an indication that the initiative's priority has been to develop the basics of a bond market and that the development of securitization as part of what might be called an "applied market" has been considered of secondary importance and therefore is still at a primitive stage.

Concentration of Risk in the Banking System

One of the distinctive features of Asian corporate finance is that companies still depend heavily on banks for their funds. Figure 7-1 shows that bank loans account for a relatively high proportion of the funds raised by Asian companies.

SMEs play a more important role in emerging market economies such as China and India than in Western economies. SMEs have few alternatives to bank loans as a source of funds and are vulnerable to loan restrictions and recalls during credit crunches. A smoothly functioning corporate bond market would therefore be an attractive option for Asian companies (and especially SMEs) looking to raise funds. However, as most SMEs have a low credit rating, only a small proportion of any bonds that they issued would qualify as investment grade. Also, possible shortcomings in their disclosure and accounting standards would probably make it difficult for individual SMEs to issue bonds.[2] In addition, there is the problem, as mentioned, that Asian bond (and especially corporate bond) markets are underdeveloped.

The response of the Asian Development Bank and individual governments has therefore been to consider ways of originating bonds that would relieve the cash flow difficulties of Asian SMEs, on the one hand, and meet investors' needs, on the other, by bundling (that is, securitizing) small amounts of low-grade corporate debt. The aforementioned moves under the Asian Bond Markets Initiative, including the moves to establish asset-backed securities markets, are part of this response.

---

2. This section is based on Kokusai Tsuukamondai Kenkyuujo, *Ajia ni okeru Saikenshijou Kenkyuukai Houkokusho (Zaimushou Ishoku)* [Report from Asian Bond Markets Study Group (commissioned by Japanese Ministry of Finance)] (Japan: Institute for International Monetary Affairs, March 2005).

Figure 7-1. *Sources of Funds for Asian Companies*[a]

Percent

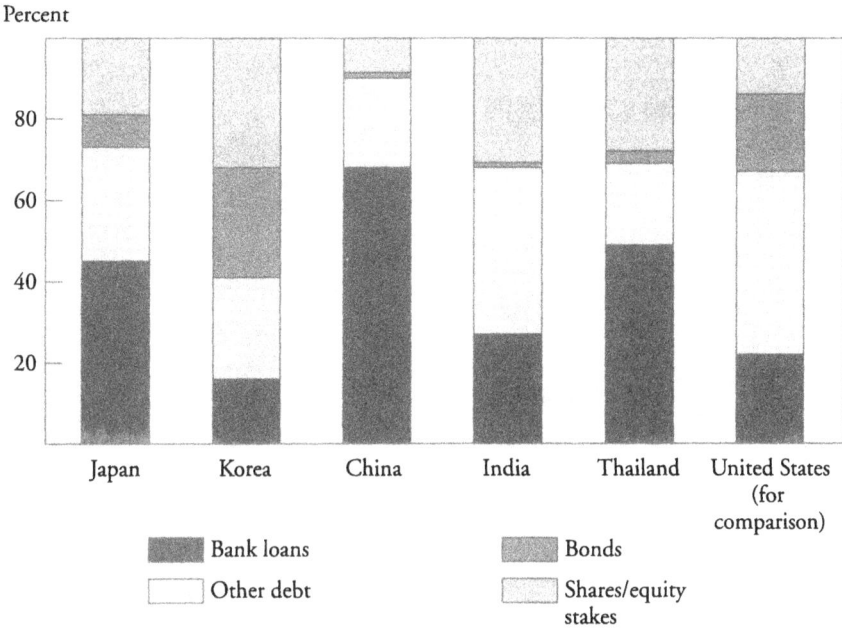

Source: Nomura Institute of Capital Markets Research, based on data from the Japanese Ministry of Finance and the Reserve Bank of India.

a. Data are for the five years through 2003 (FY2003, in the case of India).

Current State of Asian Securitization Markets

Securitization in Asia has been led by Japan and Korea, followed by countries such as India, China, and Malaysia. The amount of securitized products issued by the main Asian countries involved in securitization (Japan, Korea, India, and China) has been increasing and had reached nearly $120 billion by the end of 2006 (figure 7-2). Nevertheless, according to figures from the Bank for International Settlements (BIS), while the United States issued some $800 billion of securitized products in 2005, securitized products in Asian markets in 2005 were worth only as much as such products in the U.S. market in 1995.[3] However, Asian securitization markets are not only relatively small in scale but also underdeveloped.

3. "Securitisation in Asia and the Pacific: Implications for Liquidity and Credit Risks," *BIS Quarterly Review*, June 2006.

Figure 7-2. *Size of Main Asian Securitization Markets*

$100 millions

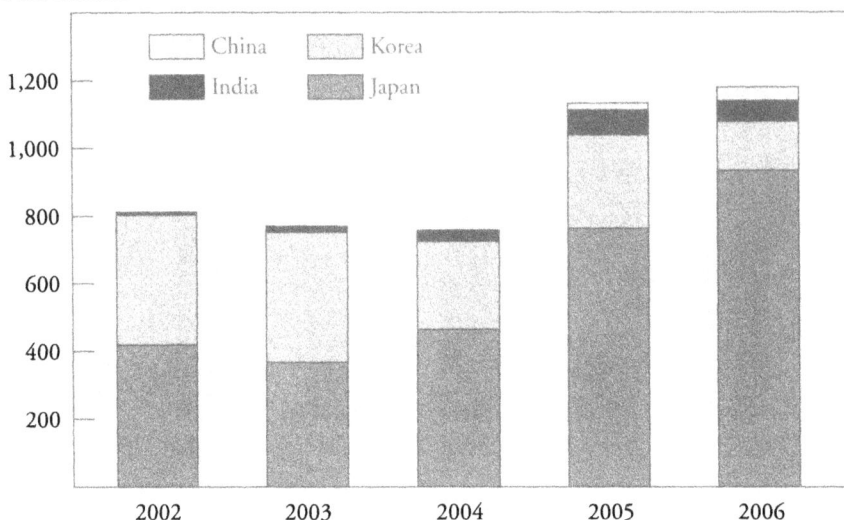

Source: Nomura Institute of Capital Markets Research, based on data from Nomura Securities, "Rating and Investment Information"; ChinaBond (www.chinabond.com.cn/Site/cb/en); and Vinod Kothari, "Indian Securitisation Market" (www.vinodkothari.com/India_securitisation_vinodkothari.pdf).

While it is convenient to talk about Asian securitization markets, the state of the markets varies from country to country. One example of that variation is the underlying assets used in the products. While mortgages are the main asset in Japan and Malaysia and auto loans are the main asset in India, nonperforming loans, project finance loans, mortgages, and auto loans compete for first place in Korea. And even in Japan and Malaysia, where mortgages are the main underlying asset, the history that led to the current situation is completely different.

What is common to all the Asian securitization markets is that the products that they offer are underdeveloped. While the issue of single-loan collateralized loan obligations (CLOs) in India is perhaps an extreme example of the use of securitization for what, for all intents and purposes, is a loan sale, it is not uncommon in South and Southeast Asia for senior and subordinated tranches not to be issued. And even when such tranches are issued, the originator usually keeps the subordinated tranche, selling only the senior tranche to investors. One example of this is the repackaging of nonperforming loans by Korea Asset Management Corporation (KAMCO). Resecuritized products, such as are issued in the United States, also are rarely seen in Asia. While these factors make it less likely that

Asian countries will experience a subprime mortgage crisis, they restrict the freedom of Asian investors to choose financial products that match their personal risk profile.

Another distinctive feature of Asian securitization markets is the lack of investor sophistication and a shortage of originators. Asian investors generally are considered to have a short horizon, and securitized products create no exception to that rule. One of the reasons cited for the failure of India's mortgage-backed securities (MBS) market to take off is lack of investor interest in such long-term products. Another example of a short investment horizon is Korea, where 73 percent of the asset-backed securities issued in 2004 had a maturity of less than two years. As for the lack of originators, Japan's MBS market has, for all intents and purposes, fewer than five originators, while in India 80 percent or more of securitized products are issued by top banks such as ICICI Bank, Sundaram Finance, and Standard Chartered. Increasing the number and improving the quality of investors and originators is therefore one of the challenges facing the development of securitization markets in Asia.

Similarly, emerging Asian economies in particular face a number of infrastructure problems, including a shortage of credit enhancement tools (for example, monoline insurers), underdeveloped credit rating agencies (with either none or only one in some countries), and inadequate legal infrastructure.

Development of Asian Securitization Markets

Asia's securitization markets were established to deal with the nonperforming loans left by the Asian currency crisis. In 1998, asset-backed securities were issued in the countries that had triggered the crisis (such as Korea, Malaysia, Thailand, and the Philippines) in an attempt to unbundle the excessive concentration of credit risk in the banks, which found themselves saddled with a mountain of nonperforming loans. Although the asset-backed securities issued in the late 1990s initially targeted foreign investors and were denominated in foreign currencies, since the turn of the century most securitized products (currently about 80 percent) have been denominated in the local currency. In the meantime, countries that were affected by the crisis also have established securitization markets, according to their own particular needs. Now that the crisis has passed, both groups of countries have gone their separate ways.

Countries That Triggered the Asian Currency Crisis

Korea. In Korea, the Asian country that has made the greatest use of securitization (apart from Japan), the Asset-Backed Securities Law was passed in 1998 to encourage the banks to dispose of their nonperforming loans. The following year, 42 percent of the securitizations in Korea involved such loans, but the figure declined to 5 percent by 2002 as the impact of the crisis faded. That was also the period when issuance of securitized products in Korea peaked, falling from KRW509 trillion in 2001 to KRW16.8 trillion in 2005.

Consumer loans and credit card receivables replaced nonperforming loans as the main underlying assets in Korean securitizations. In 2003 and the following years, however, the collapse of a number of credit card and consumer loan companies led to a decline in the issuance of such securities, while the number of CDOs issued to refinance corporate bonds and the number of securities backed by auto loans increased.

More recently, efforts have been made to create an even more diversified securitization market in Korea. In 2003 the country's first security backed by student loans was issued, and in 2004 the country's first residential mortgage–backed security was issued by the Korean Housing Finance Corporation, which had been established the same year. That was followed in 2005 by the issuance of a synthetic CDO by Korea Development Bank (KDB) and the issuance overseas of a U.S. dollar–denominated security backed by Korean credit card receivables.

Malaysia. The largest securitization market among the ASEAN countries is Malaysia's. Malaysia created the regulatory framework necessary for a securitization market following the Asian currency crisis in order to encourage the use of securitization. In 2001, the Securities Commission of Malaysia published guidelines for the issuance of asset-backed securities, and amendments to the guidelines were published in 2003 and 2005. The amendments were designed to make the securitization process smoother and more flexible by abolishing the requirement for central bank approval of the issue and sale of asset-backed securities and by allowing the use of a wider range of underlying assets.

In 2001, following the enactment of the guidelines, Malaysia's national asset management company, Danaharta, issued MYR310 million of securitized products backed by nonperforming loans. The range of underlying assets subsequently increased, and, in 2004, Cagamas MBS issued MYR1.56 billion of the country's first residential mortgage–backed securities.[4] As of 2005, commercial and residential mortgage–backed securities accounted for the largest proportion (45 percent) of securitized products issued in Malaysia.

---

4. Cagamas was established in 1986 to securitize property loans from Malaysian banks. At the beginning, it enjoyed certain privileges (for example, a credit line from the central bank and exemption from stamp duty), but those privileges were abolished in 2004.

Another distinctive feature of the securitized products issued in Malaysia is the development of shariah-compliant products. In 2005, Cagamas issued the world's first Islamic residential mortgage–backed securities. As of 2007, 30 percent of the outstanding securitized products issued in Malaysia were shariah-compliant— although that includes so-called *sukuks* (Islamic bonds), and therefore the share of shariah-compliant securitized products is well below 30 percent.

Other countries. Although Thailand, Indonesia, and the Philippines all en- acted laws and guidelines to encourage the use of securitization following the Asian currency crisis,[5] their securitization markets are still small. The largest issue of securitized products in these countries has been a THB24 billion deal by Thai- land's Dhanarak Asset Development Company to finance the construction of a government complex; the deal is backed by lease payments on the complex.

Countries Affected by the Asian Currency Crisis

Japan. In Japan, securitization came into its own in 1996 following the enact- ment of the Specified Credits Act in 1993. When the asset boom of the 1980s turned to bust in the early 1990s, nonbanks found it increasingly difficult to obtain bank loans because banks became increasingly reluctant to lend. The aim therefore was to use securitization to make it easier for nonbanks to raise funds. Japan's securitization market expanded rapidly during 2004–05 following the enactment of the Act on Liquidation of Specified Assets by Special Purpose Com- panies (SPC Act) in 1998. The reason for the increase in securitization was the expansion of the Government Housing Loan Corporation's role to include assis- tance with the securitization of residential mortgages. In 2006, issuance of secu- ritized products in Japan topped ¥10 trillion for the first time. Roughly half of those securities were backed by residential mortgages.

China. China has only very recently begun to issue securitized products. A pilot program was conducted in 2005–06 in which bank loan assets and nonper- forming loan assets held by asset management companies were securitized and traded on China's interbank bond market, while specific cash flows of nonfinan- cial companies were securitized by securities companies and traded on the coun- try's stock exchanges. Further details of the securitization markets of Japan and China are discussed later in the chapter.

India. In India, securitization came into its own only earlier in this decade. India's asset-backed securities market has expanded as a result of the strong

---

5. For example, in Thailand, a securitization law was enacted in 1992, an ABS law in 2003, and an SPV law in 2004; in Indonesia, guidelines were issued by the Capital Market Supervisory Agency in 2002–03; and in the Philippines, a special purpose vehicle (SPV) act was enacted in 2002 and a securitization act in 2004.

Figure 7-3. *Issuance of Securitized Products in India*

INR billions

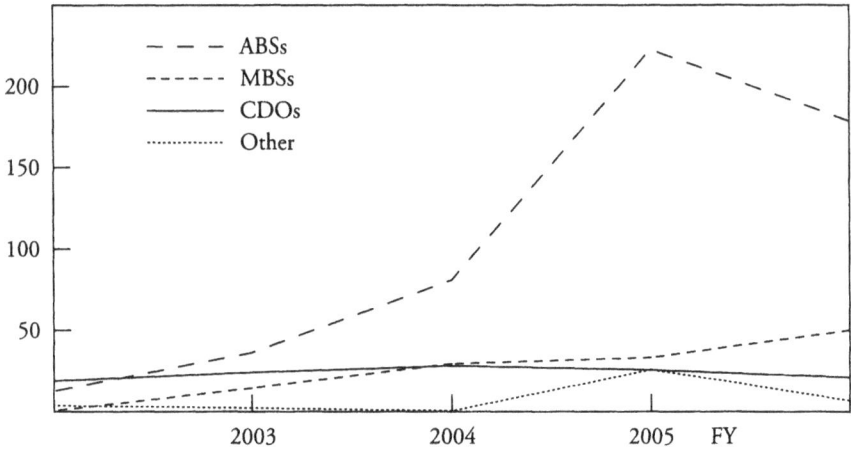

Source: Nomura Institute of Capital Markets Research, based on data from Vinod Kothari, "Indian Securitisation Market" (www.vinodkothari.com/India_securitisation_vinodkothari.pdf).

domestic demand for automobiles and auto loans, and most securitized products are still backed by such loans (figure 7-3). Since 2006, however, issuance of collateralized loan obligations (CLOs, not shown in figure 7-3) has increased to the point that it is now neck and neck with that of asset-backed securities. However, 45 percent of the CLOs issued in 2007 were single-loan CLOs (simple deals involving assignment of a single corporate loan by a bank or a finance company to a special purpose vehicle, which issues pass-through certificates against receivables). That is not exactly what securitization was developed to do.[6] Issuance of residential mortgage–backed securities also has increased. However, unlike in Korea, in India the range of underlying assets (for example, credit card receivables) remains quite limited.

Rules Governing Securitization

The rules governing securitization in Asian countries vary according to each country's legal system and the reasons why each national market has been obliged

6. Single-loan CLOs are issued to enable issuers to avoid the disclosure and onerous paperwork required when issuing bonds and to allow originators to transfer credit risk despite the underdeveloped state of India's credit derivatives market.

to expand. International comparisons of legal systems often distinguish between civil law jurisdictions and common law jurisdictions. When it comes to specifics (for example, securitization), however, we do not find that distinction very appropriate. In fact, as shown in table 7-2, the differences between civil law and common law jurisdictions do not necessarily correspond to the development of rules governing securitization. Furthermore, some Asian countries that have traditionally adopted civil law systems base their financial regulations on U.S. practice (for example, Japan and Korea).

Nevertheless, the distinction between civil law jurisdictions and common law jurisdictions does give a general idea of the way in which legal systems as a whole are organized, with civil law jurisdictions regulated by statutes and common law jurisdictions regulated by rules and guidelines. The rules and regulations governing securitization in Korea are an example of the former and those in India are an example of the latter.

As mentioned previously, the basic rules governing securitization in Korea are contained in the Asset-Backed Securities Law (ABS Law) of 1998. This law lays down who can be involved in a securitization: namely, securitization vehicles (asset-backed security special purpose vehicles, offshore special purpose vehicles, and trusts) and originators (government agencies and financial institutions and internationally known nonfinancial companies approved by Korea's Financial Supervisory Commission). In addition, it contains rules for mitigating risks such as transfer denial risk, commingling risk, and offset risk.

Also, originators have to register a "securitization plan" with the Financial Supervisory Commission (FSC) when securitizing. Registration involves providing details of any issues of asset-backed securities, the underlying assets, the originator, and the management and operational procedures for the securities or assets. Under the ABS Law, in order to ensure the effectiveness of the transfer of underlying assets against any third-party objections, all an originator needs to do is register the transfer with the FSC. If a transfer is conducted according to the Civil Code, originators are required to inform each debtor in writing or to obtain its agreement; hence there is an incentive to comply with the ABS Law. Korea therefore can be said to have all its rules governing securitization systematically organized under one statute law. Hence, its high score in table 7-2.

India, in contrast, does not have any systematic rules and regulations governing securitization. Instead, it has a collection of rules in the form of guidelines and partially amended laws going back to the early years of this decade. The Securitization and Reconstruction of Financial Assets and Enforcement of Security Interests Act of 2002 sets out the rules and regulations governing the purchase of nonperforming assets by asset reconstruction companies (that is, asset management

Table 7-2. *Provisions for Securitization in East Asia*[a]

Nation	Source of law	Sale, assignment, or other conveyance of assets by originators to securitization vehicles				Creation, maintenance, and operation of SPVs		Restrictions on securitization vehicles to issue multiple tranches with varying characteristics
		Legal framework for creating, transferring, and perfecting ownership interests	Restrictions on types or terms of financial assets that can be transferred	Taxation and gain recognition issues	Default and foreclosure and/or repossession at level of individual assets	Legal and regulatory impediments (for example, bankruptcy remoteness)	Taxation or licensing requirements	
China	Civil law	1/2	1	1	1	1	1	1
Indonesia	Civil law	2/3	2	2	2	2	2	2
Korea	Civil law	5	4	3/4	4	5	5	5
Malaysia	Common law	5	4	4	3/4	4	4	5
Philippines	Common law	2/3	2/3	1/2	2/3	2/3	2/3	2/3
Thailand	Common law	3/4	3	3/4	3/4	2/3	4/5	2/3
Hong Kong	Common law	5	5	4	5	5	5	5
Singapore	Common law	5	5	5	4	5	5	5

Source: Douglas W. Arner and others, "Property Rights, Collateral, and Creditor Rights in East Asia," Asian Institute of International Financial Law, University of Hong Kong (May 15, 2006), with additions by Nomura Institute of Capital Markets Research.

a. The number 5 indicates the maximum degree of provision; the number 1, the minimum.

companies) from bank balance sheets.[7] "Guidelines on Securitization of Standard Assets," a document issued in 2006 by the Reserve Bank of India, sets out the central bank's policies on what constitutes a true sale, a bankruptcy-remote special purpose vehicle, credit enhancement, and disclosure. Similarly, the Securities Contracts (Regulation) Amendment Act of 2007 sets out the rules governing the listing on a stock exchange of asset-backed financial products issued by special purpose vehicles; it also includes such products in its definition of "securities." That has paved the way for the creation of a secondary market for securitized products.

The biggest challenge facing the Indian authorities in their attempts to establish rules and regulations governing securitization has been taxation (and especially stamp duty). Any transfers of assets to special purpose vehicles have to be recorded in a document on which a stamp duty is payable at different rates (ranging from 3 percent to 16 percent) in different states. While some states charge a preferential rate of tax of only 0.1 percent on the transfer of assets involved in a securitization, eligibility for that rate is restricted because the rate depends on where the underlying assets (not the special purpose vehicle) are located. That has proved an obstacle to securitizing assets, especially credit card receivables. Enlarging India's securitization market is one of the items on the agenda of a Ministry of Finance project to develop the country's domestic bond market, and that is one of the reasons why there have been calls for applying the same tax rate throughout the country.

The preceding general overview of the size, distinctive features, and rules and regulations of Asian securitization markets is followed below by a more detailed look at the markets in Japan and China.

Japan's Securitization Market

Japan's securitization market really took off around 1996, and in the following decade annual securitization issuance grew to more than ¥10 trillion (figure 7-4). In the United States, development of the securitization market was driven by the issuance of RMBSs in the 1970s, but in Japan it was the issuance of ABSs backed by leases and credit receivables that really started the structured finance ball rolling. Subsequently, CDOs backed by corporate loans and bonds were structured, and then even Japan got into the act, issuing RMBSs as well as commercial mortgage–backed securities (CMBSs), which are backed by either commercial real

---

7. Following the act, the Asset Reconstruction Company of India was established as part of the infrastructure of the banking industry. As of March 2006, it had purchased INR211 billion of assets from thirty-one banks.

Figure 7-4. *Annual Securitization Issuance in Japan*[a]

¥ trillions

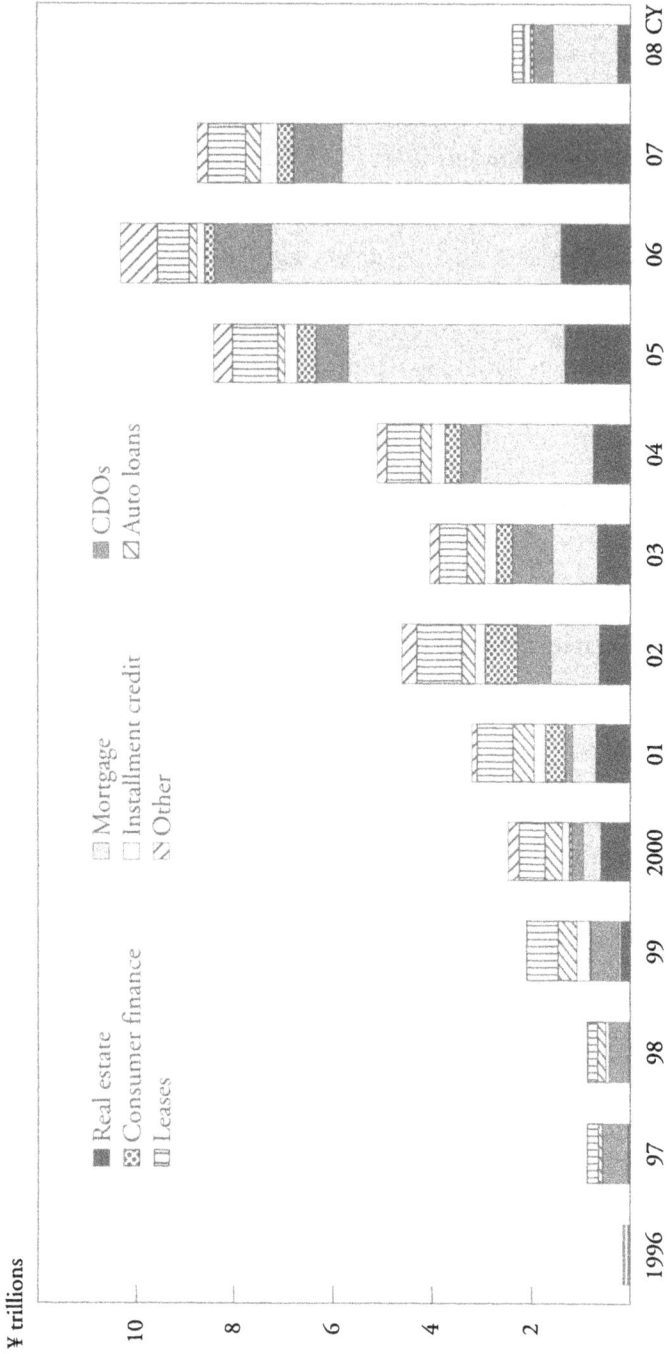

Source: Nomura Securities.

a. 2008 figures are the total from January to June. Figure does not include asset-backed commercial paper or asset-backed loans; CDO numbers show only funded portion. Figure includes euro bonds and foreign currency–denominated bonds. Figure includes total value of rated issues, both publically and privately placed. Information on undisclosed issues included only to the extent known.

estate or loans that use commercial real estate as collateral. In 2002, total issuance of RMBSs overtook that of other structured products. Over the past few years, RMBSs have been the core product in Japan's securitization market, accounting for between 40 percent and 60 percent of issuance.

Although Japan's securitization market had consistently generated solid growth, issuance has stagnated since the subprime loan mess that surfaced in the summer of 2007. The more than ¥10 trillion in securitized products issued in 2006 included a whole business securitization (WBS) backed by the future cash flow of a mobile phone business, which explains in part the 15 percent year-over-year (YoY) decline to ¥8.7 trillion in securitization issuance in 2007, which is only slightly higher than total issuance in 2005. Issuance has remained weak, and it was down approximately 30 percent YoY in January-June 2008. That suggests that securitization market conditions in Japan are as weak as those in Europe and the United States.

On the other hand, although the issuance of securitized products has declined, it is still fairly strong when compared with financing based on the issuance of other types of securities. Domestic issuance in 2007 totaled only ¥2.2 trillion for stocks, ¥9.2 trillion for nonfinancial corporate bonds, and ¥2.2 trillion for yen-denominated overseas bonds, so the ¥8.7 trillion in securitized products issued in that year compares very favorably with the level of corporate bonds issued (figure 7-5). Although securitization issuance has been weak recently, securitized products already play an important role in funding, and they appear to have established a solid footing in the Japanese market.

History of Japan's Securitization Market

The liberalization of interest rates in Japan increased the risk that financial institutions would develop mismatches between liabilities and investments, and the increased use of securities for both investing and procuring funds, as well as the sale of loan assets, led to a gradual awareness of the need for securitization. Full-scale development of securitization did not occur until the issuance of ABSs backed by lease and credit receivables, which was sparked by establishment of the Act on Regulation of Businesses Concerning Specified Credits and So Forth (Specified Credits Act).

The Specified Credits Act was passed because of the deterioration, coincident with the collapse of Japan's economic bubble, in the funding environment for nonbanks, which had greatly expanded their businesses during the bubble of the late 1980s. At the time, nonbanks depended primarily on bank loans to obtain funding, and therefore the bubble's collapse clearly worsened their funding environment. In order to make funding easier, the Ministry of Economy, Trade, and

Figure 7-5. *Issuance of Private Sector Securities, by Type, 2007*

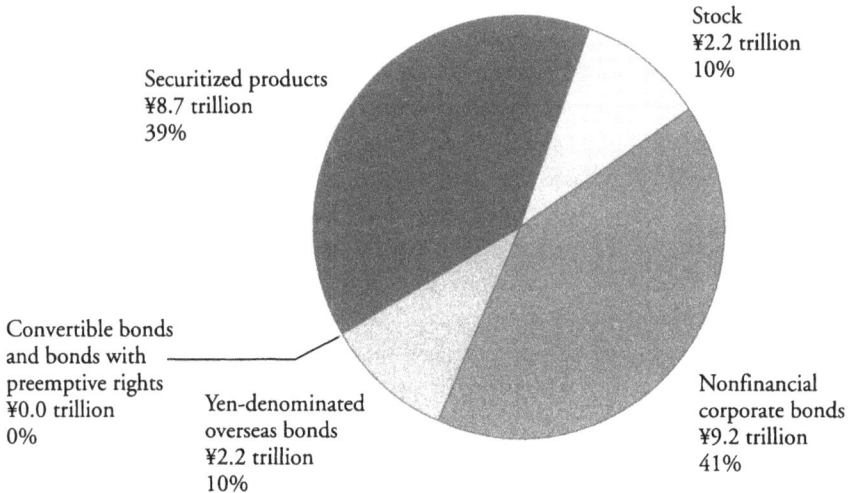

Stock
¥2.2 trillion
10%

Securitized products
¥8.7 trillion
39%

Convertible bonds
and bonds with
preemptive rights
¥0.0 trillion
0%

Yen-denominated
overseas bonds
¥2.2 trillion
10%

Nonfinancial
corporate bonds
¥9.2 trillion
41%

Source: Nomura Institute of Capital Markets Research, based on data from Tokyo Stock Exchange, Japan Securities Dealers Association, and Nomura Securities.

Industry (called the Ministry of International Trade and Industry at the time) implemented the Specified Credits Act in 1993 in order to open another door to funding through the securitization of lease and credit receivables.[8]

The Specified Credits Act's introduction of simplified procedures for allowing third parties to object to the transfer of lease and credit receivables was a pivotal moment in the development of Japan's securitization market. That is because Article 467 of the Civil Code, which governs the transfer of receivables, included as a requirement for third-party objections the administratively onerous and costly requirement to notify debtors with a fixed-date certificate; the Specified Credits Act, however, simplified the procedure, requiring only public notice in a daily newspaper to meet the requirement for third-party objections. Because the Specified Credits Act was designed to help nonbanks obtain funding, it covered only lease and credit receivables, but by establishing exceptions to the rules in the Civil Code concerning the transfer of receivables, it turned out to be revolutionary legislation that established a precedent for securitization laws (table 7-3).

It was later realized that having a legal framework in which the rules differ depending on the business, as in the case of the Specified Credits Act for non-

8. The Specified Credits Act was repealed in 2004 because development of the securitization market made the procedures stipulated in the law more complicated and eventually rendered the law ineffective. The repealed law's functions are now covered by the revised Trust Act.

Table 7-3. *Laws and Regulations on Securitization*

1993	Act on Regulation of Businesses Concerning Specified Credits, Etc. (Specified Credits Act) is implemented.
1998	Act on Liquidation of Specified Assets by Special Purpose Companies (SPC Act) is implemented. Act on Special Exceptions to the Civil Code Related to Objections to the Transfer of Receivables (Receivables Transfer Exceptions Act) is implemented.
1999	Act on Special Measures Related to Debt Collection Businesses (Servicer Act) is implemented.
2000	SPC Act is revised, and its title is changed to the Securitization Act. Securities Investment Trust Act is revised, and its title is changed to Act on Investment Trust and Investment Corporations.

Source: Nomura Institute of Capital Markets Research.

banks, would hold up progress in the securitization market, and that led to the realization of the need for a general law on securitization that included no constraints based on type of business. In 1998, the passage of the SPC Act introduced the TMK (*tokutei mokuteki kaisha*) scheme as a special purpose vehicle (SPV) for securitization. The new law recognized securities issued by a TMK as exchange-tradable securities and legally protected the right of investors to acquire them. To improve its usefulness to TMKs and ensure greater bankruptcy remoteness, the SPC Act was amended in 2000 and renamed the Act on Securitization of Assets, making it possible to use a TMK scheme for securitization. The Act on Special Exceptions to the Civil Code Related to Objections to the Transfer of Receivables, implemented in 1998, introduced, as an exception to the Civil Code, more simplified procedures for registering third-party objections to transfer of receivables.

Once the securitization laws were implemented, Japan's securitization market began to grow. Starting in 1997, the declaration of bankruptcy by a series of major financial institutions amid instability in the financial system led to tighter bank lending and an overall credit crunch. That motivated nonbanks and nonfinancial corporations to concentrate on securitized products as a new way to procure funds without bank loans and led to their participation in the securitization market as originators. The financial sector also saw securitization as a new business opportunity, and both domestic and foreign banks and securities firms began participating in the market as originators and arrangers. It was at that point that Japan's securitization market really took off.

The government implemented securitization laws and other policy measures in response to the need for more diverse ways to obtain funding that resulted from the bursting of Japan's bubble and the accompanying deterioration of the macroeconomic environment, as well as from the destabilization of Japan's financial system caused by the large number of nonperforming loans held by financial institutions. That regulatory framework can probably be seen as the catalyst for full-scale development of Japan's securitization market.

Development of Japan's Securitization Market and Involvement of the Public Sector

Although securitization in Japan was initially built around asset-backed securities backed by leases and credit receivables, residential mortgage–backed securities have been the driving force behind Japan's securitization market since 2002. In the beginning, most RMBSs were originated and issued by banks, but those issued by public institutions have been playing an increasingly important role in the securitization market.

The Government Housing Loan Corporation of Japan (GHLC), a government-sponsored agency established in 1950 to assist with home loans, provided consumers with long-term, fixed-rate home loans at low interest, a type of loan that was difficult to get in the private sector. Home loans from the GHLC were seen as a key component of the government's housing policy. Because of the robust demand for funds from the corporate sector during the post–World War II recovery period, a period of high economic growth, no lenders had enough resources to devote to home loans; therefore a public sector provider of low-rate home loans was needed. The GHLC became the largest originator of home loans, far larger than any private sector financial institution, holding assets of more than ¥70 trillion.

When the Koizumi administration took office in April 2001, administrative and fiscal reform became a hot topic, and during reforms of the Fiscal Investment and Loan Program (FILP), the rationale for the continued existence of government-affiliated financial institutions (FILP agencies) came into question. As a result of revisions to the GHLC's home loan policies and the Japanese government's determination that the need for home loans remained high,[9] the GHLC turned to a complementary role in housing finance and began specializing in providing assistance with the securitizing of home loans written by private sector financial institutions. As a part of the change, the GHLC stopped directly writ-

9. Kokudokoutuushou, *Shijyoukinou wo Sekkyokuteki ni Ikashita Jyutaku Kinou no Arikata Kondankai Houkokusho* [Report of the Working Group on How to Make Housing Finance Function More in Accordance with Market Principles] (Japan: Ministry of Land Infrastructure, Transport, and Tourism, April 2002).

ing home loans. The way that the U.S. housing government-sponsored enterprises (GSEs) operated was used as a guide in reforming the GHLC.

The GHLC was dismantled in April 2007 and replaced by an independent administrative agency, the Japan Housing Finance Agency (JHF). JHF's purpose, like that of the GHLC, is to assist with the securitization of home loans written by private sector financial institutions. It provides assistance in two primary ways: by purchasing home loans written by private sector financial institutions and repackaging those loans for issuance as RMBSs (the purchase program) and by providing guarantees on the principle and interest payments for RMBSs issued by private sector financial institutions (the guarantee program).

The GHLC began issuing RMBSs in a pilot program in March 2001 and was fully into the securitization assistance business by October 2003, years before it was reorganized as the JHF. JHF took that business over and continues to issue RMBSs. In addition, in order to reduce the home loan assets held by the agency, since FY2005 the GHLC had been issuing S-series RMBSs, which are backed by home loans issued previously by the GHLC. (The JHF continues to do so.)

Cumulative outstanding RMBS issuance from the GHLC and JHF combined was about ¥8 trillion as of the end of March 2008. Including the S-series bonds that the GHLC began issuing in FY2005, annual RMBS issuance has been ¥2 trillion yen (figure 7-6). Based on its FY2008 budget, JHF's funding plan included ¥900 billion in funding obtained by issuing FILP agency bonds and by borrowing from private sector financial institutions and ¥2.9 trillion in financing obtained by issuing RMBSs. JHF thus has made the securitization market its base, and it is now making active use of that market.

In addition, as a measure to stimulate public sector use of the securitization market, the Japan Finance Corporation for Small and Medium Enterprises (JASME), which is rolled into the new Japan Policy Finance Corporation,[10] began offering securitization support services. The primary business of JASME, a government-affiliated financial institution established to help SMEs obtain financing, used to be providing loans to SMEs. Because of rising instability in the financial system caused by the epidemic of nonperforming loans in the banking system in the late 1990s, SMEs dependent on bank loans started having trouble getting financing. To deal with the credit crunch, the government offered a ¥20 trillion guaranteed lending facility through the credit guaranty corporations, and it also provided enhancement to the lending mechanisms of JASME and

---

10. On October 1, 2008, JASME was dismantled and merged with three other government-affiliated financial institutions—the National Life Finance Corporation (NLFC), the Agriculture, Forestry, and Fisheries Finance Corporation of Japan (AFC), and the Japan Bank for International Cooperation (JBIC)—to form a new organization, the Japan Policy Finance Corporation.

Figure 7-6. *RMBS Issuance by Japan Housing Finance Agency*[a]

¥ billions

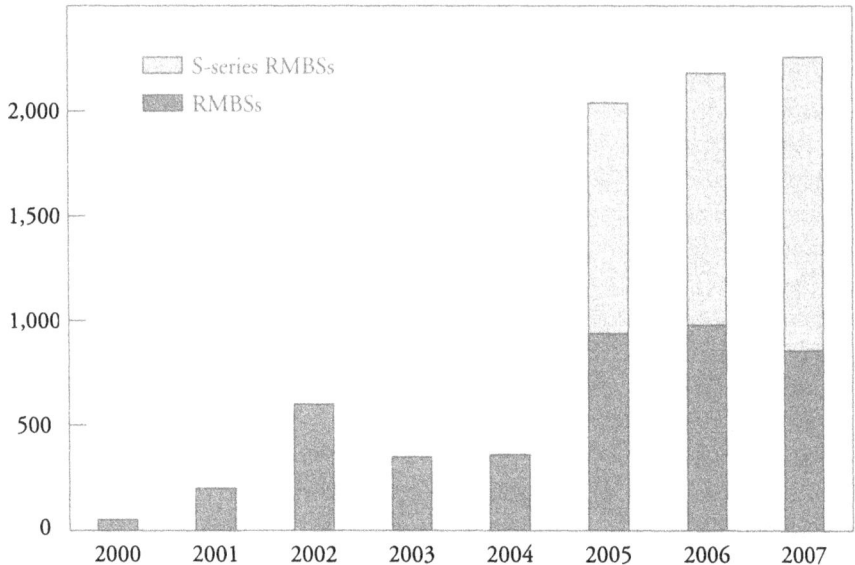

Source: Nomura Institute of Capital Markets Research, based on materials from Japan Housing Finance Agency.

a. S-series bonds are securitizations of existing loans.

other government-affiliated lenders. On the basis of that experience, JASME started concentrating on securitization in order to provide SMEs with a way to obtain funding other than through bank loans, and in 2004 it began offering securitization support for small business loans written by regional banks, the *shinkin* banks, and other regional financial institutions. As of March 2008, JASME's cumulative securitization issuance was approximately ¥300 billion.

In addition to government-affiliated financial institutions, the government itself is trying to make active use of the securitization market. In order to shrink its balance sheet, which is considerably larger than that of other countries, the Japanese government, pursuant to the Regulatory Reform Law implemented in June 2006, announced a July 2006 cabinet decision called Basic Policies for Economic and Fiscal Management and Structural Reform 2006 (Basic Policies 2006). That decision included a plan for reforming the nation's balance sheet, including by reducing assets by about ¥140 trillion by the end of March 2015 and reducing FILP loans to government-affiliated financial institutions by more than

¥130 trillion. One of the ways proposed to achieve those goals was through the use of securitization.

To accommodate the policy of reducing FILP loan assets, in February 2008 the Ministry of Finance began issuing securitized products in a master trust format, with FILP loans serving as the underlying assets. Two deals involving issuance of ¥200 billion in securitized products known as fiscal loan fund ABSs had been concluded as of August 2008, and further issuance is planned.

Local governments also are becoming quite active in the securitization market. Metro Tokyo, which has experienced periods during which banks were reluctant to lend to SMEs in the past, came up with its Tokyo financial market initiative in 1999. Aimed at helping smaller companies obtain unsecured, nonguaranteed funding, this initiative introduced a scheme for issuing CLOs and collateralized bond obligations backed by loans to SMEs—and privately placed corporate bonds issued by SMEs—with Metro Tokyo as the sponsor. Then in 2005, Metro Tokyo and a number of other local governments formed an alliance to introduce a program for the issuance of CBOs backed by privately placed bonds issued by SMEs from various regions of Japan.[11] Approximately 16,000 smaller firms have obtained funding totaling more than ¥700 billion under the alliance program thus far.

The public sector thus has been trying to make active use of Japan's securitization market. The idea behind the shift in the nature of public finance is for the public sector to move away from directly providing credit to the final borrower and instead to start supplementing the provision of credit by private sector financial institutions. Another unique aspect of Japan's securitization market is that it is being used as a way to streamline the national balance sheet and reduce the amount of assets and liabilities held by the government.

Characteristics of Japan's Securitization Market

Although Japan's issuance of securitized products has declined as a result of the subprime loan problem, the decline has not occurred because of any direct impact on securitized products in Japan from exposure to subprime loans in the United States. The amount of securitized products issued in Japan that include subprime RMBSs in their loan pool is negligible.

Furthermore, the performance of Japan's securitized products has been stable. Of the rating actions on Japan's securitized products announced by Moody's in 2007, 104 were upgrades and only nine were downgrades (table 7-4). Compared with the

11. As part of the Tokyo financial market initiative, Metro Tokyo formed an alliance with Osaka Prefecture and the cities of Kawasaki, Yokohama, Shizuoka, Osaka, Kobe, Chiba, and Sakai to issue CBOs and CLOs backed by loans to and privately placed bonds issued by SMEs.

Table 7-4. *Credit Downgrade and Upgrade Rates for Japan's*
Securitized Products
Percent

Securitized products	Twelve-month downgrade rate			Twelve-month upgrade rate		
	2007	2006	2000–07	2007	2006	2000–07
Securitized products in Japan	0.4	0.1	0.3	6.0	5.7	4.9
ABS	0.7	0.0	0.1	2.8	2.3	2.7
CDOs	1.6	0.8	0.4	19.0	19.3	14.8
CMBS	0.0	0.0	0.8	7.6	8.4	7.1
RMBS	0.0	0.0	0.2	5.6	5.4	7.6
Securitized products worldwide	7.4	1.2	2.7	2.2	3.6	2.6

Source: Moody's.

structured products rated by Moody's worldwide, those issued in Japan had on aver-age a lower rate of downgrades and a higher rate of upgrades. Japan's securitized products also have outperformed products in the global securitization market. Japan's securitized products have been stable over a sustained period, and there has not been a single case of default since several defaults that occurred in 2001.

The recent decline in issuance of securitized products, despite the fact that Japan's securitized products have virtually no exposure to subprime-related prod-ucts and have demonstrated stable performance over an extended period of time, can be attributed in part to the deterioration in investment sentiment caused by the subprime crisis. Participants in Japan's securitization market include domes-tic insurance companies, trust banks, regional banks, *shinkin* banks, and mega-banks, as well as the Japan operations of overseas financial institutions. Participa-tion thus is dominated by domestic financial institutions, with little participation by nonresident investors. The lack of a diverse investor base with a diverse risk profile may be one explanation for the recent sluggishness of Japan's securitization market.

Securitized Product Characteristics and Recent Trends

The characteristics of securitized products structured and issued in Japan as well as recent related trends are summarized below. There has been a substantial reduction in the size of Japan's market for certain classes of securitized products. We attribute that to worsened investment sentiment caused by the subprime cri-sis combined with factors specific to Japan.

Figure 7-7. *RMBS Originators*

¥ trillions

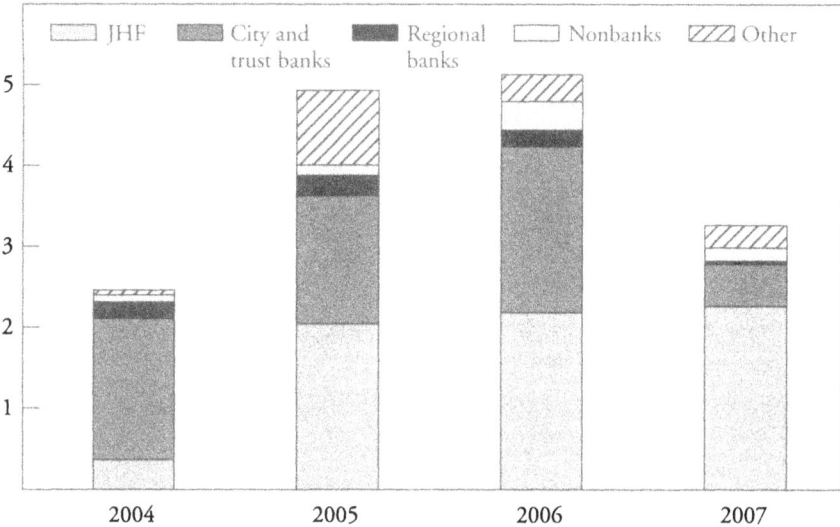

Source: Japan Security Dealers Association.

RMBSs. RMBSs are the biggest single category within Japan's securitization market, accounting for between 40 percent and 60 percent of total issuance. JHF is the largest originator of RMBSs, after which come the major banks (figure 7-7). In FY2007, JHF issued more than ¥2.3 trillion in RMBSs, while major banks issued only ¥0.5 trillion (down dramatically from ¥2.1 trillion in FY2006). JHF therefore accounted for roughly 70 percent of the total RMBS market. In the United States, mortgage bankers and mortgage brokers played a major role in the origination of subprime loans, but the share of RMBSs issued by mortgage companies and other nonbanks is not very large in Japan.

The lending criteria used for home loans backing RMBSs are generally the loan-to-value (LTV) ratio, the debt-to-income (DTI) ratio, the maximum loan amount, and the loan applicant's age, years of employment, and minimum annual income. The home loans purchased from private sector financial institutions by JHF as part of its securitization support business are long-term, fixed-rate loans known as Flat 35 loans. The lending standards for Flat 35 loans are predefined, and if the private sector financial institution writing the loan does not meet those standards, JHF will not purchase the loan (table 7-5). There is no notable difference in the lending standards for home loans written by banks and other private

Table 7-5. *Overview of Flat 35 Loans*

Target borrowers	In principle, below age 70, with a stable income. When annual income is less than ¥4 million, the maximum DTI is 30 percent; when annual income is ¥4 million and above, the maximum DTI is 35 percent.
Use of funds	To fund the construction or purchase of a new home; to fund the purchase of an existing home.
Loan amount	Up to 90 percent of the construction cost or purchase price, between ¥1 million and ¥80 million.
Loan term	Between fifteen and thirty-five years.
Loan interest rate	Fully fixed rate; the rate varies depending on the financial institution.
Repayment method	Equal principal and interest payments or equal principal payments.
Collateral	Japan Housing Finance Agency is the first lien holder on the mortgaged home or land.

Source: Nomura Institute of Capital Markets Research, based on materials from Japan Housing Finance Agency.

sector financial institutions and those for JHF's Flat 35 loans. There also is little variation among financial institutions in the mortgage rates offered for their mortgages, nearly all of which are fully amortized with either equal principal and interest payments or just equal principal payments.[12] Virtually no nonconforming mortgages—mortgages that do not meet normal JHF and bank standards— are originated in Japan.

Furthermore, traditional lending practice in Japan is to provide credit through recourse loans. As the securitization market has developed, nonrecourse loans have come to be used for loans backed by commercial real estate, but residential mortgages are still based on recourse loans. In a recourse loan, if the proceeds from the sale of the collateral property are insufficient to pay back the debt, the borrower is obligated to make repayment by means other than the collateral property, an arrangement that probably helps to prevent moral hazard on the borrower's side. Consequently, the borrower's income is an important component of the credit approval process for a home loan, and the borrower is expected to have

12. Fitch Ratings, "Japanese Nonconforming Mortgage Loan Spotlight," April 27, 2007 (special report on RMBSs in Japan).

a stable source of income. A borrower with a past history of delinquent payments normally has a hard time getting approved for a mortgage. Japan's home loans are limited to the prime market, and therefore they are treated as quality assets. Looking at it from a different perspective, one could say that the demand for home loans from subprime borrowers is not being met.

Recently, however, some financial institutions have been using a scoring model that takes account of the borrower's needs and risk/return in the mortgage approval process. So far, individuals who did not meet the credit standards also have been able to take out a mortgage, and securitization of those mortgages also is being tried. Currently, however, such nonconforming mortgages account for only a very small share of RMBSs.

CDOs. CDO issuance began relatively early in Japan, around 1997, and even now CDOs still account for a reasonable share of the market. As noted earlier, CDOs structured in Japan are almost entirely primary securitized products (securitized, not resecuritized, products) backed by corporate credit; there is little issuance of resecuritized products, which have securitized products as underlying assets. Moody's says that it has a rating on only five CDO deals backed by Japanese securitized products (ABS-CDOs).[13]

Normally, CDOs structured in Japan are synthetic CDOs, which use credit default swaps (CDSs) that reference investment-grade corporate credit. The reference assets for this type of CDO are high-quality credit and normally comprise either subordinated debentures from the banks or the credit of international blue-chip nonfinancials, ranging from such infrastructure businesses as electric power companies and railroad companies to automobile manufacturers. Recently, because of the subprime mess, investors have become wary of the impact on valuations from correlation, and the tendency has been for the number of underlying credit issues to be reduced to five and in some cases to only three. Furthermore, because of some mergers between major banks, many of the CDOs originated by those banks have been structured with the objective of adjusting balance sheets to maintain better control of asset–liability management and credit portfolios.

One characteristic of Japan's CDO market appears to be the large number of CDO issues in which the public sector is involved as a sponsor. During the period of financial system instability that began in the late 1990s, the banks lost their ability to provide funding because of the large amount of nonperforming loans in their portfolios. That made them reluctant to lend, which in turn made access to

---

13. Moody's, "U.S. Subprime Crisis: Impact—or Lack of—on Japanese Structured Finance Market," September 2007 (special report on international structured finance).

funding considerably more difficult for SMEs that were dependent on bank loans. Consequently, with the aim of assisting smaller firms and diversifying their sources of funding beyond bank loans, public sector institutions, including JASME and local governments, began sponsoring the issuance of CDOs backed by loans to—and corporate bonds issued by—SMEs.

JASME's securitization business provides securitization support to private sector financial institutions by either providing guarantees or purchasing loan assets. The guarantee program is a securitization scheme whereby JASME provides guarantees of up to a maximum of 70 percent of the value of CLOs backed by loans to SMEs made by multiple financial institutions spread across more than one region, thereby achieving regional diversification. JASME's purchase program is a scheme for securitizing CLOs by packaging SME loans purchased from various individual regional financial institutions that would have trouble doing securitization deals on their own. Under the purchase scheme, JASME plays the lead role in securitization while taking on the risk of subordinated tranches jointly with multiple financial institutions. In addition to providing securitization assistance to private sector financial institutions, JASME also originates and issues synthetic CDOs backed by SME loans, structured as CDS agreements with special purpose companies (SPCs), known as TMKs in Japan (figure 7-8).

In addition, Metro Tokyo has been the lead sponsor for the issuance of CBOs and CLOs aimed at facilitating and increasing the diversity of SME funding, and it also has introduced a structure through which it jointly issues CBOs and CLOs with multiple other local governments. Initially, JASME provided credit guarantees, but recently it has been issuing CBOs and CLOs based only on credit enhancements from a senior-subordinated structure.

One of those deals has recently been at risk of default, however. The collateralized bond obligation All Japan was jointly issued by Metro Tokyo and multiple other local governments in March 2006 (table 7-6). This CBO is backed by a pool of corporate bonds issued by SMEs and underwritten by multiple banks, including some of the major banks, while the super-senior A class is offered to individuals. Under this securitization scheme, there is no external credit enhancement and the subordinated beneficial interests are sold to investors.

The CBO All Japan was first downgraded about one year after it was issued, and it has had several more credit downgrades since then. The senior B– class, which was rated AAA by S&P at issuance, has been downgraded eighteen notches, down to CCC–.

The CBO All Japan is backed by a pool of corporate bonds issued by 1,200 SMEs diversified across regions and industries, and its potential for default was analyzed

Figure 7-8. *Securitization Issuance by Japan Finance Corporation for Small and Medium Enterprises*[a]

¥100 millions

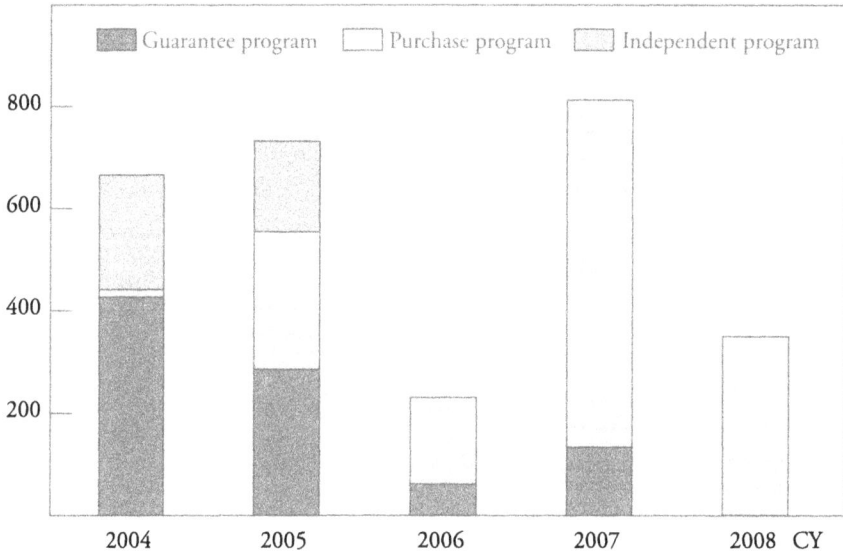

Source: Nomura Institute of Capital Markets Research, based on materials from Japan Finance Corporation for Small and Medium Enterprises.
a. 2008 figures reflect the total from January to August.

using the law of large numbers, which typically is used to analyze pools that benefit from diversification.[14] Ultimately, however, defaults have been considerably higher than expected, and the deal is at increased risk of suffering a loss of principal by the final maturity date in July 2009 (figure 7-9). This situation has depressed the issuance of CDOs backed by SME credit in Japan, and there have been no such issues since the JASME CDO issued in March 2008.

CMBSs and ABSs. Securitized products for which issuance has been declining include commercial mortgage–backed securities and asset-backed securities backed by lease and consumer finance receivables. The decline can be attributed to factors specific to Japan as well as to the weakening of investment sentiment caused by the subprime crisis.

14. Default analysis of the CBO All Japan is based on the SME credit model developed jointly by the Risk Data Bank of Japan and S&P, which is used by the major banks as well as the regional banks.

Table 7-6. *Overview of CBO All Japan*

Overview of issuance

Issuance amount	¥88.1 billion
Number of companies	1,269

Bond issuance	Issuance amount	Credit rating (S&P)	Final maturity
Class A	¥4 billion	AAA	April 2009
Class B	¥83.1 billion	AAA	July 2009
Class C	¥700 million	AA	July 2009
Class D	¥300 million	A	July 2009

SPC	CBO All Japan TMK
Arranger	Mizuho Bank
Originators	Mizuho Bank/Bank of Ikeda/Sumitomo Mitsui Banking Resona Bank/Shizuoka Bank/Shimizu Bank/Suruga Bank
Interest rate	Average of 3.3 percent (fixed, all-in)
Issuance format	Public ABS
Term/repayment	Three years/bullet repayment
Funding amount	Maximum of ¥100 million per company

	Class A	Class B	Class C	Class D
Ratings history				
Initial March 2006	AAA	AAA	AA	A
July 2007	↓	AA	A–	BBB–
September 2007	↓	BB+	BB+	B
April 2008	↓	B–	CCC–	CCC–
July 2008	↓	CCC–	↓	↓

Source: Nomura Institute of Capital Markets Research, based on S&P data.

CMBSs issued in Japan are structured primarily by foreign-capitalized securities firms and nonbanks. The CMBSs structured by foreign-capitalized securities firms are normally broken down into a larger number of tranches than are securitized products structured by domestic firms, and their subordinated portions also are sold to investors, making them similar to securitization deals structured in the United States.

The CMBS market is made up of a limited number of participants, most of which are foreign-capitalized securities firms. Because of that, the CMBS market

Figure 7-9. *Delinquency Rate of CBO All Japan's Underlying Pool of Assets*

Percent

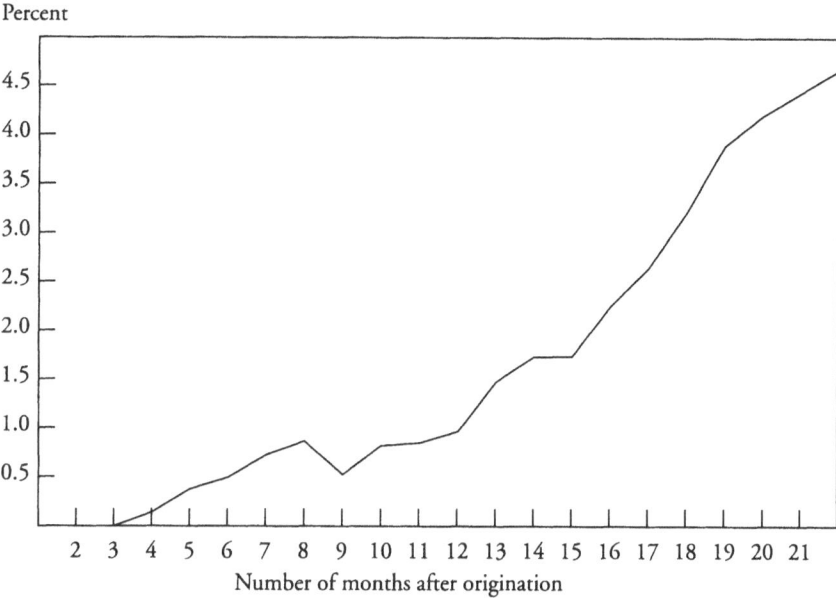

Number of months after origination

Source: Nomura Institute of Capital Markets Research, based on TMK's interim report on CBO All Japan.

has shrunk by a considerable margin, for two reasons: participants affected by the subprime crisis have reduced their commitment to the market and the market itself has become less attractive because of increased oversight by the Financial Supervisory Agency (FSA) and the higher level of due diligence being exercised by financial institutions investing in real estate securitization products. This shrinkage in Japan's securitization market is indicative of the narrow range of investors in the market.

Also issued in Japan are ABSs backed by lease, consumer loan, and automotive loan receivables. Issuance of ABSs backed by lease receivables has been weak owing to changes in lease accounting rules. Weak issuance of ABS backed by consumer finance loans can be attributed to changes in the law—specifically the elimination of gray-zone interest rates, which arose from the gap in coverage between the Investment Deposit and Interest Rate Law and the Interest Rate Restriction Law—that have led to claims for excess interest payment reimbursements by borrowers. That is an example of an external factor, in this case legislative changes, affecting the securitization market by creating uncertainty over the cash flow from underlying assets.

Structural Characteristics

The vast majority of securitized products structured in Japan are primary, with RMBSs accounting for roughly half of all issuance and CMBSs and ABSs accounting for most of the rest. Nearly all of the CDOs issued in Japan are primary products; either they are backed by corporate loans or corporate bonds or they make use of CDSs to reference corporate credit. In the United States, the problem with subprime loans wound up having a huge impact on re-securitized products, such as ABS-CDOs (SF-CDOs) and CDOs^2 with subprime exposure, but in Japan virtually no securitized products are issued that have other securitized products as underlying assets.

Many securitized products use a senior-subordinated structure for credit enhancement. Generally, the senior-subordinated structure used on securitized products in Japan contains few tranches, normally only between two and five. Considerably more tranches are used for CMBSs and other products structured by foreign-capitalized securities firms, and some products are structured with as many as eight or sixteen tranches, as is the case with U.S. subprime RMBSs.

One possible reason for Japan's relatively simpler senior-subordinated structure is that investors tend to want the originators to hold the subordinated portion in order to prevent originator moral hazard. Consequently, in many of the deals in Japan the originators hold the subordinated tranches, although they are not bound by restrictions on the sale of those tranches. Looked at from a different perspective, that indicates a fairly thin investment class for Japan's securitization market—that is, not very many investors are willing to invest in subordinated tranches or equity.

In addition, although in some cases guarantees are provided through the securitization support businesses of such public institutions as JHF and JASME, there is little resort to the private sector for external credit enhancement such as that provided by the monoline insurers in the United States, partly because resecuritization schemes are almost nonexistent in Japan.

Characteristics of Issuance Types

Because of their inclusion in the Nomura-BPI and other bond performance indices, securitized products issued in Japan for public subscription wind up attracting investment from pension funds and other institutional investors using index-linked models. Nevertheless, because only a narrow class of investors invests in Japan's securitized products and the size of each deal is still small, several tens of billions of yen at the most, few of the issues are offered through public subscription. Most are placed privately and limited to either qualified investors or a small number of investors. Almost all of the securitized products issued publicly are sponsored by the public sector—such as JHF's RMBSs and the Ministry of Finance's fiscal loan fund ABSs—and they tend to have large issuance amounts and attract participation by a relatively large number investors.

Although in some cases involving privately placed issues institutional investors are able to sign confidentiality agreements and obtain information on the performance of the underlying assets, normally investors are able to obtain little ongoing information. The Bank of Japan (BOJ) addressed the problem with securitized product disclosures at a forum that it held for participants in the securitization market, where it recommended a format for securitized product disclosures.[15] The recommended format was only voluntary, however, and it never caught on. Nevertheless, one approach to improving disclosure that resulted from debate at the forum—making a BOJ survey of trends in the securitization market available to the general public—was implemented in January 2004. The BOJ compiled the survey based on voluntary monthly reporting on securitized product issuance by arrangers, sponsors, and rating agencies. The survey has since been taken over by the Japan Security Dealers Association (JSDA), and it is now widely used by market participants as a source of core data in trying to understand trends in the securitization market.

Enhancement of Securitized Product Disclosures

Securitized products structured in Japan have not been directly affected by the subprime crisis in the United States. Nevertheless, Japanese financial institutions have suffered considerable losses as a result of their investment in RMBSs, CDOs, and other structured products issued overseas. As of the end of March 2008, deposit-taking financial institutions had booked total losses on their securitized product holdings of ¥1.453 trillion, and they had valuation losses of ¥983 billion. To address that, the FSA asked the JSDA to look into how it can ensure the traceability of information on securitized products.[16] In response to the FSA's request, the JSDA formed a working group on the distribution of securitized products, exchanged ideas with market participants, and announced an interim report in July 2008.

---

15. Bank of Japan Financial Markets Department, *Shokenka Shijou Fooramu—Houkokusho* [Securitization Forum Report] (Japan: April 22, 2004).

16. To ensure food safety, the Ministry of Agriculture, Forestry, and Fisheries had instituted a "traceability mechanism" to track food products and information on those products at every level of the food chain, including production, preprocessing, processing, distribution, and sales. The debate over how to ensure traceability in the sale of securitized products was based on use of that mechanism.

The report proposed guidelines for a "unified information disclosure format" (UIDF) to standardize the way that information is presented on the content and risks of the assets that underlie the primary securitized products that have become common in Japan, namely RMBSs, CMBSs, ABSs, and CLOs. The JSDA plans to define the UIDF as part of its self-regulatory rules after further discussions on specific details. To further ensure use of the UIDF for disclosures as well as the proper transmission of information on the content and risks of the underlying assets to distributors of securitized products, the JSDA has intensified debate over establishing new self-regulatory rules governing actions before, during, and after the sale of such products.

That effort is heading in the following basic direction: Prior to the sale of securitized products, distributors would be required to collect the information that they deem necessary to transmit to the investors and to obtain analyses, including by others, of the risks of the underlying assets deemed to be material to investors. During the sale, distributors would be required to transmit to the investor of their own accord the information deemed necessary as well as information regarding risks deemed material but not reflected in the credit ratings of the securitized products involved. If after the sale an investor requested information for the purpose of forming an investment rating or market valuation, the distributor would be required to transmit to the investor detailed information on the underlying assets and their risks. Thus, in Japan, self-regulatory disclosure rules will be formulated by the JSDA.

New Regulations for the Credit Rating Agencies

Japan has a system of designating credit rating agencies modeled after the Nationally Recognized Statistical Rating Organization (NRSRO) designation used in the United States, where ratings by an agency approved as an NRSRO by the U.S. Securities and Exchange Commission (SEC) can be used for certain regulatory purposes. Likewise in Japan, ratings issued by agencies designated by the FSA commissioner are approved for use for various regulatory purposes. Designated credit rating agencies include the multinationals, Moody's, S&P, and Fitch, as well as the Japan-based credit rating agencies, Rating and Investment Information, Inc. (R&I) and Japan Credit Rating Agency (JCR), all of which are also designated credit rating agencies under Basel 2.

Debate over how to regulate the credit rating agencies has taken center stage worldwide as a result of the subprime loan crisis. In the United States, there is talk of beefing up previously introduced regulations governing the NRSRO, while in Europe the debate has been over introducing new rating agency regulations. In response, Japan's FSA is now trying to introduce new such regulations.

The Possibility of a Subprime Loan Crisis in Japan

In the United States, exposure to subprime loans is not limited to subprime RMBSs but extends to resecuritized products such as ABS-CDOs and CDO²s that are structured on mezzanine tranches of subprime RMBSs. Because of that, the risks from subprime loans in the U.S. mortgage market have spread to financial and capital markets throughout the globe.

As noted above, however, the Japanese securitization market consists almost entirely of simple structured products based on simple senior-subordinated structures, and few securitized products in Japan are highly leveraged. Another feature of securitization in Japan is that because investors tend to prefer that the originator hold the subordinated tranche, in most cases that is what happens, resulting in an alignment of incentives between investors and originators. Japan therefore is unlikely to suffer from transmission of risk from primary securitized products through resecuritization, which is what occurred in the U.S. subprime crisis.

That said, the CBO All Japan was similar in structure to the structure of CBOs involved in the subprime mess in that there was an error in the credit model. CBO All Japan, backed by a pool of corporate bonds issued by more than 1,000 SMEs, was issued with a rating based on a credit model using the law of large numbers. Defaults in the underlying pool exceeded the level assumed by the credit rating agencies based on their credit model, thereby triggering substantial credit downgrades.

The corporate bonds backing this CBO were assessed using SME scoring, but the use of scoring to assess credit does not have a very long history. Financial institutions began putting together an extensive database on defaults in the late 1990s, when they introduced internal mechanisms for assessing nonperforming loans, and by the early 2000s, when the quantity of data in the database had built up to critical mass, the banks began actively using business models predicated on providing loans based on credit scores. Credit models are generally thought to have some degree of accuracy based on statistical testing, but it has been noted that the data may have been insufficient in quantity and quality for tracking the model's performance.

A number of specific problems have been identified as the cause.[17] To begin with, the data did not include any information on companies that did not take out loans, thereby introducing bias in the sample. In addition, when there are differences in economic conditions between the time that a model is built and the

17. Hideaki Hirata, *Chuushou Kigyou Muke Sukoaringu Kashidashi no Shippai ni Manabu* [Learning from Mistakes in Score-Based Lending to SMEs] (Japan: Kinzai Institute for Financial Affairs, July 2008).

time that it is used, results can be affected. In Japan, because the data were accumulated during an economic contraction and the scored loans were written during an economic recovery, there may be related problems that have not yet been exposed. We think that the same can be said of the problems with default data on subprime RMBSs and CDOs.

CBO All Japan's problems are specific and do not appear to be at risk of spreading immediately to other securitized products, but we do see almost the same disputes that surfaced during the subprime crisis, including over the suitability of the credit model and the ratings based on it, as well as problems with due diligence by the originators. A thorough examination of these problems will probably be necessary in the future.

The Future of Japan's Securitization Market

Overall issuance in Japan's securitization market has slowed as a result of not only weakened investor sentiment caused by the subprime crisis but also problems specific to Japan. At this point, we think it would be difficult to take the optimistic view that the current market conditions are only temporary and that the market will soon resume strong growth.

When contemplating the future of securitization in Japan, we think that the relationship between the securitization market and the banks, the largest segment of Japan's financial sector, is an important factor to consider. For many years following World War II, Japan's financial sector had been relatively slow to develop securities markets because of policies that promoted a pattern in which surplus funds from the household sector were accumulated in bank deposits and then lent by the banks to the corporate sector, which was short of funds. Even today, loans account for the largest share of corporate financing in Japan. In 2007, domestic banks lent a total of ¥41.6 trillion to fund business investment, while securities issuance by the private sector was worth only approximately ¥22.3 trillion. The destabilization of Japan's financial system caused by the nonperforming loan problem in the late 1990s can be seen as exposing the concentration of systemic risks in Japanese banks and the frailty of Japan's financial structure, and making better use of securities markets is one of the major challenges now facing Japan. In fact, the government has been promoting a shift of household financial assets out of bank deposits and into investment products.

Under these conditions, the banks play a critical role in the securitization market as either originators or arrangers, and their participation is clearly essential to the market's future development. Nevertheless, considering the path toward development that the securitization market has taken thus far, the relationship between the banks and the market has not always been marked by the healthiest behavior.

For example, there were times during Japan's period of instability in the financial system when the banks securitized the mortgages on their balance sheets in order to generate upfront fees to make up for losses from the disposition of nonperforming loans. In addition, leading up to the introduction of Basel 2 at the end of March 2007, there was a rush by banks to securitize their loans in order to reduce the amount of risk assets that entered into calculations of regulatory capital.

In addition, financial institutions gradually became less profitable during the extended period of low interest rates, and amid overall weak demand for business investment funding, there was a tendency for lenders to become more aggressive in offering home loans, a relatively more profitable line of business. That created intense competition among financial institutions in the home loan market. In fact, a fairly large mismatch in terms between the investment and the source of funding occurs when securing funding for long-term, fixed-rate mortgages, which creates difficulties from an asset–liability management perspective. The concern, particularly for the regional financial institutions, which have limited means for hedging, is that the sector now finds itself with balance sheets that are quite vulnerable to an increase in interest rates.

Not until the banking sector makes its decisions based not only on profitability but also on asset–liability management will it start looking seriously at the choice between using its own balance sheet or using the securitization market. Once that happens, the healthy growth of Japan's securitization market should follow.

The public sector has come to play a greater role in Japan's securitization. While the overall securitization market has been languishing, JHF has continued to issue RMBSs and has become a key pillar of the market. Nevertheless, if the public sector maintains this high level of involvement for an extended period, there is a risk that the market will lose autonomy; an even bigger danger is that the government will use the securitization market as a way to shrink its balance sheet. The public sector should take care not to focus too hard on asset reduction in order to avoid crowding out securitized products sponsored by the private sector. It probably needs to proceed in a way that is consistent with the capacity of the securitization market for absorbing funds.

China's Securitization Market

The most distinctive feature of China's securitization market, which began as a pilot in 2005, is that the securities are issued with the approval of China's financial authorities. The market is divided into two sections. The first is the interbank bond market, which is supervised by the central bank, the People's Bank of China

Figure 7-10. *Issuance of Securitized Products in China*[a]

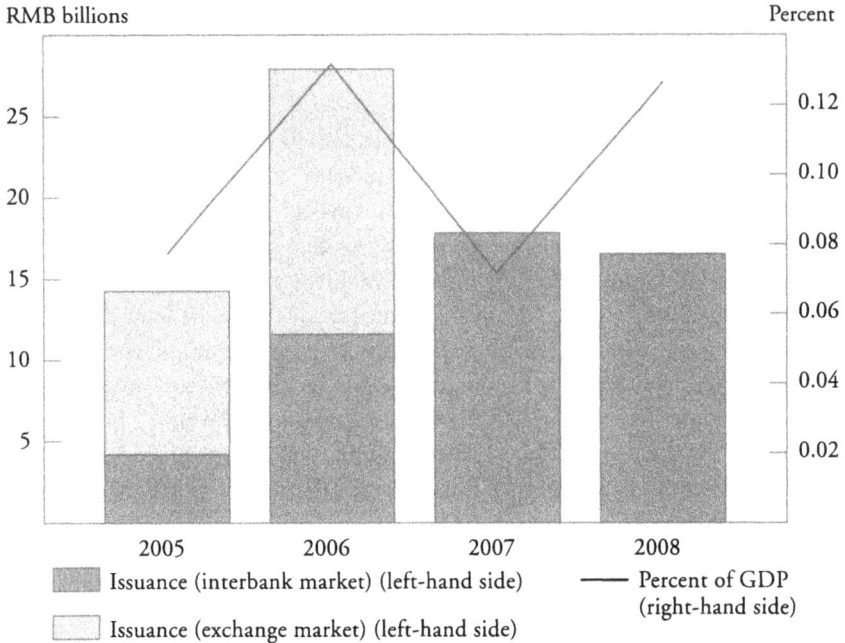

Source: Nomura Institute of Capital Markets Research, based on data from ChinaBond (www.china
bond.com.cn/Site/cb/en) and China National Bureau of Statistics.
a. 2008 data as of the end of June.

(PBC); the issuance of securitized products (in this case, by financial institutions) is subject to the approval of the China Banking Regulatory Commission (CBRC). The second is the stock exchanges, which are supervised by the China Securities Regulatory Commission (CSRC), whose approval is necessary for the issuance of securitized products (in this case, by nonfinancial companies).

Following enactment of the necessary legislation, RMB4.2 billion of securities was issued on the interbank bond market in 2005, RMB11.6 billion in 2006, and RMB17.8 billion in 2007; during the first six months of 2008, RMB16.5 billion was issued (figure 7-10). On the stock exchange market, RMB10.1 billion of securities was issued in 2005 and RMB16.3 billion during the first nine months of 2006, but no securities have been issued since then.

China's securitization market is still in its infancy, and it is much smaller in relation to its economy than that of either the United States or Japan. Issuance of securitized products was equivalent in value to 0.08 percent of GDP in 2005,

0.13 percent in 2006, 0.07 percent in 2007, and 0.127 percent during the first six months of 2008.

Securitization in the Interbank Bond Market

On the interbank bond market, financial institutions issue bonds but also participate as investors. Although the main instrument traded on this market has been bank debentures (issued by both the policy banks and the commercial banks), commercial paper (issued by nonfinancial companies and classified as "bank debentures") has been issued and traded since 2005.

The issuance of securitized products on this market is still in its infancy. On April 20, 2005, the PBC and CBRC promulgated the Administrative Rules for Pilot Securitization of Credit Assets (Administrative Rules), which came into effect the same day (see table 7-7 for relevant legal documents).[18] As a result, the regulatory authorities have to vet each loan securitization separately.

The Administrative Rules apply to securitization activities within China in which financial institutions, as originators, entrust credit assets to trustees, and trustees issue beneficiary securities in the form of asset-backed securities through special purpose trusts (figure 7-11). The aim is to use the bankruptcy-remote framework, which, in turn, uses the trust function of the existing Trust Law.[19] Bankruptcy remoteness enables the securitized assets to be shielded from the risk that either the owner of the underlying assets (that is, the originator) or the issuer will go bankrupt and allows the creditworthiness of the underlying assets to be reflected directly in the credit rating of the securitized assets.

Only a trust and investment company (TIC) with a track record that meets the CBRC's requirements can become a trustee. In order to ensure the smooth continuation of a trustee's securitization responsibilities, Article 20 of the Administrative Rules provides that the CBRC will appoint a temporary trustee in circumstances in which a trustee's qualifications as a trustee are revoked according to law or in which the trustee is dissolved, ordered to be terminated, or announced to be bankrupt according to law.

18. Even before the Administrative Rules of 2005 were enacted, two packages of nonperforming loans were securitized: a package belonging to Huarong Asset Management Company, an affiliate of Industrial and Commercial Bank of China (ICBC), in 2003 and a package belonging to the Ningbo branch of ICBC in 2004.

19. Article 15 of the Trust Law states that "the trust shall be differentiated from other property that is not put under trust by the settler." Similarly, Article 16 states that "the trust property shall be segregated from the property owned by the trustee (hereinafter referred to as his 'own property,' in short) and may not be included in, or made part of his own property of the trustee. Where the trustee dies or the trustee as a body corporate is dissolved, removed, or is declared bankrupt according to the law, and the trusteeship is thus terminated, the trust property shall not be deemed his legacy or liquidation property."

Table 7-7. *Rules and Regulations Pertaining to Interbank Bond Market in China*[a]

Name of rule/regulation	Promulgating department	Promulgation	Implementation
Special purpose trusts			
Trust Law	Standing Committee of the Ninth National People's Congress of the People's Republic of China	April 28, 2001	October 1, 2001
Securitization of loan assets			
Administrative Rules for Pilot Securitization of Credit Assets	PBC, CBRC	April 20, 2005	April 20, 2005
Supervisory Rules for Pilot Securitization of Credit Assets of Financial Institutions	CBRC	November 7, 2005	December 1, 2005
Rules for the Information Disclosure of Asset-Backed Securities	PBC	June 13, 2005	June 13, 2005
Provisions on the Accounting Treatment for Securitization of Credit Assets	MOF	May 16, 2005	May 16, 2005
Circular on Relevant Taxation Policy Issues Concerning the Securitization of Credit Assets	MOF, State Administration of Taxation	February 20, 2006	February 20, 2006
Trust companies			
Rules Governing Trust Companies	CBRC	January 23, 2007	March 1, 2007
Rules on Trust Schemes of Collective Funds by Trust Companies	CBRC	January 23, 2007	March 1, 2007
Auto finance companies			
Revised Rules Governing Auto Finance Companies	CBRC	January 24, 2008	January 24, 2008
Rules for Implementing the Rules Governing Auto Finance Companies	CBRC	November 12, 2003	November 12, 2003
Administrative Rules for Automotive Loans	PBC, CBRC	August 16, 2004	October 1, 2004

Source: Nomura Institute of Capital Markets Research, based on information from the Chinese government departments concerned.
a. PBC = People's Bank of China; CBRC = China Banking Regulatory Commission; MOF = Ministry of Finance.

Figure 7-11. *Schematic Diagram of Securitization of Chinese Bank Loans*

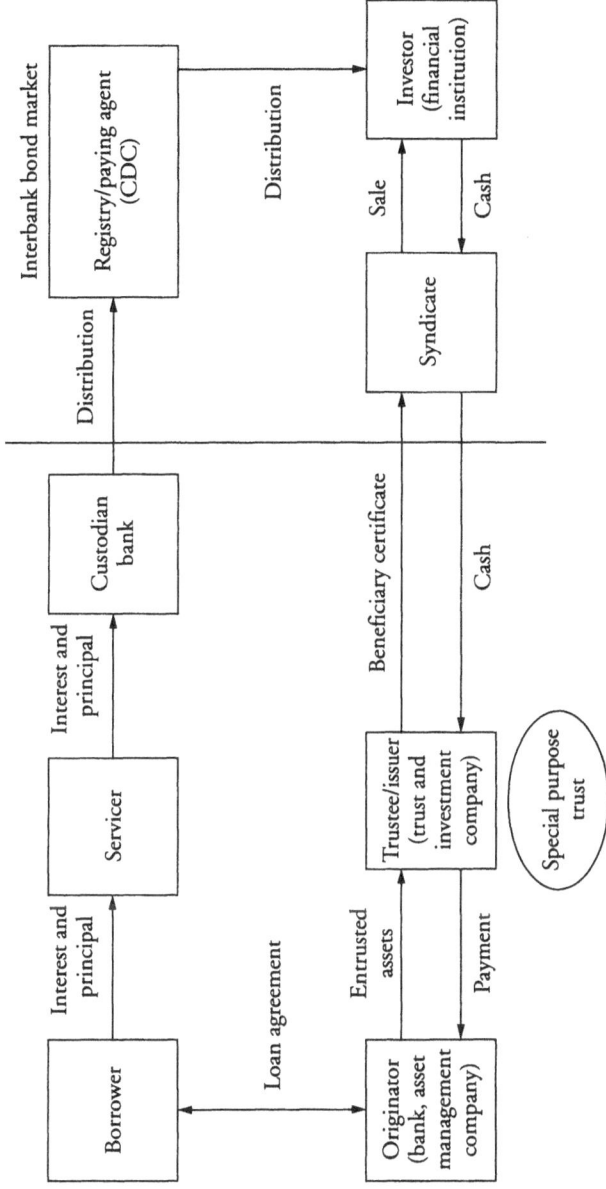

Source: Nomura Institute of Capital Markets Research.

The CBRC is responsible for assessing the suitability of the originator owning the underlying assets. The following financial institutions may act as originators: commercial banks, asset management companies, policy banks, trust and investment companies, finance companies,[20] and credit cooperatives.[21]

Investors are the financial institutions that are allowed to participate in the interbank bond market, including commercial banks, trust and investment companies, finance companies, credit cooperatives, fund management companies, securities companies, and China Postal Savings Bank. While insurance companies are allowed to participate, they are prohibited from investing in securitized products by the guidelines of the China Insurance Regulatory Commission (CIRC), the body that administers and regulates China's insurance industry.[22]

While securitized loans are issued and traded on the interbank bond market, bond issuance and trading has to be registered with the China Government Securities Depository Trust and Clearing Company (CDC).[23] Disclosure is made through websites designated by the regulator.[24] On the taxation side, the issuer avoids double taxation on corporate income and bond holders receive preferential treatment on stamp duties and business taxes.

Securitization in the Stock Exchange Market

China has no special law governing the securitization of specific cash flows of nonfinancial companies. However, under the CSRC's Pilot Rules Concerning the Business of Client Asset Management of Securities (promulgated on December 18, 2003, and implemented on February 1, 2004), securities companies are allowed to solicit subscriptions from private investors and manage those assets under a client agreement. There are three types of asset management agreements: one-to-one "predirected asset management" agreements between a securities company and one of its clients; one-to-many "collective asset management" agreements between a securities company and various of its clients; and "specific asset management plans" (SAMPs). Securitization of the specific cash flows of nonfinancial companies falls into the third category.

Although the pilot rules have been in force since 2004, it was not until 2005 that the first SAMPs were issued. They can therefore be said to be a relatively new product—just like the securitized products on the interbank bond market.

20. Financial subsidiaries of nonfinancial companies.
21. There are two types: urban and rural.
22. However, insurance companies have been calling for the rules to be relaxed to allow them to invest in securitized products.
23. The designated clearing system for the interbank bond market.
24. Namely, http://www.chinamoney.com.cn and http://www.chinabond.com.cn.

SAMPs are sold by securities companies to their clients on an agency basis;[25] they are a securitized form of the specific cash flows that nonfinancial companies transfer to the securities companies (figure 7-12). Only "pilot securities companies" authorized by the CSRC may act as asset managers and purchase and manage those assets.[26]

There are no particular rules stipulating who may be an originator or what assets may be securitized; all that is required is authorization from the CSRC. Moving assets off the balance sheet, however, is complicated by the fact that a number of legal, tax, and accounting issues must be resolved first. Nor are there any particular rules governing investors. However, neither banks (because they are not members of a stock exchange) nor insurance companies (because of the aforementioned CIRC rules) may invest in SAMPs. SAMPs are issued and traded on the stock exchange market (that is, the Shanghai and Shenzhen stock exchanges), but registration is with the China Securities Depository and Clearing Corporation (CSDCC).[27] There is no requirement to disclose information to the general public, only to SAMP investors.

Types of Interbank Bond Market Securitized Products and Their Issuance

RMBSs. There have been two issues of residential mortgage–backed securities in China to date, both by China Construction Bank (CCB): an RMB3,020 million issue in December 2005 and an RMB4,160 million issue in December 2007, for a total issuance of RMB7,180 million.

When China's was still a planned economy, the state and companies built and owned public housing that they rented to employees for a modest amount. Since China's transition to a market economy, however, housing has become a commodity that can be bought and sold for cash. That has involved the creation of a housing market and a system to provide purchasers with the necessary cash. At the heart of the system are mortgages provided by private sector commercial banks. However, CCB, which is one of the Big Four state-owned commercial banks, has the largest share of the market (21.7 percent), with RMB557.8 billion in outstanding mortgages as of June 30, 2007.

25. Not on a trust basis.

26. These are one of the categories of blue chip securities companies to emerge from the CSRC's reorganization of China's securities industry. They also receive the most operational and financial support. The next-highest category is "standard securities company." As of January 16, 2007, there were nineteen pilot and thirty standard securities companies. For further details, see Nomura Institute of Capital Markets Research, *Chuugoku Shouken Shijou Handobukku* 2007 [Handbook of Chinese Securities Markets 2007] (Japan).

27. The designated clearing system for the stock exchange market.

Figure 7-12. *Schematic Diagram of SAMP Securitization in China*

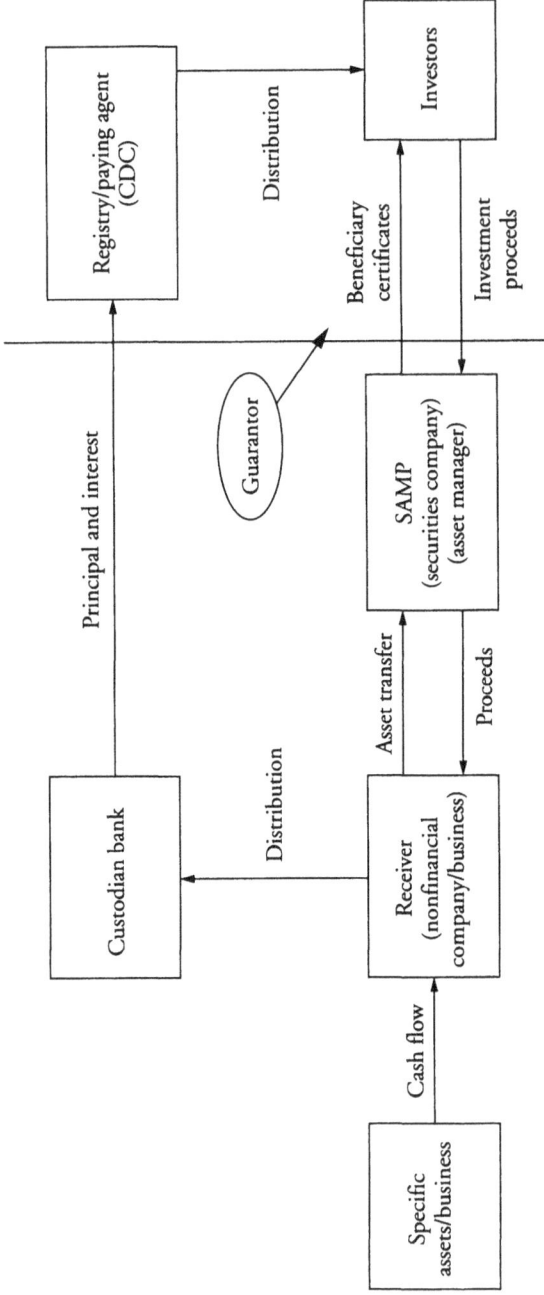

Source: Nomura Institute of Capital Markets Research.

In addition to private sector mortgages, local governments have public housing reserve funds, to which employers and employees contribute every month and which provide the funds for preferential housing loans. The rate of interest on those loans is set by the PBC in consultation with the Ministry of Housing and Urban-Rural Development. As of year-end 2007, RMB507.4 billion in such loans was outstanding.

CLOs. One type of product that has been used to securitize bank loan assets is CLOs, which have been issued by both policy and commercial banks. While China Development Bank (CDB), one of China's three policy banks, has issued ABSs totaling RMB13.68 billion (RMB4.18 billion in December 2005, RMB5.73 billion in April 2006, and RMB3.77 billion in April 2008), Industrial Bank (IB) and Shanghai Pudong Development Bank (SPDB), both commercial banks, have issued CLOs: the former, RMB5.24 billion in December 2007; the latter, RMB4.38 billion in September 2007.

The role of CDB, which was established in 1994, along with China's two other policy banks, is to provide financing and financial services for China's basic infrastructure, major industries, and major companies. Originally regional banks, IB and SPDB are now commercial banks with a nationwide branch network.

Nonperforming loans. Both asset management companies and CCB have securitized nonperforming loans. In December 2006, Xinda Asset Management Corporation (an affiliate of CCB) issued RMB3.0 billion and Orient Asset Management Corporation (a Bank of China affiliate) issued RMB700 million of securitized nonperforming loans, while in January 2008, CCB issued RMB2.765 billion of such loans.

Beginning in 1999, asset management companies were established for each of the Big Four state-owned commercial banks—China Construction Bank, Bank of China (BOC), Industrial and Commercial Bank of China (ICBC), and Agricultural Bank of China (ABC)—to dispose of their nonperforming loans. Although their initial task was to purchase nonperforming loans from their banking affiliates in accordance with the decision of the administrative authority, they have extended their operations to include investment banking, and some have even been reported to be considering becoming full-blown financial service companies.

Auto loans. After China joined the World Trade Organization (WTO), demand for automobiles increased rapidly. In response, foreign automakers not only stepped up their exports and local production but also petitioned the Chinese authorities to allow them to offer auto loans to prospective buyers. In October 2003, the CBRC promulgated Measures for the Administration of Auto Finance Companies, followed soon afterward by a set of implementing rules (table 7-7). In August 2004, the PBC and the CBRC promulgated Measures for the Administration of Auto Loans. Following those measures, GMAC-SAIC Automotive Finance was established both as China's first auto finance company and as its first joint-venture (J/V) auto finance company. In January 2008, GMAC-SAIC Automotive Finance issued RMB1.993 billion of securitized auto loans. Since then, nine other (all J/V) auto finance companies have been established in China. Most recently, Chery Automobile Company has been reported to be in the process of establishing such a subsidiary.

Types of Stock Exchange Market Securitized Products

In August 2005, China Unicom issued China's first SAMP, for RMB9.5 billion. The specific cash flows backing the securities are receivables from the lease of China Unicom's CDMA mobile telephone network for a specific period in the future, and investors can receive an expected return as well as their initial investment. Although China Unicom has to pay the receivables into its designated SAMP account every time it receives them, the payments are guaranteed by a third party (BOC).

Since this first issue, nine SAMPs (worth a total of RMB26.4 billion) have been issued. They are backed by specific cash flows from a range of receivables: highway tolls, equipment lease payments, electricity charges, payback fees on build-and-transfer projects, and sewage treatment charges.

However, because the relationship between investors and the securities company is that of client-agent, no fiduciary duty necessarily exists nor is bankruptcy remoteness guaranteed. That is why the CSRC has not approved any new SAMP issues since September 2006 and apparently has been examining these problems with a view to possibly issuing detailed guidelines.

Assessing China's Securitization Market

China's securitization market was established with the approval of the country's financial authorities for four reasons: to transfer and spread the risk that banks face from their loan assets; to dispose of banks' nonperforming loans; to make it easier for nonfinancial companies to raise funds; and to give investors a greater choice of investments.

Transferring and Spreading Risk

We think that China's banks are well aware of the importance of securitization because of the following benefits that accrue to them as originators from the securitization of their loan assets: it helps them to improve asset–liability management; it reduces regional overdependence on bank loans; it enables them to

Figure 7-13. *Bank Deposits and Loans as Percent of GDP in China*

Percent

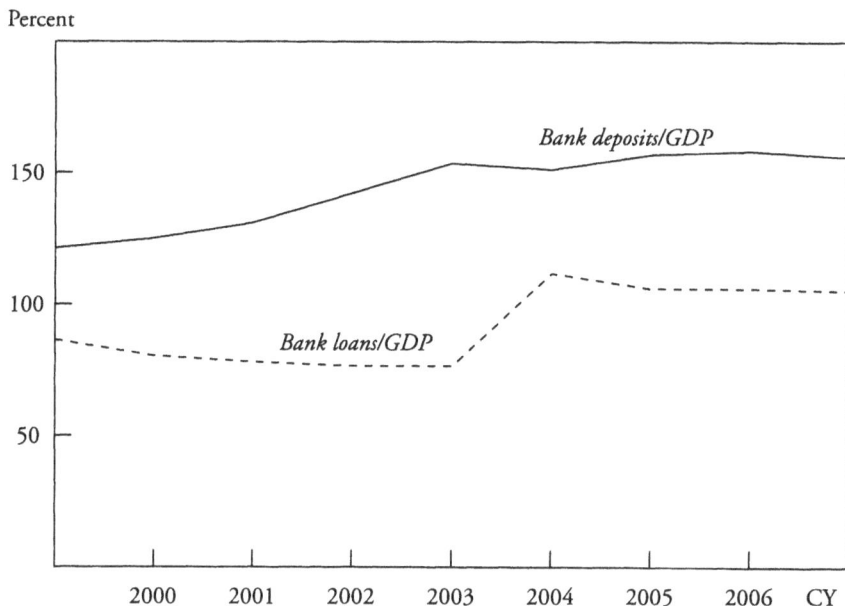

Source: Nomura Institute of Capital Markets Research, based on data from China Statistical Yearbook and People's Bank of China.

enhance their own capital; it enables them to achieve a better profit structure; and it gives them an opportunity to develop new sources of funds.[28]

Figure 7-13 shows the ratio of bank deposits and loans to GDP in China over the past few years. Since 2004 the gap between the ratio of bank deposits to GDP and the ratio of bank loans to GDP has been steadily widening, suggesting that banks have been taking in deposits at a faster rate than they have been able to lend. The growth in deposits has put pressure on the banks to increase lending, and that pressure is seen by the financial authorities as one of the factors that generates excessive liquidity in the economy.

The Chinese financial authorities apparently want to encourage the banks to use sound assets when they originate new products in order to foster the development of a securitization market and to avoid mistakes. We assume, however,

28. Comments of Shen Bingxi, deputy director of the People's Bank of China Financial Market Division, at the China Securitization 2007 symposium held in Beijing in March 2007.

that the banks would prefer to keep sound credit assets on their balance sheets. A perception gap such as this between the financial authorities and the banks could be one factor inhibiting the growth of China's securitization market.

Resolving Nonperforming Loans

Although the nonperforming loan ratio of China's commercial banks (both state-owned and joint-stock) has been declining (figure 7-14), the Big Four state-owned commercial banks have not yet repaid the capital infusions that they received from the government, which were funded by issuance of special government bonds or by the country's foreign exchange reserves. Without taking those infusions into consideration, it is as important as ever for the banks to put their house in order. In fact, in absolute terms, the amount of the banks' nonperforming loans has not declined significantly (figure 7-15).

With the Chinese economy expected to slow as a result of the global economic slowdown and the central bank's tightening policy, we think that China's financial authorities are probably concerned that after declining for several years, banks' nonperforming loan ratio could begin to rise again. If it did, that might be an incentive to the banks to dispose of those loans (including by means of securitization). However, the financial authorities would have to approve any issues of securitized products, and disagreements with the banks over which loans to use as underlying assets could delay the launch of new products.

Ability of Nonfinancial Companies to Raise Funds

Reducing companies' dependence on indirect financing (the banking system), which was the main source of funds when China's economy was planned, and encouraging them to make increasing use of direct financing is one of the challenges facing China's financial authorities today, when roughly 80 percent of the funds raised by nonfinancial companies is still in the form of bank loans (figure 7-16). Although we can see that the proportion of funds raised by issuing corporate bonds has increased, it is still quite small. Nonfinancial companies therefore are very interested in using securitization, as well as corporate bonds, to raise the funds that they need to keep pace with the rapid rate of economic growth. For its part, the Chinese government is also still keen to foster the development of both of these markets.

As for the level of bank lending, which still is the main source of funds for nonfinancial companies, the CBRC is reported to have been instructing commercial banks not to increase their loan balances since the Communist Party Congress in mid-October 2007.[29] An analysis of month-end renminbi loan balances in 2007

---

29. *Nihon Keizai Shimbun* [Nikkei newspaper], December 2, 2007.

Figure 7-14. *Chinese Banks' Nonperforming Loans, Ratio*

Percent

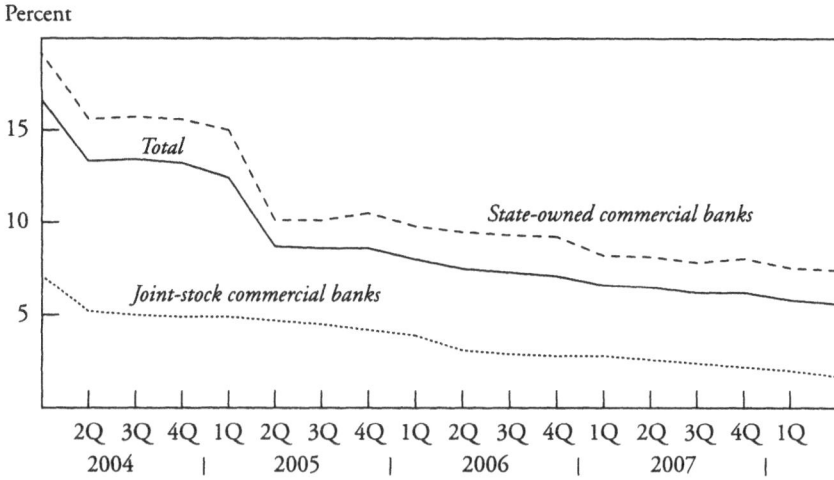

Source: Nomura Institute of Capital Markets Research, based on data from China Banking Regulatory Commission.

Figure 7-15. *Chinese Banks' Nonperforming Loans, Amount*

Number

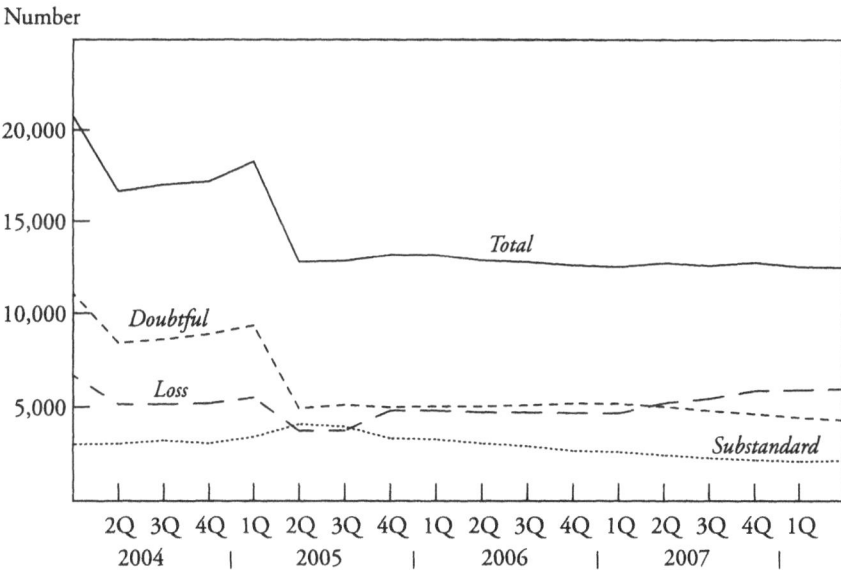

Figure 7-16. *Sources of Funds for China's Nonfinancial Sector, Flow Basis*

Percent

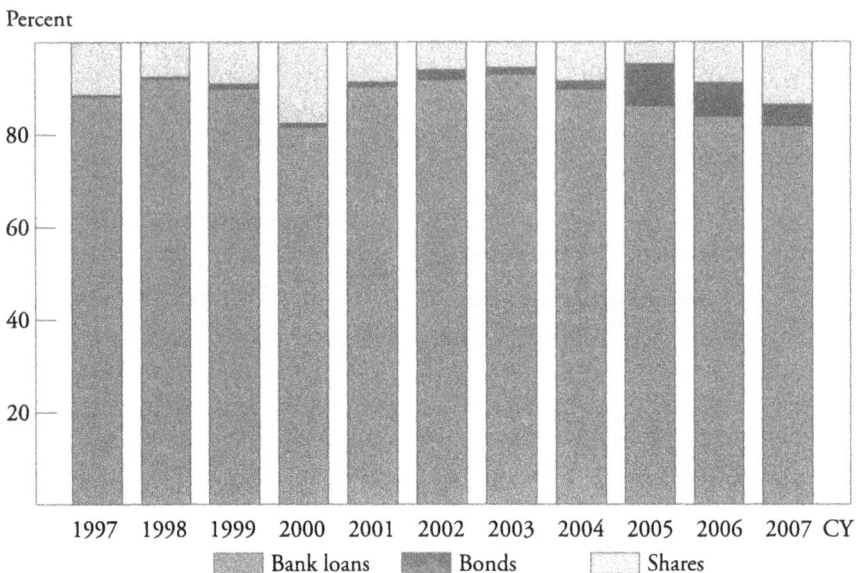

Source: Nomura Institute of Capital Markets Research, based on data from People's Bank of China.

reveals that the net increase declined as the year end approached. Similarly, an analysis of the cumulative change in loan balances in the same year reveals that the net annual increase was more or less unchanged, at about RMB3,500 billion, from the end of October, indicating that the net annual increase in loan balances was, for all intents and purposes, capped at the equivalent of a ten-month increase as a result of the ceiling imposed by financial authorities (figure 7-17). In 2008, however, loan balances increased by a net RMB800 billion in January alone and by a cumulative RMB2,450 billion in the January–June period. That means that, if the same ceiling is applied as in 2007 (RMB3,500 billion), 70 percent of the 2008 ceiling had already been used as of the end of June and that, in the second half of the year, financial institutions were likely to become increasingly reluctant to lend. While nonfinancial companies therefore are probably considering making greater use of direct financing, the fact that bond issues (as an alternative to securitization) also require the approval of the financial authorities means that they are unlikely to be a flexible alternative. Furthermore, it has been reported that the financial authorities are concerned that nonfinancial companies might try to use bond issues as a way of getting around the cap on bank lending. The outlook for issuance of

Figure 7-17. *Change in Renminbi Loan Balances, January 2007–June 2008*

RMB 100 million

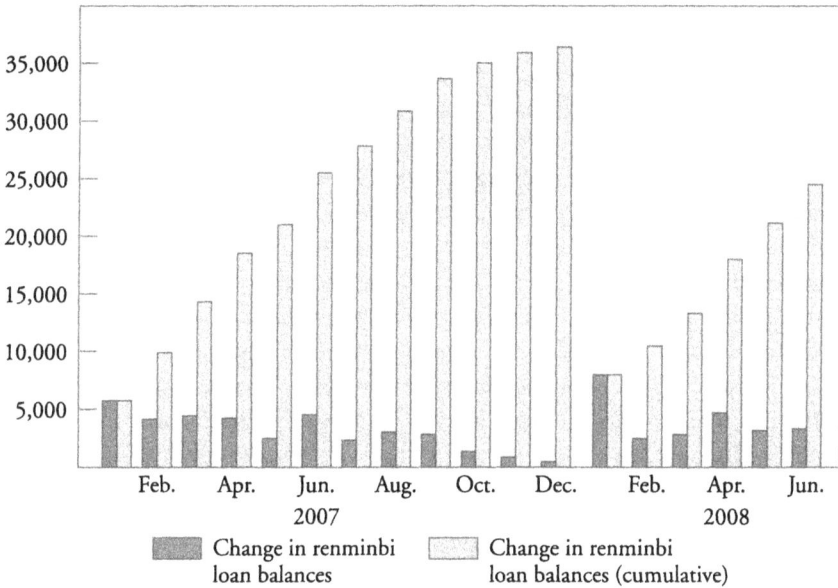

Source: People's Bank of China.

securitized products is therefore likely to continue to be dominated by the stance of the financial authorities.

Giving Investors a Greater Choice of Investments

Expanding China's securitization market would also give investors a greater choice of investments. For example, China's National Social Security Fund (NSSF), which is responsible for providing for future social security payments, has invested in securitized products since they were first issued in 2005. Although the return from those investments accounts for less than 1 percent of its total investment return, the actual numbers (RMB1.97 million in 2005, RMB28.8 million in 2006, and RMB282 million in 2007) represent a steady source of income.

However, critics point to a lack of liquidity in the securitization market, which, while partly the result of the low volume of issuance, also is partly the result of the restrictions on who may invest in such products. For example, insurance companies are not allowed to invest in securities backed by bank loans.

Impact of Subprime Mortgage Crisis on China's Securitization Market

Although securitized products continued to be issued in China even after the subprime mortgage crisis erupted in the summer of 2007, China's financial authorities began a careful and rigorous assessment of the damage in 2008. On February 4, 2008, the CBRC issued a notice to the banks to tighten up their controls on securities backed by loan assets (Notice of China Banking Regulatory Commission on Further Improving the Management of Credit Assets Securitization Business) (see box 7-1). The notice covers eight "needs": to pay attention to asset quality and to steadily promote securitization; to control credit risk and ensure that sales are "true"; to accurately judge transfer risk and strictly comply with capital requirements; to improve risk management and internal controls; to work out a proper mechanism for assessing loan service performance in order to prevent moral hazard; to standardize the procedures for transferring creditors' rights in order to mitigate legal risk; to improve disclosure; and to improve investor education. As can be seen from Article 1 of the Administrative Rules for Pilot Securitization of Credit Assets, promulgated by the PBC and CBRC on April 20, 2005, which states that "these rules are formulated . . . so as to regulate the pilot securitization of credit assets, protect legitimate interests of investors and relevant involved parties, improve the liquidity of credit assets, and enrich securities products," the aim of the financial authorities has always been to allow the gradual introduction of securitized products.

Thus far, the underlying assets used to back securitized products in the interbank bond market have ranged from loan assets and nonperforming loans to auto loans. However, our interviews with market participants in China indicate that they do not expect the financial authorities to approve more complicated securitized products that use assets such as leasing and credit card receivables in the near future. Some suggested that the volume of leasing and credit card receivables was still too small to allow their use in securitized products. A further consideration in the case of credit card receivables is that the use of such assets for securitization would require access to and sharing of credit data on individuals, and at the moment, China does not have the necessary infrastructure. We therefore expect China's securitization market to continue to depend mainly on loan assets, nonperforming loans, and auto loans.

Whether approval is granted to specific issues is likely to depend, in our opinion, on factors such as whether they use a senior-subordinated structure, whether the originator retains the subordinated tranche, and whether there is any (internal) credit enhancement in the form of a cash reserve. Regarding the possibility of resecuritization issues in the aftermath of the subprime mortgage crisis, we see

---

Box 7-1. *Notice from China Banking Regulatory Commission on Further Improving the Management of the Credit Asset Securitization Business, February 4, 2008*

Banks to which notice applies

China Development Bank, Industrial and Commercial Bank of China, Agricultural Bank of China, Bank of China, China Construction Bank,

Required efforts

Bank of Communications and joint-stock commercial banks.

Pay attention to asset quality and steadily promote securitization.

Control credit risk and ensure that sales are "true."

Accurately judge transfer risk and strictly comply with capital requirements.

Improve risk management and internal controls to prevent operational risk.

Work out a proper mechanism for assessing loan service performance in order to prevent moral hazard.

Standardize the procedures for transferring creditors' rights in order to mitigate legal risk.

Improve disclosure and protect investors' legitimate interests.

Improve investor education.

Source: Nomura Institute of Capital Markets Research, based on information from the China Banking Regulatory Commission.

---

little prospect of such issues because securitization in China is still in the pilot stage; however, there have been no official statements regarding that possibility. We conclude from all this that while China's securitization market may not expand rapidly, major problems are unlikely to occur as long as the current system—under which issuers, investors, and intermediaries are all located in China—remains in place and the issuance of securitized products remains under the control of the financial authorities.

Conclusions

As this chapter shows, Asia's securitization markets are still in their infancy relative to those in the United States and because of that there is little risk that Asia will experience an event similar to the U.S. subprime crisis.

One characteristic of securitization markets in Asia is that in principle they comprise primary securitized products and the concept of resecuritized products has yet to take hold. Consequently, at least from the standpoint of product design, the risk is fairly low that in Asia originators of and investors in resecuritized products will become unable to determine what their underlying assets are, as occurred in the United States.

A second characteristic is that the senior-subordinated structures in Asia are built so that in most cases the originator holds the subordinated portion. That is, Asian securitization does not normally follow the U.S.-style business model of originating to distribute; that is one reason why the moral hazard that arises when the originator does not monitor the underlying assets is less likely to be an issue. From the investors' side, that implies a narrow range of investment choices. Consequently, we see a need to implement rules and design products in a way that minimizes the risk of moral hazard, regardless of whether the originator continues to hold the securitized product.

A third characteristic is that, unlike in the United States, where the originator often is a mortgage bank or mortgage broker, in Asia the banks play a critical role as originators and arrangers. Domestic financial institutions also play an important role as investors. We attribute that to the fact that the banks have played the central role in financial systems in Asia for many years. Although having risk concentrated in the banking system is not desirable, we think that banks, provided that they are listed and have a diverse stakeholder base, have a greater incentive to conduct strict due diligence than do mortgage brokers, particularly when taking reputational risk into account.

On the other hand, Asian securitization markets have some of the same problems found in the United States. For example, just as the government-sponsored enterprises Fannie Mae and Freddie Mac have become key players in the U.S. securitization market, JHF in Japan, Cagamas in Malaysia, and state-owned banks in China are all public or quasi-public institutions that play an important role in Asian securitization markets. There is a risk, however, that such a large public sector presence will destroy the market's autonomy and wind up crowding out the private sector. For example, Cagamas, of which the central bank owns 20 percent, dismisses the suggestion that it has an "implicit guarantee" by the government, although the market defines the Cagamas bonds as "quasi-government" bonds. In addition, the percentage of total outstanding loans owned by JHF in Japan that are classified as nonperforming loans has been rising; it was at 3.58 percent in FY2007. Thus there are signs even in Japan that a portion of the mortgage pool is becoming nonperforming.

In overall terms, however, the special characteristics described above make it unlikely that Asian securitization markets will experience an event similar to the subprime crisis that occurred in the United States. Hence, the United States and Europe can learn from some elements in the Asian securitization markets. If we were to summarize the lesson, it would be to advise them to get "back to basics."

On the other hand, the fact that Asia has not experienced such a crisis can be interpreted as a mere consequence of the underdeveloped state of Asian securitization markets. Thus far, securitization regulations and products in Asia have not been designed in a way that will avoid the types of problems that have occurred in the United States. Many of the regulatory reforms and product innovations occurring in the United States in response to the subprime crisis are worth considering in Asia, even though Asia has yet to experience the same sort of crisis.

Contributors

Jennifer E. Bethel
Babson College

Robert E. Eisenbeis
Federal Reserve Bank of Atlanta

Allen Ferrell
Havard Law School

Günter Franke
Konstanz University, Germany

Yasuyuki Fuchita
*Nomura Institute of Capital Markets
   Research, Tokyo*

Jack Guttentag
University of Pennsylvania

Richard J. Herring
University of Pennsylvania

Gang Hu
Babson College

Tetsuya Kamiyama
*Nomura Institute of Capital Markets
   Research, Tokyo*

Kei Kodachi
*Nomura Institute of Capital Markets
   Research, Tokyo*

Jan P. Krahnen
Goethe University Frankfurt, Germany

Robert E. Litan
*Kauffman Foundation and Brookings
   Institution*

Joseph R. Mason
Louisiana State University

Igor Roitburg
Default Mitigation Management

Eiichi Sekine
*Nomura Institute of Capital Markets
   Research, Tokyo*

.

Index

Brookings Institution

The Brookings Institution is a private nonprofit organization devoted to research, education, and publication on important issues of domestic and foreign policy. Its principal purpose is to bring the highest quality independent research and analysis to bear on current and emerging policy problems. The Institution was founded on December 8, 1927, to merge the activities of the Institute for Government Research, founded in 1916, the Institute of Economics, founded in 1922, and the Robert Brookings Graduate School of Economics and Government, founded in 1924. Interpretations or conclusions in Brookings publications should be understood to be solely those of the authors.

Nomura Institute of Capital Markets Research

Established in April 2004 as a subsidiary of Nomura Holdings, Nomura Institute of Capital Markets Research (NICMR) offers original, neutral studies of Japanese and Western financial markets and policy proposals aimed at establishing a market-structured financial system in Japan and contributing to the healthy development of capital markets in China and other emerging markets. NICMR disseminates its research among Nomura Group companies and to a wider audience through regular publications in English and Japanese.

Wharton Financial Institutions Center, University of Pennsylvania

The Wharton Financial Institutions Center is one of twenty-five research centers at the Wharton School of the University of Pennsylvania. The Center sponsors and directs primary research on financial institutions and their interface with financial markets. The Center was established in 1992 with funds provided by the Sloan Foundation and was designated as the Sloan Industry Center for Financial Institutions, the first such center designated for a service-sector industry. It is now supported by private research partners, corporate sponsors, and various foundations and nonprofit organizations. The Center has hundreds of affiliated scholars at leading institutions worldwide, and it continues to define the research frontier, hosting an influential working paper series and a variety of academic, industry, and "crossover" conferences.

Tokyo Club Foundation for Global Studies

The Tokyo Club Foundation for Global Studies was established by Nomura Securities Co., Ltd., in 1987 as a nonprofit organization for promoting studies in the management of the global economy. It sponsors research, symposiums, and publications on global economic issues. The Tokyo Club has developed a network of institutions from Europe, the United States, and Asia that assists in organizing specific research programs and identifying appropriate expertise. In recent years, the research agenda has strongly focused on emerging trends in global capital markets as well as current issues in macroeconomic stability and growth. Information about past and future programs may be viewed on the Foundation's website, www.tcf.or.jp/.

www.ingramcontent.com/pod-product-compliance
Lightning Source LLC
Chambersburg PA
CBHW021549210326
41599CB00010B/375